Lecture Notes in Computer S

Commenced Publication in 1973
Founding and Former Series Editors:
Gerhard Goos, Juris Hartmanis, and Jan van Leeuwen

Editorial Board

David Hutchison
   Lancaster University, UK

Takeo Kanade
   Carnegie Mellon University, Pittsburgh, PA, USA

Josef Kittler
   University of Surrey, Guildford, UK

Jon M. Kleinberg
   Cornell University, Ithaca, NY, USA

Friedemann Mattern
   ETH Zurich, Switzerland

John C. Mitchell
   Stanford University, CA, USA

Moni Naor
   Weizmann Institute of Science, Rehovot, Israel

Oscar Nierstrasz
   University of Bern, Switzerland

C. Pandu Rangan
   Indian Institute of Technology, Madras, India

Bernhard Steffen
   University of Dortmund, Germany

Madhu Sudan
   Massachusetts Institute of Technology, MA, USA

Demetri Terzopoulos
   New York University, NY, USA

Doug Tygar
   University of California, Berkeley, CA, USA

Moshe Y. Vardi
   Rice University, Houston, TX, USA

Gerhard Weikum
   Max-Planck Institute of Computer Science, Saarbruecken, Germany

Mokrane Bouzeghoub   Carole Goble
Vipul Kashyap   Stefano Spaccapietra (Eds.)

Semantics of a Networked World

Semantics for Grid Databases

First International IFIP Conference, ICSNW 2004
Paris, France, June 17-19, 2004
Revised Selected Papers

 Springer

Volume Editors

Mokrane Bouzeghoub
CNRS - Université de Versailles, Laboratoire PRiSM
45, avenue des Etats-Unis, 78035 Versailles, France
E-mail: mok@prism.uvsq.fr

Carole Goble
University of Manchester, Department of Computer Science
Oxford Road, Manchester, M13 9PL, UK
E-mail: carole@cs.man.ac.uk

Vipul Kashyap
Clinical Informatics R&D, Partners HealthCare System, Inc.
93 Worcester St., P.O. Box 81905, Wellesley, MA 02481, USA
E-mail: vkashyap1@partners.org

Stefano Spaccapietra
Swiss Federal Institute of Technology Lausanne, EPFL-IC-LBD
1015 Lausanne, Switzerland
E-mail: stefano.spaccapietra@epfl.ch

Library of Congress Control Number: 2004113830

CR Subject Classification (1998): H.2, H.3, H.4, C.2.4, D.2.12, D.4.3-4

ISSN 0302-9743
ISBN 3-540-23609-0 Springer Berlin Heidelberg New York

This work is subject to copyright. All rights are reserved, whether the whole or part of the material is
concerned, specifically the rights of translation, reprinting, re-use of illustrations, recitation, broadcasting,
reproduction on microfilms or in any other way, and storage in data banks. Duplication of this publication
or parts thereof is permitted only under the provisions of the German Copyright Law of September 9, 1965,
in its current version, and permission for use must always be obtained from Springer. Violations are liable
to prosecution under the German Copyright Law.

Springer is a part of Springer Science+Business Media

springeronline.com

© 2004 International Federation for Information Processing, Hofstrasse 3, A-2361 Laxenburg, Austria
Printed in Germany

Typesetting: Camera-ready by author, data conversion by PTP-Berlin, Protago-TeX-Production GmbH
Printed on acid-free paper   SPIN: 11339694   06/3142   5 4 3 2 1 0

In Memory of Professor Yahiko Kambayashi

Prof. Kambayashi was for many years an active member of the IFIP 2.6 Working Group, which organized the conference whose proceedings make up this volume.

Prof. Kambayashi suddenly passed away in February 2004. He leaves us with the memory of a wonderfully competent, energetic and kind colleague.

The members of the Working Group are very sad to lose one of their best friends. They wish to offer this volume to his memory as a testimony of their esteem for the late Prof. Kambayashi.

Preface

The explosion in data exchange fostered by the success of the Web has restated semantics as a kernel issue in the development of services providing data and information to users and applications worldwide. This newly designated conference series on "Semantics for the Networked World" unifies into a single framework the previous series on "Database Semantics" and "Visual Database Systems" that the IFIP WG 2.6 has been offering since 1985. Whereas the intent of the conference series is to explore interesting research issues related to semantics, the theme for the 2004 edition is "Semantics for Grid Databases". Grid computing, a new field concentrating on "flexible, secure, coordinated resource sharing among dynamic collections of individuals, institutions, and resources (also referred to as virtual organizations)", has gathered momentum in the context of providing shared infrastructures for large-scale scientific computations and data analysis. Similarly, P2P computing has attracted substantial attention.

Currently, attention is devoted to the provision of middleware services to make computational resources interoperable at the technical level and to increase the efficiency of use of physical resources. However, as Grid and P2P computing infrastructures are being increasingly adopted, they are likely to have typical problems of information overload that manifest themselves in any large-scale infrastructure for information and application sharing (e.g., the WWW). The need for resource discovery, application and service interoperability, integration and composition manifest themselves in these infrastructures. The ability to interoperate at the semantic level will largely determine the continued success and utilization of these infrastructures.

This working conference focused on issues of semantic interoperability of the information and services provided and manipulated by Grid and P2P computing systems. The purpose of the conference, as for its predecessors, was to provide an active forum for researchers and practitioners for presentation and exchange of research results and practical management of databases, this time applied to large-scale systems used for managing and sharing scientific information. The technical program of the conference, which was held during June 17–19, 2004 in Paris, represented the state of the art in developing principles and practices related to the management of semantics in large-scale networked (Grid and P2P) information infrastructures. It featured two invited talks, by Norman Paton (Databases and the Grid: JDBC in WSDL, or Something Altogether Different?) and Karl Aberer (Emergent Semantics Systems), a tutorial by Dave Berry (The State of the Grid), and a panel on "What Can and Should We Do for the Grid?". The rate of acceptance of the research track was 1 out of 3, and the papers were presented in the following sessions: integration, peer-to-peer computing, semantics for scientific applications, interoperability and mediation, and global services and schemas. This was followed by a posters program that sought to showcase research ideas that are in various stages of progress and show promise.

Finally, the conference chairs would like to thank all the people who worked hard to bring this conference into being. This includes the members of the Program Committee, the invited and tutorial speakers and the authors of the various submissions who put forth their research ideas. Last, but not least, we would like to thank the local organizers in Paris — Daniela Grigori, Stéphane Lopes and Annick Baffert — whose efforts made this conference feasible and operational. We hope the attendees had stimulating and interesting exchanges of innovative ideas, possibly with some meaningful advances in this new and emerging area of research.

June 2004

Mokrane Bouzeghoub
Carole Goble
Vipul Kashyap
Stefano Spaccapietra

Organization

General Chair

Mokrane Bouzeghoub, University of Versailles, France

Program Co-chairs

Carole Goble, University of Manchester, UK
Stefano Spaccapietra, Federal Institute of Technology, Lausanne, Switzerland
Vipul Kashyap, National Library of Medicine, Bethesda, MD, USA

Steering Committee

Tiziana Catarci, University "La Sapienza", Rome, Italy
Karl Aberer, Swiss Federal Institute of Technology, Lausanne, Switzerland
Marc Scholl, University of Konstanz, Germany

Local Arrangements

Daniela Grigori, University of Versailles, France
Stéphane Lopes, University of Versailles, France

Program Committee Members

Karl Aberer, EPFL Lausanne, Switzerland
Mario Cannataro, University Magna Græcia, Catanzaro, Italy
Isabel Cruz, University of Illinois at Chicago, USA
Vassilis Christophides, ICS-FORTH, Crete, Greece
Christine Collet, Institut National Polytechnique de Grenoble, France
Nigel Collier, National Institute of Informatics, Tokyo, Japan
Isabel F. Cruz, University of Illinois at Chicago, USA
Ewa Deelman, University of Southern California, USA
Peter Fankhauser, IPSI, Darmstadt, Germany
Ian Foster, Argonne National Laboratory, USA
Alon Halevy, University of Washington, USA
Maurizio Lenzerini, University "La Sapienza", Rome, Italy
Ling Liu, Georgia Institute of Technology, USA
Bertram Ludaescher, San Diego Supercomputing Center, USA
Robert Meersman, Free University of Brussels (VUB), Belgium
Reagan Moore, San Diego Supercomputer Center (SDSC), USA

James Myers, Pacific Northwest National Laboratory, USA
John Mylopolous, University of Toronto, Ontario, Canada
Aris Ouksel, University of Illinois at Chicago, USA
Norman Paton, University of Manchester, UK
Dave Pearson, Oracle, UK
Munindar Singh, North Carolina State University, Raleigh, USA
Steffen Staab, Karlsruhe University, Germany
Paul Watson, University of Newcastle upon Tyne, UK
Hai Zhuge, Chinese Academy of Sciences, China
Esteban Zimanyi, Free University of Brussels (ULB), Belgium

Table of Contents

Semantics for Scientific Applications

Interoperability and Mediation

Global Services and Schemas

Posters

Databases and the Grid: JDBC in WSDL, or Something Altogether Different?

Norman W. Paton

Department of Computer Science, University of Manchester,
Manchester, M13 9PL, UK
norm@cs.man.ac.uk

Abstract. The Grid is rising to prominence both as a vision and as an infrastructure. The vision is of dynamically formed virtual organisations that collaborate to address shared goals. The infrastructure, although still a work in progress, is a middleware that facilitates the sharing of networked resources on a global scale. Databases are important resources that are central to many organisations, and as such must be able to be accessed, integrated and managed in a Grid environment. How should this be done? What problems must be overcome when working in a Grid environment? What new expectations, opportunities and patterns of use come to the fore? This presentation both discusses core grid data access services and the wider implications and opportunities of Grids for database technologies.

1   Introduction

The Grid [10] is rising to prominence both as a vision and as an infrastructure. The vision is of dynamically formed virtual organisations that collaborate to address shared goals. Although often associated with scientific applications, for example in particle physics and astronomy, the need for incremental, secure, easily managed and efficient resource sharing across organisations is present whenever collaboration takes place, so the potential reach of the Grid is extremely broad. The infrastructure, although still a work in progress, is a middleware that facilitates the sharing of networked resources on a global scale. There is no single Grid middleware; there are several commercial (e.g., Avaki (www.avaki.com), Platform (www.platform.com)) and not for profit (e.g., Globus (www.globus.org), UNICORE (www.unicore.org)) offerings, although Globus [12] is widely credited with providing the principal proving ground for many of the core functionalities that Grids require.

The name, and much of the original focus, was based on the idea of a global computational Grid, analogous to an electricity Grid, which would provide users with transparent access to remote computing resources. A CPU-hungry application could be moved to a suitable, available computer and executed without the need for micromanagement by the user. As the set of Grid-enabled resources, and their loads, will change over time, so decisions on resource selection must be made dynamically. This raises the possibility of computational marketplaces, in

M. Bouzeghoub et al. (Eds.): ICSNW 2004, LNCS 3226, pp. 1–13, 2004.
© IFIP International Federation for Information Processing 2004

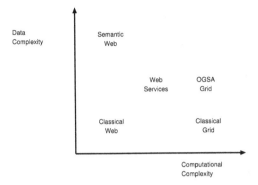

Fig. 1. The grid in context.

which service providers offer computational resources, and users select a resource based on criteria including price and quality of service offered.

The initial application drivers for the development of a Grid infrastructure were in large-scale scientific and engineering applications. For example, the first production grid was probably NASA's Information Power Grid (IPG) [19], which was developed in the context of a vision to simulate the US national air space, including, for example, detailed models of airframes and landing gear. Supporting such an application involves the integration of many existing computational resources, and the provision of a large collection of inter-related services to help in the management of the resources. These services include security services, uniform data access services, global event services, co-scheduling, etc. There has also been considerable interest in the use of Grids in Particle Physics (e.g., [18]) and Astronomy (e.g., [26]).

As these initial Grid applications were often closely associated with devices or tools that read and/or generated flat files, support for files rather than for the management of structured data had the highest profile in early Grid toolkits. However, file management systems and the registries associated with Grid toolkits themselves quickly became complex, and database management systems were increasingly used to store metadata (e.g., [7]). However, where databases are currently used as components within Grid toolkits, it is rarely the case that the database is a first-class citizen – for example, the Grid authentication and data transfer mechanisms may not be closely integrated with those of the database. As such, early Grid toolkits can be seen as providing effective facilities for accessing and sharing low-level data and computational resources, but to provide only limited support for complex data, as illustrated in Figure 1. The figure illustrates the level of support provided by different internet scale software architectures for managing the data and computational complexity of applications. In essence, early Grid middlewares provided operating system style functionalities, in a distributed and heterogeneous environment, over which higher-level application-oriented functionalities could be built.

It became clear, however, that the capabilities being developed for use in Grid middlewares overlapped with those that are under development in the web services community to support e-Business transactions (e.g., for authentication, protocol-neutral communication, resource description, etc). As such, a proposal has been made for a service-oriented architecture for the Grid, known as the Open Grid Services Architecture (OGSA) [11]. While the specific services that will constitute such an architecture are not yet fully understood, the OGSA will include interfaces for capabilities such as resource description, monitoring, negotiation, deployment, fault management and logging. As such, the OGSA will make available classical grid functionalities using the service description and invocation standards of the web services community, as illustrated in Figure 1. The OGSA architecture will form the core of activity within the Global Grid Forum (GGF) (www.ggf.org), the principal standards body for Grid computing. As databases are important resources that need to be deployed, accessed and managed within a Grid setting, the Database Access and Integration Services Working Group (DAIS-WG) has been set up within the GGF to develop standards for service-based interfaces to databases. It is not yet clear precisely what will occupy the top right hand corner of Figure 1, but work is underway to identify how semantic web technologies can be applied to the description of Grid resources, to yield a "semantic grid" [15].

This paper discusses the relationship between databases and the Grid under two headings:

1. *Deploying databases on the Grid:* identifying how databases can be made available as Grid resources.
2. *Deploying database technologies on the Grid:* identifying how functionalities and abstractions developed in the database community can be deployed in a Grid setting to provide higher level data access and integration services.

As such, with reference to the title, this paper discusses both core grid data access services ("JDBC in WSDL", to a first approximation) and the wider implications and opportunities of Grids for database technologies ("something altogether different"). Henceforth, the focus will largely be on service-based Grids, as the momentum behind the integration of web and Grid services seems great. The remainder of the paper is structured as follows. Section 2 discusses the requirements for database access in a Grid setting, outlines several proposals that have been made, and provides some concrete examples form the OGSA-DAI project. Section 3 discusses the role that Grids can play in supporting the development of higher level data integration and provisioning, and provides some concrete examples from the OGSA-DQP project. Some conclusions and pointers to future work are presented in Section 4.

2   Deploying Databases on the Grid

Deploying databases on the Grid means that databases are supported as first class citizens in a Grid setting. What does it mean for databases to be "first class citizens"? As in life, citizenship brings with it both rights and responsibilities. In a Grid setting, a database access middleware might expect to be able to benefit from other Grid functionalities, such as for service discovery and data movement, but might also be expected to conform to community norms in areas such as authentication, monitoring and transaction management. As such, a database access service could potentially implement a significant number of web and grid service interfaces, few of which have been formally standardised at the time of writing. Relevant proposals in the web services arena include those for transaction management (e.g. WS-Transaction [6] or WS-TXM [4]) and for context management (e.g. WS-Coordination [5] or WS-Context [4]), and in the Grid Services arena include many of the capabilities identified in the OGSA Architecture proposal (https://forge.gridforum.org/projects/ogsa-wg). However, as such specifications are intended to be composable, it is possible to discuss the specific operations and access patterns of a data access service with minimal direct reference to the potentially numerous related specifications, on the assumption that a database service will also implement, for example, a transaction management interface, and thereby behave in the manner required by the corresponding specification.

The behaviour of a data access service is characterised in [13] as having the following principal aspects:

1. *Data Description:* the description of the key characteristics of the data made available by the service.
2. *Data Access:* the interface that permits access to and modification of the data made available by the service.
3. *Data Factory:* the interface by which a new data resource can be derived from an existing resource.
4. *Data Management:* the interface by which operations manage the relationship between the data access service and the underlying data management infrastructure.

Data Description is important in service-oriented architectures as, at least in principle, it should be possible to dynamically discover, interrogate and make use of a service from a running application. For example, in the case of databases, a data federation could be dynamically constructed from the data services in an organisation that record information on customers. As such, services should be able to make available enough information about themselves to allow an informed choice to be made as to their suitability for a specific purpose. Use cases for data description in a Grid setting are described in [22].

Data Access is important, as interfaces must be developed that allow remote requesters to make convenient and efficient use of a data resource. Traditionally, database access interfaces assume a client-server interaction model. However, it is possible to envisage a wide range of different access patterns that are equally valid in a Grid setting. For example, the usage scenarios illustrated in Figures 2 and 3 are not only valid, but quite common in distributed applications [25]. In Figure 2, a query evaluation request is sent to a data service, but the result is delivered to a party other than the requester. The third party recipient of

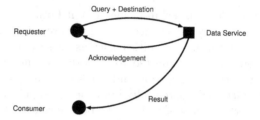

Fig. 2. A data access request with third party push delivery.

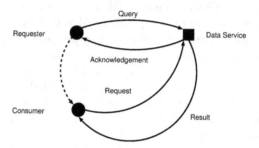

Fig. 3. A data access request with third party pull delivery.

the result could, for example, be a service through the use of a standard data delivery interface, or could be a file in a remote filesystem. In Figure 3, the result is not so much delivered to, but obtained by, a third party consumer. In this scenario, a way of identifying the result is passed from the requester to the consumer, who then invokes operations on the data service to access the result. As such, there might be somewhat more to data access in a Grid setting than at first meets the eye – although JDBC provides a useful guide to the kinds of capability that are at the core of data access, as a client library for client-server access it provides less comprehensive functionality than one might hope to see in grid data access services.

Data Factory functionality is important, as it is often necessary for services to create data resources that are to some extent independent of the interaction or the resources that brought them into being. As Grid middleware is very much focused on computational and data resources, there has been considerable discussion as to how best to represent networked resources in a service-oriented architecture. The most recent proposal in this regard is the Web Services Resource Framework [9], which characterises a WS-Resource as an association between a web service and some state that is accessed through the web service. In a data services context, a WS-Resource could be used, for example, to represent the result of a query evaluated by a requester who wants to make the result known to a third party consumer, as in Figure 3.

Data Management is important because the coordinated deployment and maintenance of a collection of data services in a distributed environment requires systematic support for management of the services. It is anticipated that groups

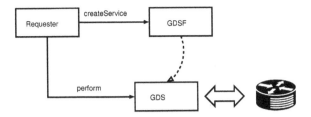

Fig. 4. Basic service interactions in OGSA-DAI.

such as the Web Services Distributed Management Working Group of OASIS (`http://www.oasis-open.org/committees/tc_home.php?wg_abbrev=wsdm`) will provide generic interfaces both for managing services and for managing resources using services.

As such, the development of data access services in the Grid can be seen to touch on a range of design issues, which complement the functionality of initial vendor offerings for web service access to databases (e.g., [21,23]), which principally addressed a narrower range of functionalities, such as making stored procedures available as web services.

The OGSA-DAI project (`http://www.ogsa-dai.org.uk/`) provides an early example of service-based access to databases [2], and now forms part of the Globus toolkit. Figure 4 illustrates the basic interactions between services in OGSA-DAI using the grid service creation facilities of Globus Toolkit 3. A client (referred to here using web services terminology as a *Requester*), first invokes the *createService* operation on a Grid Database Service Factory (*GDSF*), which leads to the creation of a Grid Database Service (*GDS*). The *GDS* represents a session over a particular database, to which the *Requester* can then submit requests using the *perform* operation.

A single request to a GDS, conveyed as a parameter of *perform*, is capable of evaluating a collection of linked activities. Each activity describes an atomic capability provided by the service. For example, there are activities that can query a database, apply a transformation to a result, or deliver a result to a third party. The request in Figure 5 makes use of *sqlQueryStatement* and *deliverToGFTP* activities to retrieve data from a *frogGenome* database and deliver the result using GridFTP (`http://www.globus.org/datagrid/gridftp.html`) to a third party, thereby implementing the scenario illustrated in Figure 2. The result of the `sqlQueryStatement`, which is named *statementresponse*, is explicitly used as input to the `deliverToGFTP` activity. As such, OGSA-DAI provides a coarser-grained interface than JDBC, providing a means of grouping data movement, database access and data transformation operations in a single request.

The deployment of databases in service-based grids can thus be seen to raise a wide range of design issues, relating, for example, to the granularity of requests, the support provided for handling of query results, the delivery scenarios supported directly by the data access service, and the level of detail provided for service description. Furthermore, as Grids are often concerned with the timely

```
<gridDataServicePerform ...>
  <request name="requestAsynchPush">

    <sqlQueryStatement name="statement">
      <dataResource>frogGenome</dataResource>
      <expression>
        select * from chromFrag where num = 30
      </expression>
      <webRowSetStream name="statementresponse"/>
    </sqlQueryStatement>

    <deliverToGFTP name="d1">
      <fromLocal from="statementresponse"/>
      <toGFTP host="ogsdai.org.uk"
              port="8080" file="path/to/myfile.txt"/>
    </deliverToGFTP>

  </request>
</gridDataServicePerform>
```

Fig. 5. An OGSA-DAI perform document for a data access request with third party push delivery.

provisioning of data, it can also be speculated that subscription-based data access [8] is likely to have a more prominent role in Grid computing than it has to date. The Information Dissemination Working Group of the GGF is developing proposals in this space.

3   Deploying Database Technologies

Database technologies, techniques and principles can be applied in a Grid setting in various ways. This section makes a case that Grid and database technologies each have something to offer the other, by discussing how the development of data management systems can benefit from Grids in Section 3.1, and how Grids stand to benefit from effective deployment of database technologies in Section 3.2. OGSA-DQP [1] is used as a concrete example of a database middleware developed over a service-based Grid in Section 3.3.

3.1   Database Technologies Need the Grid

Database technologies might be considered likely to benefit from Grid technologies for several reasons. For example, database management systems, as complex pieces of software operating in a networked environment, stand to benefit from systematic access to computational and storage resources, and from facilities for dynamic resource discovery and allocation. Furthermore, the study of systems developed without access to service-based Grids can be used to make the case that Grid services provide capabilities that are required to enable the effective development of information integration platforms.

As an example, ObjectGlobe [3] provided a platform for executing distributed queries, using web technologies to provide access to data stores and computational resources ("cycle providers"). ObjectGlobe consists of a collection of distributed Java components that communicate with each other using messages encoded in XML. In so doing, ObjectGlobe, which largely predated the web and grid service activities, developed registries, database wrappers and cycle providers with a view to supporting distributed query processing, in which query plan partitions could be allocated to widely distributed nodes on the internet. Many of the components that were developed from scratch for ObjectGlobe now form part of a service-based Grid middleware, such as Globus. For example, Globus provide registries for describing both services and the capabilities of computational resources, and is shipped with the OGSA-DAI database wrappers. In addition, it inherits from the web services community consistent techniques for describing and invoking operations on heterogeneous platforms. As such, the developers of distributed query processors for the Grid have significantly less work to do than was required to construct ObjectGlobe over the internet only a few years ago.

The highest profile association to date of Grid technologies with a commercial database management system is in Oracle 10g (the "g" is for "grid"). Here the emphasis is on using Grid functionalities to ease the deployment, management and adaptation of the database management system as a complex software system in a distributed environment [17].

As such, data management systems can be seen as complex software artifacts in a distributed, heterogeneous setting, and thus able to benefit from the dynamic, flexible and consistent access to computational resources that the Grid is promising to provide.

3.2   The Grid Needs Database Technologies

Database management systems provide high-level facilities for managing large and potentially complex data resources. In so doing, many details as to how and where the data is physically stored are hidden from users. In a distributed setting, database systems further exploit the notion of transparencies to characterise aspects of the management of data that are hidden from users (e.g., the presence of replicas, the language used to access specific portions of the data, etc). This notion of transparencies can also be applied in the design of data grids [24], and the level of abstraction at which Grid resources are accessed can be seen as steadily increasing with time.

The classical representation of a collection of dependent tasks that are to be executed together in a Grid setting is as a Directed Acyclic Graph (DAG), and systems such as Condor can be used to queue and schedule jobs on a Grid [14]. However, such representations tend to refer to jobs and resources in terms of the programs to be executed and the files to be acted on, rather than in terms of higher level abstractions. As such, work is underway to develop higher level

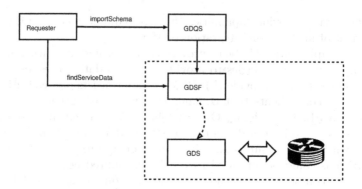

Fig. 6. Initialising a GDQS in OGSA-DQP.

representations for data intensive tasks. For example, Chimera [11] supports the notion of *virtual data* by describing how a data product is produced, and scheduling the jobs required to produce the data product on demand. With a view to integrating database access and management more fully with this process, the GridDB project [20] has developed a language that combines facilities for database access with those for the invocation of programs on a Grid. In essence, a relational representation of data is used to model data of relevance to an application, and analyses are wrapped to act on tuples that may be initial inputs or intermediate values in a workflow, all of which can be managed using standard relational database facilities. The work described in the next section, on OGSA-DQP, has a similar motivation to that of GridDB, but is acting in the context of service-based Grids. As such, a key difference is that OGSA-DQP uses existing service interfaces to access remote resources, and thus does not require custom wrapping of analysis programs.

3.3 OGSA-DQP as a Case Study

OGSA-DQP (http://www.ogsa-dai.org.uk/dqp/) is a service-based distributed query processor for the Grid, which supports the evaluation of queries over one or more OGSA-DAI wrapped databases and other web services [1]. In essence, OGSA-DQP allows a single query to access data from multiple resources, and to invoke web service operations on data extracted from database services. As such OGSA-DQP can be seen as providing declarative service orchestration, in a manner that complements that of, for example, workflow systems.

Figure 6 illustrates the initialisation of a Grid Distributed Query Service (*GDQS*). It is assumed that the *GDQS* service has already been created in a similar manner to that illustrated for an OGSA-DAI GDS in Figure 4. The *Requester* then identifies a number of Grid Database Service Factories (*GDSFs*), for example by looking them up in a registry, that are associated with databases that may be required to participate in a distributed query processing activity. The specific properties of a database that can accessed using a *GDS* created by

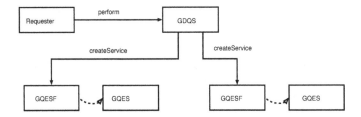

Fig. 7. Creating evaluators for a specific query in OGSA-DQP.

a *GDSF* can be ascertained by invoking the GDSF's *findServiceData* operation. When a suitable *GDSF* has been identified, the *Requester* can then invoke the *importSchema* operation on the *GDQS*, which leads to a *GDS* being created that is used to access the relevant database by queries submitted to the *GDQS*.

Once the resources have been identified over which queries are to be run, specific queries can be submitted by the *Requester* to the *GDQS* using the *perform* operation, as illustrated in Figure 7. The *GDQS*, as described in [1], compiles the query, to yield a collection of query partitions, each of which must be evaluated using a Grid Query Evaluation Service (*GQES*). Thus the *GDQS* then creates a collection of *GQES*s, as illustrated in Figure 7, to each of which is assigned a single partition. Invoking *perform* on the root evaluator leads to a cascaded collection of evaluation requests, which execute the query in a distributed fashion, potentially with both pipelined and partitioned parallelism.

The deployment of database technologies in a Grid setting can thus be seen as having implications both for the Grid and for the way in which the technology is used. In OGSA-DQP, data intensive tasks that involve access to multiple data and computational resources can be expressed using queries, providing a new, more declarative mechanism for describing data intensive requests over the Grid. In addition, parallel database query processing technology is adapted to work in a highly heterogeneous setting, where the Grid middleware provides useful abstractions for hiding details of the resources used in the evaluation of requests. Thus database technologies can have a significant role as part of the Grid middleware stack, and Grids can impact on the way database technologies are engineered, deployed and used.

4   Conclusions

So, are databases for the Grid principally JDBC in WSDL, or something altogether different? Well, there is a need for service-based interfaces to databases for use as part of the Grid middleware stack, which in many cases will involve functionality that is familiar from existing database access middlewares such as JDBC. However, as discussed in Section 2, it is possible to identify scenarios and thus opportunities to explore somewhat more expressive data access interfaces, both for request-response and publish-subscribe access to data. In addition, as discussed in Section 3, it is possible to envisage a much closer association of Grid and data management technologies. This can be not only to increase the flexibility and manageability of existing database software, but also to allow database infrastructure to be deployed more widely for information and process integration in Grids. Although initial work has taken place to deploy database technologies for service orchestration in Grids, as in GridDB and OGSA-DQP, this work can be seen as being at an early stage, with scope for significant additional developments. For example, wide deployment of queries for service orchestration in Grids is likely to require further work on adaptive query processing to take account of the unpredictability of resource availability and computational costs associated with Grids [16], and providing automatic support for varying quality of service requirements is likely to involve significant additional work on how these requirements are both described and supported.

Acknowledgements. The work reported in this paper has emerged from ongoing interactions in the OGSA-DAI, myGrid and OGSA-DQP projects, and in the DAIS Working Group of the GGF. Research on grid data management is supported at Manchester by the Engineering and Physical Sciences Research Council and the UK e-Science Programme.

References

1. N. Alpdemir, A. Mukherjee, N. W. Paton, P. Watson, A. A. A. Fernandes, A. Gounaris, and J. Smith. Service-based distributed querying on the grid. In *Proc. of ICSOC*, pages 467–482. Springer-Verlag, 2003.
2. A. Anjomshoaa et al. The design and implementation of grid database services in ogsa-dai. In S. Cox, editor, *Proc. UK e-Science Programme All Hands Meeting*, pages 795–801.
   http://www.nesc.ac.uk/events/ahm2003/AHMCD/ahm_proceedings_2003.pdf, 2003.
3. R. Bramandl, M. Keidl, D. Kossman, A. Kreutz, S. Seltzsam, and K. Stocker. ObjectGlobe: Uniquitous query processsng on the Internet. *VLDB Journal*, 10:48–71, 2001.
4. D. Bunting et al. Web Services Composite Application Framework (WS-CAF) Version 1.0. Technical report, Arjuna Technologies Ltd., Fujitsu Limited, IONA Technologies Ltd., Oracle Corporation and Sun Microsystems Inc.,
   http://developers.sun.com/techtopics/webservices/wscaf/primer.pdf, 2003.
5. L. F. Cabrera et al. Web Services Coordination (WS-Coordination). Technical report, IBM developerWorks Report,
   ftp://www6.software.ibm.com/software/developer/library/ws-coordination.pdf, 2002.
6. L. F. Cabrera et al. Web Services Transaction (WS-Transaction). Technical report, IBM developerWorks Report,
   http://www-106.ibm.com/developerworks/library/ws-transpec/, 2002.
7. P. Dinda and B. Plale. A unified relational approach to grid information services. Technical Report GWD-GIS-012-1, Global Grid Forum, 2001.
8. P. Eugster, P. Felber, R. Guerraoui, and A.-M. Kermarrec. The many faces of publish/subscribe. *ACM Computing Surveys*, 35(3):114–131, 2003.

9. I. Foster et al. Modeling Stateful Resources with Web Services. Technical Report Version 1.1, Computer Associates International, Fujitsu Limited, Hewlett-Packarg Development Company, IBM, University of Chicago, http://www.ibm.com/developerworks/library/ws-resource/ws-modelingresources.pdf, 2004.

10. I. Foster and C. Kesselman. *The Grid 2: Blueprint for a New Computing.* Morgan Kaufmann Publishers Inc., 2004.

11. I. Foster, C. Kesselman, J. Nick, and S. Tuecke. Grid Services for Distributed System Integration. *IEEE Computer*, 35:37–46, 2002.

12. I. Foster, C. Kesselman, and S. Tuecke. The Anatomy of the Grid: Enabling Scalable Virtual Organizations. *Int. J. Supercomputer Applications*, 15(3), 2001.

13. I. Foster, S. Tuecke, and J. Unger. OGSA Data Services. Technical Report Informational Draft, Global Grid Forum, Database Access and Integration Services Working Group, https://forge.gridforum.org/projects/dais-wg/document/OGSA_Data_Services-ggf9/en/1, 2003.

14. J. Frey, T. Tannenbaum, I. Foster, M. Livney, and S. Tuecke. Condor-G: A Computation Management Agent for Multi-Institutional Grids. In *Proc. 10th Int. Conf. on High Performance Distributed Computing*, pages 55–66. IEEE Press, 2001.

15. C. Goble, D. DeRoure, N. Shadbolt, and A. Fernandes. Enhancing Services and Applications with Knowledge and Semantics. In I. Foster and K. Kesselman, editors, *The Grid 2: Blueprint for a new computing infrastructure*. Morgan Kaufmann, 2004.

16. A. Gounaris, N. Paton, A. Fernandes, and R. Sakellariou. Adaptive query processing and the grid: Opportunities and challenges. In *Proc. 1st Intl. Workshop on Grid and Peer-to-Peer Computing Impacts on Large Scale Heterogeneous Distributed Database Systems*. IEEE Press, 2004. To be published.

17. B. Goyal. Oracle Database 10*g* - The Database for the Grid. Technical Report 40123, Oracle White Paper, http://otn.oracle.com/tech/grid/collateral/10gdbgrid.pdf, 2003.

18. G. Graham, R. Cavanaugh, P. Gouvares, A. D. Smet, and M. Livney. Distributed Data Analysis: Federated Computing for High-Energy Physics. In I. Foster and K. Kesselman, editors, *The Grid 2: Blueprint for a new computing infrastructure*. Morgan Kaufmann, 2004.

19. W. Johnston, D. Gannon, and B. Nitzberg. Grids as Production Computing Environments: The Engineering Aspects of NASA's Information Power Grid. In *8th IEEE Symposium on High Performance Distributed Computing*. IEEE Computer Society, 1999.

20. D. Liu and M. Franklin. GridDB: A Data-Centric Overlay for Scientific Grids. Technical Report CSD-04-1311, UC Berkeley, http://www.cs.berkeley.edu/ dtliu/pubs/griddb_tr.pdf, 2004.

21. S. Malaika, C. Nelin, R. Qu, B. Reinwald, and D. Wolfson. DB2 and Web Services. *IBM Systems Journal*, 41(4):666–685, 2002.

22. S. Malaika and N. Paton. CIM Database Model for Data Access and Integration Services: Scenarios. Technical Report Informational Draft, Global Grid Forum, Database Access and Integration Services Working Group, https://forge.gridforum.org/projects/dais-wg/document/DAIS_CGS_Scenarios-ggf10/en/1, 2004.

23. K. Mensah and E. Rohwedder. Database Web Services. Technical Report Informational Draft, Oracle Corporation White Paper,
    http://otn.oracle.com/tech/webservices/htdocs/dbwebservices/
    Database_Web_Services.pdf, 2002.
24. V. Raman, I. Narang, C. Crone, L. Haas, S. Malaika, T. Mukai, D. Wolfson, and
    C. Baru. Services for Data Access and Data Processing on Grids. Technical Report
    GFD.14, Global Grid Forum,
    http://www.ggf.org/documents/GWD-I-E/GFD-I.014.pdf, 2003.
25. G. Riccardi, M. Subramanian, S. Misra, and S. Laws. DAIS Usage Scenarios.
    Technical Report Informational Draft, Global Grid Forum, Database Access and
    Integration Services Working Group,
    https://forge.gridforum.org/projects/dais-wg/document/DAIS_Usage_Scenarios-
    ggf10/en/1, 2004.
26. A. Szalay, P. Z. Kunszt, A. Thakar, J. Gray, and D. R. Slut. Designing and mining
    multi-terabyte astronomy archives: The sloan digital sky survey. In *Proc. ACM
    SIGMOD*, pages 451–462. ACM Press, 2000.

Emergent Semantics Systems*

Karl Aberer[1], Tiziana Catarci[2], Philippe Cudré-Mauroux[1]**, Tharam Dillon[3],
Stephan Grimm[4], Mohand-Said Hacid[5], Arantza Illarramendi[6],
Mustafa Jarrar[7], Vipul Kashyap[8], Massimo Mecella[2], Eduardo Mena[9],
Erich J. Neuhold[10], Aris M. Ouksel[11]***, Thomas Risse[10],
Monica Scannapieco[2], Fèlix Saltor[12], Luca de Santis[2], Stefano Spaccapietra[1],
Steffen Staab[4], Rudi Studer[4], and Olga De Troyer[7]

[1] Swiss Federal Institute of Technology (EPFL), Switzerland
`Philippe.Cudre-Mauroux@epfl.ch`
[2] Univ. of Roma La Sapienza, Italy
[3] Univ. of Technology, Sydney, Australia
[4] Univ. of Karlsruhe, Germany
[5] Univ. of Lyon 1, France
[6] Univ. of the Basque Country, Spain
[7] Vrije University of Brussels, Belgium
[8] National Library of Medicine, USA
[9] Univ. of Zaragoza, Spain
[10] Fraunhofer IPSI, Germany
[11] Univ. of Illinois at Chicago, USA
[12] Univ. Politècnica de Catalunya, Spain

Abstract. With new standards like RDF or OWL paving the way for
the much anticipated Semantic Web, a new breed of very large scale
semantic systems is about to appear. Traditional semantic reconciliation techniques, dependent upon shared vocabularies or global ontologies, cannot be used in such open and dynamic environments. Instead,
new heuristics based on emerging properties and local consensuses have
to be exploited in order to foster semantic interoperability in the large. In
this paper, we outline the main differences between traditional semantic
reconciliation methods and these new heuristics. Also, we characterize
the resulting *emergent semantics* systems and provide a couple of hints
vis-à-vis their potential applications.

1 Introduction

Global economics needs global information. The time is over when enterprises
were centralized and all the information needed to operate an enterprise was

---

* The work presented in this paper reflects the current status of a collaborative effort
initiated by the IFIP 2.6 Working Group on Databases. It was partly carried out as
part of the European project KnowlegeWeb No 507482. A previous version of this
work was published in the proceedings of DASFAA04.
** Corresponding author. Phone: +41-21-693 6787
*** The research of this author is partially supported by NSF grant IIS-0326284.

stored in the enterprise database. Nowadays, all major economic players have decentralized organizational structures, with multiple units acting in parallel and with significant autonomy. Their information systems have to handle a variety of information sources, from proprietary ones to information publicly available in web services worldwide. Grasping relevant information wherever it may be and exchanging information with all potential partners has become an essential challenge for enterprise survival. Shortly stated, information sharing, rather than information processing, is IT's primary goal in the 21st century. Not that it is a new concern. It has been there since data has been made processable by a computer. What is (relatively) new is the focus on semantics, which takes the issue far beyond the syntactic functionality provided by exchange standards or standard formatting à la XML. The reason that makes semantics re-emerge so strongly is that now information has to be sharable in an open environment, where interacting agents do not necessarily share a common understanding of the world at hand, as used to be the case in traditional enterprise information systems.

Lack of common background generates the need for explicit guidance in understanding the exact meaning of the data, i.e., its semantics. Hence the current uprising of research in ontologies, for instance. Ontologies are the most recent form of data dictionaries whose purpose is to explain how concepts and terms relevant to a given domain should be understood. However, ontologies are not the panacea for data integration [1]. Consider a simple example from traditional data management: an enterprise database will most likely contain data about employees, and every user will be expected to understand the concept of "an employee". Yet a closer look at the concept reveals a number of possible ambiguities, including whether specific types of personnel (e.g., students in their summer jobs, trainees, visitors) have to be considered as employees. Without an agreement between the interacting units as to the correct mapping between these concepts, interpretation may not be decidable.

Ontologies are forms of "a-priori" agreements on concepts, and therefore, their use is insufficient in ad-hoc and dynamic situations where the interacting parties did not anticipate all the interpretations and where "on-the-fly" integration must be performed [2]. In fact, the commensurability of knowledge and the desirability of developing efficient solutions for the open environment preclude an approach which realistically captures the space of interpretations in a finite structure. Semantic errors compound even intuitively well understood concepts. In the absence of complete definitions, elicitation of explicit and goal-driven contextual information is required for disambiguation. In human conversations, the context may be implicit, elicited through a dialogue between the interlocutors, or gathered from additional information sources. The new computing environment in the Internet demands similar capabilities. Increasingly, information systems are represented by agents in their interactions with other autonomous systems. These agents must therefore be capable of building the context within which "on-the-fly" integration could occur. What ought then be the appropriate mechanisms and tools that agents must possess to accomplish the task of resolving semantic conflicts in a dynamically changing environment, such as the Internet and the Web?

The above discussion serves as a motivation for the general principles enunciated thereafter which could drive the development of the next generation of semantic reconciliation methods. The rest of this paper is organized as follows: We first take a look back at classical data integration techniques in Section 2 and summarize the rationales and principles of the new *emergent semantics* trend in Section 3. Section 4 gives some details on an important aspect of emergent semantics systems, namely *self organization*. Opportunities and challenges related to emergent semantics systems are outlined in Section 5 and 6. Finally, we present three case studies in Section 7 before concluding.

2 Classical Information Integration

The need to integrate heterogeneous information sources is not new; For decades, researchers have been working on building data integration systems providing uniform query interfaces to a multitude of data sources, thereby freeing the user from the tedious task of interacting and combining data from the individual sources. Given a user query that is formulated in the query interface (also called the mediated schema), these systems use a set of semantic mappings to translate the query into queries over source schemas, then execute the queries and combines the data returned from the sources, to produce the desired answers to the user. Numerous research activities have been conducted along those lines, both in the artificial intelligence and database communities. Much progress has been made in terms of developing conceptual and algorithmic frameworks; query optimization; constructing semi-automatic tools for schema matching, wrapper construction, and object matching; and fielding data integration systems on the Internet.

2.1 Information Integration from a Database Perspective

The motivation for data integration from a database perspective is old and reflects the activities from the 90s, when various databases were integrated. Most of the databases integration systems described in the literature (see, e.g., [3,4,5, 6,7]) are based on a unified view of data, called mediated or global schema, and on a software module, called mediator that collects and combines data extracted from the sources, according to the structure of the mediated schema. The existing mediator-based information integration systems can be distinguished according to: 1) the type of mappings between the mediated schema and the schemas of the sources (Global As View versus Local As View), and 2) the languages (therefore, the expressivity) used for modeling the mediated schema and the source descriptions.

2.2 Global as View Versus Local as View

According to [8], information integration systems can be related to two main approaches for modeling inter-schemas correspondence: Global As View (GAV) and Local As View (LAV). The GAV approach has been the first one to be proposed and comes from the Federated Databases world. The mediated schema is defined in function of the schemas of the sources to integrate, i.e., each relation of the mediated schema is defined as a view on the relations of the sources schemas. The advantage of this approach is the simplicity of query reformulation which simply consists of replacing each atom of the query by its definition in terms of the relations of the sources schemas. Its drawback is its lack of flexibility with respect to the addition or deletion of sources to the mediator: adding (or deleting) a source to the mediator may affect the definitions of all the relations of the mediated schema. The LAV approach is dual and has opposite advantages and drawbacks. It consists of describing the contents of the sources in function of the mediated schema. In such an approach, adding a new source is quite straightforward because each source is described independently of each other. The price to pay for this flexibility is the difficulty of the query answering processing which requires a more complex process of rewriting queries using views (see [9] and [10] for more details on the problem of answering queries using extensions of views).

2.3   Relational Versus Object-Based Mediated Schema

The selection of the language used to modeling the mediated schema and the source descriptions is a very important aspect: the expressitivy of such a language will restrict the kind of semantic relationships that can be described among data elements. We can distinguish between those approaches providing a relational view of data sources and those systems using an approach based on objects. The most representative information integration systems of the relational approach are: Razor [11], Internet Softbot [12], Infomaster [13] and Information Manifold [14]. They all follow a LAV approach. The Razor and Internet Softbot systems use datalog (without recursion) for modeling the mediated schema, the views describing the sources contents and the users queries. Infomaster and Information Manifold are based on extensions of datalog. Infomaster exploits integrity constraints in addition of datalog rules. Information Manifold extends datalog by allowing that some predicates used in the rules are concepts defined by using description logics constructors. The most representative information integration systems of the object-based approach are: TSIMMIS [6], SIMS [15,16], OBSERVER [17] and MOMIS [18]. TSIMMIS is based on the object-oriented language OEM for describing the mediated schema and the views, and on the OEM-QL query language. It follows a GAV approach. The SIMS and OBSERVER systems use a description logic for modeling the mediated schema, the views and the queries. SIMS follows the LAV approach while OBSERVER follows the GAV. The MOMIS system is based on the use of a very expressive description logic (ODL-I3) for describing the schemas of the sources to integrate. It follows the GAV approach.

2.4   Information Integration from Knowledge Representation Perspective

The schematic and semantic heterogeneity is one of the difficulties in the integration of heterogeneous information sources. Normally, the information in every information source is stored with regards to its users' requirements, disregarding access from other sites or their integration. Two critical factors for the design and maintenance of applications requiring Information Integration are conceptual modeling of the domain, and reasoning support over the conceptual representation. It has been demonstrated that knowledge representation and reasoning techniques can play an important role for both of these factors. Two relevant works that follow the knowledge representation approach are from Calvanese et al. [19] and Rousset and Reynaud [20].

2.5   Information Integration and the World Wide Web

With the progress in global interconnectivity, the scale of the problem has changed from a few databases to an open and dynamic environment of millions of heterogeneous information resources. Current keyword-based approaches are usually found to provide a poor quality of result. However, the key challenges to be faced are at the semantic level, where people would increasingly expect the information systems to help them not at the data level, but at the information, and increasingly knowledge levels which call for semantic interoperability. In essence, we need an approach that reduces the problem of knowing the contents and structure of many information resources to the problem of knowing the contents of easily-understood, domain-specific ontologies, which a user familiar with the domain is likely to know or understand easily. Recent papers focused on some of the issues characterizing data integration over the Web. For example [21] identifies the problem of similarity matching among XML data. The proposed algorithm is able to find the commonalities and differences which give rise to a numerical rank of the structural similarity. [22] investigates the heterogeneity problem of information sources from the query answering point of view. To handle semantics inconsistencies between the same attributes used at different sites, task ontologies are used as a communication bridge between them. Information Retrieval is also a well established domain [23] that now has a new field of application: Web-based IR. [24] isolates four different approaches of this problem in the Web context: (1) human or manual indexing, (2) automatic indexing using classical IR techniques, (3) intelligent or agent-based indexing such as using Crawlers and Robots and (4) meta-data, RDF (Resource Description Framework) and annotation-based indexing. Meta information (and hence semantic Web) can also be important in the prospect of information integration: [25] proposes web servers export specific meta-data archives describing their content. In order to offer better processing and integration of information, a unified representation for Web resources (data and services) is becoming a necessity. The use of ontologies to provide the means to machines of understanding the data they are manipulating is increasing. With the emergence of Semantic Web [26], the study of ontologies and their uses has increased, since they provide a shared and common understanding of a domain that can be communicated between people and application systems.

2.6 The Future of Data Integration

To date, all the integration technologies have been offered by various independent vendors and products. Even if the information technology organizations can appropriately match the right integration technology to the problems related to information integration, it still has the problem of how many skilled, specialist resources are needed to implement these technologies and integration scenarios, as well as how many different vendors must be contracted. Each of these separate technologies has its own user interface to the developer, brings its own development environment (often graphical), has its own meta data repository to document the interface, its own security framework, and its own management framework. Developing intelligent tools for the integration of information extracted from multiple heterogeneous sources is a challenging issue to effectively exploit the numerous and dynamic sources available on-line in global information systems.

3   The Emergence of Emergent Semantics

Nowadays, several research areas such as peer-to-peer data management, information agents, Semantic Web or Web data mining and retrieval all address the problem of semantic interoperability in widely distributed information systems with large numbers of agents[1] [27,28] using remarkably similar ideas. Global information is seen as highly evolutionary: documents of already existing sources may be updated, added or deleted; new sources and services may appear and some may disappear (definitively or not). Semantic interoperability is viewed as an emergent phenomenon constructed incrementally, and its state at any given point in time depends on the frequency, the quality and the efficiency with which negotiations can be conducted to reach agreements on common interpretations within the context of a given task. We refer to this type of semantic interoperability as "emergent semantics". In the following we outline what we believe are the key characteristics underlying this concept.

3.1   Principle 1: Agreements as a Semantic Handshake Protocol

Meaningful exchanges can only occur on the basis of mutually accepted propositions [29]. The set of mutual beliefs constitutes the "agreement" or "consensus" between the interacting agents. It is the semantic handshake upon which shared

---

[1] The term "agents" refers to both humans through computed-mediated communication and to artificial surrogates acting as information and/or service consumers and producers. The term "peers" is used as a synonym.

emerging and dynamic ontologies can be established and exchange context can be constructed. In practice, the agreement can be over the real-world meaning of some model, as it is typically assumed in conceptual modeling, on schema mappings, on consistent data usage or on any other meta-data information relevant to the task at hand. The strength of the agreement will depend on the strength of the accepted propositions, their quality and trustworthiness.

3.2   Principle 2: Dynamic Agreements Emerge from Negotiations

Information exchange between agents is necessary to negotiate new agreements or to verify preexisting ones. This is a recognition that the information environment is dynamic, and thus, assumptions must be constantly validated. Agreements evolve as agents learn more about each other and as interests broaden or become more focused. Interaction is required to identify and resolve semantic conflicts, to negotiate and establish consensus on the data interpretation, and to verify whether a consensus leads to the expected actions. Communication can be realized in terms of explicit message exchanges or implicitly by reference to distributed information resources.

Note that in our context, agreements are no longer "static". Unlike ontological commitments, these agreements are likely to change dynamically as the network of information parties evolves. Also, agreements do not need to be "binary", i.e., it is not the case that either there is or isn't consensus about the meaning of a particular term. In fact there might be fuzzy notions of consensus, such as weak, strong, etc. which may have a bearing on the semantics. Finally, agreements do not necessarily result from negotiations of "equals". In general it is assumed that (in the committee approach) all the people contributing to creation of ontology/enterprise model have equal expertise. This is definitely not the case in an emergent semantics scenario, where different people from a variety of backgrounds will be contributing to the negotiations, and thus to the agreements generated.

3.3   Principle 3: Agreements Emerge from Local Interactions

The principles stated so far are analogous to those formulated for introducing the concept of ontological commitments [30], except that "emergent semantics" assumes that commitments are dynamic and are established incrementally. The key challenge for emergent semantics remains scalability. The complexity of "emergent semantics" and communication costs preclude the option for an agent to seek agreements simultaneously with a large number of other agents. The combinatorial nature of such an endeavor will limit the viability of the approach in distributed environment. Thus, pragmatics dictate that "emergent semantics" be kept local to reduce communication costs and that global agreements are obtained through aggregations of local agreements. As a result, even if agents are only aware of a small fraction of a network directly, they will nevertheless be able to interoperate over the whole network indirectly by exploiting aggregate information. This raises the immediate question on how to technically perform aggregation and inference of new agreements.

3.4 Principle 4: Agreements Are Dynamic and Self-Referential Approximations

Making an appeal to context in resolving semantic conflicts is a recognition that traditional schema or conceptual analysis leave open several possible interpretations of a mapping between the information sources of two interacting agents. However, the problem with context in general is that the space of possibilities is very rich, and that it has no well defined boundary. Since agreements rely on the context of interaction, their boundaries are also fuzzy. The way out of this conundrum may lie in the fact that we view "emergent semantics" as an incremental and goal or query-directed process which sufficiently constrains the space of possibilities.

Two interacting agents may achieve an agreement in one application and fail in another even if the set of identified semantic conflicts are basically the same. Interpretations may depend on the context. In turn, agreements are dynamic. Local consensus will be influenced by the existing context of existing global agreement, thus the process of establishing agreements is self-referential.

3.5 Principle 5: Agreements Induce Semantic Self-Organization

Considering the dynamics and self-referential nature of emergent semantics, it is not far-fetched to view it as the result of a self-organization process. Self-organization is a principle that has been studied in many disciplines, in particular physics, biology, and cybernetics for a long time, and has been attracting substantial attention in computer science as well (see Section 4. Informally, self-organization can be characterized by a complete distribution of control (which corresponds to complete decentralization) and by the restriction to local interactions, information and decisions. Global structures can then emerge from such local interactions.

Francis Heylighen characterized self-organizations as follows: "The basic mechanism underlying self-organization is the noise-driven variation which explores different regions in a system's state space until it enters an attractor." In the case of emergent semantics, the state space consists of all local communication states reached in consensus building. The attractor is obtained when agents locally reach acceptable agreements that are as consistent as possible with the information they receive. The attractor actually embodies what we call the global semantic agreement. The noise-driven variation results from randomness of interactions induced by environmental influence (e.g., network connectivity) and autonomous decisions.

3.6 A Canonical and Well-Known Example

We illustrate the principles of emergent semantics by referring to one particularly successful example of emergent semantics, namely link-based ranking as used in

Google [31]. A global semantic agreement is obtained for a simple property of Web documents, namely their "general importance". The local communication is performed by Web document authors implicitly by referring to other Web documents through hyperlinks. The global agreement is determined by using the PageRank algorithm.[1] It provides a ranking of all Web documents. This ranking is approximate, as surely not all authors would agree on it, it is dynamic as the Web evolves, and it is self-referential as the impact of a link is derived from the importance of its Web document. The self-referential nature of link-based ranking actually leads to problems when link spammers exploit their knowledge on the Google ranking method in order to influence the rankings in their interests.

We can compare Google's approach to the one taken by Web directories, such as Yahoo. In web directories the decision on importance of Web documents with respect to some ontological concept (the directory) is taken globally, manually and centrally. This clearly limits the scalability of the approach.

Other approaches similar to Web document ranking are currently appearing in other Web applications. For example, several works on trust and reputation mechanisms relies on similar principles as Google's ranking approach. A practical application of reputation-based trust management is found with Ebay. More complex tasks, such as Web document classification and clustering based on emergent semantics principles are reported in the literature.

3.7   Extending the Scope of Emergent Semantics

A next natural step beyond ranking-based methods ignoring the structure of the content would be to apply the principle of emergent semantics to obtain interpretations for structured data. The Semantic Web is currently laying foundations for the use of semantically richer data on the Web, mainly through the use of ontologies for meta-data provisioning. The effort of establishing semantic agreement is largely related to the development of shared ontologies. The question we pose is whether principles of emergent semantics could be a solution for obtaining semantic agreement in the Semantic Web with its richer data models in a more scalable fashion.

One possible avenue of how this might be achieved is currently being opened in the area of peer-to-peer data management, where local schema mappings are introduced in order to enable semantic interoperability. We may see such local schema mappings as the local communication mechanisms for establishing consensus on the interpretation of data. Once such infrastructures are in place, the principles of emergent semantics become directly applicable. Relying on local consensus, automated methods may then be employed in order to infer more expressive and accurate global semantic agreements.

---

[1] The fact that the ranking is computed on a central server is from the perspective of establishing a semantic agreement just an implementation issue.

4   Self Organizing Systems in Nature and Computer Science

As stated above, self organization is an essential property of emergent semantics systems. A self organizing system essentially consists of a system that evolves towards displaying global system behaviours and structures that are more than an aggregation of the properties of its component parts. Such systems generally have complex dynamic characteristics that allow them to evolve from a given state towards attractors, which exhibit stable patterns in structure and behaviour. There can be more than one attractor, in a given self organizing system each having its region of attraction. An important element of these self organizing systems is that there is no external influence or central controller that leads to these patterns. Rather these patterns are arrived at through interactions between components such that these components only have local information, knowledge or local rules. The collection of information arising from local rules and knowledge leads to the emergent properties of the global system as a whole.

Several examples can be found in science and nature of self organizing systems. A few examples are discussed below: Two examples from Physics are [32] a) magnetization and b) Bernard Rolls. In magnetization, spins (the equivalent of tiny magnets) are randomly changing orientation at high temperatures. At a lowered temperature these align themselves to reinforce each other's magnetization leading to a magnetized bar. Bernard rolls are circular movements of liquid flows, which result from the heated liquid moving from a hot bottom of the container to the top whilst the cooler liquid from the surface moves down setting up a circular pattern. In each case the particles are reacting locally without an external or central controller but their interactions lead to the stable patterns at the global system level. Examples from biology or chemistry [33] include the stripped patterns in Zebras, Fish and the ocular dominance columns of the brain. These patterns are produced due to the individual responses of the cells to local conditions and the response of the neighbouring cells. Again there is no central controller involved and the patterns are an emergent property of the collection of cells. An example from nature consists of a flock of birds that flies in a certain formation. These birds develop into this formation and preserve it despite several changes in direction and environmental factors. Again there is no leader or controller that marshals the birds into these formations.

There are several different examples of self organizing systems in computer science and related disciplines. Specifically one can distinguish: a) Self Organizing Neural Networks such as Kohonen Nets and Edelman Nets b) Hopfield Neural Nets and Boltzmann Nets c) Particle Swarms d) Evolutionary Computation e) Cellular Automata f) Peer to Peer Networking. The self-organizing feature map, also known as Kohonen network [34], was developed by Teuvo Kohonen. The Kohonen network has the ability to find clusters in the data as well as structure and to perform an ordered or topology-preserving mapping, thus revealing existing similarities in the inputs. The topology preserved with this network need not correspond to a physical arrangement; it can correspond to a statistical feature of the input set. In a typical Kohonen network, units are arranged in a two-dimensional grid. However, it is possible to use one or more dimensions. This grid of units is usually referred to as a Kohonen layer. All units in the input layer are fully connected to the units in the Kohonen layer of Feature Map. Feedback is restricted to lateral interconnections with immediately neighbouring units in the Kohonen layer. Each link between an input and a Kohonen layer node has an associate weight. The net input into each neuron in the Kohonen layer is equal to the weighted sum of the inputs. Learning proceeds by modifying these weights from an assumed initial distribution with the presentation of each input pattern vector. A central aspect of a Kohonen network is that it uses competitive learning. As learning involves adjustment of weight vectors, the importance of determining the winner resides in the fact that only the neurons within a small region around the winner are allowed to learn this particular input pattern. There are two types of Hopfield networks [35], the first is a discrete output, stochastic network whilst the second has a deterministic continuous form. A key element of the Hopfield network is feedback. This essentially means that the weighted output from every neuron in the network is fed back to the input of each neuron. Another important element is the network's updating technique, i.e., for a modified input, when does the network change its output? In the discrete stochastic network, each neuron samples its input at random times. Furthermore the sampling times of each neuron are independent of every other neuron, i.e., the system is asynchronous. The motion of the state of the system with N neurons in state space describes the computation being performed. Any model must describe evolution of the state with time. Hopfield proposed a model with stochastic evolution. In analogy to spin glass models, Hopfield introduced the generalized energy function. Therefore the iteration must lead to stable states. The energy function can be visualized as a surface. The stable states correspond to the local minima on this surface. Each stable state can be considered as an attractor with its own basin of attraction. A Hopfield net can converge to a local minimum that is not an optimal solution. A process described by metaphor from metal annealing can be applied using a net algorithm similar to Hopfield's to encourage convergence to a global minimum. The network, a Boltzmann machine, has a probabilistic update rule which sometimes allows jumps into higher energy states rather than lower ones as a strategy to escape local minima. The thermal noise added to the network is initially high and it is slowly decreased to encourage thermal equilibrium in the net.

Particle Swarm [36] and evolutionary computation are both adaptive optimization techniques. Particle Swarm is inspired by bird flocking and fish schooling phenomena whilst evolutionary algorithms are inspired by genetic evolution. Particle Swarm and Evolutionary Computation both start from an initial randomly generated population, have a fitness function which represents closeness to the optimal volume and carries out selection from the current population based on the best fitness value until a stopping criteria is met. In evolutionary computation and genetic algorithms, these operators namely reproduction, crossover and mutation are utilized to generate new candidates for the population. Note that the whole retained population is used to search for the optimum. In contrast in particle swarms each particle's velocity is updated by the best historical value and the current global best value.

Cellular automata consist of a two dimensional arrangement of cells. Each cell interacts with cells in proximity and has transition rates that determine its state. Camazine et al. [33] have shown how cellular automata can be used to model stripped and mottled patterns that appear in animals.

Peer to Peer networks and their self organizing properties are discussed later in this paper.

5   Opportunities

Despite the specificities mentioned in Section 3, Emergent Semantics can still benefit from the heuristics and results of many different research fields. We detail below how dynamics in decentralized settings, data mining or lexical resources can all in their own ways help building Emergent Semantics systems.

5.1   Dynamics in Decentralized Settings

Semantics do not emerge from purely random settings, but rather from environments exhibiting specific, well-known properties. Locality has been referred to (Section 3) as an essential component of emergent systems. Semantic networks – as many social or natural networks – build up from large numbers of purely local, pair-wise interactions. *Scale-free* networks [37] have been designed specifically for studying systems resulting from such a construction process. These networks differ from random networks in the sense that they first start from a small nucleus of nodes, and expand then with the arrival of new nodes that join the network following some preferential attachment law. We can expect semantic networks to expand following a similar process, where new nodes connect to already existing nodes because of some semantic affinity. Results from *scale-free* graph theory range from network formation to statistical connectivity and could be directly applied to model the shaping of semantic networks as well as to highlight some of their essential attributes, like scalability which is one of the inherent properties of such graphs.

Also, locality may be seen as a real opportunity to leverage investments while establishing semantic interoperability. This is important both in cases where communication used to establish semantic agreement requires human intervention or when it is automated. When human intervention is required, it is instrumental to minimize it, as human attention is one of the scarcest resources today [38]. On the other hand, automated methods to locally establish semantic interoperability (e.g., schema matching or natural language translations) are computationally very intensive and would directly benefit from decentralization and from localized view on global agreements.

The fact that no central component is at hand for coordinating the various interactions in the semantic system imposes some autonomous behaviors on its constituents. Autonomy has been studied in bio-inspired [39] and decentralized peer-to-peer [40,41] approaches, which are particularly good at decomposing large or complex problems otherwise hard to tackle using standard centralized solutions. Autonomy also directly refers to intelligent and multi-agent systems [42] in general, where coordination and distributed problem planning/solving are tackled using distributed artificial intelligent techniques.

Randomness clearly induces a certain loss of efficiency but leads to a higher failure resilience and robustness of the system. This relates to the dynamics of decentralized environments and to the fact that a large fraction of nodes may be faulty or off-line at any given point of time in such settings. Built-in load-balancing and replication algorithms [43] usually handle the problem from a data-availability point of view, while overall connectivity is typically not at stake, as long as a reasonable fraction of preferred (i.e., highly connected, cf. above) nodes still function properly in the system.

Naturally, locality, autonomy and randomness may all be seen as harmful to different degrees to the global integrity and completeness of the system. Even if algorithms have been devised for taking care of data availability and integrity in highly dynamic environments [44], global semantic integrity in heterogeneous environments remains for the time being a challenging research problem. The lack of any agreed-upon global schema or ontology makes it very difficult for the participating parties to reach a global consensus on semantic data. Initial approaches rely on some pre-defined corpus of terms serving as an initial context for defining new concepts [45] or make use of gossiping and local translation mappings to incrementally foster interoperability in the large [46,47].

5.2   Data Mining

Once some initial level of semantic agreement has been reached, individual entities can make use of data mining techniques to refine the agreements. *Data Mining for Emergent Semantics* aims at enhancing semantic interoperability by exploiting:

1. content data (of texts, multimedia, relational table);
2. structural data (e.g. links between texts, coordination between multimedia objects, multirelational structures, network data);
3. usage data (e.g. usage of texts, video, data).

In addition, to overcome data sparseness, which is often a problem for achieving semantic descriptions from data mining, there is the possibility to

4. *actively collect data* (also cf. Active Learning [48]).

For instance, data mining based on Web resources to achieve emergent semantics uses globally available Web data and structures to define new local semantics. Blueprints for this paradigm are found in works such as the following:

1. Web Content Mining: Some researchers use explicit, linguistically motivated natural-language descriptions to propose semantic relationships ([49,50,51, 52]).

2. Web Structure Mining: In [53,54], the Web structure itself is used to determine a focus for harvesting data. Thus, specialized semantic relationships, such as recommendations coming from a particular Web community can be derived.
3. Web Usage Mining: [55]
4. Active Learning: Others use the Web to cope with data sparseness problems in tasks that require statistics about possible semantic relationships ([56,57, 58,59]).

Currently, people work on combinations, e.g. content and structure mining [60] or content mining and active learning [61].

Particularly relevant work in this area of global approaches of emergent semantics are the areas of 'traditional' Ontology Learning — mostly, though not only, from texts (see [51,62]).

Other techniques for bilateral semantic alignment can also be used. The basic idea of bilateral semantic interoperation is to generate an alignment between two different semantic descriptions based on a number of heuristics (see in particular the survey [63]). These generations can be based on identity of lexical labels, agreements on common semantic structures, indirect mapping via thesauri or overlap of extensional descriptions such as found through machine learning. Multi-lateral consensus tries to generalize from bilateral semantic interoperation. Some of the basic ideas here include the composition of individual bilateral agreements — be it by forwarding through gossiping [46,47] or by more centrally directed algorithms [64,65,66].

5.3   The Influence of Usability Perspectives on Locally Axiomatized Semantics

We use the term semantic axiomatization in order to refer to a formal description accounting for the intended meaning of a vocabulary, represented in a machine-processable manner[2]. Same semantics can be axiomatized in different ways. This usually reflects different usability perspectives, such as granularity, scope, representation primitives and constructs, reasoning and computational scenarios, and so forth. In other words, local semantic axiomatizations are substantially influenced by "what the semantic is being axiomatized for" and "how it will be used". Bylander and Chandrasekaran argued in [68] that: "Representing knowledge for the purpose of solving some problem is strongly affected by the nature of the problem and the inference strategy to be applied to the problem." We believe that establishing formal semantic interoperability among different *local* semantic axiomatizations mostly fails due to the diversity of usability perspectives, although all axiomatizations might *intuitively* agree at the domain/knowledge level[3].

---

[2] This definition is derived from Guarino's definition of the term ontology as found in [67]
[3] See [69] for the definition of "knowledge level"

Intuitive definitions and agreements about the intended meaning of certain vocabularies are implicit assumptions shared among human cognitive agents. Such informal definitions and agreements can be found in lexical resources (e.g., dictionaries, lexicons, glossaries, lexical databases). Linking or grounding the vocabulary used in local axiomatizations with terms found in lexical resources can help achieving basic semantic interoperability between different axiomatizations. For example, by using (euro)WordNet synsets [70] as a shared vocabulary space, autonomous semantic axiomatizations will be able to interoperate at least freely from language ambiguity and multilingualism.

Using lexical resources as shared vocabulary spaces could be seen as an attachment law of emergent semantics networks; or, it could be advised in case of failure or uncertain semantic interoperations. The basic (or maybe the only) requirement for a lexical resource to be used as such, is that it should provide (1) a discrimination of word/term meaning(s) (2) in a machine-referable manner. Lexical resources that only list vocabularies and their similarities are irrelevant to our purposes. Semantic or linguistic relationships between word forms (such as hyponymy, meronymy, and synonymy) could be significant but not essential. Our basic target is to enable emergent semantics networks to communalize word/term senses, which are largely independent of usability perspectives.

In comparison of using lexical resources with the use of axiomatized domain theories (i.e., ontologies), building adequate ontologies is difficult and very expensive, while many reliable and comprehensive lexical resources are available. Further, lexical resources are generally easier to extend than ontologies.

As a related work, Jarrar et al proposed in [71,72] an ontology engineering approach that uses the notion of "ontology base" as a controlled vocabulary space shared between application axiomatizations. An ontology base is intended to capture context-specific domain vocabularies, i.e., lexical rendering of domain concepts.

6   Threats and Limitations

In this section, we investigate characteristics and problems of emergent semantics systems from two distinct points of view. We first illustrate which are the threats and limitations strictly inherent to emergent semantics systems. Then, we describe issues related to decentralized and peer-to-peer architectures and how those issues can influence emergent semantics systems. Table 1 summarizes the results of our analysis.

6.1   Emergent Semantics Systems: Threats and Limitations

Representational Model. First, there is the need to commit to a particular representational model, i.e., a relational data model like the relational algebra, a semi-structured data model like Lore [73], a semi-structured data model like RDF [74] with its schema language RDFS [75], or a full-blown knowledge representation language like OWL (Web Ontology Language) [76]. The trade-off along

Table 1. Emergent semantics systems and P2P Infrastructures: threats and limitations

	Threats and Limitations
ES Systems	Representational Model
	Common Upper Ontology & Extensibility
	Data Integration & Querying
	Provenance Information & Trust
	Incompleteness
	Consensus Derivation
P2P Infrastructures	Degree of Centralization
	Degree of Inter-Peer Coupling
	Data Availability & Updates
	Anonymous Entities

these lines is one between expressiveness and efficiency. While on the one end the relational algebra is a model for which highly efficient systems exist, it will hardly be sufficient to prescribe semantic definitions. At the other end, OWL allows for comprehensive definitions, including e.g. cardinalities and arbitrary Boolean expressions for defining classes — but currently there is no system on the horizon that efficiently handles more than several dozen of tuples at the instance level. Furthermore, there are currently no algorithms that would infer complex constraints from observed data with reasonable accuracy. Thus, representational models like RDF(S) currently appear to constitute the appropriate paradigm for defining some semantics as well as handling reasonably sized data stores.

Common Upper Ontology & Extensibility. Emergent semantics systems can make use of text mining and existing lexical information to incrementally come up with a consensus on the data they share (cf. Section 5). However, some common understanding is usually necessary to bootstrap the process, thus the need to agree on some upper-ontology (e.g., [77]).

Furthermore, once mining has yielded new conceptual structures, the results should be added in an appropriate way to the existing background information for later re-use. This second step requires extensible representations. In addition, to counter the need for integrating multiple mining results, the second step requires an agreement on how the conceptual structures are stored (according to the representational paradigm) and how the very particular lexicon structures are named (according to the upper ontology or a vocabulary of meta metadata for emergent semantics systems).

For instance, WordNet [70] allows for one concept to be referred to by several lexical terms (e.g. the lexical terms 'hard' and 'difficult' may refer to one concept) and it allows for on lexical term to refer to multiple concepts (e.g. 'hard' may refer to the concepts for 'difficult' and for 'non-soft'). There exist first considerations to provide a data model to this end (cf. [78]), but no final conclusion exists yet in this matter.

Data Integration & Querying. In an emergent semantics system, different entities may have different knowledge levels on other parties schemas and mappings. The problem of defining how to answer to a query posed on the schema of a specific entity arises.

One approach to solve this problem is the one used in traditional data integration systems [79]: a global schema is constructed starting from the schemas locally exported by the different data sources (see also Section 2). The assumptions in the case of the emergent semantics paradigm are completely different: no global schema is a-priori constructed in order to make the system work, instead it is an inherent function of the system to construct a global knowledge "dynamically" while working. In this case, mappings cannot be defined with respect to a global schema, therefore the research problem of mappings definition and resolution arises. Semantic Gossiping [46,47] could be a promising approach to reach semantic interoperability in a network of semantically heterogeneous parties.

Provenance Information & Trust. Provenance information may be important in order to cluster or categorize data according to where they came from. Results could be that particular quality/trust ratings are given for particular provenances or that semantic structures are treated individually based on where they came from. Such pieces of information are particularly difficult to gather and verify in open and dynamic environments such as emergent semantics systems. Ehrig et al. [80] present a quite specific metadata model based on RDF(S) to this end. Siebes and van Harmelen[81] and Tempich et al.[82] are examples on how to exploit such models for negotiating meanings and routing semantic queries, respectively.

It is also on provenance information that one can build trust mechanisms or ratings for the various entities in the system. Also, mechanisms should be developed in order to check mappings and results received from other peers; Misbehaving peers could populate the community with erroneous mappings or bogus schemas and could answer queries with fake data. Such situations must be detected and actions must be taken to exclude malicious peers and remove fake data from the system. Coming up with good heuristics for solving these issues is especially complex given the dynamics of emergent semantics infrastructures (cf. also Section 6.2 below).

Incompleteness. Incompleteness in an emergent semantics context is related to the impossibility to obtain all the information available in the system due to a lack of knowledge on the information that peers commonly share and to a lack of global semantic interoperability. In a traditional data integration system, with a global schema summarizing all the available information, the incompleteness problem does not occur in these terms: It is usually known *a priori* which pieces of information can be provided by whom. The absence of complete indexes on resources in emergent semantics systems and the presence of replicated copies of the same semantic information, could cause system inefficiency. Therefore, on one hand we have to assure a high level of completeness in information searching; on the other hand, it is also desirable to avoid network request flooding. The adoption of specific semantic query models need to be investigated in order to consider possible tradeoff among search strategies, optimal request load balancing and system robustness to failures.

Consensus Derivation. Related to the Incompleteness problem presented above, Consensus Derivation can be considered as a key component when deriving semantics that emerge from the interactions of people and from the various messages generated to express their opinions. Given a set of observations by a set of people, requirements on a consensus computation scheme could be:

- The ability to compute the consensus semantics or reality based on an analysis and aggregation of the individual events observed.
- Based on the computed reality, estimate the individual expertise of the people involved based on how close their opinions corresponded to the central reality.
- Update the consensus and associated expertise estimates whenever current observations change and new observations are added to the mix.

Work done in cultural anthropology and approaches such as Delphi methods and Repertory Grids need to be explored to come up with effective algorithms for consensus derivation. Besides semantics, consensus computation might also have some impact on other issues such as trust, quality and assessment of satisfaction. All these issues can in turn influence the computation of new consensus, thus outlining once more the self-referential property of agreements in emergent semantics systems.

6.2   Peer-to-Peer Systems as Infrastructure for Emergent Semantics Systems: Threats and Limitations

As stated above (Section 5), we expect emergent semantics properties to appear in large-scale, decentralized and dynamic environments. Thus, P2P systems represent a natural infrastructure on which to base emergent semantics systems. By *P2P*, we do not only consider the well-known file-sharing applications, but also all the access structures and distributed systems where participating nodes can be both clients and servers. In other words, all nodes provide access to some of the resources they own, enabling a basic form of interoperability. Below, we illustrate some peculiarities and issues of P2P infrastructures and we analyze how they could influence emergent semantics systems.

Degree of Centralization. A first architectural problem in P2P systems is related to the *degree of decentralization*: decentralized, centralized and hierarchical models are all possible [83]. The topology of centralized systems causes the well-known problems of bottlenecks and single points of failure. On the other hand, fully decentralized systems are difficult to implement and their performances are relatively low. This is also proven by the fact that many P2P systems are built with an hybrid approach (such as Napster, KaZaA, or eDonkey). Also, P2P softwares should not require any significant set up or configuration of either networks or devices [84]. Though much progress has been made in designing P2P systems, such constraints still complicate the implementation of "actual" emergent semantics systems.

Degree of Inter-Peer Coupling. The degree of inter-peer coupling takes into account how much *tight* can a peer interaction be. For example, with systems such as Kazaa, the interaction is not tight since users only search for data and establish temporary connections. On the other hand, with distributed workflow systems, each node can have significantly more sophisticated and longer interactions with other nodes, thus originating tighter interactions. We can expect some applications of emergent semantics systems to require such tight interactions, thus the necessity for the system infrastructure to support various inter-peer coupling models.

Data Availability & Updates. Even if an efficient indexing mechanism is developed, in many cases data can be unavailable, simply because the peers storing such data are offline or unreachable. In order to achieve better data availability, peers should replicate their own data in the community. The replication could be controlled by the originator or the data could be replicated through gossiping mechanisms by other peers. Very popular data might need to be highly replicated. It is also possible to exploit standard fault tolerance techniques, such as software replication [85] in order to enhance data availability and reliability.

Introducing replication makes updates more complicated, because of the necessity to update replicas as well. Some approaches already exist that work under probabilistic guaranties [44].

Anonymous Entities. Anonymity is often associated to P2P systems, because of their open nature and the lack of any central authority. Anonymity can be defined with respect to a communicating pair in the P2P system. Specifically, three kinds of anonymity are possible: *sender anonymity*, which hides the sender's identity; *receiver anonymity*, which hides the receiver's identity; and *mutual anonymity*, in which the identities of the sender and the receiver are hidden to each other and to other peers.

From a system perspective, the major drawback of peer anonymity is the limitation in implementing security controls in upper layers. In an emergent semantics context, retrieving the peers' identity might be essential to enable trust mechanisms or counter malicious attacks (see above Section 6.1).

7   Examples/Cases Studies Evaluation

In this section we present three possible application scenarios for the concept of emergent semantics. The case of Service Discovery shows how emergent semantics could help to improve data freshness and quality of the discovery process. The second example from the digital library area indicates in which way emergent semantics can support the integrated access on heterogeneous libraries. Elicitation of interpretation semantics in scientific collaborations is presented in the last example.

7.1   Semantic Service Discovery

Semantic Web Services combine Web Services technology with machine-understandable meta data annotation emerging in Semantic Web research. Just as the WWW moves towards offering dynamic content and Web Services instead of static content alone, part of the Semantic Web vision is to establish a network of semantically annotated services. In such a network agents are able to combine the functionality of several Web Services in order to achieve complex high-level goals in an automated way without human intervention.

This fully automated scenario involves discovery, composition and execution of Web Services [86] and requires formal descriptions of service semantics for software agents to reason about. Discovery includes the task of locating Web Services that provide certain capabilities and fulfil the constraints specified by the requestor. Composition comprises the combination of several services to a more complex one [87]. Execution involves the invocation of an identified service by an agent including proper message exchange with the service's interface [88].

The usage of Web Services involves a requesting and a providing party both of which can be either human users or software agents. Automated discovery is a means for the requestor to find potential providers by querying a registry. Providers advertise the capabilities of their services to the registry whereas requestors formulate the goals they want to achieve. For a description of the semantics of goals and capabilities they make use of an ontological vocabulary based on some underlying knowledge representation formalism. Doing so they refer to commonly used domain ontologies that capture general knowledge about the corresponding domain of discourse, as e.g. delivery of products. Discovery then reduces to the task of matching goals and capabilities expressed as ontological descriptions [89].

Besides the actual business-level semantics of a service, aspects of choreographic or compositional semantics can be taken into account as well in the context of discovery. Part of the discovery semantics of a service could, for example, be characterised by its pre and post conditions or by certain parameters being part of the protocol, as e.g. the occurrence of a credit card number in the choreography of the service interface.

A concrete service instance determines all parameters - nothing is left open for the two parties to decide about. In the book-selling example a service instance specifies exactly which book is going to be delivered to which address and which amount of money has to be paid in which form. In this sense descriptions of goals and capabilities are templates for service instances - they allow several possibilities of how the service can be carried out. For example, the provider of the service decides to accept several payment methods and does not specify in the capability description which one is finally being used. The semantics of discovery matchmaking can be defined in terms of sets of service instances: a goal and a capability match if the sets of service instances they allow intersect. In this case there is at least one possible service instance which they both agree on. This approach is followed in [90].

In the general case discovery does not directly lead to a concrete service instance. Once a service has been discovered its parameters have to be negotiated between the requestor and the provider. The outcome of the discovery is not a service instance to be carried out but just the fact that the two parties can potentially do business with each other [90]. After discovery, negotiation might lead to a concrete service instance but it does not necessarily have to. For example, a book selling service provider advertises that it sells books, which is sufficient for successful discovery involving a requestor who searches for a book selling service in the internet. However, the particular book the requestor is looking for might be out of stock.

Currently, several ontological languages for declarative description of Web Service semantics emerge, such as OWL-S[91] and WSMO [92]. They provide top-level ontologies for Web Services covering the specification of service profile, process control flow, message exchange and mediation. Goals and capabilities can be expressed combining these upper level service ontologies with domain ontologies.

Considering such a top-level ontology for Web Services there are several technical approaches to discovery and appropriate description of service semantics. One of them is to model knowledge about services on the ontological level of concepts and relations and then perform schema matching. An example is given in [93] where description logic reasoning is used. Both, goals and capabilities, are described as description logic concept expressions. To check the intersection of the two concepts for satisfiability reduces matchmaking for discovery to standard description logic inferences. Another idea is to use the stronger subsumption inference and to check whether the goal describes a specialized form of the service advertised by the capability or vice versa. In [89] and [94] modified structural subsumption algorithms are applied in frameworks that support partial matches on a discrete scale. Subsumption in either direction is considered stronger than satisfiability of concept intersection but weaker than an exact match. An alternative approach to schema-level matching is to model knowledge about services on the level of instances. In this case discovery is achieved by querying the extension of a goal concept expression and applying ontology-based information retrieval techniques.

Discovery of Web Services benefits from ontological descriptions of service semantics in that reasoning based on formal semantics can be applied in matchmaking algorithms for goals and capabilities. The knowledge captured in domain ontologies can potentially be used to derive a match where the facts stated in the goal and capability alone would not be sufficient to do so. Formal semantics helps to derive facts that are not explicitly stated.

Incorporating semantics into Web Services is quite a new field and it is still an open issue how to semantically describe and annotate services in order to properly discover them by appropriate techniques - two aspects that go hand in hand. Application of discovery approaches to concrete case study scenarios have to show which aspects of service semantics have to be exploited and which reasoning techniques have to be applied to yield good solutions.

7.2 Digital Libraries

The growing availability of cyber infrastructures like GRID, Peer-to-Peer and Web Services, will lead to more open and flexible digital library (DL) architectures, e.g. BRICKS [95]. Hence DL will opened to a wider clientele by enabling more cost-effective usage and better tailored DL. Furthermore new types of infrastructures allow dynamic federative models of content and service provision involving a wide range of distributed content and service providers. This has implications for the realization of digital library functionalities mainly rooted in the increased heterogeneity of content, services and metadata. Future distributed DL infrastructures will consists of a large number of loosely coupled DL systems all over the world. Users of these infrastructures will be able to retrieve information from all involved DL. Due to the high degree of distribution, these infrastructures will often omit centralized management systems. Hence no central retrieval service and no central authority, which has a complete system overview, will exist. The decentralization approach poses new challenges to various areas like information retrieval, security, etc.

One major problem in decentralized DL infrastructures is that most DLs are using different data schemas as well as different classification systems. The standard data integration strategies like Global As View resp. Local As View or approaches to define standards for schemas or ontologies works for many specialized applications very well but is problematic in decentralized and highly dynamic environments. DL Nodes may appear and disappear in the system for several reason like network problems, economic problems, etc.. In these environments many local data schemas and ontologies exist. The local DL owners have their own semantic understanding of their data. Due to the diversity of information, reaching a global agreement among all is difficult. By viewing semantics as a form of agreement the emergent semantics approach is to enable the participating data sources to incrementally develop a global agreement in an evolutionary process that solely relies on pair-wise interactions.

The idea behind to use the emergent semantics approach is the assumption that local experts have the best knowledge about their data. Hence they know best the semantic interpretation of the data. Furthermore they have preferred collaboration partners, whose information and semantic interpretation the local experts know quite well. This assumption belongs to all nodes within the DL infrastructure. Hence local experts are able to generate high quality mappings between their own schema and classifications and those of their partners. Often the mappings are already available from previous collaborations and can be reused in the process.

The mappings are distributed together with the query to the queried library. The queried library will integrate the mapping in their local mapping table and performs the query. In addition the query will be send also other neighbours, which also receive the mapping in this way. The neighbours learn from the received mappings how to interpret the semantics of other DL. They are also able to derive mappings, e.g. the DL A sends a mapping $A \rightarrow B$ to the DL B. DL C knows already the mapping for $B \rightarrow C$ and receives the mapping for $A \rightarrow B$. Hence DL C will be able to derive a mapping $A \rightarrow C$ by using $A \rightarrow B \rightarrow C$. In this way every DL will learn about the new mapping, which can be used later on.

Nevertheless also the method of emergent semantics has prerequisites and limitations. First limitations arise from the mapping itself. So it is not always possible to generate a complete and 100% accurate mapping, e.g. due to missing fields or ambiguous semantics. Furthermore mappings between heterogeneous standards, e.g. between Dublin Core and MPEG7, also leads to problems. Hence a good practice is to restrict the process to a specific domain, e.g. science of art. With this restriction several semantic problems can be avoided as all involved persons have a similar understanding domain and of the semantics. Even if the emergent semantics approach will not solve all interoperability problems in digital libraries, will it be a very useful method to support ad-hoc collaborations.

7.3   Scientific Collaboration

Semantic reconciliation is crucial in scientific collaboration [96]. Consider the case of integrated environmental models. These models represent the consensus understanding of earth systems reached by scientists in the field at some period in time. They are composed of sub-models, which attempt to capture particular environmental systems. For example, ground water models describe subsurface water flow; infiltration models describe the movement of water into soils, and so on. These sub-models alone describe only small parts of the environment, but together they can address questions concerning the environment as a whole. The challenge is to find ways of integrating successfully a subset of these sub-models to deal with a specific goal while preserving the autonomy of the individual models. In other words, integration of sub-models must be goal-driven between peers, and similarly integration of heterogeneous information sources must be query-driven, while also preserving the autonomy of the individual models and/or information sources and services. Each goal and each query may require the elicitation of different interpretations of the models and the information sources and services within specific contexts [28]. The semantics necessary for integration emerges incrementally from the interaction of peers, as additional queries are posed and information sources and services become available. Thus, semantic reconciliation in model integration is an emergent phenomenon.

Consider, for example, query "Where do the sub-models agree on soil moisture at the beginning of the season?". The answer will depend on the models used and their context assumptions, which in this case include at least the spatial context (where), the attributes' context (soil moisture), and the temporal context (at the beginning of the growing season) [97]. These same observations about the role of context in model integration process recur in other scientific domains. Integration may be triggered by the activity of a scientist exploring the Internet and the web for models or services related to a specific real-time experiment. The models are likely to have been developed autonomously. Model autonomy must be preserved, as models in natural sciences have deeply rooted assumptions to allow representation of processes that may only be partially understood. If the underlying assumptions are not always completely specified, which is usually the case, then the integration of sub-models may result in semantic errors. In geographic applications or satellite-based information systems, for example, a variety of semantic errors resulting from model integration have been investigated [98,99]. Their occurrences are generally pegged to the lack of unified theories of space, time and accuracy [100]. However, this cannot be the only reason, as ontologies, constructed on the basis of the potential theories, will not feasibly be able to capture every possible application context of model integration. Thus, reliance on ontologies alone will be insufficient to entirely resolve the problem of semantic conflict [1].

Semantic analysis will require that models be able to self-evaluate to determine the level of violation of their own underlying assumptions with respect to an expected behavior defined within an application context. This analysis is performed within an application context guided by ontologies from cognate fields. In the environmental example, the application context consists of information such as field measurements, remotely sensed imagery, and maps. The collected information is interpreted within ontologies from cognate fields such as meteorology, geology, soil science, and ecology. They contribute contextual information about the properties of a natural environment and their aggregation, scale and resolution of observations, and generalization. Consider the example of the RHESSysd system [101]. One spatial aggregation is land unit, which represents a scale that captures long-range spatial variability. Ground water is stored at this level, but a refined semantic analysis may require disaggregating a land unit into its constituent components at lower resolution, such as the land patch. The disaggregation will be performed on the basis of assumed relations between water movement and landscape position. Observe that the ontology knowledge used for disaggregation are assumptions about water movements. These assumptions, which are simply process models, may be only ephemeral estimations subject to reevaluation as new results in the field are obtained. Collectively, all the knowledge gained represents the application context.

Users of environmental databases and models may have had no role in the development of the information sources, but nevertheless, need to use them. End-users contribute contextual information in the form of queries to the information services. The concept of context elicitation [28,29] is a process, which allows incremental extraction of relevant information to the query from the information sources and services. There is need for a notion of semantic distance to measure the compatibility of queries with the elicited information.

Queries of scientific literature may not be simple searches for information in a given topic. At the frontier of scientific discovery, investigators may wish to assess untested scientific hypotheses, or to uncover hereto unknown relations between two lines of inquiry. The semantics necessary to validate (or invalidate) these hypotheses may not be readily available. They are constructed incrementally. They form the context elicited from the information sources and services through an interactive (and often non-monotonic) semantic reconciliation process, which incrementally refines the evidence gathered at each stage.

In summary, context in scientific collaboration is elicited from the application context through an incremental query-directed semantic reconciliation process. It is thus emergent. A semantic distance measure is necessary to continuously measure at any state the semantic compatibility between this context and the user query. The challenge in the area is the development of scalable convergent context elicitation algorithms or heuristics.

8   Conclusions

The preceding work results from a large collaborative effort initiated more than one year ago by the IFIP 2.6 Working Group on Databases. The project has since then evolved to include external contributions as well. The field of Emergent Semantics is still clearly in its infancy, and we would welcome remarks as well as any kind of feedback based on this material.

References

1. A. M. Ouksel and I. Ahmed. Ontologies are not the panacea in data integration: A flexible coordinator for context construction. *Journal of Distributed and Parallel Databases*, 7,1, 1999.
2. A. M. Ouksel. In-context peer-to-peer information filtering on the web. *SIGMOD Record*, 32,3, 2003.
3. M. Vincini S. Bergamaschi, S. Castano and D. Beneventano. Semantic integration of heterogeneous information sources. *Data and Knowledge Engineering*, 36(3):215–249.
4. S. E. Madnick C. H. Goh, S. Bressan and M. D. Siegel. Context interchange: New features and formalisms for the intelligent integration of information. *ACM Trans. on Information Systems*, 17(3):270–293.
5. Y. Vassiliou M. Jarke, M. Lenzerini and editors P. Vassiliadis. *Fundamentals of Data Warehouses*. Springer, 1999.
6. H. Garcia-Molina Y. Papakonstantinou and J. Widom. Object exchange across heterogeneous information sources. In *International Conference on Data Engineering (ICDE)*, 1995.
7. J. Widom (ed.). Special issue on materialized views and data warehousing. *IEEE Bull. on Data Engineering*, 18(2), 1995.
8. J. D. Ullman. Information integration using logical views. In *International Conference on Database Theory (ICDT)*, pages 19–40, 1997.
9. G. De Giacomo D. Calvanese and M. Lenzerini. Answering queries using views in description logics. In *Proceedings of AAAI*, 2000.

10. A. Halevy. Answering queries using views: a survey. *VLDB Journal*, 10(4), 2001.
11. M. Friedman and D. S. Weld. Efficiently executing information-gathering plans. In *International Joint Conference on Artificial Intelligence*, 1997.
12. O. Etzioni and D. Weld. A softbot-based interface to the internet. *Communications of the ACM*, 37(7):72–76, 1994.
13. A. M. Keller M. Genesereth and O. M. Duschka. Infomaster: an information integration system. In *ACM SIGMOD International Conference on Management of Data*, 1997.
14. A. Levy J. Ordille and A. Rajaraman. Querying heteregeneous information sources using source descriptions. In *International Conference on Very Large Data Bases (VLDB)*, 1996.
15. A. Tate (editor). *Advanced Planning Technology*. AAAI Press, 1996.
16. Y. Arens and C. A. Knoblock. Sims: Retrieving and integrating information from multiple sources. In *ACM SIGMOD International Conference on Management of Data*, 1993.
17. E. Mena, A. Illarramendi, V. Kashyap, and A. Sheth. OBSERVER: An approach for query processing in global information systems based on interoperation across pre-existing ontologies. *International journal on Distributed And Parallel Databases (DAPD)*, 8(2):223–271, 2000.
18. S. Castano A. Corni R. Guidetti G. Malvezzi M. Melchiori D. Beneventano, S. Bergamaschi and M. Vincini. Information integration: The momis project demonstration. In *International Conference on Very Large Data Bases (VLDB)*, 2000.
19. D. Calvanese, G. De Giacomo, , M. Lenzerini, D. Nardi, and R. Rosati. Knowledge representation approach to information integration. In *AAAI workshop on AI and Information Integration*, pages 58–65, 1998.
20. M. Rousset and C. Reynaud. Knowledge representation for information integration. *Information Systems*, 29(1), 2004.
21. G. Guerrini E. Bertino and M. Mesiti. A matching algorithm for measuring the structural similarity between an xml document and a dtd and its applications. *Information Systems*, 29(1):23–46, 2004.
22. Z. W. Ras and A. Dardzinska. Ontology-based distributed autonomous knowledge systems. *Information Systems*, 29(1):47–58, 2004.
23. G. Salton and M. McGill. *Introduction to Modern Information Retrieval*. McGraw-Hill, 1983.
24. R. Baeza-Yates and B. Ribeiro-Neto. *Modern Information Retrieval*. ACM Press, 1999.
25. H. Garcia-Molina O. Brandman, J. Cho and N. Shivakumar. Crawler-friendly web servers. In *Workshop on Performance and Architecture of Web Servers (PAWS)*, 2000.
26. A. Vakali E. Terzi and M. S. Hacid. Knowledge representation, ontologies and semantic web. In *Asia-Pacific Web Conference (APWeb)*, 2003.
27. K. Aberer, Ph. Cudre-Mauroux, and M. Hauswirth. A framework for semantic gossiping. *SIGMOD Record*, 31(4), 2002.
28. A. M. Ouksel and C. Naiman. Coordinating context building in heterogeneous information systems. *Journal of Intelligent Information Systems*, 3,1:151–183, 1994.
29. A. M. Ouksel. *A Framework for a Scalable Agent Architecture of Cooperating Heterogeneous Knowledge Sources*. Springer Verlag, 1999.
30. T.R. Gruber. Toward principles for the design of ontologies used for knowledge sharing. *International Journal of Human-Computer Studies*, 43(5-6):907–928.

31. S. Brin and L. Page. The anatomy of a large-scale hypertextual Web search engine. In *International World Wide Web Conference (WWW)*, 1998.
32. F. Heylighen. Principia cybernetica web. http://pespmc1.vub.ac.be.
33. S. Camazine et al. *Self Organization in Biological Systems.* Princeton University Press, 2001.
34. T. Kohonen. *Self Organising and Associative Memory.* Springer Verlag, 1989.
35. J. J. Hopfield. Neural networks and physical systems with emergent collective computational abilities. *Proc. Nat. Acad. of Sciences*, 79:2554–2558, 1982.
36. J. Kennedy, R. Eberhart, and Y. Shi. *Swarm Intelligence.* Morgan Kaufmann Academic Press, 2001.
37. R. Albert and A. Barabasi. Statistical mechanics of complex networks. *Rev. Mod. Phys.*, 74:47–97, 2001.
38. M. Goldhaber. The attention economy and the net. In *First Monday, Vol 2, No 4*, 1997.
39. A. Martinoli and F. Mondada. Probabilistic modelling of a bio-inspired collective experiment with real robots. In *Proceeding of the Third International Symposium on Distributed Autonomous Robotic Systems.*
40. K. Aberer. P-Grid: A self-organizing access structure for P2P information systems. *Lecture Notes in Computer Science*, 2172:179–185, 2001.
41. S. Ratnasamy, P. Francis, M. Handley, R. Karp, and S. Shenker. A scalable content addressable network. In *Proceedings of ACM SIGCOMM 2001*, 2001.
42. G. Weiss (ed.). *Multiagent Systems.* MIT Press, 2000.
43. K. Aberer, A. Datta, and M. Hauswirth. The quest for balancing peer load in structured peer-to-peer systems. Technical report ic/2003/32, EPFL, 2003.
44. A. Datta, M. Hauswirth, and K. Aberer. Updates in highly unreliable, replicated peer-to-peer systems. In *Proceedings of the 23rd International Conference on Distributed Computing Systems, ICDCS2003*, Providence, Rhode Island, USA, 2003.
45. R. McCool and R. V. Guha. Tap, building the semantic web. http://tap.stanford.edu/.
46. K. Aberer, P. Cudré-Mauroux, and M. Hauswirth. The Chatty Web: Emergent Semantics Through Gossiping. In *International World Wide Web Conference (WWW)*, 2003.
47. K. Aberer, P. Cudré-Mauroux, and M. Hauswirth. Start making sense: The Chatty Web approach for global semantic agreements. *Journal of Web Semantics*, 1(1), 2003.
48. V. S. Iyengar, C. Apte, and T. Zhang. Active learning using adaptive resampling. In *Proceedings of the sixth ACM SIGKDD international conference on Knowledge discovery and data mining*, pages 91–98. ACM Press, 2000.
49. M.A. Hearst. Automatic acquisition of hyponyms from large text corpora. In *Proceedings of the 14th International Conference on Computational Linguistics*, 1992.
50. E. Charniak and M. Berland. Finding parts in very large corpora. In *Proceedings of the 37th Annual Meeting of the ACL*, pages 57–64, 1999.
51. A. Mädche and S. Staab. Ontology learning for the semantic web. *IEEE Intelligent Systems*, 16(2):72–79, March/April 2001.
52. Googlism, 2003. http://www.googlism.com.
53. G.W. Flake, S. Lawrence, C.L. Giles, and F.M. Coetzee. Self-organization and identification of web communities. *IEEE Computer*, 35(3):66 –70, March 2002.

54. E. J. Glover, K. Tsioutsiouliklis, S. Lawrence, D. M. Pennock, and G. W. Flake. Using web structure for classifying and describing web pages. In *Proceedings of the eleventh international conference on World Wide Web*, pages 562–569. ACM Press, 2002.
55. M. Spiliopoulou. Web usage mining for web site evaluation. *Commun. ACM*, 43(8):127–134, 2000.
56. G. Grefenstette. The WWW as a resource for example-based MT tasks. In *Proceedings of ASLIB'99 Translating and the Computer 21*, 1999.
57. E. Agirre, O. Ansa, E. Hovy, and D. Martinez. Enriching Very Large Ontologies using the WWW. In *Workshop on Ontology Construction of the ECAI*, 2000.
58. F. Keller, M. Lapata, and O. Ourioupina. Using the web to overcome data sparseness. In *Proceedings of EMNLP-02*, pages 230–237, 2002.
59. K. Markert, N. Modjeska, and M. Nissim. Using the web for nominal anaphora resolution. In *EACL Workshop on the Computational Treatment of Anaphora*, 2003.
60. S. Chakrabarti. Data mining for hypertext: a tutorial survey. *ACM SIGKDD Explorations Newsletter*, 1(2):1–11, January 2000.
61. P. Cimiano, S. Handschuh, and S. Staab. Towards the self-annotating web, 2003. Submitted for publication.
62. A. Maedche. *Ontology Learning for the Semantic Web*. Kluwer Academic Publishers, 2002.
63. E. Rahm and P. A. Bernstein. A survey of approaches to automatic schema matching. *VLDB Journal*, 10(4):334–350, 2001.
64. C. Behrens and V. Kashyap. The "emergent" semantic web: A consensus approach for deriving semantic knowledge on the web. In *proceedings of the International of the Semantic Web Working Symposium (SWWS), Stanford University, California, USA 2001*, 2001.
65. E. Cohen, A. Fiat, and H. Kaplan. Associative search in peer to peer networks: Harnessing latent semantics. In *IEEE INFOCOM*, 2003.
66. D. Beneventano, S. Bergamaschi, F. Guerra, and M. Vincini. Building an integrated ontology within sewasie system. In *Semantic Web and Data Bases (SWDB) Workshop*, 2003.
67. N. Guarino. Formal ontology in information systems. In *International Conference On Formal Ontology In Information Systems (FOIS)*, 1998.
68. T. Bylander and B. Chandrasekaran. Generic tasks in knowledge-based reasoning: The right level of abstraction for knowledge acquisition. *Knowledge Acquisition for Knowledge Based Systems*, 1:65–77, 1988.
69. Newell A. The knowledge level. *Artificial Intelligence*, 18(1), 1982.
70. G. A. Miller. Wordnet: A lexical database for english. *Communications of the ACM*, 38(11):39–41, 1995.
71. M. Jarrar, J. Demey, and R. Meersman. On using conceptual data modeling for ontology engineering. *Journal on Data Semantics*, LNCS, Vol. 2800, 2003.
72. M. Jarrar and R. Meersman. Formal ontology engineering in the dogma approach. In *International Conference on Ontologies, Databases and Applications of Semantics (ODBase)*, 2002.
73. S. Abiteboul, D. Quass, J. McHugh, J. Widom, and J. Wiener. The lorel query language for semistructured data. *Int. J. on Digital Libraries*, 1(1):68–88, 1997.
74. Resource description framework (rdf) model and syntax specification, 1999. W3C Recommendation 22 February 1999. http://www.w3.org/RDF/.
75. Rdf vocabulary description language 1.0: Rdf schema, 2003. W3C Working Draft 10 October 2003. http://www.w3.org/RDF/.

76. Owl web ontology language reference, 2003. W3C Candidate Recommendation 18 August 2003. http://www.w3.org/TR/owl-ref/.
77. A. Pease and I. Niles. Ieee standard upper ontology: A progress report. *Knowledge Engineering Review, Special Issue on Ontologies and Agents*, 17:65–70.
78. E. Bozsak, M. Ehrig, S. Handschuh, A. Hotho, A. Maedche, B. Motik, D. Oberle, C. Schmitz, S. Staab, L. Stojanovic, N. Stojanovic, R. Studer, G. Stumme, Y. Sure, J. Tane, R. Volz, and V. Zacharias. Kaon - towards a large scale semantic web. In *Proc. of EC-Web 2002*, LNCS, pages 304–313. Springer, 2002.
79. M. Lenzerini. Data Integration: A Theoretical Perspective. In *21st ACM Symposium on Principles of Database Systems (PODS 2002)*.
80. M. Ehrig, P. Haase, F. van Harmelen, R. Siebes, S. Staab, H. Stuckenschmidt, R. Studer, and C. Tempich. The swap data and metadata model for semantics-based peer-to-peer systems. In *Proceedings of MATES-2003. First German Conference on Multiagent Technologies. Erfurt, Germany, September 22-25*, LNAI, pages 144–155. Springer, 2003.
81. R. Siebes and F. van Harmelen. Ranking agent statements for building evolving ontologies. In *Proceedings of the AAAI-02 workshop on meaning negotiation, Alberta, Canada, July 28 2002*, 2002.
82. C. Tempich, S. Staab, and A. Wranik. REMINDIN': Semantic query routing in peer-to-peer networks based on social metaphors. In *International World Wide Web Conference (WWW), New York, USA*, 2004.
83. K. Aberer and M. Hauswirth. Peer-to-peer information systems: Concepts and models, state-of-the-art, and future systems. In *18th International Conference on Data Engineering (ICDE), San Jose, California, 2002*.
84. D. S. Milojicic, V. Kalogeraki, R. Lukose, K. Nagaraja, J. Pruyne, B. Richard, S. Rollins, and Z. Xu. Peer-to-peer computing. Technical report, HPL, 2002.
85. R. Guerraoui and A. Schiper. Software-based replication for fault tolerance. *IEEE Computer Journal*, 30(4):68–74, 1997.
86. Sheila A. McIlraith, Tran Cao Son, and Honglei Zeng. Semantic web services. *IEEE Intelligent Systems*, 16(2):46–53, 2001.
87. D. Berardi, D. Calvanese, G. DeGiacomo, M. Lenzerini, and M. Mecella. E-service composition by description logics based reasoning. In *Proceedings of the International Workshop on Description Logics*, 2003.
88. A. Eberhart. Ad-hoc invocation of semantic web services. In *Proceedings of the IEEE International Conference on Web Services*, San Diego, 2004.
89. M. Paolucci, T. Kawmura, T. Payne, and K. Sycara. Semantic matching of web services capabilities. In *First Int. Semantic Web Conf.*, 2002.
90. D. Trastour, C. Bartolini, and C. Preist. Semantic web support for the business-to-business e-commerce lifecycle. In *Proceedings of the eleventh international conference on World Wide Web*, pages 89–98. ACM Press, 2002.
91. OWL Service Coalition. *OWL-S: Semantic Markup for Web Services, November 2003*. http://www.daml.org/services/owl-s/1.0/.
92. *Web Service Modeling Ontology*. http://wsmo.org/.
93. L. Li and I. Horrocks. A software framework for matchmaking based on semantic web technology. In *Proceedings of the twelfth international conference on World Wide Web*, pages 331–339. ACM Press, 2003.
94. T. Di Noia, E. Di Sciascio, F. M. Donini, and M. Mongiello. A system for principled matchmaking in an electronic marketplace. In *Proceedings of the twelfth international conference on World Wide Web*, pages 321–330. ACM Press, 2003.
95. *Bricks - Building Resources for Integrated Cultural Knowledge Services, EU-IST 507457*. http://www.brickscommunity.org/.

96. A. M. Ouksel. Emergent semantics and in-context peer-to-peer information filtering and model calibration on the web. In *Workshop on Semantic Web Technologies for Searching and Retrieving Scientific Data, Sanibel Island, Florida*, 2003.

97. A. M. Ouksel and D. S. Mackay. Environmental modeling within a scalable multi-agent architecture for semantic cooperation amongst autonomous and heterogeneous information sources. In *NSF Proposal 1004213-9978386. (PI: A. M. Ouksel). UIC-IDS-CRIM/Tech-Report 99-07*, 1999.

98. V. B. Robinson and A. U. Frank. About different kinds of uncertainty in collections of spatial data. In *Auto-Carto 7, American Society for Phtogrammetry and Remote Sensing and American Congress on Surveying and Mapping*, Falls Church, VA, 1985.

99. M. F. Worboys and S. M. Deen. Semantic heterogeneity in distributed geographic databases. *ACM SIGMOD Record*, 20(4), 1991.

100. G. C. Roman. Formal specification of geographic data processing requirements. *IEEE Transactions on Knowledge and Data Engineering*, 2(4), 1990.

101. D. S. Mackay. Semantic integration of environmental models for application to global information and decision-making. *ACM SIGMOD Record*, 28(1), 1999.

User-Specific Semantic Integration of Heterogeneous Data: The SIRUP Approach

Patrick Ziegler and Klaus R. Dittrich

Database Technology Research Group, Department of Informatics,
University of Zurich, Winterthurerstrasse 190, CH-8057 Zürich, Switzerland
{pziegler,dittrich}@ifi.unizh.ch

Abstract. We give an overview of the SIRUP (Semantic Integration Reflecting User-specific semantic Perspectives) approach to semantic data integration that takes into account heterogeneity of data receivers. Our goal is to provide means that allow data from heterogeneous sources to be integrated in a way that it perfectly fits to a particular user's information needs, emphasizing his individual way to perceive a domain of interest. To achieve this, we propose to use a semantic multidatasource language to declaratively manipulate so-called *IConcepts*; these are basic conceptual building blocks to which attribute data that refers to the same real-world concept is linked by data providers. We provide explicit, queryable semantics by connecting IConcepts to concepts of ontologies. Additionally, pre-integrating data on a conceptual level through IConcepts shields SIRUP end-users from low-level heterogeneity and technical details of underlying data sources.

1 Introduction

In today's ever increasing abundance of online data sources, integration is becoming more and more indispensable in order not to drown in data while starving for information. In general, the goal of data integration is to combine data from different sources by applying a global data model and by detecting and resolving schema and data conflicts so that a homogeneous, unified view can be provided. The reason for data integration is twofold: First, given a set of existing data sources, an integrated view is to be created to facilitate data access and reuse through a single data access point. Second, given a certain information need, data from different complementing sources is to be combined to gain a more comprehensive basis to satisfy the information need.

There is a remarkable history of research projects in the area of data integration. The spectrum ranges from early multidatabase systems (e.g., Multibase [18]) over mediator systems (e.g., Garlic [4]) to ontology-based integration approaches (e.g., OBSERVER [19]). These approaches have in common that autonomy of the data sources to be integrated is considered to be of paramount importance.

Besides this autonomy of data sources, there is the often neglected autonomy and sovereignty of data receivers, i.e., human users and applications [11].

M. Bouzeghoub et al. (Eds.): ICSNW 2004, LNCS 3226, pp. 44–64, 2004.
© IFIP International Federation for Information Processing 2004

Data receivers are autonomous in the sense that they typically have different information needs and vary in the ways they perceive their particular domain of interest. Sovereignty of data receivers refers to the fact that using integrated data must be *non-intrusive* [25]; i.e., users should not be forced to adapt to any standard concerning structure and semantics of data they desire. Therefore, to take a "one integrated schema fits all" approach is definitely not a satisfactory solution. We address the problem of how user-specific ways to perceive a particular application domain can be taken into account in the process of semantically integrating data from heterogeneous data sources.

In this paper, we give an overview of the SIRUP (Semantic Integration Reflecting User-specific semantic Perspectives) approach to data integration that supports semantic integration by modeling user-specific ways to perceive an application domain. The focus of this paper is on the general foundations of our approach; advanced integration concepts and query processing are not covered. Note that we generally concentrate on querying, not on manipulation of integrated data. For integration, we consider alphanumeric data from a broad range of data sources (i.e., database systems, web services, application interfaces, file systems, and the web).

Our general goal is to provide means that allow data from heterogeneous sources to be integrated in a way that it perfectly fits to a particular user's information needs, emphasizing his individual way to perceive a domain of interest. Additionally, we aim at abstracting the user from low-level heterogeneity and technical details of underlying data sources. In contrast to traditional ex-post definition of views on top of already existing integrated global schemas, we advocate a method called *ex-ante view definition* which allows that only data items are integrated which are semantically related according to the user's individual perception of the particular application domain. In the end, we aim at providing well-structured user-specific schemas with extensive metadata and explicit, queryable semantics for integrated data from selected sources:

- By extensive metadata, explicit information on structural aspects of integrated data is given (attributes of classes/relations, attribute data types, measurement unit, precision, constraints, etc.). Additionally, we aim at providing data lineage information for all integrated data items.
- By explicit, queryable semantics, information on the real-world semantics (see Sect. 3) of the integrated data items is given. By making such semantic metadata retrievable through queries, users do not have to interpret schema and data elements themselves, which is generally erroneous. Misinterpretations can therefore be avoided.

This paper is structured as follows: The following Sect. 2 discusses integration mistakes that can occur when integration approaches are applied that provide only a predefined global schema. Sect. 3 deals with semantics and ontologies. The foundations of our solution are presented in Sect. 4 and Sect. 5 discusses some aspects in more detail. Sect. 6 describes the software architecture of the SIRUP prototype. In Sect. 7, an overview of related work and a comparison between SIRUP and related approaches is given. Sect. 8 concludes the paper.

2   Global Schema Approaches to Data Integration

Data from heterogeneous sources is often integrated by defining one single global schema that represents a unified view over this data. Global schema approaches can be classified as follows:

Traditional Global Schema Approaches. These approaches use a data model that originates from the era before object-orientation, such as the functional or relational data model, to provide one single global schema for all users. As in Multibase [18] and Mermaid [30], export schemas from the data sources are directly mapped to the global schema.

Object-Oriented Global Schema Approaches. Data sources provide interfaces which can be used to define a global schema using an object-oriented data model. These approaches generally employ integration by creating superclasses to subsume related data from several data sources. Examples for this type of approach are Pegasus [1], TSIMMIS [5], and Garlic [4].

Single Domain Model/Ontology Approaches. These approaches use a single domain model or ontology against which all data is integrated, e.g., as in SIMS [2], Carnot [6], and PICSEL [10]. A "semantic" approach to integration is chosen by integrating against one general domain model.

Different users often have diverse views of reality — i.e., they perceive and conceptualize the same real-world part differently, according to their relative points of view, their information needs, and expectations [23,29,15]. It is due to this fact that imposing a single global schema for all users can have severe limitations that seriously interfere with the users' individual work. We illustrate these limitations with the MOMIS [3] approach to data integration. In general, MOMIS can be considered as an object-oriented global schema approach in our classification. In MOMIS, a common thesaurus for terminological relationships is built from source schemas and clusters of similar classes from the source schemas are identified. Then, for each cluster a single unifying class is defined and an integrated global schema consisting of these unified classes is built.

For example, assume that there are three classes C_1, C_2, and C_3 concerning educational meetings, each from a different data source, as shown in Fig. 1. Semantically, these three classes are very similar in name. Additionally, the attributes they provide are very similar in name semantics and data type. Due to this high similarity, it is very likely that a single class is created to represent the three classes in a global schema. An example of such an integrated class $C_{integrated}$ is shown in Fig. 1.

A first drawback of such a global schema approach is that users may be given a global schema providing a unified view over data that may be – from the users' perspective – inappropriately collected and selected. In general, it is up to the designer of the global schema to choose what information from a particular local schema is relevant to be available in the global schema. Differences between these choices and the information a particular user expects can lead to situations where the global schema is inappropriate for the information needs of certain users. We refer to this problem as a *data selection mistake*.

Class C_1 from data source 1:
lecture(id_number:int, theme:varchar, auditorium:varchar, time:time,
        lecturer:varchar)

Class C_2 from data source 2:
colloquium(identifier:int, topic:varchar, location:varchar, date:date,
        speaker:varchar)

Class C_3 from data source 3:
seminar(id:int, subject:varchar, seminar_room:varchar, time:time,
        professor:varchar)

Integrated class $C_{integrated}$ in the global schema:
course(id:int, subject:varchar, room:varchar, date:date, lecturer:varchar)

Fig. 1. Example Schema Parts from Different Data Sources[1]

The same problem of inappropriate data selection can occur not only within single source schemas, but also with entire data sources. It is up to the designer of the global schema to select from which local data sources data is integrated. However, users may differ in their preference for data from different origins (due to quality, reliability, etc.) from the preference of the global schema designer. Regardless of this, all users are given the same single global schema. We refer to this problem as a *source selection mistake*.

Second, even if the global schema generally provides all the information to satisfy a certain information need, the granularity in which this information is presented may be inappropriate. On the one hand, the view provided by the global schema may be too coarse-grained; i.e., the available information can be too general. In our example, the resulting global schema class $C_{integrated}$ may be useful for users who are satisfied with the global **course** class and do not need to distinguish between different types of educational meetings. However, the global **course** class is of very limited benefit for other users who need a more fine-grained distinction between different types of courses. On the other hand, entity information provided by the global schema can also be too fine-grained.[2] We refer to this problem as an *entity granularity mistake*.

The same problem of inappropriate granularity can occur not only with entities, but also with attributes. For example, the integrated class $C_{integrated}$ only offers information on rooms where the courses take place. The information whether this is an auditorium or a seminar room, which was originally available in the source schemas C_1 and C_3, respectively, is lost. We refer to this problem as an *attribute granularity mistake*.

Third, classes in the global schema may provide an integrated view on data that is semantically not related according to the individual perception of specific

---

[1] We assume data type **date** to consist of information on year, month, day, and time.
[2] In this case, the user might try to define a unifying external view for subsumption, if supported.

users. We refer to this problem as a *data semantics mistake*. Assume that in our example, class `lecture` and `seminar` are implicitly defined in their respective data sources to consist of a series of class meetings, whereas a `colloquium` is implicitly defined to consist only of a single meeting. In this case, the global class `course` – designed to encompass all available information on educational meetings regardless how many times they take place – is inappropriate for users who care about this distinction. Even worse, important underlying assumptions concerning source schemas and the global schema may be fully implicit due to the lack of explicit metadata and documentation.

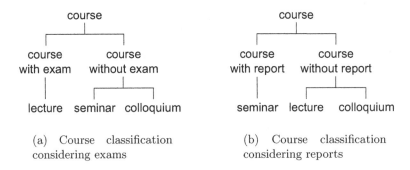

(a) Course classification considering exams

(b) Course classification considering reports

Fig. 2. Different Ways to Classify Courses

Fourth, there may be users who need completely different taxonomies of entities than provided by the global schema. For instance, assume a secretary who works for a university needs information on all the courses where students have to pass a final exam. In this case, a classification as shown in Fig. 2(a) can be suitable to provide a schema for queries. On the other hand, another secretary might need information on all the courses where a written report has to be handed in. In this case, a different classification of courses as shown in Fig. 2(b) can be preferable. However, in both cases, there is only the global `course` class $C_{integrated}$ available that cannot satisfy the two different information needs. We refer to this problem as a *taxonomy mistake*.

We have seen six types of integration mistakes that lead to situations where a global schema is inappropriate for particular users. We refer to problems of this type with the general notion of *perspectual integration mistakes*. Note that perspectual integration mistakes can be independently combined to form *combined perspectual integration mistakes*. All six integration mistakes presented are generally caused by differences between the ways a global schema designer and a particular user perceive a certain application domain for which data is integrated; i.e., they are caused by data receiver heterogeneity. *Data receiver heterogeneity* refers to the fact that users are generally situated in different real-world contexts and widely differ in both, their conceptual interpretation and data preference [11]. Regardless how sophisticated a predefined global schema is, there is no global schema that fits all the needs of all potential users. Therefore, users must be able to specify their individual information needs. Based on this, user-specific integration should take place to give the user access to information in a way that perfectly fits his perception of an application domain of interest.

3 Semantics and Ontologies

Semantics refer to meaning, in contrast to syntax that refers to structure. In the database area, semantics can be regarded as people's interpretation of data and schema items according to their understanding of the world in a certain context. In data integration, the type of semantics considered is generally real-world semantics. According to [21], real-world semantics are concerned with the "mapping of objects in the model or computational world onto the real world [. . .] [and] the issues that involve human interpretation, or meaning and use of data and information." Differences in interpretations of the same schema or data item between data providers and data users lead to semantic heterogeneity.

One idea to overcome semantic heterogeneity is to exhaustively specify the intended real-world semantics of all data and schema elements. Unfortunately, it is impossible to completely define what a data or schema element denotes or means in the database world [27]. Therefore, database schemas do typically not provide enough explicit semantics to interpret data always consistently and unambiguously [28]. Moreover, there are no absolute semantics that are valid for all potential users; semantics are relative [9]. Nevertheless, a means in form of semantic metadata is necessary to explicitly and semantically characterize in adequate form the information content provided for integration so that it can be reasonably interpreted by humans and computers.

Ontologies are one way to represent explicit, formal semantics. An ontology is "an explicit specification of a conceptualization" [12]. In other words, an ontology is an explicit, formal description of concepts and their relationships that exist in a certain universe of discourse and provides a shared vocabulary to refer to these concepts. Compared with other classification schemes, such as taxonomies, thesauri, or keywords, ontologies allow more complete and more precise domain models [14].

In the area of data integration, ontologies can be applied to ensure semantic interoperability between data sources. By using ontologies, the semantics of data provided by data sources for integration can be made explicit with respect to an ontology a particular user group commits to. Based on this shared understanding, the danger of semantic heterogeneity can be reduced. Note that to avoid problems similar to single global schemas, no single global ontology should be predetermined for all possible user groups. Such an approach would force users to adapt to one single conceptualization of the world. Therefore, a proper approach to data integration should support different ontologies so that different community-specific semantics can be used in parallel.

4   Foundations of the SIRUP Approach

We propose a novel approach to data integration (see Fig. 3) that mainly aims at avoiding perspectual integration mistakes. It is based on the following principles:

Semantic Perspectives. A Semantic Perspective is a user-defined conceptual model of an application domain with explicit queryable semantics for all entities and relationships appearing in it. In particular, a Semantic Perspective expresses user-specific taxonomies and categorizations of real-world entities that belong to a specific application domain according to a particular user's notion. Semantic Perspectives are built on top of data from data sources that are selected by the user and reflect an individual way to perceive a particular real-world part. With such an explicit specification of the desired view, data from user-selected data sources can be integrated reflecting the desired entities and structures defined in the Semantic Perspective.

Bipartite Integration Process. In a data integration system, there are generally two main roles: data providers and data users. Data providers know the semantics, local structure, and technical access information[3] of the data they provide and data users know their own information needs for which they want integrated data. Except for small sample cases, none of these two groups has the full knowledge of the other group.

To reflect this dichotomy between the two main roles in data integration systems, the integration process in our approach is separated into two distinct phases: (1) A *data provision phase* where administrators of local data sources explicitly declare the data and its semantics that is offered for integration and (2) a *Semantic Perspective modeling phase* where users who know their application domain for which data is to be integrated define the desired Semantic Perspective.

IConcepts. An IConcept (short for *Intermediate Concept*[4]) is a basic conceptual building block that acts as a linking element between data providers and data users interested in data for their information needs. Each IConcept has a queryable link to at least one concept of an ontology to explicitly define the semantics of the real-world concept it represents (e.g., "professor" or "lecture", etc.). Data sources can provide attributes for an ontological concept represented by a particular IConcept. That way, data sources can declare what attribute data they are capable and willing to provide concerning a given IConcept. For each of these attributes, additional structural metadata (data type, measurement unit, precision, constraints, etc.) is provided.

For data providers, IConcepts provide a means to explicitly specify semantics and structure of the data they offer for user-specific integration. Using an ontology index (see Sect. 5.5), data providers identify IConcepts which they

---

[3] Such as network addresses, protocols, interfaces/APIs, login information, etc.

[4] "Intermediate", because an IConcept is (1) not a fully-fledged user-specific concept (see the next paragraph) but just a building block to construct user-specific concepts and (2) it has an intermediate position between data sources/data providers and data users/query issuers.

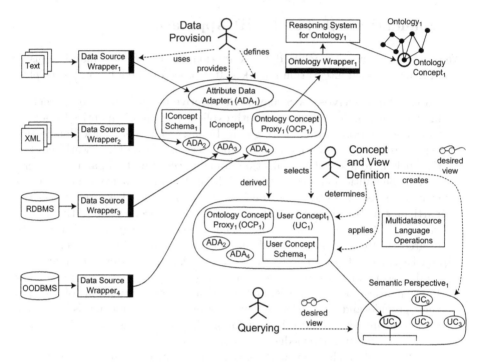

Fig. 3. Overview of the SIRUP Approach to Data Integration

are willing to provide data for. For data users, IConcepts are an access point to retrieve data from different data sources referring to the same real-world concept. Additionally, IConcepts hide technical and structural heterogeneity from data users and help to resolve semantic conflicts according to the user's perception of the application domain. Starting from an ontology index, users can browse for IConcepts relevant for their information needs and select, combine and restructure IConcepts to build user-specific concepts and concept hierarchies that define the users' individual Semantic Perspectives.

User Concepts. A User Concept is a user-specific concept that is built by selecting and combining user-specific copies of IConcepts. Whenever a user selects an IConcept for his own perspective modeling, a copy of that selected IConcept (together with all its metadata and subcomponents, see Sect. 5.6) is assigned to a namespace private to the user. Using selection, projection, join, cartesian product, and set operators (union, set difference, intersection), users can declaratively define User Concepts based on the selected IConcept copies and already existing other User Concepts. That way, IConcept copies constitute the root nodes on top of which users can incrementally build in a bottom-up manner user-specific concepts and concept hierarchies that form together the desired Semantic Perspective. In query processing, relevant attribute data can be retrieved from the data sources by the IConcept copies which user-specific concept hierarchies are based on. During concept definition, ontology links inherited from underlying IConcept copies as well as attribute metadata are automatically maintained for User Concepts so that explicitly defined queryable semantics and up-to-date structural metadata are still available. By this metadata, each User Concept possesses a highly structured, explicit schema that describes the attributes that are available. In case the User Concept's ontology link that is inherited from its underlying IConcept does not exactly fit the user's own intended semantics for that User Concept, the intended semantics of the derived User Concept can be changed by modifying the concept's ontology link and documentation.[5] However, each User Concept must always be assigned to at least one existing ontological concept to ensure that explicit, queryable semantics is anytime available.

In the SIRUP approach, users are abstracted from technical, structural, and semantic integration issues by IConcepts that provide a conceptually homogeneous view on data. However, users who want to define their own Semantic Perspective have to do schema integration on a conceptual level by selecting and combining IConcept copies. In contrast to classical approaches to schema integration, users in our approach can benefit from explicit semantics and from conceptual-level pre-integration of data according to ontological concepts. That way, users are enabled to effectively do the necessary integration activities to build their individual Semantic Perspectives.

Semantic Multidatasource Language. In our approach, a declarative language is provided for data provision as well as for specifying User Concepts and Semantic Perspectives. This language supports querying of explicit semantics and metadata assigned to User Concepts and IConcepts. Additionally, data queries against integrated data from Semantic Perspectives are supported. For data providers, our semantic multidatasource language offers the means to perform integration of semantically equivalent IConcept attributes that originate from different data sources. Our semantic multidatasource language supports IConcept definition and linking of attributes from structured, semi-structured, and unstructured data sources. For metadata and data access from these data sources, we employ data source wrappers.

Ex-ante View Definition. In traditional view definition in both centralized and distributed database environments, users can specify views only on top of already existing schemas, e.g., using the `create view` command of SQL. We refer to this approach as *ex-post view definition* since the view is created after a (global) schema is defined. When data from different data sources is integrated, perspectual integration mistakes have to be avoided. We believe that the best way to prevent these mistakes is to allow the user to specify his own individual way to perceive the application domain of interest, i.e., his own Semantic Perspective. Therefore, integrated schemas or predefined views should not be offered to the user for later refinement but the

---

[5] Note that this is not intended for arbitrarily changing source data semantics, e.g., from "course" to "cat", but for cases where User Concepts are defined by generalizing or specializing other User Concepts or IConcepts, e.g., specializing from "course" to "database course". Here, it is desirable that the ontology link can be adjusted to refer more precisely to the intended *database* course semantics.

integrated schemas have to built *before* by the user himself according to his information needs. In our approach, the definition of Semantic Perspectives and declarative integration of IConcept-attributed data are mutually intertwined processes.

Pragmatic Data Integration. Approaches that integrate data against one or more global ontologies assume an ideal world in which data for all ontology concepts is available. If data sources do not provide data for all the ontology concepts, issuing queries against ontologies acting as a query schema is not of much use. Our approach is pragmatic in that sense that only concepts for which data that is actually provided by one or more data sources is available for building Semantic Perspectives. That way, data for all concepts appearing in Semantic Perspectives can really be provided in general.[6]

Based on these foundations, perspectual integration mistakes can be avoided by enabling user-specific semantic data integration and restructuring. This is illustrated in the example in Fig. 4: Data on seminars, lectures, colloquia, and conferences from local data sources at a university is linked to IConcepts. That way, this data can be used in Semantic Perspective modeling to provide integrated information in a way that it perfectly fits the secretary's desired view from Fig. 2(a)[7]. At the same time, a completely different Semantic Perspective concerning database technology research meetings can be supported based on selected (i.e., specialized) local colloquium and external conference data.

5   A Closer Look at the SIRUP Approach

In this section, more details on several aspects and components of our integration approach are given.

5.1   Roles in the SIRUP Approach

In the SIRUP approach to data integration, there are three roles in which human users appear (see Fig. 3):

Data Provision. Each data provider is assumed to have detailed technical knowledge about his particular data source (e.g., about its location in a network, how to access it and its data, etc.) and the structure and semantics of all the data it provides for integration. On that basis, data providers create IConcepts[8] and supply metadata for the attributes their data sources are capable and willing to provide for a given IConcept.

---

[6] In practice, some data sources may nevertheless be temporarily unavailable due to server failure or maintenance, etc.

[7] For local course data, we assume that the (local) Semantic Perspective modeler can easily determine — based on his knowledge of the local domain — which courses require a final exam.

[8] Note that for each ontological concept, only one single IConcept can be created.

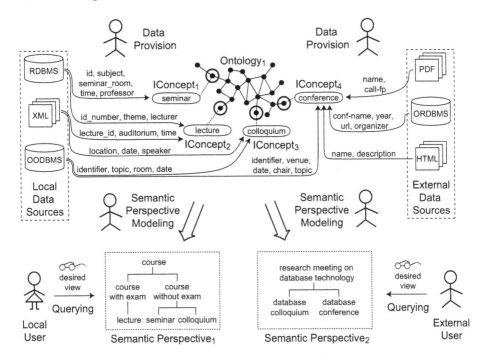

Fig. 4. Example on Applying the SIRUP Approach to Provide Tailored Semantic Perspectives on Course and Conference Data

Concept and View Definition. Each person defining User Concepts for a Semantic Perspective can select from the attributes that are provided by IConcepts and other publicly available User Concepts. For this conceptual modeling process, we assume that the particular person has a clear idea of the relevant concepts to be modeled for the desired Semantic Perspective. Concept and view definition can be done by (sufficiently knowledgeable) end-users as well as by information architects or information engineers who define tailored views for particular user communities.

Querying. After a Semantic Perspective is defined, queries against the global schema it represents can be asked. Note that this global schema is application- or user-specific; i.e., there are *several* co-existing user-specific schemas available in SIRUP, in contrast to traditional integration approaches providing a *single* global schema for all users. For querying, we assume the user has a clear idea what data is desired as a query result.

5.2   Data Sources and Source Data

For the type of data to be integrated in our approach, we focus on alphanumeric data. Other types of data, such as images, audio and video data, or binary data files (Word, Excel, PDF, etc.) are only considered as atomic files with no additional internal structure. Therefore, this type of data can only be available to users as entire files that appear as "file" attributes of IConcepts (i.e., a data source can provide images of professors as a "professor_image" attribute for an IConcept representing the ontological concept of "professor").

We aim at supporting a broad range of data sources in our approach. First, data sources can be traditional database systems (relational, object-oriented, etc.). Besides this, data from web services and applications that provide data export facilities (e.g., an API to retrieve XML data) are to be supported. Last, but not least, data from text files (i.e., XML, SGML, HTML, plain text, etc.) provided by file systems as well as data from the WWW shall be available for integration.

5.3 External Ontologies

For making semantics of data explicit, ontologies are used in the SIRUP approach (see Fig. 3). In order not to constrain the set of applicable ontologies, we intend to support different ontology languages [7]. That way, ontologies that are specified in various ontology languages can be used in SIRUP for data content explication. We employ ontology wrappers to cope with heterogeneity caused by differences in these ontology languages. Concerning their content, the set of available ontologies is generally open and extensible so that general foundational ontologies as well as specialized domain-specific ontologies can be used for accurate data content explication.

To provide a sophisticated query service on data semantics, we plan to use the reasoning systems provided for the various supported ontology languages. Hence, our semantic multidatasource language will act as a unified query interface for access to different ontological reasoning systems. Thus, users can be provided with explicit, queryable semantics regardless what ontology language is used to represent the intended real-world semantics of data.

5.4 Wrappers

A wrapper is a coupling software component that is specific to an external system and that bridges the gap between this external system and a target system by translating queries, commands and data between internal (local) and external (global) formats. In the SIRUP approach, all available wrappers are centrally registered and can therefore be easily accessed whenever needed. We use two types of wrappers to provide a uniform interface to data sources and ontological reasoning systems (see Fig. 3):

Data Source Wrappers. This type of wrapper is responsible for exporting metadata on the attributes a particular data source provides for an IConcept. In query processing, requested attribute data can be retrieved by the wrappers and is converted — if necessary — into XML format, which is globally used for all data in our approach.

Ontology Wrappers. By ontology wrappers, queries concerning data semantics are translated between our semantic multidatasource language and the
languages used by ontological reasoning systems. Ontology wrappers also
convert returned query results from external reasoning systems into a homogeneous format. That way, users can issue queries on data semantics without
having to use different ontology languages.

5.5 Ontology Index

In order to provide efficient access to ontological concepts, a centralized ontology
index is maintained in our approach (see Fig. 5). All ontologies whose concepts
are used to explicitly define data semantics must be registered to that index.[9]
That way, users looking for data are provided with a single point of access. Data
providers can only use ontological concepts in the data provision phase whose
ontologies are registered. During registration, at least one ontology wrapper has
to be specified in order to uniformly access the reasoning system of the particular
ontology.

When Semantic Perspectives are defined, users implicitly express which IConcepts (and, consequently, which underlying ontological concepts) they regard
as semantically equivalent or related. For instance, union operations between
IConcepts specify semantic equivalence from the particular user's point of view.
Besides this, semantic similarities and relationships between IConcepts are expressed by joins. Whenever a user applies union or join operations on IConcepts,
the expressed semantic relation between these IConcepts is automatically reported to the ontology index. That way, user-specific intra- and inter-ontological
mappings can be recorded. By offering these mappings to other users and data
providers, the process of finding appropriate ontological concepts and IConcepts
for data provision and Semantic Perspective building can be facilitated.

5.6 IConcept Components

In order to abstract users from heterogeneity of underlying data sources, IConcepts use services provided by two subcomponents (see Fig. 3):

Attribute Data Adapter (ADA). ADAs are software components that link
a certain data source wrapper to one single IConcept. Each ADA encapsulates information about which wrapper is to be accessed and which queries
or data access scripts are to be used in order to retrieve attribute data for
all attributes a data source provides for one particular IConcept.
Ontology Concept Proxy (OCP). Each IConcept contains exactly one
OCP that encapsulates information about which ontology wrapper is to be
accessed in order to retrieve data semantics information.[10]

---

[9] Additionally, all available IConcepts must be centrally registered in a global metadata repository. See Fig. 5.
[10] In case of union and join operations on User Concepts (which are derived from IConcepts), more than one OCP may be available in the User Concept since ontological
concepts from more than one ontologies may be referenced. See Sect. 5.7.

5.7   Maintenance of Ontology Links

During Semantic Perspective and User Concept building, it has to be ensured that the links to ontology concepts used for expressing explicit data semantics remain valid. In the SIRUP approach, ontology links are automatically maintained while the user declaratively specifies the desired User Concepts. In particular, the following link adjustments are made for operations supported by our multi-datasource language:

- For projection and selection on IConcepts or User Concepts, a new User Concept is created. The ontology link remains unchanged, i.e., the new User Concept is assigned a copy of the ontology link of the concept[11] the operation is performed on.
- For inner join, full outer join, and cartesian product, a new User Concept is created to which a copy of the ontology links from both involved concepts is assigned.
- For left outer join, a new User Concept is created. To the new User Concept, a copy of the ontology link from the left concept is assigned. ("Left" and "right" in this context means the following: For reference to position, we consider the position of the concepts in the following notation for join operations, as also supported by SQL: `employee join department on emp_depnr = dep_nr`. In this example, `employee` is considered as the left, `department` as the right concept.)
- For right outer join, a new User Concept is created to which a copy of the ontology link from the right concept is assigned.
- For union, outer union and intersection, a new User Concept is created to which a copy of the ontology links from both involved concepts is assigned.
- For set difference, a new User Concept is created to which a copy of the ontology link from the left concept is assigned.
- For changes in attribute metadata entries (attribute renaming, type conversion, etc.),[12] only the affected attribute metadata of the User Concept is changed. The ontology link of the User Concept remains unchanged.

5.8   Integrated Data and Querying

After Semantic Perspectives tailored for certain information needs are created, they are available for querying. In general, integrated data for querying and further use is to be provided in a data format that is widely accepted and usable. Therefore, we plan to use XML to offer all integrated data in a structurally self-describing way.

In SIRUP, two types of queries can be asked:

Data Queries. This type of query represents requests for data that is integrated and structured in a user-specific way. Data queries can be formulated by using User Concept and IConcept names as well as names of their attributes in declarative SQL-/OQL-like query statements.

---

[11] In this section, "concept" refers to both, IConcept and User Concept.
[12] Note that these changes can only be applied to User Concepts.

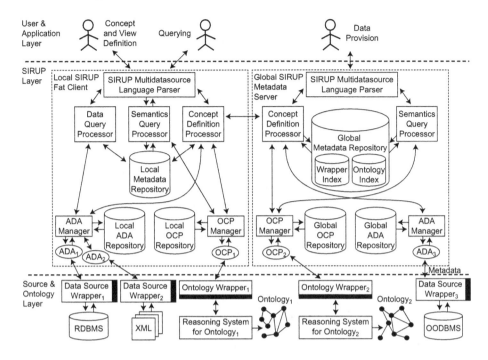

Fig. 5. Fat Client Software Architecture of the SIRUP Prototype

Semantics Queries. By semantics queries, requests for explicit data semantics for IConcepts, User Concepts, and their attributes can be expressed. Semantics queries either refer to requests for the real-world semantics of a particular IConcept or User Concept. Alternatively, semantics queries can be requests for metadata on structural aspects of IConcepts, User Concepts, and their attributes (e.g., number and names of attributes, attribute data types, data lineage information, etc.).

6   Outlook on the SIRUP Prototype Architecture

As a final proof of concept, we plan to implement a fully functional SIRUP prototype. Each SIRUP system generally consists of one central Global SIRUP Metadata Server and one or more Local SIRUP Clients (see Fig. 5):

– The Global SIRUP Metadata Server provides information on all registered IConcepts for which data is provided as well as information on all registered ontological concepts that are available to explicitly define data semantics. Additionally, it stores information about all available data source and ontology wrappers and manages central repositories for Attribute Data Adapters and Ontology Concept Proxies.

– The Local SIRUP Client is in charge of accepting and processing declarative User Concept specifications and modifications; alternatively, user input can be a query for data or semantics. For all locally defined User Concepts as well as for all IConcept copies that are in local use, the Local SIRUP Client stores all necessary metadata.

There can be more than one Global SIRUP Metadata Server instance at the same time, e.g., each one run by a different enterprise or (commercial) data provider. Each Local SIRUP Client can use IConcepts from one or more Global SIRUP Metadata Servers at the same time.

Both, the Global SIRUP Metadata Server and each Local SIRUP Client have five common subcomponents (see Fig. 5):

SIRUP Multidatasource Language Parser. The SIRUP Multidatasource Language Parser accepts declarative user input that is formulated with our semantic multidatasource language, grammatically analyzes it and produces a parse tree for subsequent processing.

Concept Definition Processor. In general, this component is capable of processing all IConcept and User Concept definition requests. The Concept Definition Processors of Local SIRUP Clients and Global SIRUP Metadata Servers communicate in order to exchange metadata.

Semantics Query Processor. The Semantics Query Processor processes all requests for explicit data semantics concerning IConcepts, User Concepts, and their attributes. For queries on the real-world semantics of IConcepts and User Concepts, the Semantics Query Processor is in charge of dispatching them via an ontology wrapper to the appropriate external ontology system for evaluation.

ADA Manager. The ADA Manager component is responsible for storing all necessary ADAs and retrieving individual ADAs whenever they are needed — e.g., when IConcepts are copied from a Global SIRUP Metadata Server to a Local SIRUP Client.

OCP Manager. Each OCP Manager has to store all necessary OCPs in its OCP Repository and to retrieve individual OCPs whenever needed.

Besides the five subcomponents that are also part of a Global SIRUP Metadata Server, each Local SIRUP Client has an additional subcomponent:

Data Query Processor. The Data Query Processor accepts parse trees concerning data queries from the SIRUP Multidatasource Language Parser as input and processes them. Note that Global SIRUP Metadata Servers do not have to be able to process data queries since they do not provide integrated data but conceptual building blocks (i.e., IConcepts) for user-specific data integration that is performed on Local SIRUP Clients.

7   Related Work

With respect to our goals (see Sect. 1), related work can mainly be found in the area of multidatabase languages and declarative integration languages, such as MSQL+ [20], SQL/M [16], SchemaSQL [17], and FRAQL [24]. Besides this, approaches that provide conceptual-level abstraction from data sources (e.g., InfoQuilt [26] and KIND [13]), object-oriented virtual integration approaches (e.g., TSIMMIS [5] and Garlic [4]), ontology-based integration approaches (e.g., SIMS [2] and OBSERVER [19]), Semantic Web approaches (e.g., On2broker [8]), and taxonomic database systems (e.g., Prometheus [22]) can be regarded as areas of related work. As we concluded in [31], no related approach is able to attain all of our main goals. Therefore, an integration approach capable of (1) preserving user sovereignty by enabling the user to express his desired view for data integration, (2) shielding the user from technical-level heterogeneities, and (3) providing explicit, queryable data semantics is desirable.

Our work in the SIRUP approach differs from related work in the following aspects:

- First, compared with multidatabase languages like SchemaSQL [17] or FRA-QL [24], users are in our approach abstracted from underlying data sources. Since multidatabase languages do not provide transparency, users have to directly locate and access the component database systems from which data is requested. Therefore, applying multidatabase languages is quite demanding since all tasks of data integration and reconciliation are solely put on the user. Additionally, multidatabase languages provide no explicit queryable data semantics to ensure semantically correct interpretations of schemas and data. Another difference to our approach is that multidatabase languages focus on data integration in homogeneous environments — usually, data from relational databases is considered.

- Second, there are integration approaches that abstract from the local data sources by providing a conceptual layer on top of which data integration can be performed, like KIND [13]. These approaches, in contrast to our approach, principally take a single global schema approach. First, data of each source is separately and conceptually described. Then, these descriptions are used as a basis for global schema creation and query processing.

  Other approaches in this category, like InfoQuilt [26], require the user to model his domain of interest. Then, it is up to the user to identify relevant data sources and to create wrappers. Our approach, on the opposite, does not require users to deal with data sources directly but shields them from underlying technical details and heterogeneity. Additionally, data in our approach is pre-integrated by linking attribute data to IConcepts.

- Third, compared with object-oriented virtual integration approaches like TSIMMIS [5] or Garlic [4], our approach provides explicit, queryable semantics on all available data. Moreover, users in our approach are more abstracted from underlying data sources and do not have to cope with low-level heterogeneities.

- Fourth, our approach can be compared with ontology-based integration approaches. In contrast to single-ontology approaches like SIMS [2], no ontological commitment is needed in our approach in that respect that a user has to accept once and for all one global ontology, i.e., a fixed way to perceive a particular domain. In contrast to multi-ontology approaches like OBSERVER [19], no mapping and similarity detection between involved ontologies is needed in our approach. Ontologies in our approach are just used as a means to explicitly define data semantics for data provision and selection; i.e., we use ontologies for data content explication. Whenever a user selects an IConcept to be a useful source of data for a desired Semantic Perspective, the user is free to change the intended Semantics of his derived User Concept by modifying the concept's ontology link and documentation.[13] Thus, Semantic Perspectives are user-specific conceptual models with ontology-based semantics as intended by a user. Apart from that, our pragmatic approach to data integration is generally capable of providing data for *all* concepts used in Semantic Perspectives, not only for certain ones as might be the case in ontology-based systems.

– Fifth, compared with approaches from the Semantic Web like On2Broker [8], our approach is not limited to data from the WWW. In our approach, data is not just annotated to represent explicit semantics, but a rich semantic multidatasource language is provided to express Semantic Perspectives that form user-specific schemas for querying well-structured data.

– Last, but not least, taxonomic database systems like Prometheus [22] do not consider integration but provision of multiple, overlapping taxonomies for single centralized database systems.

8   Conclusions and Future Work

In this paper, we presented SIRUP, a novel approach to semantic data integration that supports integration by modeling of user-specific ways to perceive an application domain. In essence, our approach provides concepts and a multidatasource language to semantically integrate data that is related according to an individual user's notion. This data is provided with explicit, queryable semantics and is structured according to the user's own conceptual model of his domain of interest. That way, schemas tailored for specific information needs and perceptions are available for querying. In our approach, structured, semi-structured, and unstructured data sources are incorporated.

Our work is not intended to be a complete replacement for existing integration approaches but as a complementing approach suitable for situations with considerable data receiver heterogeneity — e.g., for business and financial analysts with changing information needs, flexible cooperation between enterprises, virtual organizations, rapid enterprise portal development, and information support for business processes and workflows. The main intention of our approach is to provide semantically integrated data for users with heterogeneous conceptual models in mind who differ in both, their information needs and their preference for integrated data. That way, we aim at combining user-specific semantic data integration with truly individual views so that integrated data tailored to individual perceptions of a particular domain can be supplied.

---

[13] However, each User Concept must always be assigned to at least one existing ontological concept to ensure that explicit, queryable semantics is anytime available. See also Footnote 5 on this.

The distinctive features of the SIRUP approach to semantic data integration are:

- conceptual-level supply of pre-integrated data with explicit, queryable semantics and extensive metadata;
- use of an ontology-enhanced multidatasource language to support declarative modeling of data to be integrated and virtual views, both tailored to user-specific information needs.

That way, data from heterogeneous data sources can be semantically integrated and structured according to specific information needs without having to cope with low-level heterogeneity and technical details of underlying data sources. To the best of our knowledge, this combination of ontology-based pre-integration on a conceptual level with an ontology-enhanced multidatasource language is unique.

Future work includes refinement of the concepts presented in this paper as well as incorporation of additional considerations. Additionally, it is planned to implement a fully functional SIRUP prototype as a proof of concept.

References

1. R. Ahmed, P. D. Smedt, W. Du, W. Kent, M. A. Ketabchi, W. Litwin, A. Rafii, and M.-C. Shan. The Pegasus Heterogeneous Multidatabase System. *IEEE Computer*, 24(12):19–27, 1991.
2. Y. Arens, C. Y. Chee, C.-N. Hsu, and C. A. Knoblock. Retrieving and Integrating Data from Multiple Information Sources. *International Journal of Cooperative Information Systems (IJCIS)*, 2(2):127–158, 1993.
3. S. Bergamaschi, S. Castano, S. De Capitani di Vimercati, S. Montanari, and M. Vincini. An Intelligent Approach to Information Integration. In N. Guarino, editor, *1st International Conference on Formal Ontologies in Information Systems (FOIS 1998)*, pages 253–267, Trento, Italy, June 6-8, 1998. IOS Press.
4. M. Carey, L. Haas, P. Schwarz, M. Arya, W. Cody, R. Fagin, M. Flickner, A. Luniewski, W. Niblack, D. Petkovic, J. Thomas, J. Williams, and E. Wimmers. Towards Heterogeneous Multimedia Information Systems: The Garlic Approach. In *5th International Workshop on Research Issues in Data Engineering-Distributed Object Management (RIDE-DOM 1995)*, pages 124–131, Taipei, Taiwan, March 6-7, 1995.
5. S. Chawathe, H. Garcia-Molina, J. Hammer, K. Ireland, Y. Papakonstantinou, J. Ullman, and J. Widom. The TSIMMIS Project: Integration of Heterogeneous Information Sources. In *16th Meeting of the Information Processing Society of Japan (IPSJ)*, pages 7–18, Tokyo, Japan, October 1994, 1994.
6. C. Collet, M. N. Huhns, and W.-M. Shen. Resource Integration Using a Large Knowledge Base in Carnot. *IEEE Computer*, 24(12):55–62, 1991.
7. O. Corcho and A. Gómez-Pérez. A Roadmap to Ontology Specification Languages. In R. Dieng and O. Corby, editors, *12th International Conference on Knowledge Acquisition, Modeling and Management (EKAW 2000)*, volume 1937 of *Lecture Notes in Computer Science*, pages 80–96, Juan-les-Pins, France, October 2-6, 2000. Springer.

8. D. Fensel, J. Angele, S. Decker, M. Erdmann, H.-P. Schnurr, S. Staab, R. Studer, and A. Witt. On2broker: Semantic-based Access to Information Sources at the WWW. In P. D. Bra and J. J. Leggett, editors, *World Conference on the WWW and Internet (WebNet 99)*, pages 366–371, Honolulu, Hawaii, USA, October 25-30, 1999. Association for the Advancement of Computing in Eduction (AACE).

9. M. García-Solaco, F. Saltor, and M. Castellanos. Semantic Heterogeneity in Multidatabase Systems. In O. A. Bukhres and A. K. Elmagarmid, editors, *Object-Oriented Multidatabase Systems. A Solution for Advanced Applications*, pages 129–202. Prentice-Hall, 1996.

10. F. Goasdoué and C. Reynaud. Modeling Information Sources for Information Integration. In D. Fensel and R. Studer, editors, *Knowledge Acquisition, Modeling and Management, 11th European Workshop (EKAW 1999)*, volume 1621 of *Lecture Notes in Computer Science*, pages 121–138, Dagstuhl Castle, Germany, May 26-29, 1999. Springer.

11. C. H. Goh, S. E. Madnick, and M. Siegel. Context Interchange: Overcoming the Challenges of Large-Scale Interoperable Database Systems in a Dynamic Environment. In *Third International Conference on Information and Knowledge Management (CIKM 1994)*, pages 337–346, Gaithersburg, USA, November 29 - December 2, 1994. ACM.

12. T. R. Gruber. Toward Principles for the Design of Ontologies Used for Knowledge Sharing. In N. Guarino and R. Poli, editors, *Formal Ontology in Conceptual Analysis and Knowledge Representation*. Kluwer, 1993.

13. A. Gupta, B. Ludäscher, and M. E. Martone. Knowledge-Based Integration of Neuroscience Data Sources. In O. Günther and H.-J. Lenz, editors, *12th International Conference on Scientific and Statistical Database Management (SSDBM 2000)*, pages 39–52, Berlin, Germany, July 26-28, 2000. IEEE Computer Society.

14. M. N. Huhns and M. P. Singh. Agents on the Web: Ontologies for Agents. *IEEE Internet Computing*, 1(6):81–83, 1997.

15. W. Kent. *Data and Reality. Basic Assumptions in Data Processing Reconsidered.* North-Holland, 1978.

16. W. Kim, I. Choi, S. K. Gala, and M. Scheevel. On Resolving Schematic Heterogeneity in Multidatabase Systems. *Distributed and Parallel Databases*, 1(3):251–279, 1993.

17. L. V. S. Lakshmanan, F. Sadri, and I. N. Subramanian. SchemaSQL - A Language for Interoperability in Relational Multi-Database Systems. In T. M. Vijayaraman, A. P. Buchmann, C. Mohan, and N. L. Sarda, editors, *22nd International Conference on Very Large Data Bases (VLDB 1996)*, pages 239–250, Bombay, India, September 3-6, 1996. Morgan Kaufmann.

18. T. Landers and R. L. Rosenberg. An Overview of MULTIBASE. In H.-J. Schneider, editor, *Second International Symposium on Distributed Data Bases (DDB 1982)*, pages 153–184, Berlin, Germany, September 1-3, 1982. North-Holland.

19. E. Mena, V. Kashyap, A. P. Sheth, and A. Illarramendi. OBSERVER: An Approach for Query Processing in Global Information Systems Based on Interoperation Across Pre-existing Ontologies. In *First IFCIS International Conference on Cooperative Information Systems (CoopIS 1996)*, pages 14–25, Brussels, Belgium, June 19-21, 1996. IEEE Computer Society.

20. P. Missier and M. Rusinkiewicz. Extending a Multidatabase Manipulation Language to Resolve Schema and Data Conflicts. In R. Meersman and L. Mark, editors, *Sixth IFIP TC-2 Working Conference on Data Semantics (DS-6)*, volume 74 of *IFIP Conference Proceedings*, pages 93–115, Stone Mountain, Atlanta, Georgia, USA, May 30 - June 2, 1995. Chapman & Hall.

21. A. M. Ouksel and A. P. Sheth. Semantic Interoperability in Global Information Systems: A Brief Introduction to the Research Area and the Special Section. *SIGMOD Record*, 28(1):5–12, 1999.

22. C. Raguenaud, J. B. Kennedy, and P. J. Barclay. The Prometheus Taxonomic Database. In N. G. Bourbakis, editor, *1st IEEE International Symposium on Bioinformatics and Biomedical Engineering (BIBE 2000)*, pages 63–70, Arlilngton, Virginia, USA, November 8-10, 2000. IEEE Computer Society.

23. F. Saltor and M. García-Solaco. Diversity with Cooperation in Database Schemata: Semantic Relativism. In J. I. DeGross, R. P. Bostrom, and D. Robey, editors, *Fourteenth International Conference on Information Systems (ICIS 1993)*, pages 247–254, Orlando, Florida, USA, December 5-8, 1993. ACM.

24. K.-U. Sattler, S. Conrad, and G. Saake. Adding Conflict Resolution Features to a Query Language for Database Federations. In M. Roantree, W. Hasselbring, and S. Conrad, editors, *Third Workshop on Engineering Federated Information Systems (EFIS 2000)*, pages 41–52, Dublin, Ireland, June 19-20, 2000. IOS Press / infix.

25. P. Scheuermann, A. K. Elmagarmid, H. Garcia-Molina, F. Manola, D. McLeod, A. Rosenthal, and M. Templeton. Report on the Workshop on Heterogenous Database Systems held at Northwestern University, Evanston, Illinois, December 11-13, 1989. *SIGMOD Record*, 19(4):23–31, 1990.

26. A. Sheth, S. Thacker, and S. Patel. Complex Relationships and Knowledge Discovery Support in the InfoQuilt System. *The VLDB Journal*, 12(1):2–27, 2002.

27. A. P. Sheth, S. K. Gala, and S. B. Navathe. On Automatic Reasoning for Schema Integration. *International Journal of Intelligent and Cooperative Information Systems*, 2(1):23–50, 1993.

28. A. P. Sheth and J. A. Larson. Federated Database Systems for Managing Distributed, Heterogeneous, and Autonomous Databases. *ACM Computing Surveys*, 22(3):183–236, 1990.

29. J. F. Sowa. *Conceptual Structures: Information Processing in Mind and Machine*. Addison-Wesley, 1984.

30. M. Templeton, D. Brill, A. Hwang, I. Kameny, and E. Lund. An Overview of the Mermaid System - A Frontend to Heterogeneous Databases. In J. M. Walker, editor, *Sixteenth Annual Electronics and Aerospace Conference and Exposition - Technology Shaping the Future (IEEE EASCON 1983)*, pages 387–402, Washington, D.C., USA, September 19-21, 1983. IEEE Aerospace and Electronic Systems Society.

31. P. Ziegler. User-Specific Semantic Integration of Heterogeneous Data: What Remains to be Done? Technical Report ifi-2004.01, Department of Informatics, University of Zurich, 2004. http://www.ifi.unizh.ch/techreports/TR_2004.html.

Towards a Mediation System Framework
for Transparent Access to Largely Distributed Sources
The MediaGrid Project[*]

Christine Collet, Khalid Belhajjame, Gilles Bernot, Christophe Bobineau,
Gennaro Bruno, Beatrice Finance, Fabrice Jouanot, Zoubida Kedad, David Laurent,
Fariza Tahi, Genoveva Vargas-Solar, Tuyet-Trinh Vu, and Xiaohui Xue

LSR-IMAG Lab., Institut National Polytechnique de Grenoble
BP 72, 38402 Saint-Martin d'Hères, France
`Christine.Collet@imag.fr`

Abstract. This paper presents the MediaGrid project whose goal is the definition of a mediation framework for transparent access to largely distributed
sources. *Frameworks* are reusable pieces of design being expressed as a set of
interfaces and components together with the description of their collaboration.
Research topics addressed by the MediaGrid project include meta-data design,
generation of mediation queries and adaptive and interactive query evaluation.

1 Introduction

The increasing use of computers and the development of communication infrastructures have led to a wide range of information sources being available through networks. Data integration systems or mediation systems have been proposed as a solution to provide a transparent and efficient access to multiple heterogeneous, distributed and autonomous sources [DD99,Wie92]. These systems handle underlying data
source managers, operating systems and networks heterogeneity thereby giving users
and applications the illusion that they deal with a unique data source.

The complexity of mediation systems increases with respect to the number, the
types and the capacities of data sources. Moreover, huge amounts of knowledge
(source descriptions, schemas, semantic relations between schemas) have to be maintained. This increases the difficulty to design assertions between sources. Future mediation systems would be highly dynamical: hence they will have to manage data
sources evolution and the adding or removal of sources. Source availability should be
considered by the query processing, where queries may need to dynamically change
their execution plan, produce partial results or materialize results. Finally, users and
applications want to control the query processing.

---

[*] This work is supported by the French Ministry of Research through the ACI-GRID program.
Participants of the project are from: the LSR-IMAG Laboratory – Grenoble University, the
PRiSM Laboratory – Versailles University and the LaMI Laboratory – University of Evry-
Val-d'Essone.

M. Bouzeghoub et al. (Eds.): ICSNW 2004, LNCS 3226, pp. 65–78, 2004.
© IFIP International Federation for Information Processing 2004

The MediaGrid project (*http://www-lsr.imag.fr/mediagrid*) takes up these challenges. The objective is to propose a mediation framework, i.e. a reusable design (of a mediation system) expressed as a set of interfaces (or components) and the way their instances collaborate. MediaGrid mediation systems built from the framework are able to (i) support more and more available sources, (ii) consider sources containing weakly structured data, (iii) authorize partial results for queries in case of data sources unavailability and/or satisfy user interests, (iv) support a query evaluator which is able to dynamically adapt itself to the execution environment and which accepts user interaction during query execution.

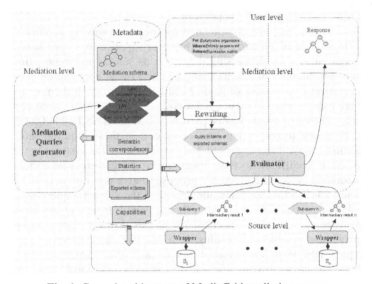

Fig. 1. General architecture of MediaGrid mediation system

The general architecture of a MediaGrid system is given in Figure 1. It follows the classical three-layer architecture. Users or applications access data contained in local sources through the mediation layer. Queries are formulated over a mediation schema (global schema) and are rewritten in terms of exported schemas. Both kinds of schemas are defined using a XML syntax. The mediation (or global) schema describes integrated data manipulated at the mediation level. The exported schemas result from the subscription of sources to the system. During this process, sources are wrapped and data descriptions (schemas, DTD, types, etc.) are translated as exported schemas. Advanced information such as source capabilities and some statistics on sources are also extracted.

Operational mappings between the exported schemas and the mediation one are specified using mediation queries. Such queries are often supposed to be generated manually, which is generally a very complex process considering the amount of knowledge to take into account. Indeed, besides knowing the content of all the sources, the designer has to know semantic links between the sources and the mediation schema (e.g., functional dependencies, referential constraints and value constraints, domains compatibility, semantic equivalence between attributes and instances of key attributes, etc.).

The complexity of this task increases with the number of data sources. A first answer has been proposed in [KBo99], followed by a valuable result from the Clio project [YMH+01]. The Mediation Queries generator automates this process.

Meta-information also plays a very important role in query processing. When querying data, mediation queries are used as input of the (unfolding) algorithm to rewrite user queries into sub-queries executed at local sources. Mediation queries have therefore to be considered as meta-data. Queries are rewritten in terms of exported schemas and evaluated by the Evaluator component. It is important that this component takes into account sources capabilities to avoid a huge data transfer over the network by delegating some tasks to the sources. Returned results from sources are then combined and sent back to applications or users.

Query evaluators may use complicated techniques resolving problems related to network delays, lack of memory, etc. Moreover, applications (or users) may have different requirements for processing data such as source preference, time limit for query evaluation, number of results being handled by an application, economic cost limit for accessing data in case of paying sources, etc. Some of them can wish to get results in brief delay even if they are not complete while others need complete and exact results. Different mechanisms [SAC+79,GM93,KD98,BFMV00,UF00,AH00] have been proposed to respond to one or several of these requirements. However, such mechanisms have been designed and implemented for systems having specific characteristics. It is difficult to have them working together in an efficient manner within a mediation layer. Therefore, we propose to give programmers of a MediaGrid system some tools to build an evaluator providing the « exact » querying capabilities for the applications requirements. The evaluator is built from a Query Broker Framework (QBF) integrating several mechanisms proposed in distributed and parallel database management systems and coming from adaptive and interactive query processing techniques [HFC+00]. This innovative approach offers different adaptation techniques which can be used over different data models (relational, semi-structured or object), in an uniform way, to reach application (or user) requirements, even if these techniques have not been originally designed for those data models.

To illustrate these aspects we consider a mediation system that allows biologists with a means to correlate expression levels of a gene -- whose data are stored within the three data sources GOLD [BEK01], SMD [SHK+01] and SGD [BDD+00] sources -- and to observe their evolution. An example of a query defined at the application level is "looks for the organisms completely published and eukaryote".

Outline of the Paper. The remaining of this paper focuses on the main contributions of the project. Section 2 discusses the meta-data supported by MediaGrid systems. Section 3 introduces the main steps of its query generation process and Section 4 describes the QBF approach to provide adaptive and interactive query evaluators. Finally, Section 5 concludes and gives some information on the current status of the project and the way we validate our approach.

2 Metadata Management

Meta-data are defined to support the generation of mediation queries and the evaluation of global queries. They describe mediation and exported schemas, mediation queries, semantic correspondences, source capabilities and statistics.

2.1 Schema Representation

Mediation and exported schemas in MediaGrid are represented using the XML model. The meta-representation of a XML schema is based on a graph modeled as a set of nodes. Thus, using meta-representation concepts a Schema is modeled as a collection of Node classes that can be linked by a relationship of type path. The Node class can be specialized into ExportedNode that represents an exported schema node, and MediationNode that represents a mediation schema node. Each of them has the Node structure presented in Figure 2.

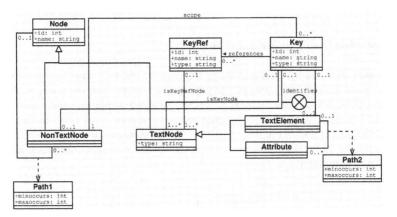

Fig. 2. XML Schema Node representation

A Node in a Schema has an identifier (id) and a name type (see Figure 2). A node is of type TextNode or NonTextNode. The TextNode class describes text nodes (i.e. integer, string) and it can be specialized into Attribute and TextElement. Constraints such as primary and foreign keys are also represented. The class Key represents primary keys. A key has an identifier (id), a type and a name[1]. It can be of type ID, Key or Unique. A foreign key is characterized by an identifier, a name and a type (IDREF or KeyRef). Relationships isKeyNode and isKeyRefNode represent the association of a key to the set of nodes that compose it. A primary key can be used either for identifying a NonTextNode or a TextElement. The relationship identifies is used for representing this situation. Finally, in a XML schema, the key scope may be limited to a part of a XML document. The relationship scope links a key to the NonTextNode representing its scope.

---

[1] This name represents the name of the primary key constraint and does not correspond to the name of the node playing the role of primary key.

2.2 Semantic Correspondences

Exported schema nodes are semantically linked with mediation schema nodes through semantic correspondences. Figure 3 illustrates the meta-representation of this type of correspondences (see for example the association between ExportedNonTextNode and MediationNonTextNode classes and ExportedTextNode and MediationTextNode ones). For the time being only one-to-one correspondences and no transformation functions are represented.

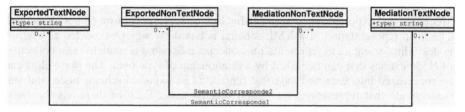

Fig. 3. Semantic correspondences

2.3 Mediation Query Representation

A mediation query represents a strategy that can be used for populating a mediation schema by integrating instances of the exported schemas from the sources. A mediation query (MediationQuery class) is described by an identifier (id) and a query definition (see Figure 4). A mediation schema can have several associated mediation queries. On the other hand, a mediation query can be associated to one and only one mediation schema. This relationship is represented by the association between the classes Schema and MediationQuery.

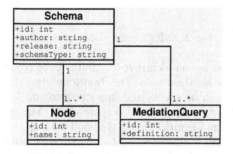

Fig. 4. Mediation Query

2.4 Source Capabilities

Figure 5 (non-grayed zone) shows the UML diagram modeling local sources capabilities. A source (DataSource class) is hosted by an access provider (Provider class) and exports one or more native interfaces (NativeInterface class). A NativeInterface class can be mapped to one or more wrapper interfaces (WrapperInterface class). Each wrapper manages only one schema and one schema definition can be shared by different wrappers. Concerning computation capabilities, the queryOperator class models all possible operators that can be applied to the nodes of an exported schema. An operator has an input (hasInput relationship) and one or two operands, according to the kind of operation. One operator is associated to one or more predicates. Each predicate is applied over a non-finite set of nodes.

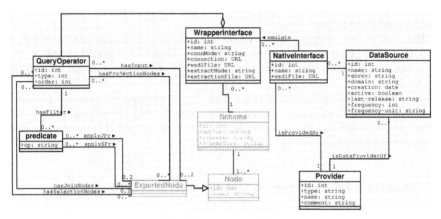

Fig. 5. Source capabilities

2.5 Statistics

Statistics play a very important role in query evaluation. They can be obtained from data sources when they registered to a mediation system or they can be derived at execution time. We propose a meta-representation for two kinds of statistics (see Figure 6): (i) the Datastatistics class linked to the Node class represents data-oriented statistics -- characterized by the node cardinality, its min value and its max value ; (ii) the SystemStatistics class represents information about communication between mediators and wrappers such as data network rate.

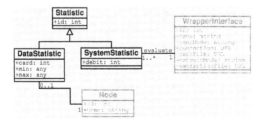

Fig. 6. Statistics UML Diagram

3   Mediation Queries Generation

In a mediation system, given the descriptions of the mediation schema and the exported schemas, mediation queries are defined in order to express how instances of the mediation schema are derived from the exported schemas. These mediation queries represent mappings between the mediation schema and the exported schemas. Mappings are used for: (i) translating queries expressed on the mediation schema to sub-queries on exported schemas, and (ii) translating and integrating sub-queries results to produce a global result.

The goal of the mediation queries generation process is to discover candidate mediation queries given the descriptions of the mediation and exported schemas, which are given using XML schema[Fal01]. Generated mediation queries are XQuery ones [CCD+01].

Our approach comprises three main steps: (i) identifying the relevant portions of each data source considering the mediation schema, (ii) identifying the candidate operations between the relevant portions of data sources and (iii) generating mediation queries from candidate operations.

3.1   Identifying Relevant Portions of Data Sources

For each exported schema, the first step identifies the relevant portion, called a relevant schema, with respect to the mediation schema. To produce such a schema, we consider that some metadata is available, consisting mainly in a set of semantic correspondences defined between elements of the exported schemas and the mediation schema. A relevant schema is composed of elements of the exported schema involved in semantic correspondences and the keys and the references defined in the exported schema. The result of this step gives, for each exported schema, a relevant schema and a query allowing deriving this schema from the corresponding source. Figure 7 shows an example of relevant schema for the exported schema of the GOLD source[BEK01].

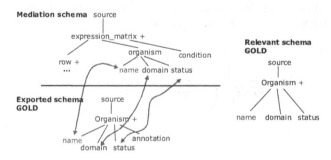

Fig. 7. Identify the relevant portion of the GOLD data source

3.2 Identifying Candidate Operations

Once all relevant schemas are defined, the next step consists in searching for some candidate operations between them. In our work we have considered the join operator.

Using the semantic correspondences, the keys and references defined in the relevant schemas, candidate join operators are derived. A join operator can either be defined in the same relevant schema or between two relevant schemas. Each pair of relevant schemas can be combined with one or several candidate joins.

Figure 8 shows an example where we have the generated relevant schema of the GOLD data source (see Fig. 7) and another relevant schema corresponding to the biological data source SMD [SHK+01]. The only candidate operation between these two relevant schemas is a join in which the path "GOLD/source/organism/name" must correspond to the path "SMD/source/expression_data/org".

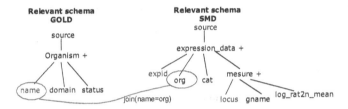

Fig. 8. Identifying candidate operations between two relevant schemas

3.3 Generating Mediation Queries

Given the set of relevant schemas and the candidate operations between them, we consider different parts in the mediation schema; each part is a sub-tree in the mediation schema such that the root n of the sub-tree is either a multi-valued node or the root of the mediation schema, and the nodes of the sub-tree are all the mono-valued children of n. For each part of the mediation schema, we define a set of partial mappings, each of them corresponding to a way of populating the considered part from the exported schemas. A mediation query is defined as a combination of partial mappings such that there is one partial mapping for each part of the mediation schema. All the combinations of partial mappings are considered, some of them will lead to mediation queries. The result of our approach is a set of mediation queries having different semantics. The union of a sub-set of the derived mediation queries is also a mediation query.

4 Query Evaluation

Mediation queries are used as input of the (unfolding) process to rewrite a global query into expressions upon local sources. These expressions are then evaluated by an evaluator, so-called a Query Broker built from QBF, a Query Broker Framework.

QBF is an innovative reusable design represented by a set of component interfaces and the way they collaborate. Its implementation provides the basic functionalities for flexibly evaluating queries. Building query brokers from QBF means creating new subclasses and instances and configuring these instances together according to application requirements. Query Brokers can also adapt themselves to changes of the execution environment and/or of user and application requirements during query evaluation.

The following concentrates on queries representation within a broker, its general architecture, and the way its components interact to provide an adaptive query evaluation and to authorize interaction during query evaluation. More details are given in [CV04,VC04].

4.1 Query Representation

The internal representation of a query is a standardized, canonical query tree so-called query plan. Query plan nodes, represented by the OperNode interface, are operators such as Select, Project, Join, Union, etc. Each operator can have one or several useable algorithms (Algorithm interface). These algorithms consume and produce sequences of items (tuples, entities or objects). More precisely, operator algorithms are implemented in the *iterator model* and provide the open, next and close operations.

Also, operator nodes are annotated by their properties such as the estimated size of the result, or the cost of operator execution. These properties are represented by the Property interface and are regrouped by an instance providing the Annotation interface.

A query also has a Context that determines constraints to be checked during query processing. Some examples of constraints are number of results handled by client, time limit or source preferences. A context is represented as a list of parameters, i.e. couples of (name, value).

Figure 9 represents a query plan for the example: "looks for the organisms completely published and eukaryote". This plan requires an evaluation on all the three biological sources (GOLD, SMD and SGD). Join nodes are used to combine data from the sources.

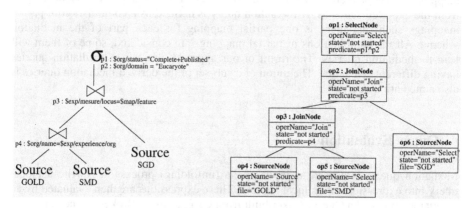

Fig. 9. Example of query

4.2 Query Broker Components

Figure 10 shows the components of any query broker: each of them is designed to cope with a well-identified query evaluation concern. The separation of concerns of query execution and optimization is based on our analyses of existing query systems and optimization techniques such as in [SAC+79,SWA89,KD98,GD87,GM93]. The QueryManager component provides the interface of a query evaluator. It coordinates other components to evaluate queries. The PlanManager and the ContextManager components provide tools for managing query plan and query context parts, respectively. The BufferManager component provides storage capability for processing queries. These base components are required for building any query evaluator.

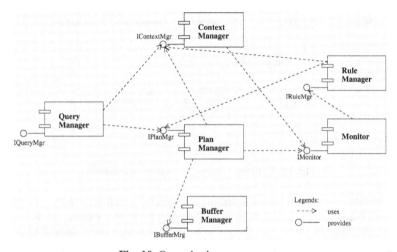

Fig. 10. Query broker components

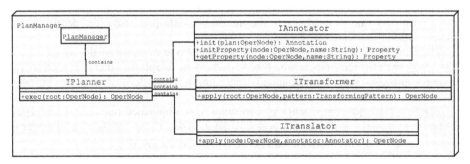

Fig. 11. Plan manager components

Building an adaptive query evaluator needs use of the Monitor and the RuleManager components. These two components enable the observation of the query execution (Monitor) and define the way in which query evaluator reacts according to changes of the environment during query execution (RuleManager).

The PlanManager defines operations for manipulating query plans. This component covers all aspects of query optimization, i.e. search space, cost estimation and search strategy. It is composed of the Planner (providing the search strategy) that coordinates the activities of some sub-components dedicated to query plan optimization such as the Annotator, the Transformer and the Translator (see Fig. 11). The Annotator allows calculating properties of query nodes including the cost of query operations. The Transformer and the Translator provide possible query plan manipulations (logical and physical, respectively) which define the search space of a query plan.

The interaction between sub-components of the PlanManager is given by the sequence diagram in Figure 12. It is important to note that the number and the order of method calls from the Planner to the Annotator, to the Transformer and to the Translator are not fixed. This depends on the search strategy supported by the Planner.

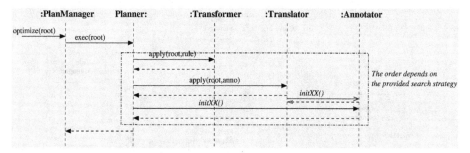

Fig. 12. Sequence diagram for query optimization

The Monitor is responsible for detecting unexpected conditions in the execution environment (such as network delays, use of resources or query context). It manages a list of observation elements which can be accessed through the PropertyMonitor interface. Each element has a check method defining how to detect unexpected condition, and a notify method being responsible of throwing events to the RuleManager. Subclasses of the PropertyMonitor have been defined to monitor specific properties, like the arrival data rate (RateMonitor), the number of data processed (SizeMonitor) and the execution time (TimeMonitor).

The RuleManager receives events and launches one or more of the set of corresponding Event-Condition-Action (ECA) rule(s) to adapt the query execution (to changes in the execution environment) according to a pre-defined strategy (Strategy interface).

The RuleManager component can also support a complicated rule model composed of an event model and a reaction model. A detailed description of the rule manager is out of the scope of this work but can be found in [CVG00,VC02].

4.3 Adaptive Evaluation

Different techniques for adaptive evaluation such as the ones in [KD98, AFT+96, HFC+00, AH00] have been integrated in a uniform way. Besides, an adaptive evaluation can also be ensured by using adaptive operators such as XJoin [UF00], ripple-join [HH99], etc. We can integrate all of these techniques in query brokers by implementing the corresponding rules and operators. For example, to provide the *query scrambling* technique initially proposed in [UFA98], we consider that network delays are detected by instances of the RateMonitor class. Query scrambling reacts to such delays in two ways: *rescheduling* and *operator synthesis* through the following two rules:

(1)   When timeout
      If   schedulable
      Do   materialize(op)

(2)   When timeout
      Do   reoptimize(root,join-related)

The first rule (1) aims at rescheduling query plan when a delay is detected. The condition is a method to verify if another operator can be executed during the detected delay. In such case, a *Buffer* operator is inserted into the query plan so as to materialize results of the op operator, i.e. op will be executed during previously detected delay (call of materialize method) in order to delay the access to the missing data source.

The second rule (2) corresponds to operator synthesis aiming at reordering join operators so as to be able to evaluate a sub-plan during detected delay. The corresponding method is called to reoptimize the query with a particular strategy. Please note that a simple rule execution strategy should be defined over these two rules: rule (2) is executed when rule (1) cannot be executed anymore.

An adaptation in the case of unavailable data could be the generation of partial results. This allows better responding to user requirements and enables user interactions during query processing. Partial results are returned using techniques for directing and/or redirecting data flows between query operators. The same approach is adopted to authorize partial results, i.e. considering specific operators such as switch, dummy and specific adaptation rules [VC03].

4.4 Interactive Evaluation

Looking at the first (incomplete) results, users can refine their long running queries as in [RRH99]. They can also modify their ongoing query (both the query context, as in [RH02], and the query plan) or request partial results.

User interaction is handled in two phases. The first one aims at preparing query evaluation for this change. It detects modifications needed at query operators and monitoring property parameters. No new input data is accessed but the system can continue to return results with data in process. This phase aims also at maintaining the coherence of data processing. The second phase directs and/or redirects data flows between query operators in order to minimize query plan updates.

For enabling user interactions, we implement the UserInteractionMonitor class specializing the PropertyMonitor one. This class defines all possible user interactions for modifying query context, adding new selection condition, removing an existing selection condition, etc. as events. Examples of user interaction events are *addOperator*, *setupContextParameter* or *requestResult*. Rules for handling these events are defined and managed by the RuleManager component. These rules define system behaviors toward user interaction. The following rule is implemented to enable building partial results according to user requests:

When requestResult Do returnResult

When the rule is launched, the system produces partial results using one of the available computing partial result strategies. For example, the simplest strategy is that each unavailable data source is replaced by a *dummy* operator, producing *any* item which can match with any item.

5 Conclusion

This paper presents results of the MediaGrid project whose objective is to contribute to the definition of an open mediation framework for accessing heterogeneous and largely distributed sources. This paper puts emphasis on the metadata management, the generation of mediation queries, and the adaptive and interactive evaluation of user queries.

Implantation of instances of the framework needed to build the specific mediation system providing a transparent access to the biological GOLD, SMD and SGD sources is in progress [Col03]. XML is used at the mediation level for meta-data and XQuery is used to formulate queries. Another on-going work concerns the architecture aspect of the framework and some tools to facilitate the construction of a mediation system itself and its deployment [BVC03].

The next step is to validate our approach considering: complexity of components, scalability, and performances (caching, context-aware operators, etc.).

References

[AH00] Avnur, R., Hellerstein, J.M.: Eddies: Continuously adaptive query processing. In Proc. of International Conference on Management Data (SIGMOD). (2000)

[AFT+96] Amsaleg, L., Franklin, M-J., Tomasic, A., Urhan, T.: Scrambling query plans to cope with unexpected delays. In: Proc. of Conference on Parallel and Distributed Information Systems (PDIS). (1996)

[BDD+00] Ball, C-A., Dolinski, K., Dwight, S-S., Harris, M-A., Issel-Tarver, L., Kasarskis, A., Scafe, C-R., Sherlock, G., Binkley, G., Jin, H., Kaloper, M., Orr, S-D., Shroeder, M., Weng, S., Zhu, Y., Botstein, D., Cherry, J-M. : Integrating functional genomic information into the Saccharomyces Genome Database. In: Nucleic Acid Res. (2000)

[BEK01] Bernal, A., Ear, U., Kyrpides N. : Genomes OnLine Database (GOLD) : a monitor of genome projects world-wide. In: Nucleic Acid Res. (2001)

[BFMV00] Bouganim, L., Fabret, F., Mohan, C., Valduriez, P.: Dynamic query scheduling in data integration systems. In: Proc. of Inter. Conference on Data Engineering.(2000)

[BVC03] Bruno, G., Vargas-Solar , G., Collet, Ch.: *ADEMS, an Adaptable and Extensible Mediation Framework: application to biological sources.* In Proceedings of the Workshop on Advances in Databases and Information Retrieval , ISBN 970-36-0070-0, Tlaxcala, Mexico, Septembre 2003.

[CCD+01] Chamberlin, D., Clark, J., Robie, J., Florescu, D., Siméon, J., Stefanescu. M.: XQuery 1.0: An XML Query Language. W3C Working Draft, June 2001. http://www.w3.org/TR/xquery/.

[Col03] Collet, C. and the Mediagrid Project team, A Mediation Framework for a Transparent Access to Biological Data Sources, In Proceedings of the ECCB 2003 Conference Poster Session, Paris, novembre 2003. Long version presented at the 2003 Entity Relationship, published in the EMISA FORUM proceedings.

[CV04] Collet, C, Vu,T-T.: QBF: a Query Broker Framework for Adaptable Query Evaluation. In Proc. of the Sixth International Conference on Flexible Query Answering Systems (FQAS), June 24-26, Lyon, France.(2004)

[CVG00] Collet, C., Vargas-Solar, G., Grazziotin-Ribeiro, H.: Open active services for data intensive distributed applications. In: Proc. of International Database Engineering and Application Symposium (IDEAS). (2000)

[DD99] Domenig, R., Dittrich, K.R.: An Overview and Classification of Mediated Query Systems. In Sigmod Record.(1999)

[Fal01] Fallside. D.C.: XML Schema Part 0: Primer. W3C Recommendation. Mai 2001. http://www.w3.org/TR/xmlschema-0/.

[GD87] Graefe, G., DeWitt, D.J.: The exodus optimizer generator. In: Proc. of International Conference on Management Data (SIGMOD). (1987)

[GM93] Graefe, G., McKenna, W.J.: The volcano optimizer generator: Extensibility and effcient search. In: Proc. of International Conference on Data Engineering.(1993)

[KBo99] Kedad, Z., Bouzeghoub, M.,: Discovering View Expressions from a Multi-Source Information System, in Proc. of the Fourth IFCIS International Conference on Cooperative Information Systems (CoopIS), Edinburgh, Scotland, pp. 57-68.(1999)

[KD98] Kabra, N., DeWitt, D.J.: Effcient mid-query re-optimization of sub-optimal query execution plans. In: Proc. of International Conference on Management Data (SIGMOD).(1998)

[HFC+00] Hellerstein, J.M., Franklin, M.J., Chandrasekaran, S., Deshpande, A., Hildrum, K., Madden, S., Raman, V., Shah, M.A.: Adaptive query processing: Technology in evolution. IEEE Data Engineering Bulletin.(2000)

[HH99] Haas, P.J., Hellerstein J.M.: Ripple Joins for Online Aggregation. Proc. of SIGMOD.(1999)

[RRH99] Raman, V., Raman, B., Hellerstein, J-M.: Online dynamic reordering for interactive data processing. In: Proc. of International Conference on Very Large Data Bases (VLDB). (1999)

[RH02] Raman, V., Hellerstein, J-M.: Partial results for online query processing. In Proc. of ACM SIGMOD.(2002)

[SAC+79] Selinger, P.G., Astrahan, M.M., Chamberlin, D.D., Lorie, R.A., Price, T.G.: Access path selection in a relational database management system. In: Proc. of International Conference on Management Data (SIGMOD). (1979)

[SHK+01] Sherlock, G., Hernandez-Boussard, T., Kasarskis, A., Binkley, G., Matese, J-C., Dwight, S-S., Kaloper, M., Weng, S., Jin, H., Ball, C-A., Eisen, M-B., Spellman, P-T., Brown, P-O., Botstein, D., Cherry, J-M. : The Stanford Microarray Database. In: Nucleic Acid Res. (2001)

[SWA89] Swami, A.: Optimization of large join queries: Combining heuristics and combinatorial techniques. In: Proc. of Int.. Conference on Management Data. (1989)

[UF00] Urhan, T., Franklin, M.J.: Xjoin: A reactively-scheduled pipelined join operator. IEEE Data Engineering Bulletin 23.(2000)

[UFA98] Urhan, T., Franklin, M.J., Amsaleg, L Cost based query scrambling for initial delays. In: Proc. of International Conference on Management Data (SIGMOD). (1998)

[VC02] Vargas-Solar, G., Collet, C.: Adees: An adaptable and extensible event based infrastructure. In: Proc. of Database and Expert Systems Applications.(2002)

[VC03] Vu,T-T., Collet, C.: Query Brokers for Distributed and Flexible Query Evaluation. In Proc. of the Conference RIVF, Hanoi, Vietnam.(2003)

[VC04] Vu,T-T., Collet, C.: Adaptable Query Evaluation using QBF. In Proc. of the IDEAS Conf. (2004)

[Wie92] Wiederhold G.: Mediator in the Achitecture of Future Information Systems. The IEEE Computer Magazine, 25(3):38—49.(2002)

[YMH+01] Yan, L.L., Miller, R.J., Haas, L.M., Fagin, R.: Data-Driven Understanding and Refinement of Schema Mappings. SIGMOD Conference. (2001)

Null Values Revisited in Prospect of Data Integration

Guy de Tré[1], Rita de Caluwe[1], and Henri Prade[2]

[1] Computer Science Laboratory, Department of Telecommunications and Information Processing, Ghent University, Sint-Pietersnieuwstraat 41, B-9000 Gent, Belgium
[2] Institut de Recherche en Informatique de Toulouse (IRIT)–CNRS, Université Paul Sabatier, 118 route de Narbonne, 31062 Toulouse Cedex, France

Abstract. A considerable part of the information available in the real world is inherently imperfect and/or incomplete. Traditionally, the most commonly adopted modelling approaches for dealing with imperfect and missing information are based on the use of default values and of null values. However, in order to deal with imperfect information in a more efficient way, a database system needs some more advanced modelling facilities that better reflect the semantics of the data. Such facilities become even more necessary if data stemming from different data sources must be integrated in a distributed, federated database system. In this paper, the concept of a 'null' value has been revisited. A semantically richer definition, based on possibility theory, is proposed together with a description of the accompanying many-valued logic. Additionally, the potentials of the new approach with respect to the integration of data in multi-database environments or grid database services are illustrated.

Keywords: Null values, many-valued logic, data semantics, database modelling, data integration.

1   Introduction

The treatment of missing information in traditional database models has been widely addressed in research and continues to be explored. A survey that gives an overview of the field is presented in [13]. The most commonly adopted technique is to model missing data with a pseudo-description, called *null*, that denotes 'missing' [4,2,5]. Once 'null' values are admitted into a database, it is necessary to define the impact of transformations and modifications in the presence of 'nulls'. On the other hand, techniques for the handling of imperfect information have been studied by the 'fuzzy' database community [3,17,9,16] and research on such techniques has been recognized as a challenge for the near future [15].

In his approach, Codd has extended the relational calculus based on an underlying three-valued logic [4,5] in order to formalize the semantics of 'null' values in traditional databases. Mainly due to the fact that the law of excluded middle no longer holds, this extension has been subject to criticism [7]. As an alternative approach, Date proposes to omit null values and to force the database

M. Bouzeghoub et al. (Eds.): ICSNW 2004, LNCS 3226, pp. 79–90, 2004.
© IFIP International Federation for Information Processing 2004

administrator or some suitable authorized user to select a specific, so-called 'default' value from the domain of the field of the missing data to denote missing information in that field [7,8].

In this paper, it is shown how possibility theory can help to overcome some of the problems encountered in a traditional 'null' value approach and moreover allows to deal efficiently with both imperfect and missing information. Furthermore, it is discussed how the presented approach supports the integration of (imperfect) data stemming from different data sources. In Section 2 a new approach for dealing with 'null' values in databases is presented. In order to define the full semantics of the new concepts a many-valued logic, based on so-called extended possibilistic truth values (EPTV's), has been used. An overview of some basic definitions and properties of EPTV's is given in Section 3. In Section 4 it is illustrated how the presented approach can contribute to semantically richer data integration techniques. Finally, some concluding remarks are given in Section 5.

2   Null Values in Databases

2.1   Traditional Approaches

Missing information in databases could be indicated and handled by using a 'null' value, which can be seen as a special mark that denotes the fact that the actual database value is missing [2,5]. In order to assign correct semantics to such a mark, it is important to distinguish between two main reasons for information being missing. As originally stated by Codd [5], information is either missing because:

- data is unknown to the users, but the data is applicable and can be entered whenever it happens to be forthcoming;
- data is missing because it pertains to a property that is inapplicable to the particular object represented by the database instance involved.

Accordingly, Codd introduces the idea of making an explicit distinction in the modelling of both cases by using two different kinds of null values, one meaning "value unknown" and the other "value not defined" [6]. Nevertheless, in many traditional approaches (and existing database systems) such an explicit distinction is not made and a single kind of 'null' values is used to handle both cases of missing data.

In formal definitions of database models null values are represented by some special symbol, e.g. by the bottom symbol '$\perp$' [1,20]. In some formal approaches, null values are considered to be domain dependent [20]: the domain dom_t of each data type t supported by the database model contains a domain specific null value $\perp_t$, which implies that an explicit distinction is made between for example a missing integer value, a missing string value, etc.

In order to define the impact of transformations and modifications in the presence of null values, a many-valued logic [19] has been used. This logic is three-valued if only a single kind of null values is used [2,5] and four-valued if two distinct kinds of null values are considered [6]. The truth values of Codd's four-valued logic are resp. true (T), false (F), unknown $(\perp_U)$ and inapplicable $(\perp_I)$. In Codd's three-valued logic, the latter two values have been combined into one truth value $\perp_{U/I}$, which stands for 'either unknown or inapplicable'.

2.2 Problem Description

A problem with many-valued logics is that the law of excluded middle and the law of non-contradiction do not hold. For example, in a three-valued Kleene logic the considered truth values are T, F and $\perp$, conjunction is defined by $T \wedge T = T$, $T \wedge F = F \wedge T = F \wedge F = F \wedge \perp = \perp \wedge F = F$ and $T \wedge \perp = \perp \wedge T = \perp \wedge \perp = \perp$; disjunction by $T \vee F = F \vee T = T \vee T = T \vee \perp = \perp \vee T = T$, $F \vee F = F$ and $F \vee \perp = \perp \vee F = \perp \vee \perp = \perp$; and negation by $\neg T = F$, $\neg F = T$ and $\neg \perp = \perp$ [19]. With these definitions $\perp \wedge \neg(\perp) = \perp \neq F$ and $\perp \vee \neg(\perp) = \perp \neq T$.

Another important observation is that considering a truth value that is interpreted as 'unknown' (as e.g. $\perp_U$ or $\perp_{U/I}$), induces a problem of truth functionality because the 'degree of' truth of a proposition can no longer be calculated from the 'degrees of truth' of its constituents. 'Unknown' stands for the *uncertainty* of whether a proposition is true or false, which differs from the idea of 'many-valuedness' in a logical format where many-valued logics are intended for: degrees of uncertainty and degrees of truth are different concepts [12].

These observations explain some of the rationales behind Date's criticism on the use of null values [7]. In the approach, presented in the remainder of the paper, unknown information —more specifically uncertainty about the value of existing information— is no longer modelled using a special 'null' value, but using possibility theory, which is intended to model uncertainty [22,11].

2.3 Revised Approach

In the revised approach, only one kind of 'null' values is considered: 'null' values that represent 'inapplicability' and denote that a regular domain value is not applicable. In accordance with [20], these 'null' values are considered to be domain dependent. Therefore, the domain dom_t of each data type t supported by the database model is considered to contain such a null value $\perp_t$.

An unknown value for an attribute A with associated type t is modelled by a possibility distribution π_A that is defined over the domain dom_t of t [22,11]. A possibility distribution can be derived from a fuzzy set, which on its turn is a generalization of a set. Each fuzzy set $\tilde{V}$ is characterized by a membership function

$$\mu_{\tilde{V}} : dom_t \rightarrow [0,1] : x \mapsto \mu_{\tilde{V}}(x)$$

which associates a membership grade $\mu_{\tilde{V}}(x) \in [0,1]$ with each element of the universe over which the fuzzy set is defined. A membership grade 0 denotes that x does not belong to the fuzzy set, a membership grade 1 denotes that x completely belongs to the fuzzy set, whereas a membership grade $\mu_{\tilde{V}}(x) \in]0,1[$

denotes that x only belongs to the set to a given extent. When representing a possibility distribution, a fuzzy set is interpreted as being disjunctive where each of its elements is a possible value and its associated membership grade denotes its degree of possibility.

For example, considering an attribute salary of an employee record, the values 'moderate' and 'unknown' can be defined by possibility distributions as given in Figure 1.

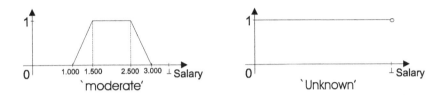

Fig. 1. Possibility distributions representing a moderate salary and an unknown salary.

This approach for modelling unknown information, is in fact the approach taken in so-called possibilistic databases as originally presented in [18]. When applied in a traditional database model, one can use the three label values 'UNK', 'N/A' and 'UNA' to represent 'unknown', 'not applicable' and 'unavailable' data. Thus, 'UNA' stands for the case where it is not even known if a considered property applies or not. The semantics of these labels is defined in terms of a possibility distribution:

– 'UNK' corresponds to the possibility distribution with membership function

$$\mu_{UNK}(x) = 1, \text{ if } x \in dom_t \setminus \{\perp_t\}$$
$$= 0, \text{ if } x = \perp_t,$$

– 'N/A' corresponds to the possibility distribution with membership function

$$\mu_{N/A}(x) = 0, \text{ if } x \in dom_t \setminus \{\perp_t\}$$
$$= 1, \text{ if } x = \perp_t \text{ and}$$

– 'UNA' and corresponds to the possibility distribution with membership function

$$\mu_{UNA}(x) = 1, \forall\, x \in dom_t.$$

Thus, beside $\perp_t$ no additional domain values are required and 'unknown' and 'unavailable' stand for uncertainty, which is conform with [12].

3   Extended Possibilistic Truth Values

An adequate logic to support the revised null value concept has been obtained by imposing the same possibilistic uncertainty to a three-valued logic with truth values true (T), false (F) and inapplicable $(\perp)$. Such a logic, based on a three-valued Kleene logic, has been developed in [10]. The resulting truth values have been called 'extended possibilistic truth values' (EPTV's). EPTV's provide an epistemological representation of the truth of a proposition, which allows to reflect knowledge about the actual truth. Their semantics is defined in terms of a possibility distribution.

Definition 1 (EPTV) *With the understanding that P represents the universe of all propositions and $\tilde{\wp}(I^*)$ denotes the set of all ordinary fuzzy sets in the universe $I^* = \{T, F, \perp\}$, the so-called extended possibilistic truth value (EPTV) $\tilde{t}^*(p)$ of a proposition $p \in P$ is formally defined by the mapping*

$$\tilde{t}^* : P \to \tilde{\wp}(I^*)$$

which associates a fuzzy set $\tilde{t}^*(p)$ with each $p \in P$. The semantics of this associated fuzzy set are defined in terms of a possibility distribution.   □

The EPTV $\tilde{t}^*(p)$ of a proposition p can thus be seen as a possibility distribution

$$\tilde{t}^*(p) = \{(T, \mu_T), (F, \mu_F), (\perp, \mu_\perp)\}, \text{ where } \mu_T, \mu_F, \mu_\perp \in [0, 1]$$

Hereby, the membership grade μ_T denotes the possibility that p is true, μ_F denotes the possibility that p is false and $\mu_\perp$ denotes the possibility that some of) the elements of p are not applicable, undefined or not supplied.

Special cases of EPTV's are:

$\tilde{t}^*(p)$	Interpretation
$\{(T, 1)\}$	p is true
$\{(F, 1)\}$	p is false
$\{(T, 1), (F, 1)\}$	p is unknown
$\{(\perp, 1)\}$	p is inapplicable
$\{(T, 1), (F, 1), (\perp, 1)\}$	information about p is unavailable

These cases are verified as follows:

- If it is completely possible that the proposition is true and no other truth values are possible, then the proposition is considered to be true.
- If it is completely possible that the proposition is false and no other truth values are possible, then the proposition is considered to be false.
- If it is completely possible that the proposition is true, it is completely possible that the proposition is false and it is not possible that the proposition is inapplicable, then the proposition is considered to be applicable, but unknown. This truth value will shortly be called 'unknown'.
- If it is completely possible that the proposition is inapplicable and no other truth values are possible, then the proposition is considered to be inapplicable.

- If all truth values are completely possible, then this means that no information about the truth of the proposition is available. The proposition might be inapplicable, but might also be true, false or unknown. This truth value will shortly be called 'unavailable'.

New propositions can be constructed from existing propositions, using logical operators. An unary operator '$\tilde{\neg}$' is provided for the negation (NOT) of a proposition and binary operators '$\tilde{\wedge}$', '$\tilde{\vee}$', '$\tilde{\Rightarrow}$' and '$\tilde{\Leftrightarrow}$' are respectively provided for the conjunction (AND), disjunction (OR), implication ($IF\ THEN$) and equivalence (IFF) of propositions. The arithmetic rules to calculate the EPTV of a composite proposition and the algebraic properties of EPTV's are presented in [10]. The rules for negation, conjunction and disjunction can be summarized as

- *Rule for negation:* $\forall\, p \in P : \tilde{t}^*(NOT\ p) = \tilde{\neg}(\tilde{t}^*(p))$ where

$$\tilde{\neg} : \tilde{\wp}(I^*) \to \tilde{\wp}(I^*) : \tilde{V} \mapsto \tilde{\neg}(\tilde{V})$$

  is defined by
  - $\mu_{\tilde{\neg}(\tilde{V})}(T) = \mu_{\tilde{V}}(F)$
  - $\mu_{\tilde{\neg}(\tilde{V})}(F) = \mu_{\tilde{V}}(T)$
  - $\mu_{\tilde{\neg}(\tilde{V})}(\bot) = \mu_{\tilde{V}}(\bot)$

- *Rule for conjunction:* $\forall\, p, q \in P : \tilde{t}^*(p\ AND\ q) = \tilde{t}^*(p)\tilde{\wedge}\tilde{t}^*(q)$ where

$$\tilde{\wedge} : \tilde{\wp}(I^*) \times \tilde{\wp}(I^*) \to \tilde{\wp}(I^*) : (\tilde{U}, \tilde{V}) \mapsto \tilde{U} \tilde{\wedge} \tilde{V}$$

  is defined by
  - $\mu_{\tilde{U}\tilde{\wedge}\tilde{V}}(T) = \min(\mu_{\tilde{U}}(T), \mu_{\tilde{V}}(T))$
  - $\mu_{\tilde{U}\tilde{\wedge}\tilde{V}}(F) = \max \begin{pmatrix} \min(\mu_{\tilde{U}}(T), \mu_{\tilde{V}}(F)), \\ \min(\mu_{\tilde{U}}(F), \mu_{\tilde{V}}(T)), \\ \min(\mu_{\tilde{U}}(F), \mu_{\tilde{V}}(F)), \\ \min(\mu_{\tilde{U}}(F), \mu_{\tilde{V}}(\bot)), \\ \min(\mu_{\tilde{U}}(\bot), \mu_{\tilde{V}}(F)) \end{pmatrix}$
  - $\mu_{\tilde{U}\tilde{\wedge}\tilde{V}}(\bot) = \max \begin{pmatrix} \min(\mu_{\tilde{U}}(T), \mu_{\tilde{V}}(\bot)), \\ \min(\mu_{\tilde{U}}(\bot), \mu_{\tilde{V}}(T)), \\ \min(\mu_{\tilde{U}}(\bot), \mu_{\tilde{V}}(\bot)) \end{pmatrix}$

- *Rule for disjunction:* $\forall\, p, q \in P : \tilde{t}^*(p\ OR\ q) = \tilde{t}^*(p)\tilde{\vee}\tilde{t}^*(q)$ where

$$\tilde{\vee} : \tilde{\wp}(I^*) \times \tilde{\wp}(I^*) \to \tilde{\wp}(I^*) : (\tilde{U}, \tilde{V}) \mapsto \tilde{U} \tilde{\vee} \tilde{V}$$

  is defined by
  - $\mu_{\tilde{U}\tilde{\vee}\tilde{V}}(T) = \max \begin{pmatrix} \min(\mu_{\tilde{U}}(T), \mu_{\tilde{V}}(T)), \\ \min(\mu_{\tilde{U}}(T), \mu_{\tilde{V}}(F)), \\ \min(\mu_{\tilde{U}}(T), \mu_{\tilde{V}}(\bot)), \\ \min(\mu_{\tilde{U}}(F), \mu_{\tilde{V}}(T)), \\ \min(\mu_{\tilde{U}}(\bot), \mu_{\tilde{V}}(T)) \end{pmatrix}$

- $\mu_{\tilde{U} \tilde{\vee} \tilde{V}}(F) = \min(\mu_{\tilde{U}}(F), \mu_{\tilde{V}}(F))$

- $\mu_{\tilde{U} \tilde{\vee} \tilde{V}}(\perp) = \max \begin{pmatrix} \min(\mu_{\tilde{U}}(F), \mu_{\tilde{V}}(\perp)), \\ \min(\mu_{\tilde{U}}(\perp), \mu_{\tilde{V}}(F)), \\ \min(\mu_{\tilde{U}}(\perp), \mu_{\tilde{V}}(\perp)) \end{pmatrix}$

These rules are obtained by applying Zadeh's extension principle [21] to the operators of the three-valued Kleene logic [19]. Kleene logics are truth-functional, which means that according to these systems, the behavior of a logical operator is mirrored in a logical function combining Kleene truth values. Therefore, the extended truth value of every composed proposition can be calculated as a function of the extended truth values of its original propositions.

In the framework EPTV's the concept 'unknown', i.e. uncertainty about a truth value is not modelled by means of an extra value, but by means of possibility theory. An extra 'null' value is no longer needed for the modelling of incompleteness due to unavailability. However, an extra 'null' value remains necessary for the modelling of incompleteness due to inapplicability.

Using a special 'null' value to handle inapplicable information brings along with it the same problem as incomplete truth-functionality [7]. The point about this problem is that a database "is" not the real world, but instead contains only (partial) knowledge about the real world. By using extended possibilistic truth values this is reflected by the inability to cope adequately with the special cases $\tilde{t}^*(p \: AND \: NOT \: p)$ and $\tilde{t}^*(p \: OR \: NOT \: p)$. In the presented approach, this inability has been accepted as a tradeoff for being able to cope explicitly with the inapplicability of information.

However, this could be solved by using a constrained version of the extension principle, where one enforces constraints expressing

i. that the truth values of p and $NOT \: p$ are a function of each other, and
ii. the piece of information, when available, that the truth value of p is different from (or is equal to) $\perp$ (since we should have $\tilde{t}^*(p \: AND \: NOT \: p) = F$, $\tilde{t}^*(p \: OR \: NOT \: p) = T$, in case of applicability of the property, and $\tilde{t}^*(p \: AND \: NOT \: p) = \perp = \tilde{t}^*(p \: OR \: NOT \: p)$ otherwise).

4   Data Integration in a Multi-database Environment

The approach presented in the previous sections is able to support a semantically richer handling of missing information in databases and is moreover consistent with the data modelling techniques for imperfect information used in possibilistic databases. Additionally, the approach allows for semantically richer techniques for combining and integrating data that stem from different (heterogeneous) data sources as for example is the case in data warehouses and grid databases.

In order to illustrate the advantages and potentials of the revised 'null' value approach for data integration, two different data sources A and B are considered. Furthermore, for the sake of the example it is assumed that each source contains, among other things, data about employee salaries. The salary attributes in both sources are respectively denoted by $salary_A$ and $salary_B$, whereas a value of $salary_A$ is denoted by v_A and a value of $salary_B$ is denoted by v_B. Further assume that it is necessary to integrate the data from both sources and that hereby a record value v_A must be combined with a record value v_B (e.g. because both records contain information about the same entity). Ten different cases could occur, all of them are described below. For each case, a comparison has been made between a *traditional approach* —where missing information is handled by one single null value, denoted by $NULL$—, the *revised null value approach* applied on a traditional data model as described in this paper and the revised null value approach applied on a *possibilistic data model*, which allows to model imprecise values and thus provides more facilities for the modelling of imperfect information.

Case 1. Both v_A and v_B are regular values.

- *Traditional approach* and *revised null value approach*.
    - If $v_A = v_B$ then both values can be combined with resulting value $v = v_A = v_B$.
    - If $v_A \neq v_B$ then the data of both sources are conflicting and the necessary precautions must be taken to prevent an inconsistent database.
- *Possibilistic approach.*
  Hereby, v_A and v_B are possibility distributions with membership functions μ_{v_A} and μ_{v_B} as described in Section 2. In order to compare two possibility distributions in prospect of integration the support function *supp* can be used. This function is defined by $supp(v) = \{x | x \in U \wedge \mu_v(x) > 0\}$ —where U is the universe over which the possibility distribution v is defined— and results in the set of all values of U that are considered to be possible within $\tilde{v}$.
    - If $supp(v_A) \cap supp(v_B) \neq \emptyset$, then v_A and v_B can be combined by applying a conjunction operator (t-norm operator [14]) for fuzzy sets. A commonly used t-norm operator is the min-operator, with which the membership function μ_v of the resulting possibility distribution v becomes $\mu_v = \min(\mu_{v_A}, \mu_{v_B})$.
    - If $supp(v_A) \cap supp(v_B) = \emptyset$ then the data of both sources are conflicting and again the necessary precautions must be taken to prevent inconsistency.

Case 2. One of the values, e.g. v_A, is a regular value and the other one is 'unknown'.

- *Traditional approach.*
  In this case $v_B = NULL$. Since $NULL$ can stand for both 'unknown' and 'inapplicable' this case can not be handled correctly without additional information.
- *Revised null value approach.*
  In this case $v_B = UNK$, as described in Section 2. The resulting value v equals v_A, which is verified by the fact that $\min(\mu_{v_A}, \mu_{UNK}) = \mu_{v_A}$, with

μ_{v_A} being the membership function of the possibility distribution that corresponds to v_A and is defined by $\mu_{v_A}(v_A) = 1$ and $\mu_{v_A}(v) = 0$, if $v \neq v_A$.

– *Possibilistic approach.*

Hereby, both v_A and $v_B = UNK$ are possibility distributions. This case can be identically handled as the possibilistic approach where both v_A and v_B are regular values. Due to the definition of 'UNK', $supp(v_A) \cap supp(UNK) \neq \emptyset$ and the resulting possibility distribution v will equal $\mu_v = \min(\mu_{v_A}, \mu_{UNK}) = \mu_{v_A}$.

Case 3. One of the values, e.g. v_A, is a regular value and the other one is 'inapplicable'.

– *Traditional approach.*

In this case $v_B = NULL$. Since $NULL$ can stand for both 'unknown' and 'inapplicable' this case can not be handled correctly without additional information.

– *Revised null value approach.*

In this case $v_B = N/A$. The data of both sources are conflicting.

– *Possibilistic approach.*

Both v_A and $v_B = N/A$ are possibility distributions. However, $supp(v_A) \cap supp(v_B) = \emptyset$, which denotes that the data of both sources are conflicting.

Case 4. One of the values is a regular value, e.g. v_A, and the other one is 'unavailable'.

– *Traditional approach.*

Again $v_B = NULL$, which can stand for both 'unknown' and 'inapplicable'. More information is necessary for a correct combination of the data.

– *Revised null value approach.*

In this case $v_B = UNA$. The resulting value v equals v_A, which is verified by the fact that $\min(\mu_{v_A}, \mu_{UNA}) = \mu_{v_A}$, with μ_{v_A} being the membership function of the possibility distribution that corresponds to v_A and is defined by $\mu_{v_A}(v_A) = 1$ and $\mu_{v_A}(v) = 0$, if $v \neq v_A$.

– *Possibilistic approach.*

Hereby, both v_A and $v_B = UNA$ are possibility distributions and can be handled as in Case 1. With the definition of 'UNA', $supp(v_A) \cap supp(UNA) \neq \emptyset$ so that the resulting possibility distribution v equals $\mu_v = \min(\mu_{v_A}, \mu_{UNA}) = \mu_{v_A}$.

Case 5. Both v_A and v_B are 'unknown'.

– *Traditional approach.*

In this case $v_A = v_B = NULL$. 'NULL' can stand as well for 'unknown' information, as for 'inapplicability'. Additional information that clarifies the correct interpretations of the 'NULLs', is required for a correct handling.

– *Revised null value approach* and *possibilistic approach.*

In both approaches $v_A = v_B = UNK$. The resulting value is $v = v_A = v_B = UNK$, which is verified by $\min(\mu_{UNK}, \mu_{UNK}) = \mu_{UNK}$.

Case 6. One of the values, e.g. v_A, is 'unknown' and the other one is 'inapplicable'.

- *Traditional approach.*
  Again $v_A = v_B = NULL$. Additional information that clarifies the correct interpretations of the 'NULLs', is required for a correct handling.
- *Revised null value approach* and *possibilistic approach.*
  In both approaches $v_A = UNK$ and $v_B = N/A$. The data of both sources are conflicting since $supp(UNK) \cap supp(N/A) = \emptyset$ and the necessary precautions must be taken.

Case 7. One of the values, e.g. v_A, is 'unknown' and the other one is 'unavailable'.

- *Traditional approach.*
  $v_A = v_B = NULL$. Additional information is required for a correct handling.
- *Revised null value approach* and *possibilistic approach.*
  In both approaches $v_A = UNK$ and $v_B = UNA$. With the definitions of 'UNK' and 'UNA', $supp(UNK) \cap supp(UNA) \neq \emptyset$ and the resulting value $v = UNK$ ($\mu_v = \min(\mu_{UNK}, \mu_{UNA}) = \mu_{UNK}$).

Case 8. Both v_A and v_B are 'inapplicable'.

- *Traditional approach.*
  $v_A = v_B = NULL$. Additional information is required for a correct handling.
- *Revised null value approach* and *possibilistic approach.*
  In both approaches $v_A = v_B = N/A$. The resulting value is $v = v_A = v_B = N/A$, which is verified by $\min(\mu_{N/A}, \mu_{N/A}) = \mu_{N/A}$.

Case 9. One of the values, e.g. v_A, is 'inapplicable' and the other one is 'unavailable'.

- *Traditional approach.*
  $v_A = v_B = NULL$. Additional information is required for a correct handling.
- *Revised null value approach* and *possibilistic approach.*
  In both approaches $v_A = N/A$ and $v_B = UNA$. The resulting value is $v = v_A = N/A$, which is verified by $\min(\mu_{N/A}, \mu_{UNA}) = \mu_{N/A}$.

Case 10. Both v_A and v_B are 'unavailable'.

- *Traditional approach.*
  $v_A = v_B = NULL$. This case is correctly handled since $NULL$ traditionally stands for UNK of N/A
- *Revised null value approach* and *possibilistic approach.*
  In both approaches $v_A = v_B = UNA$. The resulting value is $v = v_A = v_B = UNA$, which is verified by $\min(\mu_{UNA}, \mu_{UNA}) = \mu_{UNA}$.

For the cases of conflict encountered in cases 1, 3, 6, in case imprecise information would be allowed in the database, one may store the disjunction of the conflicting pieces f information.

With the previous case study it is illustrated how the presented approach for the modelling of missing information can contribute to semantically richer data integration and combination techniques and therefore can also contribute to semantically richer grid database services. Compared with a traditional approach where one 'null' value is considered —as is the case in most database models—, the revised null value approach provides a semantically richer modelling technique. At the same time the revised null value approach is completely consistent with the possibilistic data modelling approach and can therefore be easily integrated in any possibilistic database model.

Compared with an approach where two distinct kinds of null values are used to make a distinction between "value unknown" and "value not defined" (as proposed in [6]), the revised approach presented in this paper has the advantage that the case "value unknown" no longer requires an extra truth value in the underlying logic.

5 Conclusion

In this paper the semantics of null values has been revised. A semantically richer approach, based on possibility theory and an accompanying logic on extended possibilistic truth values, has been proposed. Furthermore, the usefulness of the new approach has been illustrated in prospect of the need for semantically richer data integration and data combination techniques as might be required in heterogeneous multi-database environments and advanced grid database services.

By explicitly making a distinction between uncertainty and truth, whereby 'unknown' has been modelled as standing for the uncertainty of whether a proposition is true or false, an extra truth (and 'null') value for the representation of 'unknown' has been avoided. Consequently, the problems connected with the existence of such an extra truth value, can be solved.

However, in order to be able to cope with information that is missing due to inapplicability or non-existence of information an extra truth value $\bot$ has been introduced, as well as the incorporation of an extra domain specific element $\bot_t$ in the domains dom_t of the data types t supported by the database model. This extra truth value brings along with it the same problem as incomplete truth-functionality. This is reflected by the inability to cope adequately with the special cases $\tilde{t}^*(p \; AND \; NOT \; p)$ and $\tilde{t}^*(p \; OR \; NOT \; p)$. This inability has been accepted in the paper, as a tradeoff for being able to cope explicitly with the inapplicability of information.

References

1. Abiteboul, S., Hull, R., Vianu, V.: Foundations of databases. Addison-Wesley Publishing Company, Reading, USA (1995).

2. Biskup, J.: A Formal Approach to Null Values in Database Relations. In: Advances in Data Base Theory. Gallaire H., Minker J., Nicolas J. (eds.), Plenum Press, New York, USA (1981) 299–341.

3. Bosc P., Kacprzyk J. (eds.): Fuzziness in Database Management Systems. Physica-Verlag, Heidelberg, Germany (1995).

4. Codd, E.F.: RM/T: Extending the Relational Model to capture more meaning. ACM Transactions on Database Systems **4** 4 (1979).

5. Codd, E.F.: Missing Information (Applicable and Inapplicable) in Relational Databases. ACM SIGMOD Record **15** 4 (1986) 53–78.

6. Codd, E.F.: More Commentary on Missing Information in Relational Databases (Applicable and Inapplicable Information). ACM SIGMOD Record **16** 1 (1987) 42–50.

7. Date, C.J.: Null Values in Database Management. In: Relational Database: Selected Writings. Addisson-Wesley Publishing Company, Reading, USA (1986) 313–334.

8. Date, C.J.: Faults and Defaults. In: Relational Database Writings 1994–1997. Date, C.J., Darwen, H., McGoveran, D. (eds.), Addisson-Wesley Publishing Company, Reading, USA (1998).

9. de Caluwe, R. (ed.): Fuzzy and Uncertain Object-oriented Databases: Concepts and Models. World Scientific, Signapore (1997).

10. de Tré, G.: Extended Possibilistic Truth Values. International Journal of Intelligent Systems **17** (2002) 427–446.

11. Dubois, D., Prade, H.: Possibility Theory. Plenum Press, New York, USA (1988).

12. Dubois, D., Prade H.: Possibility Theory, Probability Theory and Multiple-Valued Logics: A Clarification. Annals of Mathematics and Artificial Intelligence **32** 1–4 (2001) 35–66.

13. Dyreson, C.E.: A Bibliography on Uncertainty Management in Information Systems. In: Uncertainty Management in Information Systems: From Needs to Solutions. Motro, A., Smets P. (eds.), Kluwer Academic Publishers, Boston, USA (1997) 415–458.

14. Klir, G.J., Yuan, B.: Fuzzy Sets and Fuzzy Logic: Theory and Applications. Prentice Hall, New Jersey, USA (1995).

15. Korth, H.F., Silberschatz, A.: Database Research Faces the Information Explosion. Communications of the ACM **40** 2 (1997) 139–142.

16. Bordogna G., Pasi G. (eds.) Recent Issues on Fuzzy Databases. Physica-Verlag, Heidelberg, Germany (2000).

17. Petry, F.E.: Fuzzy Databases: Principles and Applications. Kluwer Academic Publishers, Boston, USA (1996).

18. Prade, H., Testemale, C.: Generalizing Database Relational Algebra for the Treatment of Incomplete or Uncertain Information and Vague Queries. Information Sciences **34** (1984) 115–143.

19. Rescher, N.: Many-Valued Logic. Mc.Graw-Hill, New York, USA (1969).

20. Riedel, H., Scholl M.H.: A Formalization of ODMG Queries. In: Proc. of the 7th Working Conference on Database Semantics (DS-7), Spaccapietra S., Maryanski F. (eds.), Leysin, Switzerland, (1997) 63–90.

21. Zadeh, L.A.: The concept of linguistic variable and its application to approximate reasoning Parts I, II and III. Information Sciences **8** 199–251, **8** 301–357, **9** 43–80 (1975).

22. Zadeh, L.A.: Fuzzy sets as a basis for a theory of possibility. Fuzzy Sets and Systems **1** (1978) 3–28.

Semantic-Based Query Routing and Heterogeneous Data Integration in Peer-to-Peer Semantic Link Networks

Hai Zhuge[1], Jie Liu[1,2], Liang Feng[1,2], and Chao He[1,2]

[1] China Knowledge Grid Research Group, Key Lab of Intelligent Information Processing,
Institute of Computing Technology
Chinese Academy of Sciences, Beijing, 100080, China
zhuge@ict.ac.cn
[2] Graduate School of the Chinese Academy of Sciences
{lj,feng_liang,hc}@kg.ict.ac.cn

Abstract. A semantic link P2P network specifies and manages semantic relationships between peers' data schemas. The proposed approach includes a tool for constructing and maintaining P2P semantic link networks, a semantic-based peer similarity measurement approach for efficient query routing, and peer schema mapping algorithms for query reformulation and heterogeneous data integration. The advantages of the proposed approach include three aspects: First, it uses semantic links to enrich relationships between peers' data schemas. Second, it considers not only node but also structure in measuring the similarity between schemas so as to efficiently and accurately forward queries to relevant peers. Finally, it deals with semantic heterogeneity, structural heterogeneity and data inconsistency to enable peers to exchange and translate heterogeneous information in single semantic image.

1 Introduction

The original motivation for most early P2P systems such as Gnutella and Napster is file sharing [23, 24]. Peer data management systems (PDMS) provide us with a flexible architecture for decentralized data sharing. Usually, a PDMS consists of a set of peers, and each peer has an associated XML schema. Heterogeneous data integration for large-scale P2P networks is a challenging issue due to the autonomous, scalable, dynamic and heterogeneous data characteristics of peers.

Heterogeneous data management in a PDMS concerns the following three key issues:

1. How to autonomously identify semantically relevant peers.
2. How to accurately and efficiently route a query requirement initiated by one peer to relevant peers so as to avoid network flooding.
3. How to integrate heterogeneous data flows returned from different peers so as to provide users and other peers with a single semantic image data usage mode [20, 21], because P2P systems do not have a global schema like traditional data integration systems [15].

Previous research on P2P computing systems and peer data management systems mainly concerns data models for P2P databases, peer clustering, peer searching and

M. Bouzeghoub et al. (Eds.): ICSNW 2004, LNCS 3226, pp. 91–107, 2004.
© IFIP International Federation for Information Processing 2004

query routing algorithms, and peer schema mediation mechanism. For example, the P2P-based system PeerDB for distributed data sharing [14], the scalable P2P lookup protocol [17], the local relational model for mediating between peers in a PDMS [3], approaches for controlling the distribution of peers to cluster and form super-peer networks [10, 13], the architecture supporting data coordination between peer data-bases [6], approaches to automatic schema matching [16], the semantic and algorithmic issues for mapping data in P2P systems [9], the solution to achieve semantic agreement in a P2P network [1], the generic schema-matching prototype Cupid [12], query reformulation algorithms for XML-based peers [5, 7, 8], and the approach for optimizing query reformulation in a PDMS [18]. But they are not the total solutions to the above three key issues.

This paper introduces the notion of P2P semantic link network to resolve the first issue. Semantic relationships between peers' data schemas are specified through semantic links [19]. Each peer is encapsulated as a soft-device (i.e., a software service mechanism [20]) that provides services to each other and to other virtual roles according to the content of their resources and the related configuration information through XML, SOAP (Simple Object Access Protocol) messages and WSDL (Web Service Description Language). A software tool has been implemented to assist users to construct and maintain a nested P2P semantic link network.

To resolve the second issue, this paper proposes an approach for measuring semantic similarity between peers. It considers not only the semantic similarity between nodes in peers' data schemas, but also semantic similarity between structures in peer schemas. Upon receiving a query, a peer will autonomously forward the requirement to relevant peers according to the types of the semantic links as well as the similarity between nodes and between structures of peer schemas.

To resolve the third issue, this paper establishes three mappings: *semantic node mapping*, *semantic clique mapping* and *semantic path mapping* to reformulate a query on source schema over target schemas. We apply technologies of QoP (Quality of Peers) such as response time, precision and recall to manage inconsistent data in returned data flows.

2 Approach Overview

A P2P *Semantic Link Network* (P2PSLN) is a directed network, where nodes are peers or P2PSLN, and edges are typed semantic links specifying semantic relationships between peers [19]. In a P2PSLN, each peer is an active and intelligent soft-device [20], which can dynamically and intelligently establish semantic connection with each other.

The role of a peer can be a server when it provides data, information and services, a mediator when forwarding query requirements, and a client when accessing information from other peers.

As depicted in Fig. 1, each peer in a P2PSLN has two main modules: *a communication module* and *a data management module*. Peers communicate with each other through SOAP messages. Users can query a peer through GUI (Graphical User Interface) or SSeIQL (Single Semantic Image Query Language) — an SQL-like query language designed for P2PSLN-based peer data management.

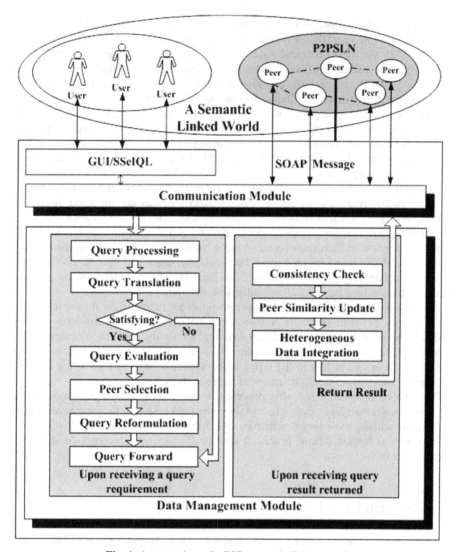

Fig. 1. An overview of a P2P semantic link network

The data management module of each peer is responsible for managing query requirements and returned query results. Upon receiving a query requirement, the data management module performs the following tasks:

1. *Query Processing* — To analyze query requirement and get query parameters.
2. *Query Translation* — To translate the query requirement against the XML schema of the current peer and check whether it can satisfy the requirement. If not, the requirement will be forwarded to the successors who are likely to answer the query and to forward the query further.
3. *Query Evaluation* — To pose the query requirement on the current peer to retrieve answers.

4. *Peer Selection* — To select approximate successors according to the semantic relationship and semantic similarity between the current peer and the selected successors.
5. *Query Reformulation* — To reformulate a query on the current peer over schemas of its immediate successors.
6. *Query Forward* — To autonomously forward the query requirement to the successors highly similar to the current peer according to the routing policy and a predefined TTL (Time_to_Live) value.

Upon receiving query results returned from the successors, the data management module of the peer who initiates the query requirement will first analyze the result to detect inconsistent data in the returned data flows. For the successors who are likely to answer the query but return fewer matching results, the current peer will send SOAP messages to inquire whether there are some schema changes, and to update the schema mapping, semantic link type and similarity degree between them. Finally, the data management module will combine or join data matching query requirement in the returned data flows and provide users or peers with data from multiple sources in a uniform view.

3 P2P Semantic Link Network Model

3.1 Semantic Link

In a P2PSLN, a *semantic link* between two peers is represented as a pointer with a type (α) directed from one peer (predecessor) to another (successor). A *semantic link* can be one of the following types:

1. *Equal-to Link*, denoted as P_i—equ→P_j, states that the semantics of P_i is equal to that of P_j. The equal-to link is reflective, symmetric and transitive.
2. *Similar-to Link*, denoted as P_i— (sim, sd) →P_j, defines that the semantics of P_i is similar to that of P_j, and sd is the similarity degree between P_i and P_j.
3. *Reference Link*, denoted as P_i—ref→P_j, defines that the semantics of P_i refers to that of P_j.
4. *Implication Link*, denoted as P_i —imp→ P_j, defines that the semantics of P_i implies that of P_j. The implication link is transitive and can help the reasoning mechanism to find new semantic implication relationships.
5. *Subtype Link*, denoted as P_i —st→ P_j, defines that the semantics of P_j is a part of P_i. The subtype link has the transitive characteristic.
6. *Sequential Link*, denoted as P_i —seq→ P_j, defines that the content of P_j is the successor of the content of P_i.
7. *Empty Link*, denoted as P_i—$\varnothing$→P_j, represents that there are no semantic relationships between P_i and P_j.
8. *Null Link* or *Unknown Link*, denoted as P_i—N→P_j, represents that the semantic relationships between P_i and P_j are uncertain or unknown.

We can chain relevant semantic links to obtain uncertain semantic relations between peers according to a set of reasoning rules [19]. The heuristic rules suitable for connecting different types of semantic links in a P2PSLN are listed in Table 1, where $\alpha \in \{equ, sim, ref, imp, st, seq, \varnothing, N\}$ denotes the semantic link type between peers.

Table 1. Resasoning rules for P2P semantic link networks

No.	Rules
Rule 1	$P_i—equ\rightarrow P_i$
Rule 2	$P_i—equ\rightarrow P_j \Rightarrow P_j—equ\rightarrow P_i$
Rule 3	$P_i—equ\rightarrow P_j, P_j—equ\rightarrow P_k \Rightarrow P_i—equ\rightarrow P_k$
Rule 4	$P_i—equ\rightarrow P_j, P_j—\alpha\rightarrow P_k \Rightarrow P_i—\alpha\rightarrow P_k$
Rule 5	$P_i—imp\rightarrow P_j, P_j—imp\rightarrow P_k \Rightarrow P_i—imp\rightarrow P_k$
Rule 6	$P_i—st\rightarrow P_j, P_j—st\rightarrow P_k \Rightarrow P_i—st\rightarrow P_k$
Rule 7	$P_i—imp\rightarrow P_j, P_j—st\rightarrow P_k \Rightarrow P_i—imp\rightarrow P_k$
Rule 8	$P_i—imp\rightarrow P_j, P_j—ref\rightarrow P_k \Rightarrow P_i—ref\rightarrow P_k$
Rule 9	$P_i—st\rightarrow P_j, P_j—imp\rightarrow P_k \Rightarrow P_i—imp\rightarrow P_k$
Rule 10	$P_i—st\rightarrow P_j, P_j—ref\rightarrow P_k \Rightarrow P_i—ref\rightarrow P_k$
Rule 11	$P_i—N\rightarrow P_j, P_j—\alpha\rightarrow P_k \Rightarrow P_i—N\rightarrow P_k$
Rule 12	$P_i—\varnothing\rightarrow P_j, P_i—\alpha\rightarrow P_j \Rightarrow P_i—N\rightarrow P_k$

3.2 Operations on P2P Semantic Link Networks

A P2PSLN supports three types of operations: peer join, peer departure and peer stabilization.

1. *Peer Join.* When a peer P_i joins a P2PSLN, it will first identify the semantic relationship between itself and a peer P_j in the network, and then take P_j as its immediate successor by calling function '$P_i.Join$ *(P2PSLN, P_j, α)*', where α denotes the semantic relationship between P_i and P_j. The detail of each function is listed in Table 2. The semantic relationships between P_i and other peers in the current P2PSLN could be derived according to rules shown in Table 1. To find other successors, P_i will ask each successor P_k of P_j by calling function '$P_i.$ *FindSuccessors (P2PSLN, P_j, α, P_k, β)*'. If $P_i —\alpha\rightarrow P_j$, $P_j —\beta\rightarrow P_k \Rightarrow P_i —\gamma\rightarrow P_k$ satisfies the reasoning rules in Table 1, then P_i makes P_k as its successor, and calls function '$P_i.FindSuccessors$ *(P2PSLN, P_k, γ, P_m, δ)*' iteratively. After establishing the semantic relationships between P_i and its successors, P_i calls function '$P_i.$ *SchemaInquiry (P2PSLN, P_j)*' to acquire the XML schemas of each successor P_j. The process to measure similarity degree between peers with *Similar-to* link type will be illustrated in Section 5.

2. *Peer Departure.* When a peer P_i leaves a P2PSLN, it may notify its predecessors and successors before its departure. In turn, predecessor P_j will remove P_i from its successor list, delete the semantic links between P_j and P_i, and add each successor P_k of P_i as its own successor provided that: (1) $P_k \notin P_j$' successor list, and (2) there is a semantic relationship between P_j and P_k. Similarly, successor P_k will remove P_i from its predecessor list, delete the corresponding semantic links, and add each predecessor P_j of P_i as its own predecessor if: (1) $P_j \notin P_k$'s predecessor list, and (2) there is a semantic relationship between P_k and P_j.

Peer Stabilization. To ensure the up-to-date semantic links between peers, each peer P_i in a P2PSLN runs function '$P_i.Stabilization$ *(P2PSLN, P_j)*' periodically in the background and updates semantic link types, predecessor pointers and successor pointers accordingly. If P_j (i.e., the predecessor or the successor of P_i) exists in the network, it will notify P_i its existence and schema change information. If P_j

Table 2. Operations on P2P semantic link networks

ID	Operation	Function
1	$P_i.Join$ ($P2PSLN, P_j, \alpha$)	To take P_j as the successor of P_i and specify the semantic link type between P_i and P_j as α in a P2PSLN.
2	$P_i.FindSuccessors$ ($P2PSLN, P_j, \alpha, P_k, \beta$)	To deduce semantic relationships between P_i and P_k in a P2PSLN provided that P_i—α→P_j and P_j—β→P_k hold.
3	$P_i.SchemaInquiry$ ($P2PSLN, P_j$)	To acquire XML schema of P_j in a certain P2PSLN.
4	$P_i.Departure$ ($P2PSLN$)	To leave a P2PSLN.
5	$P_i.Stabilization$ ($P2PSLN, P_j$)	To ask for the existence and schema change from P_j in a P2PSLN.

does not exist in the current P2PSLN, P_i will remove P_j from its predecessor/successor list and modify its neighbor index accordingly. When the XML schema of a peer changes, it will autonomously notify its predecessors and successors the new schema through SOAP messages.

3.3 P2P Semantic Link Network Definition Tool

There are two kinds of basic elements in a nested P2PSLN: nodes and semantic links. A node can be either a peer or a P2PSLN (i.e. a component), while a semantic link denotes the semantic relationship and similarity degree between two peer schemas. We have developed a tool to assist users to construct and maintain a P2PSLN. A graphical interface of the definition tool is shown in Fig.2. Users can define a P2PSLN by clicking the operation buttons arranged at the top portion and drawing on the screen. The scalable and nested node hierarchy of the current P2PSLN is arranged on the left column. The description for each peer (i.e., *PeerID, Peer Name, Peer IP, Peer Description*) and each semantic link (i.e., *Predecessor, Successor, Semantic Relationship, Similarity Degree*) is listed at the bottom.

4   Peer Schema Mapping

Peer schema mapping is to resolve the issue of the semantic inconsistency between source schemas and target schemas. Upon receiving peer schemas through SOAP messages, a peer will traverse the schemas recursively in depth-first order and extract node and path information from the target, then carry out three types of mappings: semantic node mapping, semantic clique mapping and semantic path mapping.

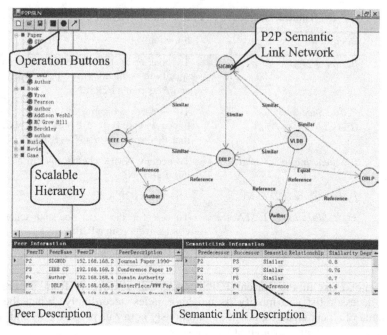

Fig. 2. An interface of the proposed P2PSLN definition tool

4.1 Semantic Node Mapping

Semantic Node Mapping is to resolve the semantic inconsistency between nodes by mapping nodes in the source schema into nodes in target schemas. A peer encapsulates a global dictionary that defines a set of semantically related terms (synonymy, abbreviations, etc.) and the similarity degree between terms. After acquiring the target peer schemas, the source peer will automatically build mapping and similarity degree between nodes according to the definition in the global dictionary. The nodes in source schemas and the mapping nodes in target schemas are called *Semantic Nodes* and *Semantic Mapping Nodes* when semantic links have been established between the source and the target. We also provide tools to enable users to manually modify the semantic node mappings automatically generated by the system, and to keep the new mappings by using a local dictionary.

4.2 Semantic Clique Mapping

A semantic clique represents the semantic structure such as the parent-child relationship and ancestor-descendant relationship between a set of closely related semantic nodes. The semantics of a node in a semantic clique is constrained by semantics of all nodes on the path from the root to it.

Semantic Clique Mapping is to identify semantic cliques (sub-trees that cover a set of closely related semantic nodes) and map each semantic clique in a source schema into the target schemas, where the mapping images are called *Semantic Mapping Cliques*. Semantic mapping nodes in a semantic mapping clique hold the semantic structure that the semantic nodes in a semantic clique hold.

To find the semantic cliques, we first divide all the semantic nodes in a source schema into a set of closely related sets, i.e., the semantic node set. The following algorithm is to identify the semantic clique corresponding to each semantic node set.

```
Algorithm SemanticCliqueRecognition (T₁, T₂, SN)
/* Given a set of closely related semantic mapping nodes, to
find semantic cliques in sub-tree rooted at T₁ and semantic
mapping cliques in sub-tree rooted at T₂ */
Input: T₁, T₂, SN={SN₁,…, SNₙ} /* SN={SN₁,…, SNₙ} is a set
of closely related semantic nodes, SNᵢ is a semantic node;*/
Output: SC={SC₁, …, SCₖ}, SMC={SMC₁,…, SMCₖ} /*Semantic
clique set in a source schema and Semantic mapping clique set
in target schemas*/
Begin
IF (T₁= =Null)
THEN Return True;
R₁=T₁.FirstChild; Temp=True;
WHILE (R₁ ! = NULL)
R₂= Semantic- Mapping-Node (T₂, R₁); /* To find semantic
                                mapping node of R₁ in T₂ */
IF (R₂= =Null)
THEN Return False;
ELSE
  Temp=Temp And SemanticCliqueRecognition (R₁, R₂, SN);
  IF Temp== False
  THEN Return False;
  ELSE
    Add R₁ To SC; /* add R1 to semantic clique set*/
    Add R₂ To SMC; /*add R2 to semantic mapping clique set*/
    R₁=T₁.NextChild;
  END IF;
END IF;
END While;
Return Temp;
End
```

The Maximum Semantic Clique is the semantic clique that is not semantically included by any other semantic clique. *The Minimum Common Sub-tree* denoted as $MCS (SC_1, …, SC_p, SN_1, …, SN_q)$ is the sub-tree that covers all the semantic cliques $(SC_1,…, SC_p)$ and all the identified semantic nodes $(SN_1,…, SN_q)$ not belonging to any semantic clique in a source schema. The root of the minimum common sub-tree is called the *Nearest Common Predecessor* of the involved semantic cliques and semantic nodes. Algorithms to find minimum common sub-tree are introduced in [11].

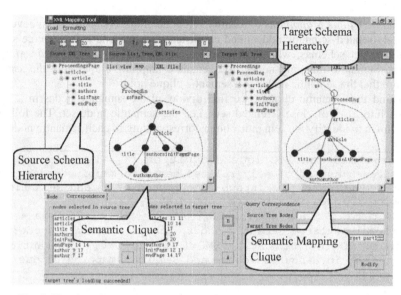

Fig. 3. User interface to define semantic cliques and semantic mapping cliques

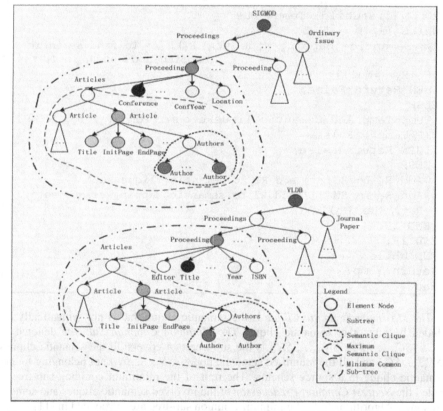

Fig. 4. XML trees conforming to the schemas of proceedings of ACM SIGMOD and VLDB

Besides the semantic cliques automatically identified by algorithm *Semantic-CliqueRecognition*, we have developed a tool to assist users to define semantic cliques that are required under certain circumstances. User interface to define semantic cliques and semantic mapping cliques is depicted in Fig. 3. The left-and-middle portion displays the source schema hierarchy and the corresponding graphical representation, while the right-and-middle portion corresponds to the target schema. The black nodes in the source schema form a user-defined semantic clique, while black nodes in the target schema are the corresponding semantic mapping cliques.

Fig. 4 depicts the schema trees of SIGMOD proceedings and VLDB proceedings. The identified semantic nodes and semantic mapping nodes are the circles in the same color. The semantic clique, the maximum semantic clique and the minimum common sub-tree are denoted by the dashed close curves as described in the legend.

4.3 Semantic Path Mapping

Semantic Path Mapping is to map each semantic path from the root to the semantic nodes in the source schema into the paths in target schemas (i.e., semantic mapping paths). Let *Semantic-Path* (N_i) be the path from *Root* (N_i) to semantic node N_i in a source schema, and *Semantic-Mapping-Path* (N_i) be the mapping path of *Semantic-Path* (N_i) in target schemas. The process of semantic path mapping can be described as follows:

```
Algorithm SemanticMappingPath (Pᵢ,Nᵢ)

Input: Pᵢ /*Schema of Pᵢ*/;
       Nᵢ /*Semantic Node in Pᵢ*/;

Output: Semantic-Mapping-Path (Nᵢ);

Step 1: For each node on Semantic-Path (Nᵢ)
        Find semantic mapping nodes in target schemas
        according to node mapping definition in
        global dictionary and local dictionary;

Step 2: Connect semantic mapping nodes in target sche-
mas to form an identified path;

Step 3: IF the identified path matches a path SMPath in
target schemas
        THEN Return (SMPath);
        ELSE
          Extend the identified path by replacing par
          ent-child relations with ancestor-
          descendant relations between adjacent
          nodes;
          IF SMPath in target schema contains the ex-
          tended identified path;
          THEN Return (SMPath);
        END IF.
```

Table 3. Semantic node mapping between the schema of SIGMOD proceedings and schema of VLDB proceedings

Source	Semantic Node	Target	Semantic Mapping Node	Similarity Degree (SD)
SIGMOD	Title	VLDB	Title	1
SIGMOD	Author	VLDB	Author	1
SIGMOD	Conference	VLDB	Title	0.5
SIGMOD	ConfYear	VLDB	Year	0.9
SIGMOD	SIGMOD	VLDB	VLDB	0.9
SIGMOD	...	VLDB	...	...

Table 4. Semantic clique mapping between the schema of SIGMOD proceedings and the schema of VLDB proceedings

Source	Semantic Clique	Target	Semantic Mapping Clique	SD
SIGMOD	Authors (Author,..., Author)	VLDB	Authors (Author,..., Author)	1
SIGMOD	Articles (Title, InitPage, EndPage, Authors (Author,..., Author))	VLDB	Articles (Title, InitPage, EndPage, Authors (Author,..., Author))	1
SIGMOD	...	VLDB		...

Table 5. Semantic path mapping between the schema of SIGMOD proceedings and the schema of VLDB proceedings

Source	Semantic Path	Target	Semantic Mapping Path	SD
SIGMOD	SIGMOD/ Proceedings/ Proceeding/ Articles/Article/ Title	VLDB	VLDB/Proceedings/Proceeding/Articles/ Article/Title	1
SIGMOD	SIGMOD/ Proceedings/ Proceeding/ Conference	VLDB	VLDB/Proceedings/Proceeding/Title	0.7
SIGMOD	...	VLDB		...

Based on the idea illustrated above, Table 3-5 respectively show the semantic node mapping, the semantic clique mapping and the semantic path mapping corresponding to schemas in Fig. 4. Table 3 is generated according to the definition in the global dictionary and local dictionary. Table 4 is generated based on the algorithm *SemanticCliqueRecognition* (Section 4.2). Table 5 is formed according to the algorithm *SemanticMappingPath* illustrated above.

5 Semantic-Based Peer Similarity Measurements and Query Routing

An effective query should forward queries only to relevant peers whose schemas are likely to match the queries. So it is necessary to have an effective similarity measurement for qualifying semantic relativity between peer schemas. We characterize the similarity degree between a set of peers according to the node similarity and structure similarity. The similarity between semantic nodes focuses on obtaining the semantic interoperability among peers, and can be measured by the methods of cycle analysis and functional dependency analysis as proposed in [1]. The similarity between semantic structures is to capture the semantic structure such as the parent-child relationship between closely related semantic nodes in a maximum semantic clique or a minimum common sub-tree. A peer determines the destination to forward a query according to the similarity between semantic nodes and between semantic structures. To define the similarity between semantic structures, we introduce the following notions:

- *Peer* (N_i) denotes the semantic mapping node for semantic node N_i.
- *Length* (N_i, N_j) denotes the number of nodes on the path from N_i to N_j.
- *MaxSC* (N_i) denotes the maximum semantic clique that semantic node N_i belongs to.
- *MinCS* (N_i) denotes the minimum common sub-tree that N_i belongs to.
- *Semantic-Node-SD* (N_i, N_j) denotes the similarity degree between N_i and N_j.

The algorithm to measure the structure similarity between the semantic node N_i in the source schema and its semantic mapping node N_j in the target schema is as follows:

```
Input:     Nᵢ, Nⱼ
    /* Nᵢ is a Semantic Leaf Node, and Nⱼ=Peer (Nᵢ) */
Output: Semantic-Structure-SD (Nᵢ, Nⱼ) /*Semantic
    structure similarity between Nᵢ and Nⱼ */
Step 1:IF Nᵢ belongs to one of the Maximum Semantic-
        Cliques
        THEN T=MaxSC (Nᵢ)
        ELSE   T= MinCS (Nᵢ)
        END IF
Step 2:Root (Nᵢ)= T
        IF Length (Nᵢ, T)=1
        THEN Semantic-Structure-SD (Nᵢ, Nⱼ)= Semantic-
            Node-SD (Nᵢ, Nⱼ)
        ELSE
            NodeSet={Nᵢ, …, Root (Nᵢ)} /* Nodes on
                    path from Nᵢ to Root (Nᵢ) */
```

$$\overrightarrow{FV} = (fv_{N_i},..., fv_{Root(N_i)}) \quad /* \text{ semantic structure}$$

similarity feature vector */

$$fv_{N_k} = \begin{cases} 0, Peer(N_k) \notin Semantic-Mapping-Path(N_i) \\ Semantic-Node-SD(N_k, Peer(N_k)), \quad Otherwise \end{cases} \quad (1)$$

$$\overrightarrow{W} = (W_{N_i},..., W_{Root(N_i)}) \quad /* \text{ weight vector to de-}$$

note node importance for node on path
from Nᵢ to Root (Nᵢ)*/

$$W_{N_k} = \begin{cases} 1/2, N_k = N_i \\ (1/2)^k, k = length(N_i, N_k), and\ N_k \neq Root(N_i) \\ 1 - \sum_{l=1}^{n-1} W_{N_l} = (1/2)^{n-1}, n = length(N_i, Root(N_i)),\quad N_k = Root(N_i) \end{cases} \quad (2)$$

$$\text{Semantic-Structure-SD } (N_i,\ N_j) = \frac{\vec{W} \cdot \vec{FV}}{\left|\vec{W}\right|\left|\vec{FV}\right|}, \quad (3)$$

where $\vec{W} \cdot \vec{FV} = W_{N_i} fv_{N_i} + ... + W_{Root(N_i)} fv_{Root(N_i)}$,

and

$$\left|\vec{X}\right| = \left\|\vec{X}\right\|_2 = \sqrt{x_1^2 + ... + x_k^2}$$

END IF

Let $SN = \{N_1, ..., N_m\}$ be semantic node set of source schema, $Semantic\text{-}Structure\text{-}SD = (SR_{N_1}, ..., SR_{N_m})$ be the feature vector for the semantic-structure similarity of each semantic node calculated according to formula (3), and $\vec{W} = (W_{N_1}, ..., W_{N_m})$ be the user-defined weight vector representing the importance of each semantic node. The semantic structure similarity between two peer schemas is defined as follows:

$$Semantic\text{-}Structure\text{-}SD\ (P_i, P_j) = \frac{\vec{W} \cdot \overrightarrow{Semantic - Structure - SD}}{\left|\vec{W}\right|\left|\overrightarrow{Semantic - Structure - SD}\right|} \quad (4)$$

6   Query Reformulation and Heterogeneous Data Integration

Upon receiving a query requirement, a peer will identify a set of relevant peers according to semantic relationships and similarity degree between peers to answer the query. We distinguish query requirements as follows:
1. A query that could be answered by separate peers.
2. A query that should be answered by joining data on multiple peers.

Query reformulation is to reformulate a peer's query over its immediate successors, then over the successors' immediate successors, and so on. Whenever the forwarded query requirement reaches a peer that stores the matching data, the query will be posed on that peer. The semantic node mapping, semantic clique mapping and semantic path mapping in Table 3-5 are used for reformulating a query over target schemas.

Within a predefined timeout, the peer initiating a query will analyze data flows returned. To solve the problem of data inconsistency, we take into account the QoP, the user-perceived qualities such as the number of returned results, response time, traffic

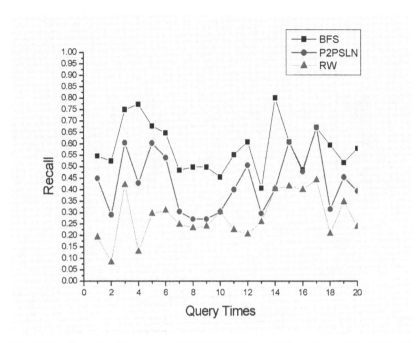

Fig. 5. Recall rate for 20 queries in BFS, P2PSLN, and RW routing policies (TTL=5)

overhead, precision and recall etc. The data returned by peers with higher QoP is considered more reliable to solve the problem of data inconsistency. Finally, the peer initiating the query will combine or join relevant data according to the pre-defined data flow and then provide users and peers with a single semantic image.

7   Experiments and Discussion

To illustrate and evaluate the proposed approach, we simulate a small but realistic P2PSLN application. The simulation environment consists of 50 peers. Each peer randomly selects a group of peers as its neighbors, and the average degree is equal to 6. The metadata of 50,000 papers collected from DBLP XML databases [4] and ACM SIGMOD XML records [2] is distributed over all peers under a uniform distribution. XML document size of each peer varies from 275K to 14, 207K. It is assumed that each peer has the same bandwidth and process ability. Twenty randomly generated queries are randomly submitted to twenty peers to test the performance of the P2PSLN with the following two types of routing mechanisms: (1) the *Breadth First Search* (BFS), each peer broadcasts query requirements to all the neighbors; and, (2) the *Random Walk Search* (RW), each peer forward the received query requests to a number of randomly selected neighbor. Our evaluation metrics are the *recall* rate (i.e., the fraction of the relevant data which has been retrieved), and the *bandwidth consumption* (i.e., the number of messages per query).

In the first experiment we measure the recall rate of three routing mechanisms when the TTL field of the request message is set to 5. Fig. 5 represents recall rate of

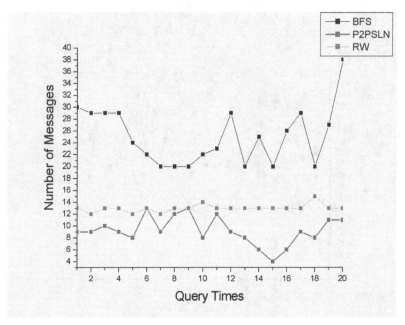

Fig. 6. Number of messages generated by 20 queries in BFS, P2PSLN, and RW routing policies (TTL=5)

the three routing mechanisms. On average, the recall rate of BFS, P2PSLN, and RW is 0.58, 0.43, and 0.28 respectively. The BFS routing policy achieves the highest recall rate. This is because the BFS broadcasts query requirements to all its neighbors and it is sure to get the most of the relevant data. The P2PSLN forwards query requirement according to the semantic relationship and the similarity degree, so it is possible to get the higher recall than the RW within a predefined TTL value.

In the second experiment we measure the number of messages that the three search mechanisms generate to process a query requirement within a predefined TTL. Fig. 6 shows that the number of messages generated by BFS is the most (25 on average). The number of messages generated by P2PSLN and RW is 9 and 13 on average respectively. We are able to reduce the number of messages by 2/3 in P2PSLN when compared to the BFS policy. In the P2PSLN search mechanism, each peer in the query path determines the neighbors according to the semantic relationship between them and then sends the query request to 3 neighbors with the highest similarity degree. Therefore, the number of messages to be forwarded can be reduced obviously.

Experimental results show that the P2PSLN is more effective and efficient in query routing than the BFS and RW routing policy in general. The major differences between the proposed approach and the previous work are as follows:

1. The P2PSLN specifies semantic relationships between peer schemas. Each peer is encapsulated as an active and intelligent soft-device, which could autonomously identify semantic relationships and dynamically interact with each other.
2. The semantic-based peer similarity measurement for efficient query routing provides a way to measure the similarity between a set of closely related nodes in peer schemas. We propose the semantic clique to denote the semantic structure between closely related semantic nodes.

3. The semantic node mapping, semantic clique mapping and semantic path mapping resolve the issues of semantic heterogeneity and structural heterogeneity between source schemas and target schemas. The data inconsistency issue in the returned data flows is resolved based on the quality of involved peers.

8   Conclusions

To resolve the issues of heterogeneous data integration in peer data management, this paper proposes a P2P semantic link network, a semantic-based peer similarity measurement for query routing, and a peer schema mapping approach for query reformulation. Results from theoretical analysis and simulations show that the proposed approach is effective. Contributions include three aspects: 1) propose the notions of P2P semantic link network and provide with a tool for constructing and maintaining a nested P2PSLN; 2) incorporate the semantic node similarity and the semantic structure similarity to measure the similarity between peers so as to improve the effectiveness and efficiency of query routing; and 3) provide users and peers with data obtained from multiple peers in single semantic image. Experiments show that the proposed approach is a promising approach for peer data management.

The proposed approach has been integrated into the China E-Science Knowledge Grid Environment IMAGINE (Integrated Multidisciplinary Autonomous Global Innovation Networking Environment), , which aims at providing access to distributed resources (i.e., information, knowledge and services) and speeding up the processes of knowledge generation, propagation, fusion and management in cooperative research [21, 22].

Ongoing work focuses on incorporating user-defined integrity constraints and query reformulation optimization into the proposed approach.

Acknowledgements. The research work was supported by the National Grand Fundamental Research 973 Program of China and the National Science Foundation. We thank all team members of China Knowledge Grid Research Group (http://kg.ict.ac.cn, http://www.knowledgegrid.net) for their diligent work and cooperation.

References

1.   K. Aberer, P. Cudre-Mauroux, and M. Hauswirth. The Chatty Web: Emergent Semantics through Gossiping. WWW 2003, Budapest, Hungary, May 2003
2.   ACM SIGMOD Xml Version.
      http://www.acm.org/sigmod/record/xml/SigmodRecord/SigmodRecord.xml
3.   P. Bernstein et al. Data Management for Peer-to-Peer Computing: A Vision. In ACM SIGMOD WebDB Workshop 2002, Madison, Wisconsin, June 2002
4.   DBLP XML Database. http://dblp.uni-trier.de/xml/
5.   Deutsch and V. Tannen. MARS: A System for Publishing XML from Mixed and Redundant Storage. Proceedings of the 29th VLDB Conference, Berlin, Germany, September 2003

6. F. Giunchiglia and I. Zaihrayeu. Making Peer Databases Interact — A Vision for an Architecture Supporting Data Coordination. In Proc. of the Conference on Information Agents (CIA 2002), Madrid, Spain, September 2002
7. Halevy et al. Schema Mediation in Peer Data Management Systems. In Proc. of ICDE 2003, Bangalore, India, March 2003
8. Halevy et al. Piazza: Data Management Infrastructure for Semantic Web Applications. In Proc. of the Intl. WWW Conf. 2003, Budapest, Hungary, May 2003
9. Kementsietsidis, M. Arenas, and R. Miller. Mapping Data in Peer-to-Peer Systems: Semantics and Algorithmic Issues. In Proc. of the ACM SIGMOD International Conference on Management of Data 2003, San Diego, California, June 2003
10. Loser et al. Semantic Overlay Clusters within Supper-Peer Networks. International Workshop on Databases, Information Systems, and P2P Computing, Berlin, Germany, September 2003
11. S.Y.Lu. A Tree-Matching Algorithm Based on Node Splitting and Merging. IEEE Transactions on Pattern Analysis and Machine Intelligence (PAMI) 6 (2) (1984) 249-256
12. J. Madhavan, P. Bernstein, and E. Rahm. Generic Schema Matching with Cupid. Proceedings of the 27th VLDB Conference, Roma, Italy, September 2001
13. W. Nejdl et al. Super-Peer-Based Routing and Clustering Strategies for RDF-Based Peer-To-Peer Networks. WWW2003, Budapest, Hungary, May 2003
14. W.S. Ng et al. PeerDB: A P2P-Based System for Distributed Data Sharing. In Intl. Conf. on Data Engineering (ICDE) 2003, Bangalore, India, March 2003
15. B.Ooi, Y. Shu, and K. Tan. DB-Enabled Peers for Managing Distributed Data. 5th Asia-Pacific Web Conference, APWeb2003, Xian, China, April 2003
16. E. Rahm and P. Bernstein. A Survey of Approaches to Automatic Schema Matching. VLDB Journal 10(4) (2001) 334-350
17. Stoica et al. Chord: A Scalable Peer-to-Peer Lookup Protocol for Internet Applications. IEEE/ACM Transactions on Networking 11 (2003) 17-32
18. Tatarinov and A. Halevy. Efficient Query Reformulation in Peer-Data Management Systems. ACM SIGMOD 2004, Paris, France, June 2004
19. H. Zhuge. Active E-Document Framework ADF: Model and Tool. Information and Management 41 (1) (2003) 87-97
20. H. Zhuge. Clustering Soft-Devices in Semantic Grid. IEEE Computing in Science and Engineering 4 (6) (2002) 60-63
21. H. Zhuge. China's E-Science Knowledge Grid Environment. IEEE Intelligent Systems 19 (1) (2004) 13-17
22. H.Zhuge, Future Interconnection Environment — Dream, Principle, Challenge and Practice, Keynote at The 5th International Conference on Web-Age Information Management, Dalian, China, July, 2004. http://www.knowledgegrid.net
23. Gnutella website. http://www.gnutella.com
24. Napster website. http://www.napster.com

Peer Selection in Peer-to-Peer Networks
with Semantic Topologies

Peter Haase[1], Ronny Siebes[2], and Frank van Harmelen[2]

[1] Institute AIFB, University of Karlsruhe, D-76128 Karlsruhe, Germany
`haase@aifb.uni-karlsruhe.de`
[2] Vrije Universiteit Amsterdam, The Netherlands
`{ronny,frankh}@cs.vu.nl`

Abstract. Peer-to-Peer systems have proven to be an effective way of sharing data. Modern protocols are able to efficiently route a message to a given peer. However, determining the destination peer in the first place is not always trivial. We propose a model in which peers advertise their expertise in the Peer-to-Peer network. The knowledge about the expertise of other peers forms a semantic topology. Based on the semantic similarity between the subject of a query and the expertise of other peers, a peer can select appropriate peers to forward queries to, instead of broadcasting the query or sending it to a random set of peers. To calculate our semantic similarity measure we make the simplifying assumption that the peers share the same ontology. We evaluate the model in a bibliographic scenario, where peers share bibliographic descriptions of publications among each other. In simulation experiments we show how expertise based peer selection improves the performance of a Peer-to-Peer system with respect to precision, recall and the number of messages.

1 Introduction

Peer-to-Peer systems are distributed systems without any centralized control or hierarchical organization, in which each node runs software with equivalent functionality. A review of the features of recent Peer-to-Peer applications yields a long list: redundant storage, permanence, selection of nearby servers, anonymity, search, authentication, and hierarchical naming. Despite this rich set of features, scalability is a significant challenge: Peer-to-Peer networks that broadcast all queries to all peers don't scale - intelligent query routing and network topologies are required to be able to route queries to a relevant subset of peers. Modern routing protocols like Chord [15], CAN [14] are based on the idea of Distributed Hash Tables for efficient query routing, but little effort has been made with respect to rich semantic representations of metadata and query functionalities beyond simple keyword searches.

The Semantic Web is an extension of the current web in which information is given well-defined meaning, better enabling computers and people to work in cooperation [2]. In a distributed knowledge management system these Semantic Web techniques can be used for expressing the knowledge shared by peers in a well-defined and formal way.

In the model that we propose, peers use a shared ontology to advertise their expertise in the Peer-to-Peer network. The knowledge about the expertise of other peers forms a

M. Bouzeghoub et al. (Eds.): ICSNW 2004, LNCS 3226, pp. 108–125, 2004.
© IFIP International Federation for Information Processing 2004

semantic topology, independent of the underlying network topology. If the peer receives a query, it can decide to forward it to peers about which it knows that their expertise is *similar* to the subject of the query. The advantage of this approach is that queries will not be forwarded to all or a random set of known peers, but only to those that have a good chance of answering it.

In this paper we instantiate the above model with a bibliographic scenario, in which researchers share bibliographic metadata about publications. In the evaluation of our model we will show how

- the proposed model of expertise based peer selection considerably improves the performance of the Peer-to-Peer system,
- ontology-based matching with a similarity measure will improve the system compared with an approach that relies on exact matches, such as a simple keyword based approach,
- the performance of the system can be improved further, if the semantic topology is built according to the semantic similarity of the expertises of the peers,
- a "perfect" semantic topology imposed on the network using global knowledge yields ideal results.

In the remainder of the paper we will present the formal model for expertise base peer selection (Section 2), instantiate this model for the bibliographic scenario (Section 3), define evaluation criteria (Section 4), present results of the simulation (Section 5), discuss related work (Section 6) and conclude with some directions for future work (Section 7).

2   A Model for Expertise Based Peer Selection

In the model we propose, peers advertise their expertise in the network. The peer selection is based on matching the subject of a query and the expertise according to their semantic similarity. Figure 1 below shows the idea of the model in one picture.

In this section we first introduce a model to semantically describe the expertise of peers and how peers promote their expertise as advertisement messages in the network. Second, we describe how the received advertisements allows a peer to select other peers

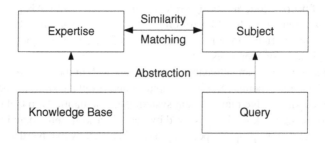

Fig. 1. Expertise Based Matching

for a given query based on a semantic matching of query subjects against expertise descriptions. The third part describes how a *semantic topology* can be formed by advertising expertise.

2.1   Semantic Description of Expertise

Peers. The Peer-to-Peer network consists of a set of peers P. Every peer $p \in P$ has a knowledge base that contains the knowledge that it wants to share.

Common Ontology. The peers share an ontology O, which provides a common conceptualization of their domain. The ontology is used for describing the expertise of peers and the subject of queries.

Expertise. An expertise description $e \in E$ is a abstract, semantic description of the knowledge base of a peer based on the common ontology O. This expertise can either be extracted from the knowledge base automatically or specified in some other manner.

Advertisements. Advertisements $A \subseteq P \times E$ are used to promote descriptions of the expertise of peers in the network. An advertisement $a \in A$ associates a peer p with a an expertise e. Peers decide autonomously, without central control, whom to promote advertisements to and which advertisements to accept. This decision can be based on the semantic similarity between expertise descriptions.

2.2   Matching and Peer Selection

Queries. Queries $q \in Q$ are posed by a user and are evaluated against the knowledge bases of the peers. First a peer evaluates the query against its local knowledge base and then decides which peers the query should be forwarded to. Query results are returned to the peer that originally initiated the query.

Subjects. A subject $s \in S$ is an abstraction of a given query q expressed in terms of the common ontology. The subject can be seen a complement to an expertise description, as it specifies the required expertise to answer the query.

Similarity Function. The similarity function $SF : S \times E \mapsto [0, 1]$ yields the semantic similarity between a subject $s \in S$ and an expertise description $e \in E$. An increasing value indicates increasing similarity. If the value is 0, s and e are not similar at all, if the value is 1, they match exactly. SF is used for determining to which peers a query should be forwarded. Analogously, a same kind of similarity function $E \times E \mapsto [0, 1]$ can be defined to determine the similarity between the expertise of two peers.

Peer Selection Algorithm. The peer selection algorithm returns a ranked set of peers. The rank value is equal to the similarity value provided by the similarity function.

    From this set of ranked peers one can, for example, select the best n peers, or all peers whose rank value is above a certain threshold, etc.

Algorithm 1 Peer Selection

---

let A be the advertisements that are available on the peer
let γ be the minimal similarity between the expertise of a peer and the topics of the query.
$subject := ExtractSubject(query)$
$rankedPeers := \emptyset$
for all $ad \in A$ **do**
  $peer := Peer(ad)$
  $rank := SF(Expertise(ad), subject)$
  if $rank > \gamma$ **then**
    $rankedPeers := (peer, rank) \cup rankedPeers$
return $rankedPeers$

2.3 Semantic Topology

The knowledge of the peers about the expertise of other peers is the basis for a semantic topology. Here it is important to state that this semantic topology is independent of the underlying network topology. At this point, we don't make any assumptions about the properties of the topology on the network layer.
The semantic topology can be described by the following relation:

$Knows \subseteq P \times P$, where $Knows(p_1, p_2)$ means that p_1 knows about the expertise of p_2.

The relation $Knows$ is established by the selection of which peers a peer sends its advertisements to. Furthermore, peers can decide to accept an advertisement, e.g. to include it in their registries, or to discard the advertisement. The semantic topology in combination with the expertise based peer selection is the basis for intelligent query routing.

3   The Bibliographic Scenario

In this section we instantiate the general model for expertise based peer selection from previous section. We use a real-life scenario for knowledge sharing in a Peer-to-Peer environment.

In the daily life of a computer scientist, one regularly has to search for publications or their correct bibliographic metadata. Currently, people do these searches with search engines like Google and CiteSeer, via university libraries or by simply asking other people that are likely to know how to obtain the desired information.

The scenario that we envision here is that researchers in a community share bibliographic metadata via a Peer-to-Peer system. The data may have been obtained from BibTeX files or from a bibliography server such as the DBLP database[1]. A similar scenario is described in [1], where data providers, i.e. research institutes, form a Peer-to-Peer network which supports distributed search over all the connected metadata repositories.

We now describe the bibliographic scenario using the general model presented in the previous section.

---

[1] http://dblp.uni-trier.de/

Peers. A researcher is represented by a peer $p \in P$. Each peer has an RDF knowledge base, which consists of a set of bibliographic metadata items that are classified according to the ACM topic hierarchy[2]. The following example shows a fragment of a sample bibliographic item based on the Semantic Web Research Community Ontology (SWRC)[3]:

```
<rdf:RDF xmlns=
  "http://www.semanticweb.org/ontologies/swrc-onto.daml#"
   xmlns:rdf ="http://www.w3.org/1999/02/22-rdf-syntax-ns#"
   xmlns:acm ="http://daml.umbc.edu/ontologies/topic-ont#">
<Publication rdf:about="dblp:persons/Codd81">
 <title>The Capabilities of
        Relational Database Management Systems.</title>
 <acm:topic rdf:resource=
    "http://daml.umbc.edu/ontologies/classification#
     ACMTopic/Information_Systems/Database_Management"/>
 <!-- ... -->
</Publication>
</rdf:RDF>
```

Common Ontology. The ontology O that is shared by all the peers is the ACM topic hierarchy. The topic hierarchy contains a set, T, of 1287 topics in the computer science domain and relations $(T \times T)$ between them: *SubTopic* and *seeAlso*.

Expertise. The ACM topic hierarchy is the basis for our expertise model. Expertise E is defined as $E \subseteq 2^T$, where each $e \in E$ denotes a set of ACM topics, for which a peer provides classified instances.

Advertisements. Advertisements associate peers with their expertise: $A \subseteq P \times E$. A single advertisement therefore consists of a set of ACM topics for which the peer is an expert on.

Queries. We use the RDF query language SeRQL [6] to express queries against the RDF knowledge base of a peer. The following sample query asks for publications with their title about the ACM topic *Information Systems / Database Management*:

```
CONSTRUCT {pub} <swrc:title> {title} FROM
{Subject} <rdf:type> {<swrc:Publication>};
  <swrc:title> {title};
  <acm:topic>
  {<topic:ACMTopic/Information_Systems/Database_Management>}
USING NAMESPACE
swrc=<!http://www.semanticweb.org/ontologies/swrc-onto.daml#>,
rdf =<!http://www.w3.org/1999/02/22-rdf-syntax-ns#>,
acm =<!http://daml.umbc.edu/ontologies/topic-ont#>,
topic=<!http://daml.umbc.edu/ontologies/classification#>
```

---

[2] http://www.cs.vu.nl/ heiner/public/SW@VU/classification.daml
[3] http://ontobroker.semanticweb.org/ontos/swrc.html

Subjects. Analogously to the expertise, a subject $s \in S$ is an abstraction of a query q. In our scenario, each s is a set of ACM topics, thus $s \subseteq T$. For example, the extracted subject of the query above would be *Information Systems/Database Management*.

Similarity Function. In this scenario, the similarity function SF is based on the idea that topics which are close according to their positions in the topic hierarchy are more similar than topics that have a larger distance. For example, an expert on ACM topic *Information Systems/Information Storage and Retrieval* has a higher chance of giving a correct answer on a query about *Information Systems/Database Management* than an expert on a less similar topic like *Hardware/Memory Structures*.

To be able to define the similarity of a peer's expertise and a query subject, which are both represented as a set of topics, we first define the similarity for individual topics. [10] have compared different similarity measures and have shown that for measuring the similarity between concepts in a hierarchically structured semantic network, like the ACM topic hierarchy, the following similarity measure yields the best results:

$$S(t_1, t_2) = \begin{cases} e^{-\alpha l} \cdot \frac{e^{\beta h} - e^{-\beta h}}{e^{\beta h} + e^{-\beta h}} & \text{if } t_1 \neq t_2, \\ 1 & \text{otherwise} \end{cases} \tag{1}$$

Here l is the length of the shortest path between topic t_1 and t_2 in the graph spanned by the *SubTopic* relation. h is the level in the tree of the direct common subsumer from t_1 and t_2.

$\alpha \geq 0$ and $\beta \geq 0$ are parameters scaling the contribution of shortest path length l and depth h, respectively. Based on their benchmark data set, the optimal values are: $\alpha = 0.2$, $\beta = 0.6$. Using the shortest path between two topics is a measure for similarity because Rada et al [13] have proven that the minimum number of edges separating topics t_1 and t_2 is a metric for measuring the conceptual distance of t_1 and t_2. The intuition behind using the depth of the direct common subsumer in the calculation is that topics at upper layers of hierarchical semantic nets are more general and are semantically less similar than topics at lower levels.

Now that we have a function for calculating the similarity between two individual topics, we define SF as:

$$SF(s, e) = \frac{1}{|s|} \sum_{t_i \in s} \max_{t_j \in e} S(t_i, t_j) \tag{2}$$

With this function we iterate over all topics of the subject and average their similarities with the most similar topic of the expertise.

Peer Selection Algorithm. The peer selection algorithm ranks the known peers according to the similarity function described above. Therefore, peers that have an expertise more similar to that of the subject of the query will have a higher rank. From the set of ranked peers, we now only consider a selection algorithm that selects the best n peers.

4   Evaluation Criteria

In this section we define a number of criteria for a Peer-to-Peer system, which will be the basis for the evaluation of our proposed model for peer selection. These criteria are mainly based on those described in [7].

4.1   Input Parameters

The following input parameters are important criteria that influence the performance of a Peer-to-Peer system:

Number of Peers.   The size of the Peer-to-Peer network is represented by this number. Typically the scalability of the system is measured in terms of number of peers.

Number of Documents.   The scalability of a Peer-to-Peer system can also be expressed in terms of the number of shared resource items, e.g. documents.

Document Distribution.   The document distribution in Peer-to-Peer networks is rarely completely random, but often has certain properties. With this input parameter we want to evaluate how the proposed model behaves with different document distributions.

Network Topology.   The performance of a Peer-to-Peer system is strongly influenced by the network topology and its characteristics. Possible topologies could for example be super-peer based, star or ring-shaped, or simply a random graph.

Advertisements.   The advertisements are responsible for building the semantic topology. There are various variables involved, e.g. whom to send the advertisments to and which received advertisements to include based on the semantic similarity between the own expertise and that of the advertisement.

Peer Selection Algorithm.   The peer selection algorithm determines which peers a query should be forwarded to. This could be a naive algorithm, which simply broadcasts a query, or a more advanced one, as the proposed expertise based peer selection.

Maximum Number of Hops.   The maximum number of hops determines how many times a query is allowed to be forwarded. It determines how much the network will be flooded by a single query.

4.2   Output Parameters

To evaluate a Peer-to-Peer system, we use precision and recall measures known from classical Information Retrieval. Here we distinguish measures on the document level (query answering) and the peer level (peer selection). These measures are defined as follows:

Document level (Query Answering)

$Precision_{Doc} = \frac{|A \cap B|}{|B|}$

indicates how many of the returned documents are relevant, with A being the set of relevant documents in the network and B being the set of returned documents. In our model we work with exact queries, therefore only relevant documents are returned. The precision will therefore always be one:

$Precision_{Doc} = \frac{|B|}{|B|} = 1.$

$Recall_{Inf} = \frac{|A \cap B|}{|A|} = \frac{|B|}{|A|}$

The recall on the document level states how many of the relevant documents are returned.

Peer Level (Peer Selection)

$Precision_{Peer} = \frac{|A \cap B|}{|B|}$

For a given query, how many of the peers that were selected had relevant information. Here A is the set of peers that had relevant documents and B is the set of peers that were reached.

$Recall_{Peer} = \frac{|A \cap B|}{|A|}$

indicates for a given query, how many of the peers that had relevant information were reached.

Further Parameters. Another important output parameters is:

$Number_{Messages}$

This output parameter indicates with how many messages the network is flooded by one query. The number of messages does not only affect the network traffic, but also CPU consumption, such as for the processing of the queries in the case of query messages.

Other output parameters that might be used as evaluation criteria, but are not considered in the following, are for example the size of messages and response times, as they are not relevant for the evaluation of our model.

5   Experimental Results

In this section we describe the simulation of the scenario presented in section 3. The evaluations are based on the criteria defined in section 4. With the experiments we try to validate the following hypotheses:

- **H1 - Expertise based selection:** The proposed approach of expertise based peer selection yields better results than a naive approach based on random selection. The higher precision of the expertise based selection results in a higher recall of peers and documents, while reducing the number of messages per query.
- **H2 - Ontology based matching:** Using a shared ontology with a metric for semantic similarity improves the recall rate of the system compared with an approach that relies on exact matches, such as a simple keyword based approach.

- **H3 - Semantic topology:** The performance of the system can be improved further, if the semantic topology is built according to the semantic similarity of the expertises of the peers. This can be realized, for example, by accepting advertisements that are semantically similar to the own expertise.
- **H4 - The "Perfect" topology:** Perfect results in terms of precision and recall can be achieved, if the semantic topology coincides with a distribution of the documents according to the expertise model.

Data Set. To obtain a critical mass of bibliographic data, we used the DBLP data set, which consists of metadata for 380440 publications in the computer science domain.

We have classified the publications of the DBLP data set according to the ACM topic hierarchy using a simple classification scheme based on lexical analysis: A publication is said to be about a topic, if the label of the topic occurs in the title of the publication. For example, a publication with the title "The Capabilities of Relational Database Management Systems." is classified into the topic *Database Management.*Topics with labels that are not unique (e.g. *General* is a subtopic of both *General Literature* and *Hardware*) have been excluded from the classification, because typically these labels are too general and would result in publications classified into multiple, distant topics in the hierarchy. Obviously, this method of classification is not as precise as a sophisticated or manual classification. However, a high precision of the classification is not required for the purpose of our simulations. As a result of the classification, about one third of the DBLP publications (126247 out of 380440) have been classified, where 553 out of the 1287 ACM topics actually have classified publications. The classified DBLP subset has been used for our simulations.

Document Distribution. We have simulated and evaluated the scenario with two different distributions, which we describe in the following. Note that for the simulation of the scenario we disregard the actual documents and only distribute the bibliographic metadata of the publications.

Topic Distribution: In the first distribution, the bibliographic metadata are distributed according to their topic classification. There is one dedicated peer for each of the 1287 ACM topics. The distribution is directly correlated with the expertise model, each peer is an expert on exactly one ACM topic and contains all the corresponding publications. This also implies that there are peers that do not contain publications, because not all topics have classified instances.

Proceedings Distribution: In the second distribution, the bibliographic metadata are distributed according to conference proceedings and journals in which the according publications were published. For each of the conference proceedings and journals covered in DBLP there is a dedicated peer that contains all the associated publication descriptions (in the case of the 328 journals) or inproceedings (in the case of the 2006 conference proceedings). Publications that are published neither in a journal nor in conference proceedings are contained by one separate peer. The total number of peers therefore is 2335 (=328+2006+1). With this distribution one peer can be an expert on multiple topics, as a journal or conference typically covers mutliple ACM topics. Note that there is still a correlation between the distribution and the expertise, as a conference or journal typically covers a coherent set of topics.

Simulation Environment. To simulate the scenario we have developed and used a controlled, configurable Peer-to-Peer simulation environment. A single simulation experiment consists of the following sequence of operations:

1. *Setup network topology:* In the first step we create the peers with their knowledge bases according to the document distribution and arrange them in a random network topology, where every peer knows 10 random peers. We do not make any further assumptions about the network topology.
2. *Advertising Knowledge:* In the second step, the semantic topology is created. Every peer sends an advertisement of its expertise to all other peers it knows based on the network topology. When a peer receives an advertisement, it may decide to store all or selected advertisements, e.g. if the advertised expertise is semantically similar to its own expertise. After this step the semantic topology is static and will not change anymore.
3. *Query Processing:* The peers randomly initiate queries from a set of randomly created 12870 queries, 10 for each of the 1287 ACM topic. The peers first evaluate the queries against their local knowledge base and then propagate the query according to their peer selection algorithms described below.

Experimental Settings. In our experiments we have systematically simulated various settings with different values of input variables. In the following we will describe an interesting selected subset of the settings to prove the validity of our hypotheses.

Setting 1. In the first setting we use a naive peer selection algorithm, which selects n *random* peers from the set of peers that are known from advertisements received, but disregarding the content of the advertisement. In the experiments, we have used n=2 in every setting, as a rather arbitrary choice.

Setting 2. In the second setting we apply the expertise based selection algorithm. The *best* n (n=2) peers are selected for query forwarding. Here the peer selection algorithm only considers *exact* matches of topics.

Setting 3. In the third setting we modify the peer selection algorithm to use the ontology based similarity measure, instead of only exact matches. The peer selection only selects peers whose expertise is equally or more similar to the subject of the query than the expertise of the forwarding peer.

Setting 4. In the fourth setting we modify the peer to only accept advertisements that are semantically similar to its own expertise. The threshold for accepting advertisements was set to accept on average half of the incoming advertisements.

Setting 5. In this setting we assume global knowledge to impose a perfect topology on the peer network. In this perfect topology the *knows* relation conincides with the ACM topic hierarchy: Every peer knows exactly those peers that are experts on the neighboring topics of its own expertise. This setting is only applicable for the distribution of the publications according to their topics, as this model assumes exactly one expert per topic.

The following table summarizes the instantiations of the input variables for the described settings:

Setting #	Peer Selection	Advertisements	Topology
Setting 1	random	accept all	random
Setting 2	exact match	accept all	random
Setting 3	ontology based match	accept all	random
Setting 4	ontology based match	accept similar	random
Setting 5	ontology based match	accept similar	perfect

Simulation Results. Figures 2 through 5 show the results for the different settings and distributions. The simulations have been run with a varying number of allowed hops. In the results we show the performance for a maximum of up to eight hops. Zero hops means that the query is processed locally and not forwarded. Please note that the diagrams for the number of messages per query and recall (i.e. Figures 5, 3, 4) present cumulative values, i.e. they include the sum of the results for *up to* n hops. The diagram for the precision (Figure 2) of the peer selection displays the precision for a particular number of hops.

In the following, we will interpret the results of the experiments for the various settings described above with respect to our hypotheses H1 through H4.

R1 - Expertise based selection. The results of Figure 2, Setting 1, show that the naive approach of random peer selection gives a constant low precision of 0.03% for the topic distribution and 1.3% for the proceedings distribution. This results in a fairly low recall of peers and documents despite a high number of messages, as shown in Figures 3, 5, 4, respectively. With the expertise based selection, either exact or similarity based matching, the precision can be improved considerably by about one order of magnitude. For example, with the expertise based selection in Setting 3, the precision of the peer selection (Figure 2) can be improved from 0.03% to 0.15% for the topic distribution and from 1.3% to 15% for the proceedings distribution. With the precision, also the recall of peers and documents rises (Figures 3, 5). At the same time, the number of messages per

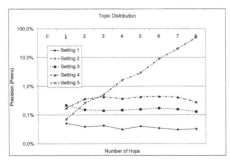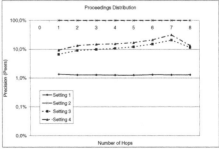

Fig. 2. $Precision_{Peers}$

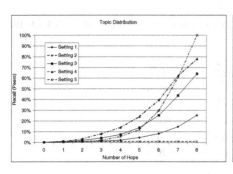
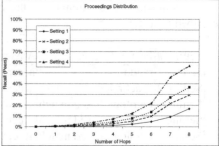

Fig. 3. $Recall_{Peers}$

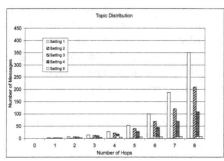
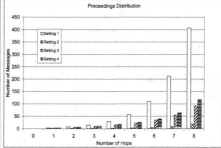

Fig. 4. $Number_{Messages}$

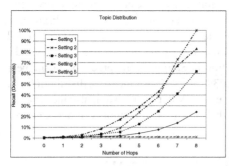
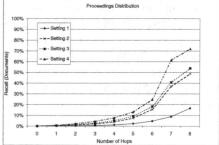

Fig. 5. $Recall_{Documents}$

query can be reduced. The number of messages sent is influenced by two effects. The first effect is message redundancy: The more precise the peer selection, the higher is the chance of a peer receiving a query multiple times on different routes. This redundancy is detected by the receiving peer, which will forward the query only once, thus resulting in a decreasing number of queries sent across the network. The other effect is caused by the selectivity of the peer selection: It only forwards the query to peers whose expertise is semantically more or equally similar to the query than that of the own expertise. With an increasing number of hops, as the semantic similarity of the expertise of the peer and the query increases, the chance of knowing a qualifying peer decreases, which results in a decrease of messages.

R2 - Ontology based matching. The result of Figure 2, Setting 2, shows that the exact match approach results in a maximum precision already after one hop, which is obvious because it only selects peers that match exactly with the query's subject. However, Figure 3 shows that the recall in this case is very low in the case of the topic distribution. This can be explained as follows: For every query subject, there is only one peer that exactly matches in the entire network. In a sparse topology, the chance of knowing that relevant peer is very low. Thus the query cannot spread effectively across the network, resulting in a document recall of only 1%. In contrary, Setting 3 shows that when semantically similar peers are selected, it is possible to improve the recall of peers and documents, to 62% after eight hops. Also in the case of the proceedings distribution, where multiple exact matches are possible, we see an improvement from 49% in the case of exact matches (Setting 2), to 54% in the case of ontology based matches (Setting 3). Naturally, this approach requires to send more messages per query and also results in a lower precision.

R3 - Semantic Topology. In Setting 4 the peers only accept semantically similar advertisements. This has proven to be a simple, but effective way for creating a semantic topology that correlates with the expertise of the peers. This allows to forward queries along the gradient of increasing semantic similarity. When we compare this approach with that of Setting 3, the precision of the peer selection can be improved from 0.15% to 0.4% for the topic distribution and from 14% to 20% for the proceedings distribution. The recall of documents can thus be improved from 62% to 83% for the topic distribution and from 54% to 72% for the proceedings distribution.

It is also interesting to note that the precision of the peer selection for the similarity based matching decreases slightly after seven hops (Figure 2). The reason is that after seven hops the majority of the relevant peers has already been reached. Thus the chance of finding relevant peers decreases, resulting in a lower precision of the peer selection.

R4 - The "Perfect" Topology. The results for Setting 5 show how one could obtain the maximum recall and precision, if it were possible to impose an ideal semantic topology on the network. All relevant peers and thus all bibliographic descriptions can be found in a deterministic manner, as the query is simply routed along the route which corresponds to the shortest path in the ACM topic hierarchy. At each hop the query is forwarded to exactly one peer until the relevant peer is reached. The number of messages required per query is therefore the length of the shortest path from the topic of expertise of the originating peer to that of the topic of the query subject. The precision of the peer selection increases to the maximum when arriving at the eight hop, which is the maximum possible length of a shortest path in the ACM topic hierarchy. Accordingly, the maximum number of messages (Figure 4) required is also eight.

6 Related Work

The idea of expertise based matching for peer selection using ontologies is similar to that of capability based matching as described in [16], where specifications of requests are matched against a set of capabilities of agents or services. Capability based matching has recently also been applied for matching of Web Services, e.g. [9].

Another approach, which does a semantic comparison between a query and a peer's context comes from [4]. They propose a Peer-to-Peer architecture, implemented as their 'KEx' system where queries can be accompanied with a 'focus' which is a part of an ontology, e.g. a small taxonomy. When a peer receives a query, its matching algorithm tries to match the focus of the query semantically and syntactically. The syntactic matching process is straight-forward by using an indexer to search for the occurrence of specific keywords into the set of documents owned by the provider. For the semantic matching a context matching algorithm is used that tries to find a correlation between a provider's context and the query focus. In particular the matching algorithm tries to find the focus in the provider's context that has a relevant semantic relation with the one sent by the seeker. Related documents that fit the focus are returned as results. If the focus points to other peers, the provider will propagate the query. The big strength of this approach is that it does not make the assumption that the ontologies should be equal and shared by all the peers, contrary to our approach. The advantage of our approach however is that it is much easier to calculate the similarity between a query's subject and the expertise of a peer.

pSearch [17] distributes document indices through the P2P network based on document semantics generated by Latent Semantic Indexing (LSI) [3]. LSI represents documents and queries as vectors in a Cartesian space and measures the similarity between a query and a document as the cosine of the angle between their vector representations. pSearch is organized as a Content-addressable network (CAN) [19]. CANs provide a distributed hash table (DHT) abstraction also distributed over a Cartesian space. The combination of the LSI representation and their network organization, the search cost (in terms of different nodes searched and data transmitted) for a given query is reduced, since the indices of semantically related documents are likely to be co-located in the network. Although the pSearch approach seems to work very well for finding documents close to a query, the vector dimensionality and the corresponding concepts for each place in the vectors need to be known beforehand. In their experiments they used a vector with a dimensionality around a few hundred concepts. This means that all the documents in the system can only be identified and matched on these corresponding concepts. In other words, the network topology is directly connected and therefore limited by the number of concepts. This is contrary to our approach where we don't make any assumption about the network topology.

A completely different approach for finding experts in a network comes from social network analysis. ReferralWeb [8] uses the social network to make a search more focused and effective. ReferralWeb attempts to uncover the existing social networks by data mining public documents found on the WWW. Such sources can include links found on home pages, lists of co-authors in technical papers and citations of papers, exchanges between individuals recorded in news archives, and organization charts. Their simulation experiments showed that automatically generated referrals can be highly successful in locating experts in a large network. Experiments performed by [19] show that when referrals are considered, better answers are found in terms of precision. They also show that it is possible to let the system evolve to a situation where peers with similar expertise and interest are grouped close towards each other, according to their own similarity function. It is probable that the number of messages needed for getting an answer on a query decreases when the system evolves, but unfortunately that isn't shown by their experiments. The main difference with our approach is that their peers express queries and expertise in a vector, in which the similarity is based on taking the cosine of both vectors.

[12] presents schema-based Peer-to-Peer networks and the use of super-peer based topologies for these networks, in which peers are organized in hypercubes. [11] shows how this schema-based approach can be used to create Semantic Overlay Clusters in a scientific Peer-to-Peer network with a small set of metadata attributes that describe the documents in the network. In contrast, the approach in our system is completely decentralized in the sense that it does not rely on super-peers.

7   Conclusions and Future Work

Summary: In this paper we have presented a model for expertise-based peer selection, in which a semantic topology among the peers is created by advertising the expertise of the peers. We have shown how the model can be applied in a bibliographic scenario. Simulation experiments that we performed with this bibliographic scenario show the following results:

- Using expertise-based peer selection can increase the performance of the peer selection by an order of magnitude (result R1).
- However, if expertise-based peer selection uses simple exact matching, the recall drops to unacceptable levels. It is necessary to use an ontology-based similarity measure as the basis for expertise-based matching (result R2).
- An advertising strategy where peers only accept advertisements that are semantically close to their own profile (i.e. that are in their semantic neighborhood) is a simple and effective way of creating a semantic topology. This semantic topology allows to forward queries along the gradient of increasing semantic similarity (result R3).
- The above results depend on how closely the semantic topology of the network mirrors the structure of the ontology. All relevant performance measure reach their optimal value when the network is organised exactly according to the structure of the topology (result R4). Although this situation is idealised and in will in practice not be achievable, the experiment serves to confirm our intuitions on this.

Summarizing, in simulation experiments we have shown that expertise-based peer selection combined with ontology-based matching outperforms both random peer selection and selection based on exact matches, and that this performance increase grows when the semantic topologies more closely mirrors the domain ontology.

Limiting assumptions: We have made a number of simplifying assumptions in our experiments. We review these assumptions, and the likely impact their relaxation may have on our results:

- **A single ontology:** clearly, the assumption that all peers agree on the use of single ontology is not in all cases realistic. We already have work in progress which allows us to relax this constraint. We expect that differences in ontologies used by different peers will *lower* our results, since the computation of the semantic distance between peers becomes less reliable across different ontologies.
- **A static semantic topology:** in our experiments, the semantic topology is determined once, during an initial advertising round, and is not adapted any further during the lifetime of the experiment. The work in [18] shows how the topology can be adjusted based on the exchange of queries and answers. We expect that such a self-adjusting network will *improve* our results, since the semantic topology will converge better towards the structure of the underlying ontology than our current one-shot advertising allows.
- **Static content distribution:** in our experiments, content was assigned statically to peers, while in a realistic network, the content of different peers is likely to evolve over the lifetime of the network. Since such changing content will also induce changes in the expertise profile of the peers, we expect that this assumption can only be relaxed in the presence of self-adjusting semantic topologies (as mentioned in the previous point). Again, we have work in progress to relax this assumption.

Future work: Besides relaxing the above assumptions, there are many other fruitful directions in which this work can be taken:

- **More complex expertise models.** The expertise model presented for the bibliographic scenario is a fairly simple one, based on the ACM topic hierarchy. Other domains may require more complex expertise models with different similarity functions. One option would be, for example, to extend the expertise model with quantitative measures to indicate how much information for a certain topic of expertise is available on the peer.
- **Merge semantic and network topology.**
  So far we have considered the semantic topology to be independent of the underlying network topology. It would however be interesting to use, for example, the extensibility mechanisms of the JXTA platform to extend its default mechanisms for discovery and query routing with the methods presented in this paper.
- **Field Experiment.** To verify the results of the simulation experiments in the real world, the model proposed in this paper is currently implemented in the Bibster system[4] and evaluated in the bibliographic scenario with a field experiment [5].

Acknowledgments. Research reported in this paper has been partially financed by the EU in the IST project SWAP (IST-2001-34103). We would like to thank our colleagues for fruitful discussions.

---

[4] http://bibster.semanticweb.org

References

1. Benjamin Ahlborn, Wolfgang Nejdl, and Wolf Siberski. OAI-P2P: A peer-to-peer network for open archives. In *2002 International Conference on Parallel Processing Workshops (ICPPW'02)*, 2002.
2. Tim Berners-Lee, James Hendler, and Ora Lassila. The semantic web. *Scientific American*, 2001.
3. Michael W. Berry, Zlatko Drmac, and Elizabeth R. Jessup. Matrices, vector spaces, and information retrieval. In *SIAM Review*, pages 335–362, 1999.
4. Matteo Bonifacio, Roberta Cuel, Gianluca Mameli, and Michele Nori. A peer-to-peer architecture for distributed knowledge management. In *Proceedings of the 3rd International Symposium on Multi-Agent Systems, Large Complex Systems, and E-Businesses MALCEB'2002*, 2002.
5. Jeen Broekstra, Marc Ehrig, Peter Haase, Frank van Harmelen, Maarten Menken, Peter Mika, Björn Schnizler, and Ronny Siebes. Bibster - a semantics-based bibliographic peer-to-peer system. In *Proceedings of the WWW'04 Workshop on Semantics in Peer-to-Peer and Grid Computing, New York, 2004*, 2004.
6. Jeen Broekstra and Arjohn Kampman. SeRQL: An RDF Query and Transformation Language. Submitted to the International Semantic Web Conference, ISWC 2004, 2004. See also http://www.openrdf.org/doc/SeRQLmanual.html.
7. Marc Ehrig, Christoph Schmitz, Steffen Staab, Julien Tane, and Christoph Tempich. Towards evaluation of peer-to-peer-based distributed knowledge management systems. In *Proceedings of the AAAI Spring Symposium "Agent-Mediated Knowledge Management (AMKM-2003)"*, 2003.
8. Bart Selman Henry Kautz and Mehul Shah. Referralweb: Combining social networks and collaborative filtering. In *Communications of the ACM*, March 1997.
9. Lei Li and Ian Horrocks. A software framework for matchmaking based on semantic web technology. In *Proceedings of the Twelfth International World Wide Web Conference (WWW 2003)*, pages 331–339. ACM, 2003.
10. Yuhua Li, Zuhair A. Bandar, and David McLean. An approach for measuring semantic similarity between words using multiple information sources. *Transactions on Knowledge and Data Engineering*, 15(4):871–882, July/August 2003.
11. Alexander Löser, Martin Wolpers, Wolf Siberski, and Wolfgang Nejdl. Efficient data store discovery in a scientific P2P network. In N. Ashish and C. Goble, editors, *Proceedings of the WS on Semantic Web Technologies for Searching and Retrieving Scientific Data*, CEUR WS 83, 2003. Colocated with the 2. ISWC-03.
12. Wolfgang Nejdl, Martin Wolpers, Wolf Siberski, Christoph Schmitz, Mario Schlosser, Ingo Brunkhorst, and Alexander Löser. Super-peer-based routing and clustering strategies for rdf-based peer-to-peer networks. In *Proceedings of the 12th International World Wide Web Conference, Budapest, Hungary, May 2003.*, 2003.
13. Roy Rada, Hafedh Mili, Ellen Bicknell, and Maria Blettner. Development and application of a metric on semantic nets. *IEEE Transactions on Systems, Man, and Cybernetics*, 19(1):17–30, 1989.
14. Sylvia Ratnasamy, Paul Francis, Mark Handley, Richard Karp, and Scott Shenker. A scalable content-addressable network. In *Proceedings of ACM SIGCOMM '01*, 2001.
15. Ion Stoica, Robert Morris, David Karger, M. Frans Kaashoek, and Hari Balakrishnan. Chord: A scalable peer-to-peer lookup service for Internet applications. In *Proceedings of the ACM SIGCOMM '01*, 2001.
16. Katia Sycara, Keith Decker, and Mike Williamson. Middle-agents for the internet. In *Proceedings of IJCAI-97*, January 1997.

17. Chunqiang Tang, Zhichen Xu, and Sandhya Dwarkadas. Peer-to-peer information retrieval using self-organizing semantic overlay networks. In *Proceedings of the ACM SIGCOMM Conference*, Karlsruhe, Germany, August 2003.
18. Christoph Tempich, Steffen Staab, and A. Wranik. REMINDIN': Semantic query routing in peer-to-peer networks based on social metaphors. In *Proceedings of the 13th Int. World Wide Web Conference, WWW 2004*, 2004.
19. Pinar Yolum and Munindar P. Singh. Dynamic communities in referral networks. *Web Intelligence and Agent Systems*, 1(2):105–116, 2003.

Autonomous Gossiping: A Self-Organizing Epidemic Algorithm for Selective Information Dissemination in Wireless Mobile Ad-Hoc Networks*

Anwitaman Datta, Silvia Quarteroni, and Karl Aberer

School of Computer and Communication Sciences (I&C),
Swiss Federal Institute of Technology (EPFL),
1015 Lausanne, Switzerland
{anwitaman.datta,silvia.quarteroni,karl.aberer}@epfl.ch

Abstract. We introduce autonomous gossiping (A/G), a new genre epidemic algorithm for selective dissemination of information in contrast to previous usage of epidemic algorithms which flood the whole network. A/G is a paradigm which suits well in a mobile ad-hoc networking (MANET) environment because it does not require any infrastructure or middleware like multicast tree and (un)subscription maintenance for publish/subscribe, but uses ecological and economic principles in a self-organizing manner in order to achieve any arbitrary selectivity (*flexible casting*). The trade-off of using a stateless self-organizing mechanism like A/G is that it does not guarantee completeness deterministically as is one of the original objectives of alternate selective dissemination schemes like publish/subscribe. We argue that such incompleteness is not a problem in many non-critical real-life civilian application scenarios and realistic node mobility patterns, where the overhead of infrastructure maintenance may outweigh the benefits of completeness, more over, at present there exists no mechanism to realize publish/subscribe or other paradigms for selective dissemination in MANET environments.

Keywords: Mobile Ad-hoc Network (MANET), Selective Information Dissemination, Content Driven Communication, Epidemic Algorithm, Self-organization, Any-to-Many Communication, Flexible casting

1 Introduction

Mobility is one of the most distinguishing traits of the present age. Infrastructure based networks have come of age, with support for online gaming in mobile devices to multimedia services. At the same time, mobile ad-hoc networks

* The work presented in this paper was supported (in part) by the National Competence Center in Research on Mobile Information and Communication Systems (NCCR-MICS), a center supported by the Swiss National Science Foundation under grant number 5005-67322.

(MANET) have, from being used exclusively in mission critical military and recovery operations, permeated into our daily life. In the recent years, mobile ad-hoc networking is gaining popularity for non critical civilian applications. This has come about with the proliferation of devices like mobile phones, PDAs, digital cameras, portable music (MP3) players which support ad-hoc networking enabled by technologies like IEEE 802.11b or Bluetooth. Infrastructure based cellular networks and MANETs have contrasting design, one based on dedicated infrastructure and global coordination, while the other is decentralized and self-organizing. But from application and usage point of view, most likely they will play complementary roles. Thus, despite the fact that most work done until now in MANET community has focussed on point-to-point routing, most likely communication with another particular node will not be the defining application for MANETs, because of the difficulties of route maintenance in a dynamic setting, and simultaneous communication between several pairs, and communication among long distance nodes. MANETs will instead do what peer-to-peer has done to the wired world, bringing the resources at the edges of the wireless network to collaborate together for better resource usage. Always using the infrastructure can be expensive, so using the MANET wherever possible can bring immense cost benefit to the end users, and also reduce the load on the infrastructure, as well as extend its coverage. Such coexistence of MANET and cellular network can be used for more purposes than one.

- Multi-hop routing in cellular networks is used to extend the coverage of cellular networks. (e.g., [20])
- The MANET can be used as a cache, such that content can be discovered in a peer-to-peer manner whenever possible, instead of each user individually downloading it using the infrastructure. (e.g. [17,25])
- Using the MANET for geographically confined information dissemination or group communication.

The focus of this paper is on information dissemination. There is an increasing opportunity for people to share resources (e.g., files) in a peer-to-peer manner, even in a wireless environment, using ad-hoc networking. One way to go about it is when a mobile node makes an explicit request for a resource, and the whole network is flooded with a query, as is the case with many mobile ad-hoc route discovery algorithms [27,38], similar to file discovery by query flooding in P2P networks like Gnutella [12]. Flooding in a wireless network is in fact relatively efficient as compared to in wired networks because of wireless multicast advantage [42]. Improvements of the basic flooding approach using advertisements and geographic information have also been recently studied [41].

The dual problem to searching resources in the network, that of disseminating resources selectively in a wireless mobile ad-hoc network is yet relatively unexplored, and is the focus of this paper. So far there exist mechanisms to broadcast information in the complete network [39], or in a specific geographic area (Geocast) [35,33], apart from to any one specific mobile node (unicast/mobile ad-hoc routing [27,38]) or any one arbitrary node (anycast). But selective dissemination paradigms based on mobile nodes' content requirement is still a relatively un-explored area. Proactive multicast group establishment, maintenance and usage can be prohibitive, particularly given the fact that membership varies over time (managing group membership is difficult), content requirement can be diverse (need for multiple multicast groups), and the network itself is very dynamic because of node mobility, capacity and energy constraints.

Recently on demand routing has been extended to flood the whole network to locate not any particular node but to rather locate all nodes with a particular content requirement [8], but it still relies on and has the overheads of broad-casting and does not scale well with respect to increasing number of content categories, nor adapts well if the population of interested parties vary over time. A similar approach where the source has global information of the destination nodes is proposed for differential destination multicast [30], but such approaches can work only in small groups.

We propose autonomous gossiping (A/G) for selective information dissemina-tion on the lines of intentional multicast [1]. However intentional multicast uses Intentional Name Resolvers to form an overlay to support routing. In contrast, A/G is a candidate solution for an infrastructure-less mobile ad-hoc networking environment. A/G's dissemination mechanism is essentially stateless, where nei-ther routing information is required nor global information like knowledge of the destination nodes is required, nor does A/G flood the whole network. It is impor-tant to note that even overlay maintenance using soft-states is very expensive, and sometimes simply impossible in a highly mobile environment. Thus, while there exists proposals like tree based multicasting for information dissemination which will work under the assumption of quasi-static environments (like sensor networks or overlays on top of internet infrastructure), we are proposing a best ef-fort mechanism for any arbitrarily dynamic environment where construction and maintenance of infrastructure (overlays) is prohibitive, while retaining the selec-tivity instead of broadcasting in the whole network. A/G spreads in the network by following a greedy mechanism much like an epidemic does, such that it spreads to immediate neighbors that are interested in the particular content (susceptible to the epidemic), and yet avoiding the ones that are not interested in the content (resistant to the epidemic). Node mobility is exploited to enable interaction with newer nodes. Thus, while mobility is detrimental to mechanisms that use states (routing information), mobility is helpful to a stateless mechanism like A/G.

Some possible applications for A/G include sharing files, directed advertise-ment [34,3] for mobile commerce and tourism supported with reduced infrastruc-ture, or dissemination of meta-data about services being provided. Meta-data so disseminated is like advertisement, which can then be used by the receivers to request for and use some other service. It is likely that lightweight infrastruc-ture (infostations [23]) is deployed to "inject" data in the MANET from time to time, for example, timetables for local transportation or menus of a restaurant. Or otherwise, some members in the MANET network may also download the resource using the cellular network, while the others avail it in a peer-to-peer manner. While at other instances the mobile nodes will already carry or generate data of their own, e.g., music files or pictures from digital camera. Or alternatively, the meta-data can be about the quality of a resource being provided by a service provider, and an user can gather such feedback from fellow users before paying for the resource. So to say, A/G can play the role of word of mouth advertisement even for resources offered by the dedicated service providers.

So far, in a decentralized environment, all advertisement mechanisms propose that sources push the information while the receivers are supposed to pull the information, and the schemes vary in how to make the push/pull efficient and reliable. These mechanisms are variously known as match making, geographic hash tables (GHT) or content based multicasting (CBM) [34,3,37,44]. From advertisement perspective, dissemination schemes in general should and A/G in particular takes this a step forward, and instead of both source and destinations participating actively (pushing and pulling), the information is pushed to targeted audience, while trying to avoid uninterested users. From dissemination perspective the novelty of A/G is that it disseminates without the need to maintain routing or other soft-states (e.g., an overlay) to support multicast, unlike [40,5,33].

Furthermore, in this paper we do not consider the mechanisms by which the data items enter the network or are annotated, nor the copyright issues of the disseminated information, but only the epidemic mechanism by which they are disseminated to other nodes that are potentially interested in the data, while scrupulously avoiding spam.

1.1   Application Scenarios

Networking the automobiles on the roads: One of the niche areas where ad-hoc networking has a promising future is the automobiles on the road. Consider that some person may be interested in the opening hour of a ski resort and the quality of snow on a particular day, while another person may be interested in the traffic information after a particular exit on the highway, while yet another person may be interested in the cultural programmes in offing in the next city, while another person may be interested in architectures. Broadcasting in the MANET network would result in everyone being informed of all the things, causing information overload, but selectively propagating it on the basis of preferences will mean that if two users with similar profiles come in contact with each other, they will exchange their information. This also means that users may not always get the information they desire, but at the same time, they won't be spammed by multiple other unnecessary information. Thus the two metrics that can be used to measure the quality of dissemination are the standard information retrieval metrics of completeness and precision [4].

Specialized units in a disaster recovery mission: Consider another application related to another niche application of MANETs, that of disaster recovery. A/G can play a significant role in effective coordination of a team of mobile units, where different units have different specializations (and hence different preferences for receiving information). If the information is about a suspected alive person, most likely an unit with a sniffer dog and an unit for removing rabbles to rescue the trapped person are needed, while, if the information is that a person has already been rescued, a medic will be needed instead. At the same time, in order to facilitate smooth working of each of the units independently, it is best if they are not distracted by information that is not of any immediate concern to them.

Apart from the completeness and precision [4], the latency of the information dissemination is also important, hence we'll measure the quality of selective dissemination based on the evolution of completeness and precision in the system with respect to time.

One of the benefits of A/G is that by tuning the dissemination criteria, users can achieve flexible casting, including broadcast, geocast, multicast and manycast. Other applications include environment monitoring and distributed aggregation, sharing content (picture, ringtones, music, gaming profiles, dating profiles) and advertisements.

1.2   Paper Organization

We give an overview of A/G in Section 2, where we elaborate A/G's salient features. The system model studied in this paper is discussed in Section 3 followed by simulation results in Section 4. In Section 5 we summarize the related work. We conclude in Section 6, along with a glimpse of future possibilities.

2   Autonomous Gossiping in Mobile Ad-Hoc Networks

The essential idea of any proactive dissemination scheme is to provide a mechanism so that mobile hosts do not have to search for resources when they are needed, but rather they automatically get the same (pushed). In autonomous gossiping, instead of mobile nodes making the decision to push data to each other, it is the data items themselves that try to identify other hosts which are suitable, based on the data item's own profile and host's advertised profile (similar to a subscription).

Hence, the dissemination aspect, which is the focus of this paper is a self-organizing mechanism whereby there is no need to explicitly build and maintain subscription lists, but dissemination is purely based on locally available information (mobile node and data profiles) and autonomous decisions.

Here we give an intuitive introduction to the concept of A/G and its distinguishing features. A more concrete description of a system model to realize autonomous gossiping for proof of concept is described in the next section.

When we travel around, we meet friends, strangers and sundry. We talk, exchange news and information, that is, we gossip. While the encounters are random, the gossip is often with only individuals with whom there is a shared interest. When we move around, similar to our social encounters, the mobile devices (mobile hosts in a MANET) we carry also come in contact with other mobile hosts as well as possibly fixed beacons. Just like the real world counterpart of "interesting information", such interacting nodes may have assets (any electronic resource, from now on referred as data items), which might be of interest for each other. By enabling these nodes to autonomously gossip among themselves according to their mutual profiles, people (their mobile devices) may come across important or at-least interesting data items. This intuition motivated us to define the notion of autonomous gossiping. A/G may possibly be implemented using various strategies. Here we describe a novel strategy which uses ecological and economic paradigms. We consider that mobile nodes are like habitats, where the node profile (interests) defines the preferred data items. Data items compete among themselves for limited resource (e.g., memory) in these mobile nodes (hosts). In order to enforce selectivity and discourage spam, hosts reward (or punish) data items required (not required) locally, thus in the long run hosting relevant data items and purging unnecessary ones. Data items, in order to survive, should move to hosts where it is required. This enforces A/G's selectivity and underlines the self-organizing aspect of the dissemination scheme. A/G has the following salient features.

Exploiting mobility: Unlike traditional approaches where node mobility is the source of difficulties, A/G utilizes the opportunity of coming in contact with new nodes arising from mobility to disseminate data. This idea of exploiting mobility is similar to Smart-Tag [6] and work being done at Media Lab Asia, like DakNet and RuralWiFi [2], where mobile objects (like buses) are equipped with Bluetooth/802.11b in order to "carry" data/e-mails back and forth between fixed points, for instance rural areas with no wired infrastructure and well connected urban localities. Other applications exploiting mobility include routing information dissemination based on encounters [24].

Selectivity: The information dissemination aspect of A/G is essentially an epidemic algorithm but unlike previous usage [31,7,15] for broadcast, A/G is selective in nature. Each unique data item may be considered as a different epidemic, and multiple epidemics spreading in the network simultaneously, each epidemic selectively infecting network members based on their vulnerability (advertised profile). Self-organization makes the selectivity (propagation of the epidemic to susceptible nodes) autonomous, thus contributing to the name "autonomous gossiping".

Self-organization: What differentiates autonomous gossiping as a selforganizing rather than just a distributed decentralized algorithm as is the case for other rumor/epidemic algorithms [31,7,15], is its use of the economic and ecological paradigms that helps it adhere to Francis Heylighen's characterization of self-organization [26]: "The basic mechanism underlying self-organization is the *noise* driven variation which explores different regions in a system's *state space* until it enters an *attractor*". The *state space* consists of any and all mobile nodes in the system being populated by any and all data items. The *noise* results from the motion of nodes which brings random nodes within radio contact of each other, random decisions at mobile hosts to use and reward (or otherwise punish) data items and autonomous local decisions by data items to migrate or replicate to neighboring nodes or do nothing. The *attractor* is the data distribution at different mobile nodes retaining the selectivity such that nodes host only data items matching their own need (profile), and mobile nodes have high utility for storing the data items locally and acting as a data carrier, and data items replicating as often as possible, and still retaining high average utility, so that they have better utility and chance of staying in the network. This is in contrast with how rumor spreading has been dealt in other contexts [7,31,15] where there is no need of self-organization since the goal is to essentially broadcasr the rumor/epidemic to a complete well-defined population, and different rumors are independent of each other, particularly, not competing among themselves for limited resources.

Flexible-casting: The self-organizing and middlewareless nature of A/G makes it suitable to support any of broadcasting, multicasting, geocasting and combinations therefrom without the need of routing information, and hence A/G is a suitable candidate for flexible casting independent of the endpoint-to-endpoint routing protocol being used. We call the resulting casting as *flexible-casting* since each of the above mentioned casting mechansims can be seen as and achieved as special cases of flexible-casting based on the context description, that is the content and location information associated with individual data items being gossiped. This is later explained in Table 1.

3   System Model

The concept of A/G based flexible casting is generic. Rest of the paper describes one way to realize such a selective dissemination. Hence the system model, and policies described next are not necessarily the unique way to realize A/G, but is one candidate solution. The results in the paper are also specific to the model described here. A/G can be used not only in the context of MANET environment, but also others, for instance, in a sensor or peer-to-peer network. For P2P networks we will then have to emulate and model random interactions among peers.

In this paper, we concentrate solely on mobile ad-hoc networks, where nodes' mobility leads to their random meetings. The objective in doing so is to give a proof-of-concept of how information can be disseminated to interested parties in a decentralized network in a self-organizing manner using local interactions, with minimal spamming.

For this paper, we assume an isolated system comprising of a fixed number of mobile nodes confined in a predefined geographic region. These nodes are mobile, and communicate with each other in a wireless ad-hoc manner. To start with each of the nodes carries some unique data items. During the period for which the system is studied, no new node or data item is introduced, nor any existing node leaves the region. However, useless data items are potentially purged from the system. Though we study a simplified system with no new data items or nodes joining it, this assumption does not affect the dissemination mechanism.

Each of the hosts m_k has a memory limit of M, and individual profile m_k^p. The profile presently comprises of abstract categories C_js. These categories may correspond to topics or more elaborate content description as in publish/subscribe systems. When using textual annotations, topics may correspond to discriminative keywords or to abstract categories extracted from larger text collec-

Table 1. Profile choice and corresponding flexible-casting scheme

Flexible-casting scheme for a data item	content profile d_j^p	location attribute d_j^l
Broadcast	any	any
Geocast	any	one destination
Multiple Geocast	any	multiple destinations
Content based dissemination	content description	any
Content and location context based dissemination	content description	one or multiple destinations

tions, e.g., using latent semantic indexing techniques [4]. Thus for instance, $m_1^p = \{C_1, C4, C7\}$. The hosts are initialized with random number of ($\leq M$) unique data items d_js, each of which has its own profile d_j^p, described in a manner similar to mobile host profile description. Data items also have a scalar called the associated utility, d_j^u. Moreover, data items are initialized with an attribute d_j^l, which defines the target geographical locations (zones) the item is supposed to belong to. d_j^l may have one or multiple entries. Thus, a data item d_j is represented as a tuple $\{d_j^p, d_j^u, d_j^l\}$. Every topic in a host profile m_k^p is associated with weighting according to the degree of interest (affinity) of the host m_k to the topic MW_k^i. Similarly profile d_j^p of data item d_j has affinity DW_j^i according to the relevance of the data item d_j to the topic i. Similarity/affinity is computed using standard techniques defined for information retrieval [4]. The use of affinity information is described later, in Section 4.2. Each host also has its next destination as its goal zone, which is used to determine whether the host is suitable for data items with nontrivial location attribute d_j^l

It is also possible for a data item to be relevant to all topics. This is modelled in the host and data item profile by the presence of a unique category, named "*any*". Similarly data items may be relevant to all locations, in which case its location context is represented as a special category "*any*". Such a model for describing profiles gives the flexibility of dissemination as described in Table 1.

Communication model. We assume a symmetric communication model, such that hosts can communicate with other hosts within a r_{comm} radius. Each host also advertises its own profile and its target destination (goal), such that data items resident at the other neighboring hosts can see the advertised profile, and thus decide to replicate, migrate or do nothing.

Host Mobility. The mobility of hosts is a hybridized version of city walk and random walk [9]. At initialization, several anchor points (A_k) are defined in the area. Each host chooses an anchor randomly as its next target destination, and moves toward the anchor at a variable speed parameterized by average speed. Occasionally perturbation is added to the host motion, such that it deviates from a linear path. Once a host reaches within a radius r_{anchor} of target anchor point, it chooses a new target destination and continues. This is intended to emulate motion in a populated area like a town or city, where most of the motion is on streets between distinct locations.

Present simulations assume that the set of possible targets for a given host coincides with the set of the possible destinations for a given data item. Further, we assume that hosts advertise their target location to neighboring nodes.

At every time step t, a host probabilistically uses some of its resident data items if their profiles have something in common (content-based match) or if the host and data item destinations coincide (location-based match).

Therefore, if d_j is residing in m_i and $similarity(d_j^p, m_i^p) \geq threshold$ where $threshold$ is a predefined threshold, or $destination(m_i) \in d_j^l$, then d_j is probabilistically used and rewarded (for example, by incrementing its utility, $d_j^u(t) = d_j^u(t-1) + 1$). The probabilistic decision to use can possibly be weighted according to the degree of similarity, or can be a constant. If similarity is below $threshold$ then data item is not used, and when any data item resides in a host for a period of time $T_{latency}$ without being used, the data item is penalized (utility is decremented). These are implementation details, and in a very general case, the choice of $similarity(.,.)$ function [4], $threshold$, and the probabilistic usage policy as well as reward/punishment policies can be decided by individual hosts.

In the simulations, we assume all hosts use the same set of functions and policies, and is elaborated in Section 4.

3.1   Policies

Depending on the hospitality received at the present host, data items decide to either continue to reside, migrate or replicate to another host with a more suitable profile and/or goal zone, and the data item's associated utility is used in the decision process.

To enable such decisions, threshold values, th_l and th_h ($th_l \leq th_h$) for utility are used by the data items, as elaborated next. The data item's present host is denoted as m_h and the neighboring mobile host where the data item may choose to migrate or replicate is denoted as m_n. These policies are essentially heuristic, and other decision criteria too may be used for defining A/G policies.

Migration: A data item decides to migrate from mobile host m_h to any mobile host m_n if $similarity(d_j^p, m_i^p) < threshold$ and $d_j^u \leq th_l$. If $d_j^u > th_l$ then the data items can afford to wait for some better host instead of migrating desperately. These conditions are implicity bio-inspired, where data items desperately migrate from a hostile environment in search of a better habitat, however if they can afford to wait for better hosts then they wait, since desperate migrations don't guarantee better environments.

The utility value d_j^u may either be incremented as a reward for making a prudent decision to leave an inhospitable host, or it may be left unchanged. In our simulations presented in this paper, we have chosen the former, that of rewarding the migrating data items.

Replication: If the data item has a high utility, it can afford to replicate and thus increase its population. This is again bio-inspired, where reproduction is possible in a favorable environment. In order to replicate, the data item is required to pay such that if a data item replicates, then both the resulting replicas have an utility value that is decremented from the original utility value before replication. This is the case if $d_j^u \geq th_h$ and $similarity(d_j^p, m_i^p) \geq threshold$. However if the utility is relatively low, $th_l \leq d_j^u \leq th_h$, the utility value is not decremented for replication, thus providing a mechanism for data items' survival. However, this case may be eliminated by choosing $th_l = th_h$ and otherwise, this should be a narrow band, so that it can not be abused by data items in order to replicate unnecessarily, since that will lead to spam.

Note that if the number of replication is restricted to a predefined number, it is also possible to realize manycast [10] (though not discussed in this paper or in Table 1).

Replica reconciliation: If a data item finds one of its own replicas being present in the new host to which it migrates or replicates, then only one replica continues to reside at the host, with the utility being one more than the maximum utility of the two replicas. Since two replicas chose the particular host, it is very likely that the host is appropriate for the data item, and though only one replica is retained (to make space for a greater diversity), incrementing the utility provides better chances for its survival as well as future replication.

Migration anyway: When location is a matching criterion and one data item is located on a host which does not match its location attribute, it tries to migrate to all neighboring hosts with that location as a goal zone, if any. The intuition is to reach the target location first. In case of Geocast that is good enough. Even for the case where both content and location are important, reaching the location first and then spreading locally to other and more significant hosts makes it easier to achieve completeness, at the cost of precision of content match.

The data items (replicas) compete with each other for the limited memory at each hosts, and the evolutionary paradigm of *extinction of the unfit* is used, so that data item with least utility value is discarded in the event of memory shortage, and in the event of a tie, it is randomly chosen. Other elimination policies like LRU (least recently used) are alternative tie-breaker.

The objective of the data items is to have as high a degree of replication as possible, and still have a high utility value. For this they must identify the suitable hosts (profiles). The hosts on the other hand need to maximize the aggregate utility value of the resident data items. This completes the ecological and economic model for data items competing for survival, and mobile nodes hosting and rewarding relevant data items while punishing and purging other data items. This ensures a symbiotic relationship rather than a parasitic one between mobile nodes and data items.

4   Simulation

A Java based discrete time simulator has been developed in order to simulate and study the effectiveness of autonomous gossiping as a information dissemination paradigm. Mathematica's J/Link extension is used to integrate display of statistical information. Since the initialization as well as the rest of the simulation is randomized, the results are not reproducible, and give only a qualitative understanding of how autonomous gossiping works. Multiple runs of the simulation though give similar qualitative results.

4.1   Initialization

A rectangular region of dimension 1000 units * 1000 units (a square) was simulated, with five randomly chosen anchor points in the region for node mobility. 20 mobile nodes with a memory for a maximum of 20 data items each, and initially storing 179 distinct data items in total were instantiated. Four anchor points were used.

Each host had a maximum of 3 content categories to be advertised, while each data item also had at most 3 content categories. There were 20 possible categories to choose from in order to describe content. For geocast, the content description of all data items were *"any"*.

Data items were penalized if not used in 10 consequent time units ($T_{latency}$). Data items with some matching profile with the host were used in every time step with a probability of 0.05. Mobile hosts could communicate with other hosts within a range of 20 units (r_{comm}). The lower and upper thresholds determining the replication/migration policies were chosen as $3(th_l)$ and $5(th_h)$. The implicit simplifying assumption for the initial study is that all data items have equal size. The random instantiation of data items, their placements in the hosts and location of anchor points and hosts had been stored in a log file, such that all simulations had the same initial condition (wherever valid). The content and location context of data items were of course in accordance to which casting technique was being simulated. All simulations were run for 500 time steps.

Note that we do not use any real life units for measuring distances or time, but use artificial ones instead (conveniently called just units), because the simulations were not meant to quantify A/G's performance if used in any particular setting or technology (IEEE 820.11b, Bluetooth or any other), but only to make a case for A/G as a selective dissemination mechanism in MANET environments in general. Consequently, it is possible that some of the assumptions made in the simulation are not yet supported by the existing technologies. Even in that case, it is our belief that the assumptions are not a fry cry from the reality, and will be realized in near future.

4.2   Results

Given space constraints and the fact that broadcast has been exhaustively investigated by many researchers, we concentrate and provide results for the other cases.

The results demonstrate the quality of information dissemination achieved using A/G. We measure the quality of information dissemination on the basis of two standard metrics used in information retrieval [4], namely *recall* and *precision*, and the latency in achieving the corresponding completeness and precision.

Recall (now onwards called *completeness* in this paper) signifies the percentage of mobile nodes reached as compared to the total target set of nodes. In this paper we use the term completeness instead of recall since it is more intuitive from the broadcasting/multicasting perspective.

Precision is determined by the percentage of the reached mobile nodes that are actually interested in the data item. Thus precision is essentially the reverse of the degree of spam caused because of the dissemination mechanism.

The target set of interested nodes comprises of all the nodes which share a commonality of interest with the data item's content (determined using similarity metric) and/or location context.

For the simulations, if data item d_j has content C_i with affinity DW_j^i and mobile node m_k has an interest in C_i with affinity MW_k^i (it is assumed that these affinities are precalculated using standard information retrieval techniques [4]), then if $|(MW_k^i - DW_j^i)| \leq threshold$ then we say that the mobile node m_k is interested in the data item d_j because of the C_i content. Thus $|(MW_k^i - DW_j^i)|$ determines the dissimilarity[1]. A smaller *threshold* means a stricter matching criteria and vice versa.

So if $\exists C_i \in d_j^p, m_k^p$ s.t. $|(MW_k^i - DW_j^i)| \leq threshold$ then we can say that m_k is interested in d_j, otherwise m_k treats d_j as spam.

For commonality of interest in location context, the intuition is to reach the target location(s) first, as has been elaborated in Section 3.1.

Note that if d_j^p or d_j^l is "any", then the respective matching condition is evaluated as true. The *x-axis* in all the figures represent time.

Content based dissemination: In Figure 1 and Figure 2 we show the completeness and precision of location based A/G for various *threshold* values, where the dissemination is content based. We observe that as far as completeness is concerned, A/G is effective as a content based dissemination scheme, with completeness value getting close to one. However precision of A/G decreases (spam increases) with stricter matching criterion (lower threshold). In order to fulfill the completeness property, a data item needs carriers, more of which consider the data items as mismatch if a stricter matching criterion is used. While it gets harder to find matching nodes, the data items need to find relatively more carriers. This conflict of interests leads to lesser precision when the matching criterion is stricter.

Geocast: Figure 3 shows the completeness and precision of A/G for Geocast. The precision is high since the choice of carrier nodes is easier to make for the data items. However, since the nodes are assumed to be continuously moving it is difficult to achieve completeness because the membership of the target

---

[1] Note the subtle difference of usage of *threshold* for dissimilarity instead of similarity (in contrast to the usage in Section3.1).

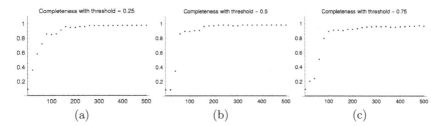

Fig. 1. Completeness of content based dissemination

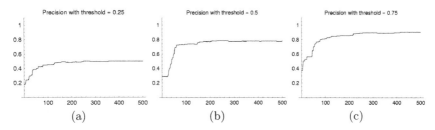

Fig. 2. Precision of content based dissemination

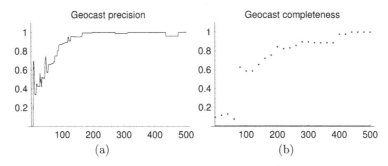

Fig. 3. Geocast - Dissemination in a targeted location

population itself keeps varying over time. Hence, in Figure 3(b) we measure completeness in a different way. If a data item belonging to a particular location reaches that location once, we consider the purpose of A/G to be achieved.

Dissemination of the data item within the zone is essentially beyond the scope of A/G, however simple extrinsic mechanism like geographically constrained broadcast may be used to that end.

The difficult part is to ensure persistence of the data item within the geographic region after reaching the region, since the carrier nodes are free to move in and out of the region. However, this will be a problem for any mechanism, since the fluctuation is purely because of the mobile nodes' movement. On the other hand, as a best effort solution to the problem, the data item migrates from the current host that is moving away from the target zone to new nodes which move towards the target zone.

Content and location context based dissemination: Next we show the precision based on both content and target location matches and completeness achieved. We show in Figure 4 and Figure 5 the cases where the content matching threshold of 0.75 and 0.5 have been used respectively. With target location and content both being matching criteria, it is even harder to find suitable mobile nodes, and as a consequence both the precision and completeness are inferior in comparison to when the dissemination is based on either one of the criteria. Noteworthy is the fact that a relatively relaxed content matching (higher *threshold*) leads to an acceptable performance.

Note that in these simulations there were only 3 content descriptors for each of host and data item profiles out of a possibility of 20, and hence the threshold of 0.75 still means that there is at least one common content in the two profiles (host and data item), even if the matching is not very tight.

The initial results described above show that A/G is a robust and effective epidemic mechanism to selectively disseminate information, where the selectivity is based on content and/or the location context of the information (data item). The precision metric is to measure the effectiveness of selectivity, and the completeness metric for the effectiveness of dissemination.

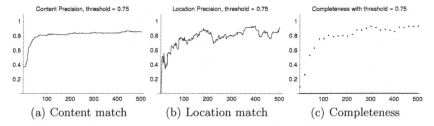

(a) Content match   (b) Location match   (c) Completeness

Fig. 4. Content and location context based dissemination (threshold = 0.75)

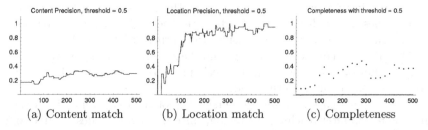

(a) Content match   (b) Location match   (c) Completeness

Fig. 5. Content and location context based dissemination (threshold = 0.5)

5   Related Work

The work presented in this paper has similarities and differences compared with several domains, as mentioned below:

- Location dependent service (LDS) [21] perspective
- Manet routing/casting perspective
- Caching [17], pre-fetching(7DS [36]) and collaborative replication [25]
- Spatio-temporally restricted dissemination [43]
- Peer-to-Peer systems like Freenet [11] and work done in the group communication and publish subscribe domain.

Because of space constraint, we only mention them above, and a more exhaustive related work can be found in the accompanying technical report [16], where we elaborate the differences in A/G and how A/G mostly complements these existing techniques.

6   Conclusion

Though research in mobile ad-hoc network is predominantly networking centric, the idea of content driven communication instead of IP driven point-to-point communication has been of interest for a while [28,1,11]. This paper extends and explores the ideas of content centric communication, particularly studying dissemination based on epidemic mechanisms, and still preserving selectivity in a self-organizing manner. Most epidemic algorithms that have so far been investigated, either in the context of wired or wireless and ad-hoc networks are for communication in the whole network, or a predefined subset (broadcast/multicast) [19,31,39,7,15,22,18,32]. Thus autonomous gossiping is a new genre of epidemic algorithm resembling more closely actual epidemic spreading, and it brings the two domains of content-based communication and epidemic algorithms together, specifically in the context of MANET. A/G spreads data items selectively based on vulnerability of other nodes, instead of treating all nodes homogeneously and flooding the network.

Self-organizing economic and ecological mechanisms of rewards and punishments and competition among the data items in order for data items to survive and propagate in the network help enforcing A/G's selectivity unlike previous mechanisms that rely on goodwill rather than enforcement of selectivity. A/G has certain characteristics that qualify it as a proactive mechanism similar to pre-fetching schemes, and at the same time has on-demand characteristic, if seen from the view-point of intentional multicast [1].

We also introduce the notion of flexible casting, such that the same mechanism can be used for either of broadcasting, multicasting, geocasting or combination of multicast and geocast. A/G's stateless nature of communication helps achieving such a flexible casting without the need to establish and maintain separate routing tables.

The system model (Section 3) including the assumption of a mobile ad-hoc network, node mobility, communication and policies are implementation details used for proof of concept, but the idea of A/G itself is more generic and applicable in environments other than MANETs.

The results presented in the paper are initial and meant to provide a qualitative study of the feasibility and effectiveness of A/G rather than comparing or quantifying performance issues like expected latency, bandwidth and energy usage of the mechanism in more realistic environment [29] models.

A/G in MANET is similar to and thus can also be used to simulate and study how diseases spread in nature, since the motion model and epidemic propagation maps to the real world unlike some of the previously studied epidemic algorithms [7,31,15]. Theoretical biologists and statistical physicists too study epidemic spreading with immunization and mutations [14], and try to discover effective immunization mechanisms [13] to prevent spread of epidemic. Our goal of information dissemination is dual to that of theirs, and hence provides complementary perspective to the same problem, and understanding either (spread/immunization) will add to understanding of and achieving the complementary goals.

Acknowledgement. The authors will like to thank Ms. Emma Frejinger for her help with writing an initial version of the simulator for autonomous gossiping during her stint as a female undergraduate summer intern (2002) sponsored by NCCR-MICS and hosted at Distributed Information Systems Laboratory (LSIR) at EPFL.

References

1. W. Adjie-Winoto, E. Schwartz, H. Balakrishnan, and J. Lilley. The design and implementation of an intentional naming system. In *Symposium on Operating Systems Principles*, pages 186–201, 1999.
2. Media Lab Asia. DakNet, Rural WiFi. http://www.medialabasia.org/.
3. I. Aydin and C. C. Shen. Facilitating match-making service in ad hoc sensor networks using pseudo quorum. In *ICCCN*, 2002.
4. R. A. Baeza-Yates and B. A. Ribeiro-Neto. *Modern Information Retrieval*. ACM Press / Addison-Wesley, 1999.
5. S. Banerjee, C. Kommareddy, K. Kar, S. Bhattacharjee, and S. Khuller. Construction of an efficient overlay multicast infrastructure for real-time applications. In *INFOCOM*, 2003.
6. A. Beaufour, M. Leopold, and P. Bonnet. Smart-tag based data dissemination. In *First ACM International Workshop on Wireless Sensor Networks and Applications (WSNA02)*, June 2002.
7. K.P. Birman, M. Hayden, O. Ozkasap, Z. Xiao, M. Budiu, and Y. Minsky. Bimodal multicast. *ACM Transactions on Computer Systems*, 17(2):41–88, 1999.
8. C. Borcea, C. Intanagonwiwat, A. Saxena, and L. Iftode. Self-routing in pervasive computing environments using smart messages. In *Proceedings of the First IEEE International Conference on Pervasive Computing and Communications (PerCom'03)*. IEEE Computer Society, March 2003.

9. T. Camp, J. Boleng, and V. Davies. A survey of mobility models for ad hoc network research. *Wireless Communications & Mobile Computing (WCMC): Special issue on Mobile Ad Hoc Networking: Research, Trends and Applications*, 2(5):483–502, 2002.

10. C. Carter, S. Yi, P. Ratanchandani, and R. Kravets. Manycast: Exploring the space between anycast and multicast in ad hoc networks. In *ACM MobiCom*, 2003.

11. I. Clarke, T.W. Hong, S.G. Miller, O. Sandberg, and B. Wile. Protecting free expression online with freenet. *IEEE Internet Computing*, 6(1):40–49, Jan./Feb. 2002.

12. Clip2. The Gnutella Protocol Specification v0.4, Jun. 2001.

13. R. Cohen, D. Ben-Avraham, and S. Havlin. Efficient immunization strategies, 2003 (Submitted at Physical Review Letters).

14. S.M. Dammer and H. Hinrichsen. Epidemic spreading with immunization and mutations. *Physics Review E*, March 2002.

15. A. Datta, M. Hauswirth, and K. Aberer. Updates in highly unreliable, replicated peer-to-peer systems. In *Proceedings of the 23rd International Conference on Distributed Computing Systems, ICDCS*, 2003.

16. A. Datta, S. Quarteroni, and K. Aberer. Autonomous Gossiping: A self-organizing epidemic algorithm for selective information dissemination in wireless mobile ad-hoc networks. Technical Report IC/2004/07, Swiss Federal Institute of Technology, Lausanne (EPFL), 2004. http://lsirwww.epfl.ch/AutoGoss.

17. N. Davies, K. Cheverst, K. Mitchell, and A. Friday. Caches in the air: Disseminating tourist information in the guide system. In *In Proceedings of Second IEEE Workshop on Mobile Computing Systems and Applications*, 1999.

18. C. de M. Cordeiro, H. Gossain, and D.P. Agrawal. Multicast over wireless mobile ad hoc networks: present and future directions. *IEEE Network Magazine*, 17(1):52–59, Jan-Feb 2003.

19. A. Demers, D. Greene, C. Hauser, W. Irish, J. Larson, S. Shenker, H. Sturgis, D. Swinehart, and D. Terry. Epidemic algorithms for replicated database maintenance. In *Proceedings of the Sixth Symposium on Principles of Distributed Computing*, pages 1–12, 1987.

20. O. Dousse, P. Thiran, and M. Hasler. Connectivity in ad-hoc and hybrid networks. In *Proc. IEEE Infocom*, June 2002.

21. M.H. Dunham and V. Kumar. Location dependent data and its management in mobile databases. In *DEXA Workshop*, pages 414–419, 1998.

22. P. Th. Eugster and R. Guerraoui. Probabilistic multicast. In *3rd IEEE International Conference on Dependable Systems and Networks (DSN 2002)*, pages 313–322, June 2002.

23. R. Frenkiel, B.R. Badrinath, J. Borras, and R. Yates. The Infostations challenge: Balancing cost and ubiquity in delivering wireless data. *IEEE Personal Communications Magazine*, Feb. 2000.

24. M. Grossglauser and M. Vetterli. Locating nodes with ease: Mobility diffusion of last encounters in ad hoc networks. In *The Proceedings of IEEE Infocom*, 2003.

25. T. Hara. Effective replica allocation in ad hoc networks for improving data accessibility. In *Proceedings of IEEE INFOCOM*, pages 1568–1576. IEEE Computer Society, 2001.

26. F. Heylighen. The science of self-organization and adaptivity. *The Encyclopedia of Life Support Systems*, 2002.

27. X. Hong, K. Xu, and M. Gerla. Scalable routing protocols for mobile ad hoc networks. *IEEE Network Magazine*, 16(4):11 –21, Jul-Aug 2002.

28. C. Intanagonwiwat, R. Govindan, and D. Estrin. Directed diffusion: A scalable and robust communication paradigm for sensor networks. In *Mobile Computing and Networking*, pages 56–67, 2000.
29. A. Jardosh, E. M. Belding-Royer, K. C. Almeroth, and S. Suri. Towards realistic mobility models for mobile ad hoc networks. In *Proceedings of Mobicom*, 2003.
30. L. Ji and M. S. Corson. Differential destination multicast - a manet multicast routing protocol for small groups. In *Proceedings of Infocom*, 2001.
31. R. M. Karp, C. Schindelhauer, S. Shenker, and B. Vöcking. Randomized rumor spreading. In *FOCS*, 2000.
32. A. Khelil, C. Becker, J. Tian, and K. Rothermel. An epidemic model for information diffusion in manets. In *Proceedings of the 5th ACM international workshop on Modeling analysis and simulation of wireless and mobile systems*, pages 54–60. ACM Press, 2002.
33. Y. B. Ko and N. H. Vaidya. Flooding-based geocasting protocols for mobile ad hoc networks. *Mobile Networks and Applications*, 7(6):471–480, 2002.
34. B. Nath and D. Niculescu. Routing on a curve. In *HOTNETS-I*, 2002.
35. J.C. Navas and T. Imielinski. Geocast - geographic addressing and routing. In *Mobile Computing and Networking*, pages 66–76, 1997.
36. M. Papadopouli and H. Schulzrinne. A Performance Analysis of 7DS, A Peer-to-Peer Data Dissemination and Prefetching Tool for Mobile Users. In *Advances in wired and wireless communications, IEEE Sarnoff Symposium Digest*, March 2001.
37. S. Ratnasamy, B. Karp, Y. Li, F. Yu, R. Govindan, S. Shenker, and D. Estrin. GHT: A Geographic Hash Table for Data-Centric Storage. In *Proceedings of the First ACM International Workshop on Wireless Sensor Networks and Applications (WSNA 2002)*, Oct. 2002.
38. E. Royer and C. Toh. A review of current routing protocols for ad-hoc mobile wireless networks. *IEEE Personal Communications*, Apr. 1999.
39. Y. Sasson, D. Cavin, and A. Schiper. Probabilistic broadcast for flooding in wireless mobile ad hoc networks. In *IEEE Wireless Comm. and Networking Conference (WCNC 2003)*, 2003.
40. M.A. Spohn and J.J. Garcia-Luna-Aceves. Exploiting relative addressing and virtual overlays in ad hoc networks with bandwidth and processing constraints. In *ICWN*, 2003.
41. J. Tchakarov and N. Vaidya. Efficient content location in wireless ad hoc networks. In *IEEE International Conference on Mobile Data Management (MDM)*, 2004.
42. J.E. Wieselthier, G.D. Nguyen, and A. Ephremides. On the construction of energy-efficient broadcast and multicast trees in wireless networks. In *Infocom*, 2000.
43. B. Xu, A. Ouksel, and O. Wolfson. Opportunistic resource exchange in inter-vehicle ad-hoc networks. In *Mobile Data Management (MDM)*, 2004.
44. H. Zhou and S. Singh. Content based multicast (cbm) for ad hoc networks. In *Mobihoc*, 2000.

Hyper: A Framework for Peer-to-Peer Data Integration on Grids

Diego Calvanese[1], Giuseppe De Giacomo[2],
Maurizio Lenzerini[2], Riccardo Rosati[2], and Guido Vetere[3]

[1] Faculty of Computer Science, Free University of Bolzano/Bozen,
`calvanese@inf.unibz.it`
[2] Dipartimento di Informatica e Sistemistica, Università di Roma "La Sapienza",
`{lastname}@dis.uniroma1.it`
[3] IBM Italia
`gvetere@it.ibm.com`

Abstract. Data Grids allow for seeing heterogeneous, distributed, and dynamic informational resources as if they were a uniform, stable, secure, and reliable database. According to this view, current proposals for data integration on Grids are based on the notion of global schema built over a collection of autonomous information sources. On the other hand, in dynamic and distributed environments, such a hierarchical and centralized architecture is not well suited for effective information integration. Peer-to-peer data integration aims at overcoming these drawbacks by modeling autonomous information systems as peers, and establishing mappings among peers without resorting to any hierarchical structure. In this paper, we present Hyper, a joint research initiative of Università di Roma "La Sapienza" and IBM Italia, which aims at developing principles and techniques for peer-to-peer data integration on a Grid infrastructure. The main contributions presented are a semantic characterization of P2P data integration, the deployment of our P2P framework on a Grid architecture, and the design of a query answering algorithm that is coherent both with the semantics and with the Grid infrastructure.

1 Introduction

Integrating heterogeneous computational resources and databases, which are distributed over highly dynamic computer networks, is the crucial challenge at the current evolutionary stage of IT infrastructures. Large enterprises, business organizations, e-government systems, and, in short, any kind of internetworking community, need today an integrated and virtualized access to distributed information resources, which grow in number, kind, and complexity. The notion of Virtual Organization denotes a set of individuals and/or institutions sharing data and computing resources by a range of collaborative strategies [10].

Grids aim at providing a suitable infrastructure for Virtual Organizations [14], based on standardized services that implement well-established and largely supported models. This kind of infrastructure hides the complexity of

M. Bouzeghoub et al. (Eds.): ICSNW 2004, LNCS 3226, pp. 144–157, 2004.
© IFIP International Federation for Information Processing 2004

heterogeneous and distributed data sources, and handles the dynamics of the underlying networking environment. This motivates the current trend of modeling complex business infrastructures as Grids, and this is why Grid technologies, which have been developed in the research community, attract today so much interest in the industry. In fact, the Open Grid Services Architecture (OGSA) [13] is part of the foundational layer of IBM's on demand operating environment.

In particular, Data Grids allow for seeing heterogeneous, distributed, and dynamic informational resources as if they were a uniform, stable, secure, and reliable database, with the aim of facilitating the application development, speeding up business integration, and ultimately for the users' sake. Grid extensions, such as OGSA's Data Access and Integration Services (DAIS) [3], specifically address the issue of modeling Data Services over a Grid, and supply a homogeneous interface to a variety of data sources, such as relational DBMS or XML documents. Basically, these services wrap the access to physical data, so that Grid-enabled applications can easily locate, connect, and query virtual data sources by means of uniform interfaces, can transparently elaborate their data, and finally provide results to either users or other applications.

Grid-based Virtual Databases [21,20] are essentially loosely-coupled database federations, which integrate heterogeneous sources, with the purpose of responding to business demands in a flexible manner. The integration logic is generally contained in specific applications (called "analysts"), that achieve integration at "functional" level. In fact, "analysts" build the integrated virtual schema based on views over the source schemas, and the integration semantics they implement is usually enmeshed in their 'ad-hoc' internal code. As a consequence, a change in data sources (i.e. adding a new node, or changing metadata) would require reprogramming "analyst" applications. Researchers in the field of Semantic Grids (see e.g. [5]) claim that this is a threat in the implementation of many real interesting application scenarios, and their effort is aimed at overcoming this limitation. Indeed, "analyst-based" Grid Databases suffer of a certain rigidity, which limits the exploitation of Data Grids in many real situations.

Current proposals for data integration on Grids are based on a traditional architecture relying on the notion of global schema built over a collection of autonomous information sources. In this paper, we present a framework for data integration in peer-to-peer (P2P) systems built on a Grid infrastructure. In our framework, each peer represents an autonomous information system, and information integration is achieved by establishing mappings among the various peers without resorting to any hierarchical structure. Queries are posed to one peer, and the role of query processing is to exploit both the data that are internal to the peer, and the mappings with other peers in the system.

The main contributions presented in this paper are the following: (i) a semantic characterization of P2P data integration (described in Section 2); (ii) the deployment of our P2P framework on a Grid architecture (presented in Section 4); (iii) the design of a query answering algorithm that is coherent both with the semantics and with the Grid infrastructure (reported in Section 3).

2   The Hyper Framework for Data Integration

In this section, we set up a general framework for P2P data integration in a Grid operating environment. We base our proposal on the work reported in [9]. We refer to a fixed, infinite, denumerable, set Γ of constants. Such constants are shared by all peers, and are the constants that can appear in the P2P system. Moreover, given a relational alphabet A, we denote with $\mathcal{L}_A$ the set of function-free first-order logic (FOL) formulas whose relation symbols are in A and whose constants are in Γ.

A *conjunctive query* (CQ) of arity n over an alphabet A is written in the form

$$\{\mathbf{x} \mid \exists \mathbf{y} \, body_{cq}(\mathbf{x}, \mathbf{y})\}$$

where $body_{cq}(\mathbf{x}, \mathbf{y})$ is a conjunction of atoms of $\mathcal{L}_A$ involving the free variables (also called the *distinguished* variables of the query) $\mathbf{x} = x_1, \dots, x_n$, the existentially quantified variables (also called the *non-distinguished* variables of the query) $\mathbf{y} = y_1, \dots, y_m$, and constants from Γ.

A *P2P system* $\mathcal{P}$ is constituted by a set of *datapeers* and a set of *hyperpeers*. Each datapeer $D \in \mathcal{P}$ is a system that exports data (possibly coming from different sources) in terms of an exported schema.

Hyperpeers instead do not have access to local data but are interconnected with both hyperpeers and datapeers from which they extract data. Formally, a hyperpeer $H \in \mathcal{P}$ is a tuple $HP = (G, M)$, where:

- G is the *schema* of HP, which is a relational schema over a relational alphabet A_G (disjoint from the other alphabets in $\mathcal{P}$) called the *alphabet* of HP.
- M is a set of *P2P mapping assertions*, each of which is an expression of the form

$$cq' \rightsquigarrow cq$$

  The query cq, called the *head* of the assertion, is a conjunctive query over the peer (schema of) HP, while the query cq', called the *tail* of the assertion, is a conjunctive query of the same arity as cq, over (the schema of) one of the other peers in $\mathcal{P}$.

In a hyperpeer $HP \in \mathcal{P}$, a P2P mapping assertion $cq' \rightsquigarrow cq$, where cq is a query over the schema of the peer HP, expresses the fact that HP can use data retrieved by cq' from the peer P' over (the schema of) which cq' is expressed. Such data are mapped to the schema of HP according to what is specified by the query cq. This form of mapping is one of the most expressive among those studied in the P2P and data integration literature. Indeed, in terms of the terminology used in data integration, a hyperpeer connected to datapeers only corresponds to a GLAV *data integration system* [15,18] managing a set of sound data sources defined in terms of a (virtual) global schema.

Observe that no limitation is imposed on the topology of the whole set of P2P mapping assertions in the peer system $\mathcal{P}$, and hence the set of all P2P mappings may be cyclic.

Finally, we assume that *queries* that are posed to the P2P system $\mathcal{P}$ are in fact posed to one of the peers (datapeer or hyperpeer) P of $\mathcal{P}$. Such queries are expressed in a certain relational query language $\mathcal{L}_P$ (which must include conjunctive queries) over the schema of P. For now, we make no specific assumption on the query language $\mathcal{L}_P$, except that the peer P can indeed process queries belonging to $\mathcal{L}_P$, and we say that the queries in $\mathcal{L}_P$ are those *accepted by* P.

We assume that the peers are interpreted over a fixed infinite domain Δ. We also fix the interpretation of the constants in Γ (cf. previous section) so that: (i) each $c \in \Gamma$ denotes an element $d \in \Delta$; (ii) different constants in Γ denote different elements of Δ; (iii) each element in Δ is denoted by a constant in Γ.[1] It follows that Γ is actually isomorphic to Δ, so that we can use (with some abuse of notation) constants in Γ whenever we want to denote domain elements.

We focus first on the semantics of a datapeer DP. We call *database* for DP a finite relational interpretation D of the relation symbols in schema of DP. Let q be a query of arity n, expressed in the query language $\mathcal{L}_{DP}$ accepted by DP, and let D be a database for DP. We denote by $ans(q, DP, D)$ the set of n-tuples of constants in Γ obtained by evaluating q in the database D, according to the semantics of $\mathcal{L}_{DP}$.

To define the semantics of hyperpeers we resort to epistemic logic[2]. The advantages of using epistemic logic instead of First Order Logic (FOL) are illustrated in [9]. In synthesis:

- While in the traditional FOL interpretation the whole is modeled as a flat theory, in our setting peers are modeled as autonomous sites that exchange information and the modular structure of the system is explicitly reflected in the definition of its semantics.
- The new semantic characterization leads to a setting where query answering is decidable, and polynomially tractable in the size of the data.
- The topology of the mapping assertions among the peers in the system is not limited in any way. In particular, while in FOL acyclicity of mapping assertions is often adopted in order to ensure decidability of query answering, in our setting we do not need to impose such a limitation.

It should be noted that the resulting semantics is weaker than the one based on FOL, but we argue that this is exactly the price to pay in order to get all the above advantages.

The use of epistemic logic is based on the idea that P2P mappings are formalized as axioms of an epistemic logic theory. More precisely, a P2P system $\mathcal{P}$ is formalized as an epistemic theory $M_{\mathcal{P}}$ formed by one axiom of the form

$$\forall \mathbf{x} \, (\mathbf{K}(\exists \mathbf{y} \, (body_{cq_1}(\mathbf{x}, \mathbf{y}))) \supset \exists \mathbf{z} \, body_{cq_2}(\mathbf{x}, \mathbf{z}))$$

for each P2P mapping assertion $cq_1 \rightsquigarrow cq_2$ in the peers of $\mathcal{P}$. Intuitively, this formalization of the P2P mapping assertions reflects the idea that only what is

---

[1] In other words the constants in Γ act as *standard names* [19].

[2] Technically we resort to epistemic FOL with standard names, and therefore with a fixed domain, and rigid interpretation of constants [19].

known by the peers (denoted by the **K** operator) mentioned in the tail of the assertion is transferred to the peer mentioned in the head.

Then, let a *system database for* $\mathcal{P}$ be a database formed by the disjoint union of the various databases of the datapeers in $\mathcal{P}$. Let a *FOL model of* $\mathcal{P}$ *based on a system database* $\mathcal{D}$ be any FOL model for the disjoint union of the schema of the peers in $\mathcal{P}$, such that the extensions of the relations in the schemas of the datapeers are those sanctioned by $\mathcal{D}$. An *epistemic model of* $\mathcal{P}$ *based on* $\mathcal{D}$ is a pair $(\mathcal{I}, \mathcal{W})$ such that $\mathcal{W}$ is a set of FOL models of $\mathcal{P}$ based on $\mathcal{D}$, $\mathcal{I} \in \mathcal{W}$, and $(\mathcal{I}, \mathcal{W})$ satisfies all the axioms of $M_{\mathcal{P}}$. In particular, the axiom

$$\forall \mathbf{x} \ (\mathbf{K}(\exists \mathbf{y} \ (body_{cq_1}(\mathbf{x}, \mathbf{y}))) \supset \exists \mathbf{z} \ body_{cq_2}(\mathbf{x}, \mathbf{z}))$$

in $\mathcal{M}_{\mathcal{P}}$ is satisfied by $(\mathcal{I}, \mathcal{W})$ if for every tuple $\mathbf{t}$ of objects in Γ, the fact that $\exists \mathbf{y} \ body_{cq_1}(\mathbf{t}, \mathbf{y})$ is satisfied in every FOL model in $\mathcal{W}$ implies that also $\exists \mathbf{z} \ body_{cq_2}(\mathbf{t}, \mathbf{z})$ is satisfied in every FOL model in $\mathcal{W}$.

Finally, given a query q over one of the peers P in $\mathcal{P}$ and a system database $\mathcal{D}$ for $\mathcal{P}$, we define the *certain answers* $ans_{\mathbf{k}}(q, \mathcal{P}, \mathcal{D})$ to q in $\mathcal{P}$ based on $\mathcal{D}$, as the set of tuples $\mathbf{t}$ of constants in Γ such that for every epistemic model $(\mathcal{I}, \mathcal{W})$ of $\mathcal{P}$ based on $\mathcal{D}$, we have that $\mathbf{t} \in ans(q, P, \mathcal{I})$, where we consider P as a datapeer and $\mathcal{I}$ as a database for P.

3   Query Answering in Hyper

In order to address query processing in Hyper, we start by defining a preliminary transformation of a P2P system. Given a hyperpeer $HP = (G, M)$, we break each P2P mapping assertion $cq' \rightsquigarrow cq$ in M between a peer P' and HP in two halves, introducing an auxiliary predicate r of the same arity as cq'. We then denote as q_r the query cq' in the tail of the corresponding P2P mapping assertion, and denote as P_r the peer P', i.e., the peer over which the query q_r is expressed. Then, we replace the mapping $cq' \rightsquigarrow cq$ by a *local* mapping assertion $\{\mathbf{x} \mid r(\mathbf{x})\} \rightsquigarrow cq$ (that has the form of a LAV mapping [18]) and a simplified P2P mapping $cq' \rightsquigarrow \{\mathbf{x} \mid r(\mathbf{x})\}$ (that has the form of a GAV mapping [18]). For each peer HP, we call *auxiliary alphabet* of HP, denoted as $AuxAlph(HP)$, the set of new predicate symbols thus defined.

Such a system modification transforms each hyperpeer $HP = (G, M)$ in a LAV data integration system $(\mathcal{G}, \mathcal{S}, M)$ [18], where the global schema $\mathcal{G}$ is the original schema G of the peer HP, the schema of the local sources $\mathcal{S}$ is constituted of the set of auxiliary predicate symbols $AuxAlph(HP)$, and the mapping from the local to the global elements is provided by the local mapping assertions introduced above.

From the semantic point of view, the local mapping assertion is interpreted (without involving the knowledge operator) simply as:

$$\forall \mathbf{x} \ r(\mathbf{x}) \supset \exists \mathbf{y} \ body_{cq}(\mathbf{x}, \mathbf{y}))$$

Informally, in each peer the local sources corresponding to the predicates in the auxiliary alphabet are used to "simulate" the effect of the P2P mapping assertions with respect to contributing to the data of the peer. It is possible to show that this new formulation of a hyperpeer is semantically equivalent to the original one.

We then define a distributed algorithm for answering queries in $\mathcal{L}_U$. Again the algorithm proposed is a version of that in [9], suitably specialized for the Hyper Framework. More specifically, we define the two main functionalities that each peer must provide in order to answer a user query to any peer in the system. Such functionalities are executed over a given source database $\mathcal{D}$, which represents the state of the datapeers when the query is issued by the user.

Each user query q to the peer P is the input of the extensionalQueryAnswering of P. If P is a datapeer, this module simply activates the query answering service of the datapeer to answer q. Therefore, in the following we assume that the query q is posed to a hyperpeer P. In such a case, this module first initiates a transaction, that is identified in the system by a unique transaction id, then passes the query q to its own intensionalQueryAnswering. Such a functionality returns a Datalog program DP (which involves queries to the datapeers of $\mathcal{P}$). The evaluation $Eval(DP)$ of such a program DP constitutes the answer set of the query q.

The intensionalQueryAnswering computes the Datalog program corresponding to the query q as follows:

1. first, a module computes the *perfect reformulation* of the query q with respect to the local mapping assertions in the peer. This step consists of expressing the query q over the schema of P in terms of an "equivalent" query q' over the local sources of P, i.e., in terms of the auxiliary alphabet $AuxAlph(P)$, which corresponds to the well-known problem of query rewriting using views [16,18].

2. then, for each predicate r in $AuxAlph(P)$ occurring in such a reformulation: (i) if the predicate r is generated by a mapping to a datapeer P_r, then a special rule $r \leftarrow q_r : address(P_r)$ is added to the Datalog program. In such a special rule, $address(P_r)$ represents the URL of the node corresponding to the datapeer P_r and q_r is the query to P_r associated with the auxiliary predicate r; (ii) if r is generated by a mapping to a hyperpeer P_r, then the P_r.intensionalQueryAnswering(q_r) is called and the resulting Datalog rules are added to the Datalog program.

As concerns $Eval(DP)$, such a procedure executes the following steps: (i) the procedure first retrieves the data corresponding to the extensional predicates of the program DP as follows. For each extensional predicate r there is a special rule $r \leftarrow q_r : address(P_r)$ in DP: the procedure asks the query q_r to the node P_r (whose URL is represented by $address(P_r)$); the answer set thus obtained constitutes the extension of the predicate r. Let D be the EDB (i.e., the set of facts) thus constructed; (ii) the Datalog program DP' obtained from DP by deleting all special rules and adding the EDB D is evaluated in the standard way.

We remark that, in order to guarantee that the intensionalQueryAnswering never processes the same mapping query twice in the same transaction, suitable checks are implemented through the procedures setTransaction and

Algorithm P.extensionalQueryAnswering
Input: user query $q \in \mathcal{L}_U$ to the hyperpeer P
Output: $ans_\mathbf{k}(q, \mathcal{P}, \mathcal{D})$
begin
   generate a new transaction id T;
   $DP := P$.intensionalQueryAnswering(q, T);
   return $Eval(DP)$
end

Algorithm P.intensionalQueryAnswering
Input: query $q \in \mathcal{L}_U$ to the hyperpeer P, transaction id T
Output: Datalog program DP
begin
   $DP :=$ computePerfectReformulation(q, P);
   for each (predicate $r \in AuxAlph(P)$ occurring in the bodies of DP)
     if (getTransaction$(r, T) = notProcessed$) {
      setTransaction$(r, T, processed)$;
      if (r is generated by a mapping to a datapeer)
        $DP := DP \cup \{r \leftarrow q_r : address(P_r)\}$
      else /* r is generated by a mapping to a hyperpeer */
        $DP := DP \cup P_r$.intensionalQueryAnswering(q_r, T);
     }
   return DP
end

Fig. 1. Algorithms extensionalQueryAnswering and intensionalQueryAnswering in hyperpeers

getTransaction. More precisely, two different states are associated to each predicate symbol r in $AuxAlph(P)$ with respect to the transaction T. If the state of r with respect to transaction T is *notProcessed*, then the mapping query q_r still has to be processed in the transaction T, therefore the intensionalQueryAnswering has to compute the answer to such a query. If the state of r with respect to transaction T is *processed*, then the mapping query q_r has already been processed in the transaction T, so the intensionalQueryAnswering does not process it again. Of course, when a new transaction is started by the extensionalQueryAnswering, all predicates are initially in the *notProcessed* state for such a transaction.

The two algorithms are reported in Figure 1. In can be shown that the result returned by extensionalQueryAnswering invoked on a hyperpeer for a query q, is exactly $ans_\mathbf{k}(q, P, \mathcal{D})$, where $\mathcal{D}$ is the system database corresponding to the extension of all datapeers.

4   Implementing the Hyper Framework on Grids

This section outlines how the Hyper Framework (as described in the previous section) can be developed as an OGSA-compliant Data Access and Integration

Service. By implementing this standard, Hyper will exploit available, well supported and understood infrastructures. On the other hand, Hyper will be easily integrated with existing environments, implementations, and tools. Although Grid and P2P computing are generally regarded as two different notions, we recognize that OGSA Grids provide a suitable infrastructure for P2P computing, in that they allow nodes discovering, binding, and exchanging data the one another in their environment, without hierarchical constraints. Furthermore, we believe that P2P architectures address many interesting Grid application problems.

4.1 OGSA Data Services

Based on the Open Grid Service Architecture [13], Grid Data Access and Integration Services (OGSA-DAI) [3] provide a reference architecture for data integration in distributed and heterogeneous environments. Before introducing OGSA-DAI, we summarize the basic Grid terminology and standards. The Open Grid Service Architecture (OGSA) specifies a framework where Grid objects and flows are designed as a set of standardized services and data models. Grid services are characterized as state-full distributed objects that can be instantiated, identified, searched, monitored, notified, and destroyed. By implementing OGSA services, applications can be integrated within a distributed operating environment, and cooperate the one another. The Open Grid Services Infrastructure (OGSI) [4] supplies a Web Services substrate for OGSA Grid functionalities, while Globus Toolkit [2] provides an open source, reference implementation of OGSI. Basically, OGSI Grid Services are Web Services that implement a set of standardized interfaces to implement Grids. Currently, enhancements to OGSI are being developed, based on the WS-Resource Framework [6], with the aim of converging with the most recent developments of Web Service standards. Anyway, Web based Grids can be viewed as special kinds of distributed object systems, which leverage Web Services standards and machineries without introducing any further binding to hosting environments, thus obtaining an unprecedented world-wide interoperability of information systems. In the OGSI setting, Grid objects (i.e., GRIDSERVICE instances) are created by invoking *Factory Services* that provide them with network identity and binding information, based on permanent handles (GSHs) and references (GSRs), which contain (possibly changing) addressing data.

Furthermore, GRIDSERVICE instances maintain *Service Data Elements* (or SDEs) that allow accommodating any kind of instance attribute, with standard access, manipulation, and search methods. Also, clients can subscribe for notifications regarding changes of specific data elements.

Based on OGSA, the Data Access and Integration (OGSA-DAI) specification details a service-oriented treatment of heterogeneous data sources, by modeling them as Grid services. The main purposes of OGSA-DAI are summarized in [3], as follows:

– Integrate data sources and resources into OGSA-compliant architectures.
– Obtain information about data that may be distributed amongst several heterogeneous database environments.

GRIDSERVICE finds service instances, manages handlers and supplies data services

DATADESCRIPTION supplies data service descriptions (e.g. metadata)
  RELATIONALDESCRIPTION supplies relational metadata (e.g. tables and columns names)
DATAACCESS manages data access
  SQLACCESS manages SQL queries
DATASERVICEFACTORY creates and configures GridService instances
  SQLDATASERVICEFACTORY creates and configures SQL Data Service instances

Fig. 2. DAI interface hierarchy

– Locate the data that may be distributed, or replicated, over many different types of databases, the locations of which may not be known beforehand.
– Integrate data models that may be different on distributed databases.
– Find the databases that hold the required data and to be in a position to be able to interpret that data.
– Access that data through uniform interfaces.
– Integrate data from various sources to obtain the required information.

In practice, Data Services are special kinds of GRIDSERVICE instances that implement a suitable set of description, access, manipulation, and query interfaces. Data Services are qualified and described by specific SDE arrays, which convey relevant information such as metadata for structured or semi-structured databases. Interestingly, Data Services standardize and virtualize the access to source metadata, as well as query interfaces, thus providing a powerful abstraction of the underlying database infrastructures. The OGSA-DAI proposal defines three main WSDL interfaces (PORTTYPES) for describing, accessing, and instantiating data sources, called DATADESCRIPTION, DATAACCESS, and DATASERVICEFACTORY, respectively, which can be specialized to support different metadata structures or access methods (cf. Figure 2). This way, specific database systems, such as RDBMS, can be wrapped by appropriate implementations of DAI interfaces. Moreover, implementations can represent virtual views instead of concrete sources, and, in turn, can get integrated by higher level virtual data services. In brief, OGSA-DAI allow data providers wrapping data sources and mediating their access, thus providing a virtualization mechanism in which different data models can be easily integrated.

4.2 Hyper Data Services

We will specify here Hyper Data Services (HDS) on the basis OGSA (DAI) standards (c.f. Figure 3). From OGSA-DAI, HDS inherits:

– peer identity, which is provided by GSHs and GSRs
– peer discovery and binding

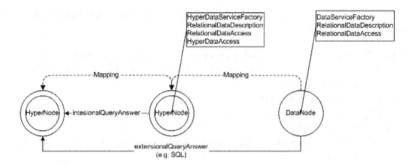

Fig. 3. Hyper Data Services

- peer typing, by means of specific SDEs
- extensional query answering services, for any suitable query language
- transaction identification for intensional queries, which relies of GSHs

First, we refer to generic DAI Service instances as *nodes*, which can be used as data sources by HDS, with provision that they supply relational metadata access services as well relational query services. We don't require nodes exposing any particular metadata format, or support any particular query language. Instead, we assume that nodes provide enough information for accessing their relational alphabets, where each relation is given, at least, a symbol and an arity. Nodes can provide such kind of information trough their DataDescription data elements. For instance, RELATIONALDESCRIPTIONS [8], are likely to expose information about relational schemas, including tables, columns, column types, and keys. As such, they would allow dealing with relational metadata according to the abstraction outlined above. Nodes will also provide extensional query answering services with their standard means.

Then, we define *hypernode* any node that supports DATAACCESS methods implementing the system-wide query answering algorithms described in Section 3. With respect to the general P2P framework, hypernodes correspond to hyperpeers, whereas nodes correspond to datapeers. Hypernode metadata will be exposed with standard DATADESCRIPTION ports, that is, WSDL PORTTYPES with no standard operations that provide a suitable structure of SDEs. Once again, the format of hyper metadata could be one of those envisioned in DAI, as long as it allows handling a basic relational alphabet. Extensional query services will be supported by standardized DATAACCESS operations as well.

The binding to DAI metadata and access methods that characterize a specific hypernode (e.g. Relational, XML) is called *hypernode's flavour*. For each supported flavour, a conversion from the specific access language to the hypernode internal relational metadata will be implemented. This will guarantee a seamless integration of hypernodes with any other agent in their Data Grid environments. At the current stage, only an SQL flavour is being designed, but future developments could include other flavours, such as XML.

HYPERACCESS: INTENSIONALQUERYANSWERING (IN TRANS, IN QUERY, OUT DATALOG, OUT FAIL)

- TRANS – the transaction identifier (GSH)
- QUERY – the body of the intensional query (conjunctive query)
- DATALOG – the resulting Datalog program
- FAIL – an error code in case of abnormal termination

Fig. 4. INTENSIONALQUERYANSWERING operation

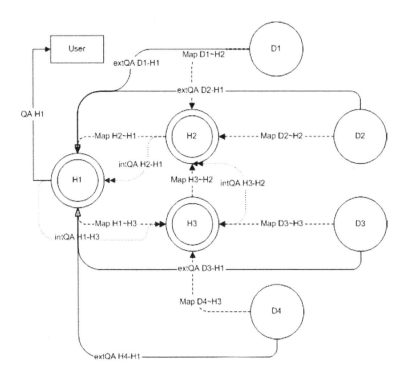

Fig. 5. Interaction among peers during query answering: an example

As mentioned above, extensional DATAACCESS operations will rely on standard DAI methods. Intensional queries, on the other hand, will require a specific support. This will be provided by the HYPERACCESS PORTTYPE, which is an extension of DAI DATAACCESS. Therefore, hypernodes will support two DATAACCESS ports, which is allowable in DAI infrastructures. HYPERACCESS defines a single operation, named INTENSIONALQUERYANSWERING (cf. Figure 5).

When a query is issued against a hypernode (cf. Figure 5), a transient DATAACCESS service is created, which allows accessing the result set of the query according to the node's flavour. The GSH of the newly created service identifies the query session. The inquired node examines the query against its internal mapping structure, and lists out nodes that are relevant for answering the query, or some of its parts. Each mapped node that is a hypernode (this can be checked at run time by accessing the node service metadata), is inquired with an intensional query, which takes as input the session GSH and the query fragment which is relevant to the mapped node. Recursively, the mapped node will invoke intensional query operations on the hypernodes, according to its mappings. Note that the evaluation of cycles in mappings can be stopped thanks to the session GSH, which allows nodes detecting if an intensional query that has already been answered is issued back because of a cycle. The distributed intensional query process results in a Datalog program, which is evaluated by the node where the query was originated. This evaluation results in Grid-wide data access plan, that is, a list of extensional queries to be posed to other nodes in the Grid in order to get the integrated response. Finally, each relevant data node will be inquired through its standard extensional query interface, and the global result will be made available to the access service associated to the query session.

5   Conclusions

In this paper we have presented Hyper, a joint research initiative of Università di Roma "La Sapienza" and IBM Italia, which aims at developing a Data Grid integration system based on peer-to-peer schema mappings, which resorts on epistemic logic for providing a semantics for the mappings among peers. Also, we have presented an OGSA-DAI extension defining data services (hypernodes) which are capable of integrating any other standard data service in a Data Grid. Thanks to the peer-to-peer architecture, hypernodes can enter and leave the Grid, or change their own structure, without enforcing any change neither in other Grid participants, nor in "analyst" nodes. In fact, they get integrated in the overall information system, as far as other hypernodes are interested in establishing and maintaining a mapping with them, in a unsupervised manner. Of course, uncontrolled dynamics in a Hyper Data Grid would cause dangling mappings. However, this would only affect the information completeness, without breaking the system functionality.

Differently from simple key-based Semantic Overlay Networks [11], Hyper does not enforce any "clustering" based on shared conceptual structures covering the entire Grid semantics. Of course, Hyper is concerned with high quality query answering on complex structured data, and should not be compared with performance-oriented infrastructures dealing with loosely structured information. With respect to enhanced, semantically rich, and self-organizing Semantic Overlay Networks such as [7], or similar data management infrastructures such as [17], Hyper uses a simple relational language for expressing both schemas and mappings, rather than new class-based languages like RDFS and OWL. This way, Hyper facilitates the exploitation of well-supported industrial standards such as OGSA-DAI, and allows for a smooth integration of legacy business databases.

Many relevant aspects of a complete P2P data integration environment are not addressed in our system so far. Above all, we would mention the problem of individual mapping [22,12], i.e., how to handle the identity of values denoted by different constants in different peers. If referred to objects denoted by network-wide identifiers (e.g. URIs), such a referential consistency could be ensured by a suitable "instance mapping" mechanism. This problem, however, is not addressed in our current framework.

Another open issue is that of discovering metadata correspondences, with the purpose of facilitating (at best, automating) the creation of metadata mappings. Simple relational metadata schemas, such as those considered here, would give just a little support to such a discovery. The adoption of rich ontology languages, such as those conceived for Semantic Web [1], if supplemented with good lexicalizations and links to reference ontologies (e.g. WordNet) would give an appropriate support to such a discovery. The way metadata mappings are established, however, is out of the scope of the Hyper Framework.

Acknowledgments. This research has been partially supported by the projects INFOMIX (IST-2001-33570), SEWASIE (IST-2001-34825) and INTEROP Network of Excellence (IST-508011) funded by the EU, by the project "Società dell'Informazione" subproject SP1 "Reti Internet: Efficienza, Integrazione e Sicurezza" funded by MIUR – Fondo Speciale per lo Sviluppo della Ricerca di Interesse Strategico, and by project HYPER, funded by IBM through a Shared University Research (SUR) Award grant.

References

1. W3C semantic web, 2001. www.w3.org/2001/sw.
2. The globus alliance, 2004. www.globus.org.
3. Open grid services architecture data access and integration, 2004. www.ogsadai.org.uk.
4. Open grid services infrastructure, 2004. forge.gridforum.org/projects/ogsi-wg.
5. The semantic grid, 2004. www.semanticgrid.org.
6. The ws-resource framework, 2004. www.globus.org/wsrf.
7. K. Aberer, P. Cudré-Mauroux, M. Hauswirth, and T. V. Pelt. Gridvine: Building internet-scale semantic overlay networks. Technical Report IC/2004/38, EPFL, 2004.
8. M. Antonioletti, A. Krause, S. Hastings, S. Langella, S. Malaika, J. Magowan, S. Laws, and N. W. Paton. Grid data service specification: The relational realisation. Technical report, DAIS Working Group, 2003.
9. D. Calvanese, G. De Giacomo, M. Lenzerini, and R. Rosati. Logical foundations of peer-to-peer data integration. In *Proc. of the 23nd ACM SIGACT SIGMOD SIGART Symp. on Principles of Database Systems (PODS 2004)*, 2004. To appear.
10. L. Camarinha-Matos, H. Afsarmanesh, C. Garita, and C. Lima. Towards an architecture for virtual enterprises. *J. Intelligent Manufacturing*, 9(2), 1998.
11. A. Crespo and H. Garcia-Molina. Semantic overlay networks for P2P systems. Technical report, Computer Science Department, Stanford University, 2002.
12. A. Doan, Y. Lu, Y. Lee, and J. Han. Profile-based object matching for information integration. *IEEE Intelligent Systems*, 18(5):54–59, 2003.

13. I. Foster, C. Kesselman, J. Nick, and S. Tuecke. The physiology of the grid: An open grid services architecture for distributed systems integration. In *Open Grid Service Infrastructure WG, Global Grid Forum*, 2002.

14. I. Foster, C. Kesselman, and S. Tuecke. The anatomy of the grid: Enabling scalable virtual organizations. *International J. Supercomputer Applications*, 15(3), 2001.

15. M. Friedman, A. Levy, and T. Millstein. Navigational plans for data integration. In *Proc. of the 16th Nat. Conf. on Artificial Intelligence (AAAI'99)*, pages 67–73. AAAI Press/The MIT Press, 1999.

16. A. Y. Halevy. Answering queries using views: A survey. *Very Large Database Journal*, 10(4):270–294, 2001.

17. A. Y. Halevy, Z. G. Ives, P. Mork, and I. Tatarinov. Piazza: data management infrastructure for semantic web applications. In *Proc. of the 12th Int. World Wide Web Conference (WWW 2003)*, pages 556–567, 2003.

18. M. Lenzerini. Data integration: A theoretical perspective. In *Proc. of the 21st ACM SIGACT SIGMOD SIGART Symp. on Principles of Database Systems (PODS 2002)*, pages 233–246, 2002.

19. H. J. Levesque and G. Lakemeyer. *The Logic of Knowledge Bases*. The MIT Press, 2001.

20. P. McBrien and A. Poulovassilis. Distributed databases. In M. Piattini and O. Diaz, editors, *Advanced Database Technology and Design*. Artech House, 2000.

21. N. Paton, M. Atkinson, V. Dialani, D. Pearson, T. Storey, and P. Watson. Database access and integration services on the grid. Technical Report UKeS-2002-03, UK e-Science Programme, National e-Science Centre, 2002.

22. G. Zhou, R. Hull, R. King, and J.-C. Franchitti. Using object matching and materialization to integrate heterogeneous databases. pages 4–18, 1995.

Semantically Linking and Browsing Provenance Logs for E-science

Jun Zhao, Carole Goble, Robert Stevens, and Sean Bechhofer

Department of Computer Science
University of Manchester
Oxford Road
Manchester
United Kingdom M13 9PL
{zhaoj,carole,robert.stevens,seanb}@cs.man.ac.uk

Abstract. e-Science experiments are those performed using computer-based resources such as database searches, simulations or other applications. Like their laboratory based counterparts, the data associated with an e-Science experiment are of reduced value if other scientists are not able to identify the origin, or provenance, of those data. Provenance is the term given to metadata about experiment processes, the derivation paths of data, and the sources and quality of experimental components, which includes the scientists themselves, related literature, etc. Consequently provenance metadata are valuable resources for e-Scientists to repeat experiments, track versions of data and experiment runs, verify experiment results, and as a source of experimental insight. One specific kind of *in silico* experiment is a workflow. In this paper we describe how we can assemble a Semantic Web of workflow provenance logs that allows a bioinformatician to browse and navigate between experimental components by generating hyperlinks based on semantic annotations associated with them. By associating well-formalized semantics with workflow logs we take a step towards integration of process provenance information and improved knowledge discovery.

1 Introduction

e-Science refers to science by scientists working collaboratively in large distributed project teams in order to solve scientific problems [1] that uses electronic resources (instruments, sensors, databases, computational methods, computers). e-Science *in silico* experiments complement traditional lab work through the use of computer-based information repositories and computational analysis to: test a hypothesis; derive a summary; search for patterns; or demonstrate a known fact [2]. Bioinformaticians, for example, perform analyses (*in silico* experiments) by submitting data (often biological sequences such as DNA or protein) to a succession of analysis tools and databases [3]. Currently when performing *in silico* experiments, bioinformaticians spend a great deal of time manually and repeatedly coordinating tools or applications to produce results.

M. Bouzeghoub et al. (Eds.): ICSNW 2004, LNCS 3226, pp. 158–176, 2004.
© IFIP International Federation for Information Processing 2004

A new software infrastructure, to form a virtual organization for sets of heterogeneous distributed data collections, computing resources and people and machines for e-Science is needed. The Grid is such a proposed infrastructure [4]. ^myGrid [1] is a project, aiming to provide middleware infrastructure for the Grid to create and orchestrate *in silico* experiments for bioinformaticans working in functional genomics, and manage and exploit the results from these experiments. ^myGrid builds sets of middleware services to automate the experiment process as *workflows* [3].

Like their laboratory based counterparts, the data associated with an e-Science experiments are of reduced value if other scientists are not able to identify the origin, or provenance, of those data. Provenance is the term given to metadata about experiment processes, the derivation paths of data, and the sources and quality of experimental components, which includes the scientists themselves, related literature, etc. For an *in silico* experiment, knowledge to be shared amongst scientists includes:

- data results and the origin of the data results: Data are of reduced value without provenance information, which are valuable resources for results verification.
- a log of all the computational processes used: This recording is analogous to the conventional recording of materials and methods in a scientist's log-book at the laboratory bench. It promotes the sharing and re-use of experimental knowledge as well as good scientific practise.

Provenance also provides "recipes" for workflow designs by enabling tracing details of workflow executions and versions of data and services. When performing *in silico* experiments by hand, such provenance recordings are often ignored. These make experiment reproduction and experiment design difficult for novice bioinformaticians. Moreover, public bioinformatics databases are frequently updated with newly discovered data resources, which may lead to different results when repeating workflow runs. Provenance information is needed to explain and analyze the impact of changes.

1.1   A Scenario

In a typical *in silico* experiment, a biologist has been using a microarray study to investigate the differences in levels of gene expression between individuals with and without the disease. The up-regulated genes[2] are identified by keys to a proprietary database. The bioinformatician needs to map these proprietary identifiers (e.g. Affymetrix_probe_set_id) onto those used in other bioinformatics databases (e.g. GenBank_id). These database resources are then used to retrieve additional data recorded about the gene, and it products. The bioinformatician will take the DNA or protein sequence from these databases and submit them to other tools, collecting further information. Most of these analyses are performed

---

[1] http://www.mygrid.org.uk
[2] Genes that have been switched on

using a separate service, and generates their own collections of results. In turn, many of these are fed into other services. In ^{my}Grid such an analysis is captured as a workflow and a collection of tools collect and co-ordinate the data generated by that workflow.

Such an experiment may be performed many times, using different datasets, in different projects or investigated with differing topics. At the end, a large repository of records about experiments will be collected. This information can be viewed from four different levels:

Organization level, which records the workflow user and creator, their organization, project, the hypothesis for this experiment/project, the experiment design, etc. For example, Dr Stevens works for the University of Manchester; he designed the workflow W21 whose purpose is to characterise an Affymetrix_probe_set_id with its predicted genomic function; this workflow is part of a greater experiment to identify the genes associated with Grave's Disease;

Process level, that collects how, when and where the workflow is run, what data are used and generated, which computational services are invoked, and the input and output data for service invocation. For example, BLAST version 3.1 run at the NCBI over SWISS-PROT version 41 on 04/05/2004 at 13:34 GMT was invoked with gene sequence identified by 1020_s_at, and successfully executed in 2.1 seconds;

Data level, most of which are inferred from the process level provenance, and describes derivation path of the data results from services. For example, a collection of pairwise sequence alignments were generated by BLAST, version 3.1, run at the NCBI over SWISS-PROT version 41, etc for a gene sequence 1020_s_at;

Knowledge level, mostly in the form of annotations, either in free text or in a structured/semi-structured form. For example, the data level view above, has the knowledge level view that the result set of *protein sequences* are *similar to* the input *gene sequence* 1020_s_at.

When a biologist reviews his or her work, these data can be used like a lab-book. Typical questions to such a resource would be:

- Which experiments used a particular workflow?
- Which experiments used gene x?
- Which experiments were performed upon Grave's disease and which upon Williams-Beuren syndrome?
- Which experiments investigated signal peptides in T-lymphocytes?

These questions are skewed towards descriptions of *what* the experiments are; *when*, *where* and *how* they are enacted; and *why* and for *whom* experiments were performed. The questions are about the analytical process. In a large collection of such data, simple keyword searches will not support such queries - we need knowledge that sequence 1020_s_at turns out to be *T-lymphocyte*, for example. Consequently, we need to include knowledge level provenance over these process provenance data in order to answer such questions.

An early version of the [my]Grid middleware generated process provenance logs as XML documents. Our ambition was to generate a web of these documents, together with related experimental components such as the home page of the scientist or the XML document describing the workflow script and so on, that could be navigated by the scientists. Biologists are familiar with the notion of *query by navigation*. Their standard way of interconnecting data sources is through web browsers and point and click navigation [5]. We emulate this by providing a browser-based navigation experience through a provenance document collection. We present the experimental holdings we wish to browse - logs, users' home pages, workflow scripts, data results, publications, notes - as a document set. We then dynamically generate a hypertext of these documents so that scientists navigate through a web of experiment data that connects enactment logs with an experiment's documents.

To do this we need a link generation mechanism. In particular we investigated the generation of links by using shared concepts associated with a document. By associating documents with domain concepts drawn from an ontology, logs can be dynamically linked together based on their shared semantic concepts. For example, even though two provenance logs have inputs with different values, they can be linked together based on the fact that both inputs are *Gene_ids*, the same semantic concept. This provides a higher level linking between these logs than just linking them based on the same data value recorded in the logs. In effect the ontology is acting as a link model for the provenance document collection.

As shown in Fig 1, the result is a dynamically generated Semantic Web of provenance, linking together a process provenance log with other logs, related workflow design templates, experiment notes, relevant literature, the scientists' home pages, as well as some organisational information about the overall experiment, through their shared semantics.

The rest of the paper is organised as follows. A brief description of the relevant [my]Grid components and the generation of process provenance, without semantic linking, is described in Sect 2. Section 3 describes how we build our semantically linked Web of experimental documents. Section 4 describes how such a Semantic Web is populated. Some related works are introduced in Sect 5. We close in Sect 6 with a discussion of our experiences and some pointers of our move to an Resource Description Framework (RDF) [6] based provenance model.

2   Provenance in [my]Grid

The [my]Grid middleware framework employs a service-based architecture, built on Web Services [7]. The platform is being used for biological investigations into gene expression and Single Nucleotide Polymorphism (SNP) analysis for Grave's disease [2] and Williams-Beuren Syndrome [3]. In addition to a workbench for creating and executing experiments, the primary services to support *in silico* experiments fall into four categories:

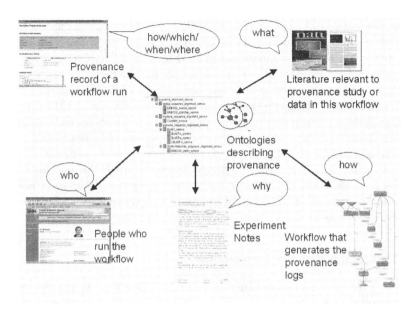

Fig. 1. A Web of provenance connected through the "Semantic Glue"

1. services that are the **tools** that will constitute the experiments, that is: external third party services such databases, computational analyses, simulations etc, presented as web services;
2. services for **forming and executing experiments**, primarily workflow management services for creating and enacting workflows, Taverna/Freefluo [3] which enact the XML-based workflow language XScufl (XML Simple Conceptual Unified Flow Language) [8], and ^{my}Grid Information Repositories (mIRs) for storage;
3. services for supporting the **e-Science scientific method**, specifically provenance management [9] and change notification [10];
4. **semantic services** for discovering services and workflows, and managing metadata, such as semantically annotated service registries and federated personalised views over those registries.

^{my}Grid services can be described as semantically aware. Ontologies represented using the DAML+OIL ontology language [11] are used to describe the inputs, outputs and tasks of web services and workflows, as well as the semantic characterisation of an object in the mIR. An ontology captures a community's understanding or knowledge of a domain and provides a common, shared understanding of that domain. For the purposes of this paper an ontology is a hierarchical classification of domain specific concepts, a set of their properties, and their internal relationships. DAML+OIL is an ontology language developed

---

³ Taverna and FreeFluo are both open source projects available from
http://taverna.sourceforge.net and http://freefluo.sourceforge.net

for the Semantic Web. Its successor OWL (Web Ontology Language) [12] is now a W3C Recommendation. DAML+OIL is based on a Description Logic, whose reasoning abilities support automated classification of terms into hierarchies [13]. ^{my}Grid uses DAML+OIL ontologies to annotate web services stored in a registry to enable service and workflow discovery and composition. These DAML+OIL semantic descriptions build on the work of the DAML-S coalition and have been used to guide the construction of workflows by constraining the choice to those services, which have semantically compatible inputs and outputs. Similarly semantic description of workflows has been used to discover relevant workflows given an item of data selected from the mIR. An ontology service provides a single point of reference for these concepts and supports reasoning over concept expressions. The use of semantic web technology such as ontology services makes this an early example of a *Semantic Grid* [14].

2.1   Producing Process Provenance

Process level workflow provenance is generated as a process graph, with services as nodes and data as arcs. The workflow description is submitted to the Freefluo workflow enactment engine to "run" the experiment. Each workflow run consumes two XML documents:

1. An XScufl document gives the low-level workflow definition, describes the ordering of process invocations and data passes, and hence plays a similar role to the DAML-S process model [15].
2. A Web service information (ws-info) document contains ontological descriptions that are associated with the inputs, outputs and services in a workflow, similar to the DAML-S profile [16]. This document has two roles: the ^{my}Grid registry uses it to advertise and hence discover Web services based on their semantics; and the ^{my}Grid workbench environment uses it when finding suitable data inputs that semantically match those of a workflow.

As shown in Fig 2 (excluding the dashed box), before running a workflow, users interact with the ^{my}Grid workbench and choose workflows through their semantic descriptions stored in the ws-info files. When a workflow is executed, the workbench retrieves from the mIR the XScufl document , and the required resources, such as input/output data and parameters, based on the ws-info file. The workbench invokes the Freefluo enactment engine with the XScufl file and an XML document containing the input data. The process provenance logs are generated at the same time as data results, in the form of XML, by the workflow enactment engine. At the end, the process provenance and the data results are returned to the mIR through the workbench.

Figure 3 shows the content of an example provenance. This is interpreted from the original XML format provenance logs. This process provenance records: the start time, end time, the user of this workflow, the service invoked in this workflow (getSequence); the parameters of the service invocations; and the inputs and outputs and their metadata of the workflow.

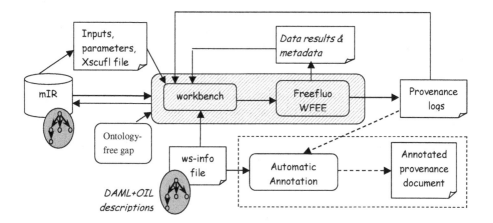

Fig. 2. The generation of provenance in ^{m y}Grid.

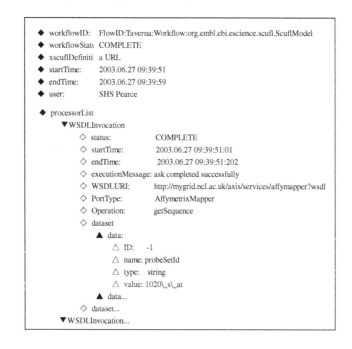

Fig. 3. An example provenance fragment.

An interface for navigating and querying these provenance logs is required by bioinformaticians. Similar experiments, using similar inputs, etc. need to be linked together semantically, at the knowledge level, in order to answer the kinds of tasks described in Sect 1. For example, what are the experiment runs using *BLAST* Web services with a *White_blood_cell* as input? Or how to find workflow runs whose outputs *contain* the *Single_nucleotide_polymorphism*? Also what is the literature that users refer to when designing an experiment for invoking sequence alignment services; what are the notes about experiment conclusions, etc. Simple keyword searching, such as asking for a particular data value to find all similar experiments, will only find experiments with that data item and not those with data values that are instances of the same concept.

To enable such tasks, we integrated explicit domain semantics with our provenance logs and presented our Web of semantically linked provenance in a browser environment. For this we used the COHSE (Conceptual Open Hypermedia Services Environment) semantic hyperlink generation tool powered by the ontologies used by the ^{my}Grid registry for service and workflow discovery and type management.

3   A Semantic Web of Provenance

In this section we describe the COHSE semantic hyperlink tool, and show it in use. In Sect 4 we give details of the ontologies we used and how we annotated the logs with the ontologies.

Detailed descriptions of the COHSE system can be found in [17]. Briefly, the COHSE approach consists of a *COHSE agent* that augments documents with links based on the semantic content of those documents. Figure 4 shows the three technologies of COHSE. *An Ontology Service*, uses rich knowledge representation techniques and reasoning abilities to provide a machine processable semantics to the conceptual metadata associated with documents and between concepts. *An Annotation Service* plays two roles: (a) annotates documents or sections of documents with concepts from the loaded ontology and (b) maintains a link base that stores bi-directional mappings between concepts and target URIs (Unique Resource Identifiers). *A Link Service* fetches target URIs for the concepts associated with documents and displays the links, supported by the reasoning of the Ontology Service.

Semantic annotations in COHSE refer to the process of identifying and associating ontological concepts with documents. These semantic metadata are not embedded in the documents. It is a Link Base that maintains the mapping from target links to concepts by storing: the URL of the document, an XPointer expression indicating the fragment of the resource being annotated, a simple textual description of the annotations, the DAML+OIL concept associated with the annotation, and the ontology selected for this annotation. This guarantees that in the process of conceptual linking, the retrieval of target links is based on explicit ontology context.

The Link Service in COHSE has the basic task of generating and presenting links to Web pages on behalf of both authors and readers. When viewing a document COHSE, the Link Service obtains the concepts that will form the link source anchors either through the *lexicon*, which holds some language terms and their mappings to the ontological concepts loaded by the Ontology Service; or through *semantic annotations*. After identifying all the concepts in the page, the Link Service in COHSE contacts the Annotation Service to identify target

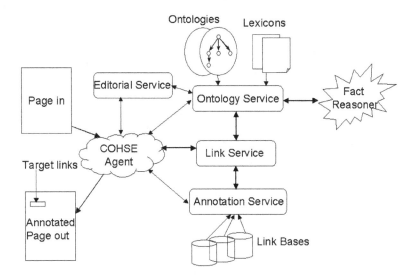

Fig. 4. The COHSE architecture.

URLs with corresponding concepts, as well as subsuming and subsumed concepts inferred by the Ontology Service.

The system employs either a specialist browser (based on Mozilla[4]) or a proxy through which all http requests are routed. In the Mozilla version, the DOM is manipulated to present the inferred links; in the proxy version the service creates a new document.

3.1   Generating Links

There are two types of entry point mechanisms to access the concepts that will form the link source anchors within a document:

1. Through the use of some language terms within the document, held in a lexicon, mapped to the concepts within an ontology provided by the Ontology Service. For example, the word *probeSetId* maps to the concept *Affymetrix_probe_set_id*. The relevant concepts in the ontology can then be used to determine appropriate targets for links out of the given document.
2. Through the use of explicitly asserted ontological annotations on regions of the document provided by an annotation service, e.g. a region is annotated directly with the concept *lymphocyte*. This approach relies on the ability to annotate resources with semantic metadata – where by semantic metadata we mean the explicit binding of concepts to resources rather than the use of terms and words as simple proxies for the concepts.

---

[4] http://www.mozilla.org

Key to the novelty of the COHSE approach is the provision of an *editorial component* within the agent. This component uses information within the ontology (such as hierarchical classification) in order to determine whether the links are suitable or to perhaps expand or cull the set of possible targets. Figure 4 shows a simplified view of the basic architecture of the system. The explicit annotations can then help guide the editorial component in its linking strategy. For example, if a passage in a web page has been annotated as being about a particular subject, say *Sequence_alignment*, the editorial component may know that there are certain terms that should be focused on within the context of that annotation (say the term *pair-wise*) – an example of an agent using semantic information to make decisions as to its behaviour.

Once an ontology is loaded, the COHSE agent contacts the Ontology Service to obtain a list of terms that are used in the lexicon to represent concepts in the ontology. One concept usually has more than one language terms corresponding to it. For example, the concept of *researcher* may have different expressions of researcher in different languages or different ways of capitalization. With the help of the lexicon we map all these into one concept *researcher*. When a new web page is viewed by COHSE, the agent grasps all the words in the page. For each word that corresponds to the term in the lexicon, the agent associates the concept with it. At the same time the agent contacts the Annotation Service to determine whether any region in the document has been annotated with any concept. Having identified all the concepts in the page, the agent contacts the Annotation Service to identify target links to other URLs with corresponding concepts as inferred by the Ontology Service using an inference reasoning service for the concepts provided by the FaCT reasoner [18]. Consequently, we are able to link web pages together based on the concepts associated with its documents. By changing the ontology we change the link anchors and link targets for the same web pages, getting different link *views* over those resources.

When the semantically annotated provenance logs are viewed through COHSE, the Link Service can identify bioinformatics concepts from the provenance log supported by the lexicon and query all the target URIs for each concept from the link base. In this way, a Web of provenance logs is built by semantically linked together. An example result is shown in Fig 5. The bioinformatics concept for the input data, 1020_s_at, — *Affymetrix_probe_set_id* — is attached to the provenance log. Since provenance logs are linked together based on the annotated semantic concepts, instead of the same data values in the logs, scientists are able to navigate from the current log to others which also use data of the type *Affymetrix_probe_set_ids* or its parent concept *Gene_id*, either as an input or an output. Using the ontology structure, links to subsumed and subsuming concepts can be fetched, supported by the reasoning ability of the Ontology Service of COHSE. Thus, users can browse the Web of provenance starting from provenance logs invoking *sequence alignment* services, to provenance logs invoking *BLAST* services or other *multiple sequence alignment services*, both of which are subsumed concepts of *sequence alignment*.

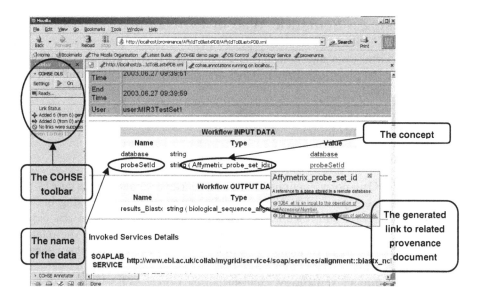

Fig. 5. Provenance discovery through semantic generation of links between provenance logs.

This Semantic Web of provenance is not limited to just provenance logs. COHSE can provide links from provenance logs to any document that can be displayed in a web browser: from a researcher's HTML home page, to a Word document or a PDF file. For example, from a workflow provenance log having invoked a *sequence alignment* service by a human geneticist, users can find links to the home page of this person describing his or her research activities in human genetics; and to a PDF file about *BLAST*, which introduces sequence alignment, etc. We imported the Gene Ontology into COHSE, for example, and were immediately able to present hyperlinks between documents based on shared GO terms.

By changing the annotation ontology, scientists can also discover computational resources beyond provenance logs. For example, when choosing viewing the Web of provenance logs with the *generic* ontology, a biologist can query the other logs that also performed upon the Grave's disease or upon the Williams-Beuren syndrome. If interested, he/she can also check out how other scientists performed the experiments which have a similar research hypothesis as his/hers. When the *biological* ontology is chosen, a higher level linking between these logs can be obtained. A biologists can query all the provenance logs which use a *Gene_id* as an input, instead of a bioinformatics term *Affymetrix_probe_set_id* (since *Affymetrix_probe_set_id* is a kind of *Gene_id*). The more general term maybe more comprehensible to a pure biologist, as opposed to a bioinformatician.

Thus this semantically linked Web of provenance logs can help answer the knowledge level questions raised in Sect 1.

4 Realising a Semantic Web of Provenance

Here we describe what and how ontologies are used to annotate the provenance logs and how the process provenance logs are semi-automatically populated with semantic concepts.

4.1 Domain Ontologies

We used three categories of ontologies, built with DAML+OIL:

- **Generic Ontology**, mainly formalizes concepts about organization, people, research topic and publishing, which supports general linking between provenance logs and documents, like experimental notes, research papers; and links between users who executed the workflows based on the relationships of their organizations or research topics. This small ontology shows a similar schema to the Dublin Core [19].
- **Bioinformatics Ontology**, conceptualizes a precise classification of bioinformatics data, web services and workflows. Services and data concepts are classified in multiple ways, for example, bioinformatics services can be classified by operation (alignment, pairwise, multiple), by the type of data source (protein, nucleotide, sequence) or by algorithm (SmithWaterman, BLAST [16].
- **Biological Ontology**, is based on the TAMBIS (Transparent Access to Bioinformatics Information Sources)[5] ontology. This ontology is used to annotate data with biological concepts, like *protein*, *acid* and *sequence*. Though large, well-established molecular ontologies as Gene Ontology [20] already exist, they mainly formalize specific data instances instead of more abstract types of data, like the biological entities processed by the bioinformatics Web services used in [my]Grid.

4.2 Acquiring the Semantic Annotations

As described in Sect 2, the process provenance logs are automatically recorded by the Freefluo workflow engine. The Freefluo workflow enactment engine is neutral about the services it enacts and only deals with WSDL (Web Service Definition Language) [21]. The ontological information in the ws-info files was not passed through the Freefluo engine to emerge in the logs or attached to the data, as shown in the Fig 2. So no domain semantics are associated with provenance entities even though the semantic information is available in ws-info files.

Here we extend the role of these ws-info files to provide domain semantics for provenance entities. This abandoned information is recovered by a post-processing annotation phase, as highlighted in the dashed box in Fig 2. From a close study of a ws-info file and its corresponding provenance log, shown in Fig 6, the semantic concept for the data 1020_s_at recorded in the provenance log can

---

[5] http://img.cs.man.ac.uk/stevens/tambis-oil.html

be retrieved from the ws-info file as *Affymetrix_probe_set_id*, based on the name of the data entity — *probeSetId*. While querying the corresponding ws-info files, the XML provenance logs can be semantically integrated with ontological concepts, defined mainly in the bioinformatics ontology. In this way, we have entries into the concepts with the instances of concepts in the provenance logs. Thus, we extend the process provenance log with a process of semantic annotation performed after the workflow run and before the provenance document is archived in the mIR, ready to be viewed by COHSE. In our prototype shown here in Fig 5 we have embedded the concepts within the document; other implementation store the concept externally using the COHSE Link Base. When the number of provenance logs increases, a Semantic Web of provenance is automatically and dynamically added to by this automatic annotation process.

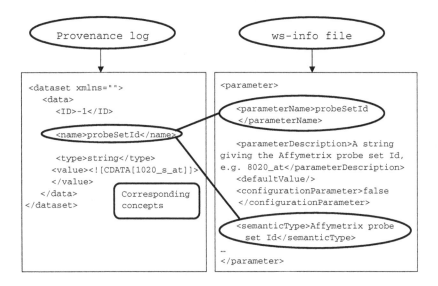

Fig. 6. The ontology concept in the corresponding ws-info of a provenance log. The annotation process transfers the concept from the ws-info file to the provenance log.

Despite the promise of this approach, there are problems. Semantically linking provenance logs based on a single *bioinformatics* ontology shows limitations for some of our users. Instead of viewing provenance logs from a bioinformatics point of view, they are more interested in more purely biological view of provenance, using semantics like *protein kinase, DNA binding, transcription,* or *carbohydrate metabolism,* alongside the bioinformatics or experimental methodological view of the data. This is because we can automatically annotate at the process and data level of provenance, but not the knowledge level.

We address this problem by semantically annotating provenance logs with *Biological* and *Generic* ontologies. This annotation is mainly a manual process. It depends on the authors of annotations to discover the *biological* relationship between data, like a DNA sequence *encodes* a protein, or a gene *expresses* a protein, a semantic property from the Biological ontology. It also depends on authors' to identify semantic concepts from documents and associate discovered resources, like reference literatures, with provenance logs. This handcrafted process has high requirements for expert knowledge of authors and demands significant effort. Also how much we should trust the manual annotations contributed by distributed users is still an open research topic. Figure 7 shows the results of linking two pages with biological ontologies.

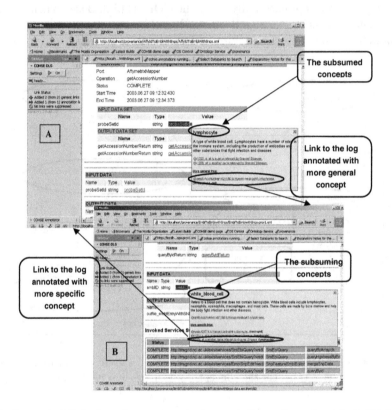

Fig. 7. Generated links based on conceptual annotations. Page A probeSetId is annotated with the concept *lymphocyte*, generating links to other pages annotated by lymphocyte and pages annotated with more general concept including page B annotated with *white_blood_cell*. Page B emblID annotated with the concept *white_blood_cell* generating links to other pages annotated by the same concept and pages annotated with more specialised concept including page A annotated with *lymphocyte*

5   Related Work

Several ontology-driven annotation tools are available, such as Magpie [22] and MnM [23]. Though Magpie is a very light annotation tool, the only annotation mechanism Magpie supports is through lexicon mapping. If we want to apply Magpie to annotating the provenance logs, first we have to populate the lexicon. But, it is difficult to build a lexicon of mapping each piece of computation data to its corresponding concept. This lexicon has to be updated each time a new piece of data needs to be annotated. MnM can support marking-up the document with semantic metadata, but its linking service can not provide target links to the subsuming/subsumed concept of the annotated concept. COHSE, on the other hand, supported by an ontology reasoner, is able to present target links to both subsuming and subsumed concepts of the annotated concept.

There are some other projects supporting knowledge discovery from provenance logs from different approaches. The Provenance Aware Service Oriented Architecture (PASOA) project aims to automatically record provenance logs and apply some reasoning algorithms over provenance logs by a provenance service client and server [24]. Their provenance logs mainly trace the process of service invocations generating a particular data in the Grid for a workflow enactment, which are similar to our process level provenance logs. They provide a tree-like provenance browsing environment, in a XML format, organized by the services and data in a workflow, without direct support for browsing linked provenance in a usable interface for e-Scientists. The focus of this project is to discover the quality and accuracy of data and services, and automatic re-execution of services in the context of e-Science based on provenance logs, instead of the semantic relationships among provenance logs, as in ᵐʸGrid.

Chimera [6] records virtual data provenance to discover available methods and fulfill on-demand data generation in the Grid computing environment. Chimera comprises two main components: a virtual data catalog and a virtual data language interpreter. Virtual Data Catalog records transformation, derivation and data underpinned by a compact virtual data schema, which has a direct support for data linking. Though ᵐʸGrid does not have direct data derivation graph in the first release, the current ᵐʸGrid achieves similar results by building a RDF data provenance graph. Chimera Virtual Data Language supports data definition and query statements, written in XML. The current querying over provenance logs is mainly keyword based, rather than from semantic point of view. Chimera contains the mechanism to locate the "recipe" to produce a given logical file, in the form of an abstract program execution graph, to support job scheduling and planning in the Grid computing environment.

6   Discussion and Future Work

By annotating provenance logs with concepts drawn from the ᵐʸGrid ontology, we built a dynamically generated hypertext of provenance documents, data,

---

[6] http://www.griphyn.org/chimera/.

services and workflows based on their associated concepts and reasoning over the ontology. We demonstrated a first implementation of semantically linking provenance logs and showed its utility in enhancing the acquisition of knowledge from data generated in ^{my}Grid. During this process, however, we came across two kinds of problems:

Knowledge provenance acquisition. The approach uses the bioinformatics ontology to annotated provenance logs with process provenance. In this way we hoped to simply reuse the bioinformatics ontology for a different task. However, it was not as reusable as first hoped in that it was good for discovering services but poor for linking logs. This ontology is too abstract to annotate data based on the *value* of the data. It only supports annotation based on the *type* of the data. Users can associate a bioinformatics concept — *Affymetrix_probe_set_id* — with the data 1020_s_at that is explicitly specified with this semantic type; but they can not say this data is a *lymphocyte*. This requires high level of text-mining technique to recognize the semantic meaning of this data or depends on time-consuming and error-prone manual annotations.

Difficulty of obtaining semantic annotations. Because our workflow enactment engine, Freefluo, is generic and neutral about the services that it enacts, and it does not preserve the ontological annotations associated with the services and their parameters. Thus we were throwing away valuable semantic annotations and were forced to recover them through post-analysis.

The work described here relates to ^{my}Grid version 1. In version 2 a Taverna Scufl workbench is extended to replace the previous workbench. It runs a workflow execution based on the XScufl script, supported by the underlying Freefluo enactment engine. Bioinformaticians can search for workflows by keywords as well as semantic concepts in Taverna, to obtain a XScufl script and a workflow graph as a recipe for experiment design. The semantic annotations for services and workflows are a) kept in the registry (for 3rd party semantics) and b) encapsulated in the metadata of services, identified by a Life Science Identifiers (LSIDs) [25]. LSID is a special Universal Resource Name (URN) proposed by the I3C consortium. The LSID resolution protocol promises persistent identification of objects. ^{my}Grid is extending the mIR with a LSID authority, to assign and resolve the LSID for each ^{my}Grid entity. The mIR exposes both a LSID data interface and a LSID metadata interface for data and metadata in the repository, which are moving to the RDF format. Thus given an LSID, both the data and its metadata can be retrieved from the mIR by resolving the LSID.

Taverna generates RDF provenance logs, which is used as a model to integrate more expressible ontological concepts with experiment resources. RDF is recommended by the W3C consortium as one of the core technologies for the Semantic Web. Each RDF triple consists of a subject, a predicate and an object, with the predicate linking the two others. A set of RDF triples forms a RDF graph model. RDF can identify resources by URI, of which URN is a type. Thus RDF can support building a graph of ^{my}Grid entities, identified by their LSIDs.

Currently the RDF provenance logs are being imported to Haystack[7], which provides a RDF file navigation and visualisation environment. In Haystack we achieve providing different views of linked provenance logs according to users' requirements. As a flexible data model, RDF can also be compatible with the syntax of XML and OWL, which promises the compatibility of our extension with existing ^{my}Grid provenance and the feasibility of the integration of ontological concepts with data.

Even if it becomes easier to identify semantic metadata for experiment resources, it is still not straightforward to annotate provenance logs with semantics. Logs are generated by the Freefluo workflow engine, which neither cares nor knows about semantics. One possible approach can be to keep the semantics with service descriptions and input parameters intact before and during the workflow execution in the workflow engine. At the end of the execution, semantics for outputs are queried from the service descriptions and attached to the result data. Thus in the end we can have semantics for services and data in the provenance logs. Another is to post-annotate the logs as what we did in the first release of ^{my}Grid, but the semantics (as part of metadata) are identified by resolving the LSIDs which are used to identify experiment resources.

The outcome of our experiments suggests that a dynamically generated Semantic Web of provenance records is a viable possibility. However, as with all the Semantic Web applications, the old story of where to get the annotations and what are the effective ontologies still stands, even for this closed problem in a closed domain.

Acknowledgments. The ^{my}Grid project, grant number GR/R67743, is funded under the UK e-Science programme by the EPSRC. The authors would like to acknowledge other members of the ^{my}Grid team for their contributions; and Yeliz Yeslida for her help in getting COHSE up and running. We also thank Mark Greenwood and Chris Wroe for their help during our annotation implementation process.

References

1. Fox, G., Walker, D.: e-Science gap analysis. Technical report, Indiana University and Cardiff University, UK e-Science Center (2003)
2. Stevens, R., Glover, K., Greenhalgh, C., Jennings, C., Li, P., Radenkovic, M., Wipat, A.: Performing in silico experiments on the Grid: a users perspective. In Cox, S.J., ed.: UK e-Science All Hands Meeting 2003 Editors. (2003) 43–50
3. Stevens, R., Tipney, H., Wroe, C., Oinn, T., Senger, M., Lord, P., Goble, C., Brass, A., Tassabehji, M.: Exploring Williams-Beuren Syndrome using mygrid. In: Proceedings of 12th International Conference on Intelligent Systems in Molecular Biology. (2004)
4. Foster, I., Kesselman, C., eds.: Blueprint for a new computing infrastructure . Second edn. Morgan Kaufmann Publishers (2003)

---

[7] http://haystack.lcs.mit.edu/

5. Moreau, L., Miles, S., Goble, C., Greenwood, M., Dialani, V., Addis, M., Alpdemir, N., Cawley, R., De Roure, D., Ferris, J., Gaizauskas, R., Glover, K., Greenhalgh, C., Li, P., Liu, X., Lord, P., Luck, M., Marvin, D., Oinn, T., Paton, N., Pettifer, S., Radenkovic, M.V., Roberts, A., Robinson, A., Rodden, T., Senger, M., Sharman, N., Stevens, R., Warboys, B., Wipat, A., Wroe, C.: On the use of agents in a bioInformatics Grid. In: The Third IEEE/ACM CCGRID'2003 Workshop on Agent Based Cluster and Grid Computing, Tokyo, Japan (2003) 653–661

6. Klyne, G., Carroll, J.J.: Resource description framework (RDF): concepts and abstract syntax. W3C Proposed Recommendation. Available at http://www.w3.org/TR/2003/PR-rdf-concepts-20031215/ (2003)

7. Lord, P., Wroe, C., Stevens, R., Goble, C., Miles, S., Moreau, L., Decker, K., Payne, T., Papay, J.: Semantic and personalised service discovery. In: Proceedings of Workshop on Knowledge Grid and Grid Intelligence (KGGI'03), in conjunction with 2003 IEEE/WIC International Conference on Web Intelligence/Intelligent Agent Technology. (2003) 100 – 107

8. Addis, M., Ferris, J., Greenwood, M., Li, P., Marvin, D., Oinn, T., Wipat, A.: Experiences with e-Science workflow specification and enactment in bioinformatics. In Cox, S.J., ed.: Proc UK e-Science All Hands Meeting 2003. (2003) 459–466

9. Greenwood, M., Goble, C., Stevens, R., Zhao, J., Addis, M., Marvin, D., Moreau, L., Oinn, T.: Provenance of e-science experiments - experience from bioinformatics. In Cox, S.J., ed.: UK e-Science All Hands Meeting 2003 Editors. (2003) 223–226

10. Krishna, A., Tan, V., Lawley, R., Miles, S., Moreau, L.: mygrid notification service. In Cox, S.J., ed.: UK e-Science All Hands Meeting 2003 Editors. (2003) 475–482

11. Horrocks, I.: DAML+OIL: a Description Logic for the Semantic Web. The IEEE Computer Society Technical Committee on Data Engineering 25 (2002) 4–9

12. Horrocks, I., Patel-Schneider, P.F.: A proposal for an owl rules language (2004)

13. Baader, F., Horrocks, I., Sattler, U.: Description Logics as ontology languages for the Semantic Web. In Hutter, D., Stephan, W., eds.: Festschrift in honor of Jörg Siekmann. Lecture Notes in Artificial Intelligence, Springer (2003) To appear.

14. Wroe, C., Goble, C., Greenwood, M., Lord, P., Miles, S., Papay, J., Payne, T., Moreau, L. In: Automating experiments using semantic data on a bioinformatics Grid. Volume 19. IEEE Intelligent Systems, Special Issue on E-Science (2004) 48–55

15. Ankolekar, A.: The DAML Services Coalition DAML-S: Web Service description for the Semantic Web. In: The First International Semantic Web Conference (ISWC), Sardinia (Italy) (2002)

16. Wroe, C., Stevens, R., Goble, C., Greenwood, M.: A suite of DAML+OIL ontologies to describe bioinformatics Web Services and data. International Journal of Cooperative Information Systems 12 (2003) 197–224

17. Bechhofer, S., Goble, C., Carr, L., Kampa, S., Hall, W., Roure, D.D.: COHSE: Conceptual Open Hypermedia Service. Volume 96. IOS Press, Frontiers in Artifical Intelligence and Applications (2003)

18. Horrocks, I.: The FaCT system. In de Swart, H., ed.: Automated Reasoning with Analytic Tableaux and Related Methods: International Conference Tableaux'98. Number 1397 in Lecture Notes in Artificial Intelligence, Springer-Verlag (1998) 307–312

19. Weibel, S., Kunze, J., Lagoze, C., Wolf, M.: Dublin Core metadata for resource discovery. In: The Internet Society. (1998)

20. Ashburner, M., et al: Gene Ontology: tool for the unification of biology. Nature Genetics 25 (2000) 25–29

21. Christensen, E., Curbera, F., Meredith, G., Weerawarana, S.: Web Services Description Language (WSDL) 1.1 (2001) W3C Note.
22. Dzbor, M., Domingue, J.B., Motta, E.: Magpie - towards a semantic web browser. In: The 2nd International. Semantic Web Conference, Florida US (2003) 255 – 265
23. Vargas-Vera, M., Motta, E., Domingue, J., Lanzoni, M., Stutt, A., Ciravegna, F.: Mnm: ontology driven semi-automatic and automatic support for semantic markup. In Gomez-Perez, A., ed.: The 13th International Conference on Knowledge Engineering and Management (EKAW 2002). (2002)
24. Szomszor, M., Moreau, L.: Recording and reasoning over data provenance in Web and Grid Services. In: ODBASE. (2003)
25. Clark, T., Martin, S., Liefeld, T.: Globally distributed object identification for biological knowledgebases. Briefings in Bioinformatics **5** (2004) 59–70

Emergent Semantics: Towards Self-Organizing Scientific Metadata

Bill Howe, Kuldeep Tanna, Paul Turner, and David Maier

OGI School of Science & Engineering at
Oregon Health & Science University
Beaverton, Oregon
{bill,kuldeep,maier}@cse.ogi.edu, pturner@ccalmr.ogi.edu

Abstract. Tasked with designing a metadata management system for a large scientific data repository, we find that the customary database application development procedure exhibits several disadvantages in this environment. Data cannot be accessed until the system is fully designed and implemented, specialized data modeling skills are required to design an appropriate schema, and once designed, such schemas are intolerant of change. We minimize setup and maintenance costs by automating the database design, data load, and data transformation tasks. Data creators are responsible only for extracting data from heterogeneous sources according to a simple RDF-based data model. The system then loads the data into a generic RDBMS schema. Additional grouping structures to support query formulation and processing are discovered by the system or defined by the users via a web interface. Discovered and imposed structures constitute emergent semantics for otherwise disorganized information.

1   Introduction

When a group of environmental scientists requested our help designing a metadata management solution for their scientific data repository, we speculated that the database community's flagship technology, relational database management systems, would solve the problem neatly. We changed our assessment after further investigation, judging that the high cost of database deployment and maintenance made the likelihood of adoption rather low. As an alternative, we present a metadata collection, organization, and query architecture that lowers the cost of entry by reordering steps in the database design methodology. Metadata is gathered and loaded immediately using a simple RDF-based data model. After the data is loaded, they are partitioned according to their *signature*, which is inferred by the system. Additional grouping structures (views) can be defined by users through a web interface. Organizing data via signatures results in a form of schema that facilitates query expression and allows efficient query evaluation. By performing schema design semi-automatically only after the data is loaded, we sidestep the primary obstacles to database adoption in a scientific environment. Additionally, the schema structures we discover can be adapted to changes in the metadata stream, avoiding schema evolution problem.

M. Bouzeghoub et al. (Eds.): ICSNW 2004, LNCS 3226, pp. 177–198, 2004.
© IFIP International Federation for Information Processing 2004

The context for our work is the CORIE Environmental Observation and Forecasting System [4], designed to support study of the physical processes of the Columbia River estuary. The CORIE system both measures and simulates the physical properties of the estuary, generating 5GB of data and over 20,000 data products and subproducts daily, including visualizations, aggregated results and derived datasets. The data products are consumed for many purposes, including salmon habitability studies and environmental impact assessments. The number of files in the repository is around 6 million and growing by tens of thousands a day. The existing repository is organized as a collection of directory structures on a Linux filesystem. Descriptions for these files are found encoded in the file name, in the content of the file itself, or in accompanying files.

For example, the data products generated from the simulation outputs have descriptive information encoded within their filenames. Figure 1 shows an example of descriptions found in and around the target file.

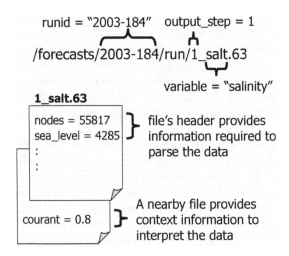

Fig. 1. Metadata encoded in file names, headers, paths, "nearby" files.

The data repository is exhibiting growth in both the number and types of files stored. We have encountered at least the following kinds of files:

- Observation data downloaded from field sensors.
- Simulation inputs downloaded from external servers, in varying stages of pre-processing.
- Simulation parameter files.
- Simulation control information such as logs, status flags, and saved checkpoints.
- Raw simulation outputs in multiple formats.
- Derived data products including reduced datasets, images, visualizations, reports, and aggregations of multiple datasets.

Additionally, there is a growing need for access to these data by people other than the data creators; the heterogeneity of the sources of metadata across these file types is an impediment.

To support general data access for non-expert users through these *scattered* metadata, we describe two alternatives. Our initial plan was to build a straightforward database application. However, there was a possibility that such a system would be difficult to deploy and maintain without considerable ongoing help from us. After further thought, we aimed higher: a system for automatically and adaptively organizing metadata.

1.1 The "Obvious" Solution

Our first thought was to define a schema to house the metadata in an RDBMS. Next, data creators populate the schema by inserting a tuple for every file in the repository. Then, a database application is constructed and tested for searching the database.

There are several disadvantages to this approach. The data creators are not necessarily data modelers; schema design requires somewhat specialized skills. Even proficient data modelers would have trouble: The schema should be tuned to declared use cases, but since new users are coming online continuously, not all use cases are known at design time. We could undertake the modeling ourselves, but the effort would still require a lot of interaction with the scientists, who do not have much time to spare.

Data loading is also problematic; we cannot ask the scientists to manually enter 6 million tuples. Portions of the data-loading task can be automated since the data creators are often proficient programmers, but their knowledge does not necessarily include RDBMS languages or APIs. Data loading constitutes a significant up-front cost to this approach which must be paid before any benefit is realized, so it is difficult to persuade the scientists to diligently record metadata during the interim. Accurate test data with which to proof the system is also needed but has an even lower priority.

Once the data is loaded, the schema may be difficult to validate since the database is free to diverge from what is encoded in the filenames, file content, etc. Database APIs and a specialized schema constitute a "wide" interface between data creators and metadata managers: Small requirements changes can result in significant interface changes. A question of responsibility also arises: if a new metadata field is required, who must update the database and possibly modify or reload data?

1.2 An Alternative

Since the metadata sources may change frequently, those responsible for the changes should also be responsible for their extraction. If we perform the extraction, we are obligated to maintain the code even as the underlying requirements and metadata encodings change. If the scientists perform the database load, they will be responsible for maintaining the interface as the schema undergoes revision. We made the observation that decoupling metadata extraction from the rest of the system was important for robustness.

In our approach, the interface between metadata extraction and database loading is as narrow as possible. Data creators extract metadata "descriptors" and deliver them through a very simple data model based on RDF. Descriptors are extracted using *collection scripts* written by the data creators (or others) in their choice of programming language. These descriptors are loaded as-is into a generic RDBMS schema. Generic schemas are difficult to query and browse, and usually exhibit poor performance. We therefore partition the data into groups according to patterns found in the metadata. These groups act as a schema to expose structure, simplify query expression, enable browsing, and improve response time. Additional groupings of data can be defined by users through a web interface providing a personalized view of the repository.

This approach offers several advantages. A narrower interface between metadata managers and data creators is valuable: To accommodate changing metadata requirements, simply update the collection scripts and the system reacts appropriately. Metadata can be harvested and exploited prior to finalizing a schema, delivering benefits much sooner. A single, generic metadata delivery interface, controlled by collection scripts, can both load new data and update existing data. Since the schema is built dynamically, new views can be easily defined to support new users or new tasks. We use the term *emergent semantics* to describe the paradigm of harvesting data first and organizing it second. By organizing and publishing the gathered metadata back to users, they retain responsibility and control over validation and adjustments. The collection scripts used to gather metadata can be modified and re-executed to update the database.

Several challenges must be overcome to realize these benefits. Queries over a generic RDF schema are expensive and difficult to express. Techniques for identifying patterns in the metadata stream must be devised. Once patterns in the metadata are found, we must convert them into structures (signatures and signature extetnts) to facilitate query expression and processing. Users may also wish to impose their own structure on the data. As new users and new use cases are introduced, requirements may change. If the metadata stream changes, can the previously found structures adapt? In some cases, users may wish to promote previously found structures into hard constraints, rejecting non-conforming metadata. This paper presents an architecture that takes initial steps towards resolving these issues.

2   Harvesting Metadata

To extract metadata from scattered sources, we rely on collection scripts to assign $\langle property, value \rangle$ pairs to each file. The output of collection scripts are then interpreted as $\langle subject, property, object \rangle$ triples. In our application, collection scripts are written primarily, but not exclusively, by the environmental scientists.

They are proficient programmers and are most familiar with the file description encoding schemes at the sources.

Collection scripts may be written in any language. To fire the collection scripts and harvest the metadata we provide a program *harvest*. The harvest program accepts a set of *applicability rules* and a target directory as input, and produces $\langle file, property, value \rangle$ triples for each file in the directory. An applicability rule consists of a regular expression, the path to a collection script, and a path to an interpreter for the collection script, if necessary. The harvest program recursively walks the target directory, testing the rules for each file. A rule is activated if its regular expression accepts the string formed by the path and file name being tested. For each activated rule, the program executes the appropriate collection script. Multiple rules may fire for the same file, and the same collection script might be triggered by multiple rules.

For the file in Figure 1, a simple rule matching the ".63" extension triggers a collection script that emits triples from the file name (e.g., `<1_salt.63, variable, salinity>`), from the content (e.g., `<1_salt.63, nodes, 55817>`), and from nearby files (`<1_salt.63, implicitness, 0.8>`). Alternatively, these three sources could have been accessed by three separate collection scripts (requiring three rules), all triggered by the same regular expression. Rules give collection script writers significant flexibility with regard to software design. For example, these three collection scripts may be written by different authors, at different locations, with different metadata requirements.

Each script is expected to accept one command line argument, a file path, and call a function `Assert(property, value, type)` for each metadata item it wishes to record for the file. The `Assert` function is provided by the system for a few languages (Perl, Python, C). If scripts are written in a language for which the assert function has not been defined, the script may simply emit the property, value, and type arguments to standard out in a comma-delimited format.

Initiating a separate process for each script execution is prohibitively expensive, as there are around 20,000 files per run and a large repository of existing runs. To improve performance, the harvest program uses embedded interpreters for the two most popular languages, Perl and Python. For simplicity, the users still write their code as if it is to be run from the command line; the harvest program wraps each script in a virtual environment and executes it in the same address space.

The `Assert` function, called from within a collection script, emits a triple through temporary files or stdout. The stream of triples produced by a series of calls made by amultiple collection scripts is then delivered to a relational database for analysis, as described in Section 4.

3   Modeling Metadata

To interpret extracted metadata, we must choose a data model to capture the descriptions. Rich data models that can capture complex relationships, constraints, and operations allow the same real world concept to be modeled in many different ways. To choose an appropriate translation into the data model's structures, modeling experts meet with domain experts, clarify the details, and construct a prototype. This offline coordination is expensive in terms of time required, and usually involves several iterations. Other confounding issues impede the data modeling efforts: dirty data, redundancy, ambiguity. Finally, if changes are expected to be frequent, this design process might be repeated several times.

We sidestep these issues at this stage by adopting a very simple data model. Very little transformation need be performed and very few initial modeling decisions need be made to get the metadata recorded and queryable. Once the descriptions are in a uniform, machine-readable format, richer modeling features can be applied. Figure 2 contrasts the manual effort required by the two approaches. In Figure 2, the term "Signature Extent" refers to the grouping structures inferred by the system and will be explained in section 4.2.

To accommodate the heterogeneity of the data sources and simplify the scientists' collection scripts, we adopt a data model based on the Resource Description Framework (RDF) [7] consisting of $\langle subject, property, object \rangle$ triples. We sacrifice expressive power for simplicity and uniformity: Simple facts can be recorded immediately without regard to overall structure.

Of course, the additional expressive power of richer data models is important for query formulation and processing. To recover these benefits, we must derive relationships encoded in the $\langle subject, property, object \rangle$ triples. For example, if several files all have the same set of properties, we can group the files together to simplify queries and improve their performance.

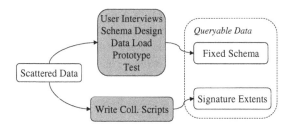

Fig. 2. Two methods of organizing data with different amounts of offline activity. Signature Extents are a form of schema inferred by the system.

3.1   RDF: Shortest Route to Machine-Processable Metadata

We have been using the RDF terminology of "subject," "property," and "object." The word "object" connotes a fundamental feature of the RDF data model: Properties can reference arbitrary resources, making the overall data model a graph. This feature distinguishes RDF from tree-based data models, e.g., LDAP [17].

RDF was designed to enable interoperability and automation by adorning web resources with simple machine-processable metadata. Our domain is similar: We adorn files, the substrate of observation and simulation systems, with metadata to enable access.

Formally, an RDF graph is a set of triples of the form (s, p, o). The property (or *predicate*) p is drawn from a set of Uniform Resource Identifiers R. The subject s is drawn from the union of R and a set of *blank nodes* B. The object o is drawn from the union of R, B, and a set of literals L. Blank nodes act as existentially quantified variables over the domain of a particular graph. RDF graphs can be drawn as a graph using the union of R, B, and L as nodes and drawing an edge for every triple. Edges are labeled with the property URI, and non-blank nodes are labeled with either the URI or the string literal in quotes. Blank nodes are, as might be expected, unlabeled.

We forego the use of more advanced features of RDF, such as RDF Schema for defining classes and class membership, and reification for asserting RDF statements about other RDF statements. Use of these features would again require the up-front modeling effort we hope to avoid. We do allow literals to carry a type as supported in RDF. Note that our interest is in the RDF model rather than the XML-based syntax for RDF [16].

Even without the advanced features, the RDF data model can be used to capture the information expressed in much richer data models, though redundancy is often introduced, and query facilities are sacrificed.

3.2 Interpreting RDF in Our Application

To model our metadata in RDF, we must first specify the sets R, B, and L. Construct a set F of URIs corresponding to files in the domain of interest. Construct a set P consisting of properties associated with a file in F. The set of URIs R is $F \cup P$. The set of literals L are simply string constants. Collection scripts will only emit triples (f, p, o) where $f \in F$, $p \in P$, and $o \in L \cup F$.

Figure 3 shows an example of an RDF graph used to model our domain.

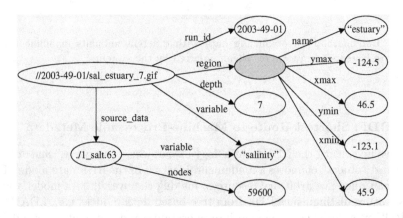

Fig. 3. An example of RDF used to model files and properties in our domain.

The RDF data model allows a URI to appear as both a property and an object in two triples x and y. In our application, however, property URIs may not appear as objects, though file URIs may. Files that reference other files are especially useful for tracking *provenance*; data products can reference the datasets they are derived from, and datasets can reference the executable of the simulation code used to generate it as well as the inputs.

The graph structure of RDF is one prominent feature RDF; the other is the concept of blank nodes. Blank nodes are used to model anonymous structured types. In Figure 3, we use a blank node (the gray oval) to capture the idea that the region named "estuary" corresponds to the bounding coordinates xmin = 45.9, ymin = -123.1, xmax = 46.5, ymax = -124.5.

By our definitions, collection scripts are not capable of emitting blank nodes directly. To retain simplicity, elements of structured property values are attached to the files directly, a decision that introduces redundancy but retains simple semantics for the collection scripts. In Section 4.4, we will describe how these structured types can be correctly abstracted *after* extraction and load.

4   Analyzing RDF Using RDBMS

We have modeled our domain of files and metadata using RDF. Our use of RDBMS technology to store and manipulate RDF data is the subject of this section. As reported in the literature, RDBMS are an appropriate choice for managing RDF data. However, since we have no schema information at this stage, we adopt a generic schema that captures the RDF triples directly. This approach has been called the *vertical representation* [3], *generic schema*, or *edge schema* [11] in the literature for various data models and applications. We discuss querying the data in terms of SQL: Query languages for RDF have been proposed [18,25], but either tend to rely on schema information encoded as RDF Schema [8], or are based on subgraph matching for which scalability has not been demonstrated.

Two variants of the generic RDF schema appear in Figure 4a. A `Triples` table stores RDF triples in terms of string representations of the URIs. To improve performance, a `Resources` table might abstract the string representations of uris and leave integer keys in the `Triples` table for faster processing of set operations on resources (Figure 4b).

4.1   Performance

The use of a single table for storing the RDF graph faithfully supports the RDF specification, but makes queries over RDF difficult to write. For example, to retrieve all the files (subjects) which exhibit the properties `variable`, `region`, and `plottype`, 2 self-joins (in standard SQL) are required. Figure 5 shows the SQL for such a query over the schema of Figure 4a. To ask for files that exhibit an n-property signature, an $(n-1)$-way join is required. More generally, each property to be viewed (projection) or used to filter results (selection) contributes a join on

a)

Triples

subject	property	object
file://forecasts/2003-184/images/anim-sal_estuary_7.gif	property:region	estuary
file://forecasts/2003-184/images/anim-sal_estuary_7.gif	property:variable	salt
file://forecasts/2003-184/images/anim-sal_estuary_7.gif	property:plottype	animation
file://forecasts/2003-184/images/anim-sal_estuary_7.gif	property:source	file://forecasts/2003-184/run/1_salt.63

b)

Resources

id	uri
1	file://forecasts/2003-184/images/anim-sal_estuary_7.gif
2	file://forecasts/2003-184/run/1_salt.63
3	property:region
4	property:variable
5	property:plottype
6	property:source
7	estuary
8	salt
9	animation

Triples

subject	property	object
1	3	7
1	4	8
1	5	9
1	6	2

Fig. 4. Two possible schemas for modeling RDF in RDBMS.

```
SELECT  r.subject as file, r.object as region,
        p.object as plottype, v.object as variable
FROM    statements r, statements p, statements v
WHERE   r.subject = p.subject
  AND   p.subject = v.subject
  AND   r.property = 'property:region'
  AND   p.property = 'property:plottype'
  AND   v.property = 'property:variable'
```

Fig. 5. Simple SQL to find resources exhibiting properties `variable`, `region`, and `plot type`.

the `Triples` table. The SQL is awkward to generate or write, and performance is terrible with respect to the number of conditions. Our current database captures 30 million RDF triples describing 6 million files, so performance is important.

Using a single `Triples` table, we can express arbitrary RDF graphs. In practice however, we observe that the files have one of several *signatures*. For example, most data products derived from simulation output are associated with a variable (e.g., salinity, velocity, temperature), a region (e.g., estuary, far, plume), and plot type (e.g., isolines, transect, timeseries). Figure 6 shows a transect plot (a) and an isolines plot (b) for the salinity variable in the estuary region.

Each of these plots exhibit the three metadata attributes involved in the query of Figure 4. If this signature is common, we can improve performance by materializing the signature extent proactively, reducing the query to "SELECT * FROM <signature name>"

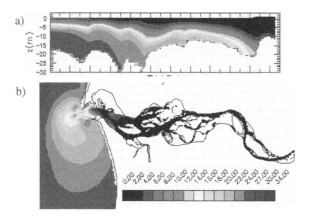

Fig. 6. Two data products from the CORIE simulation system.

4.2   Signatures

A *signature* is the set of properties used to describe a particular file. A *signature extent* is a set of files that all exhibit the same signature. Computing the extents involves finding the unique signatures exhibited in the current database instance of the `Triples` table. We materialize these extents as tables in the relational schema. This approach is only wise if the number of signatures is small relative to the number of files. Considering that there are intuitively related sets of files such as data products, simulation outputs, etc., this assumption appears valid. Note, however, that the number of signatures is not simply equal to the number of scripts. Multiple scripts, possibly written by different people, can fire for the same file. Further, nothing constrains a script to output the same properties for every file. For example, we use collection scripts that output different parameters depending on which version of the simulation is being considered.

Computing signatures is similar to extracting association rules in a data mining application. Instead of identifying which item groups tend to be found together in a single customer order, we find properties that tend to be found associated with a single file. However, we need not invoke the full power of data mining, since we are only interested in association rules of 100 percent confidence; data mining algorithms use sophisticated techniques to estimate the confidence level and prune the search space.

Computing the signatures might seem to require application code, but we can exploit set-valued attributes to express the computation using a dialect of SQL. We simulate set-valued attributes in Postgres [30] using sorted arrays. The SQL to compute all the unique signatures in the database is given in Figure 7. The outermost query simply projects out the signatures, removing duplicates. The `GROUP BY` operator in the nested query applies an aggregation function (`array_accum`) that constructs an array dynamically from the elements of the group. The result of the nested query is a set of (file, signature) pairs. To model

```
SELECT DISTINCT signature FROM (
  SELECT subject as file,
         array_accum(property) as signature
  FROM (
    SELECT DISTINCT subject, property
    FROM Triples
    ORDER BY subject, property
  )
  GROUP BY subject
)
```

Fig. 7. SQL to compute unique signatures.

sets correctly using arrays, we must remove duplicates and sort the elements; this is the purpose of the innermost query.

For each signature, a signature extent can be computed with attributes for each property in the signature. The materialized view can be computed using SQL of the form in Figure 5, but a much faster method again uses set-valued attributes and a *crosstab* operation. The crosstab operation is known by various names in the literature. The designers of the SchemaSQL language [20] propose a *fold* operator, and Online Analytical Processing (OLAP) systems include a CUBE operator [14].

The SQL in Figure 7 can be adjusted slightly to generate the profile for every subject in the triples table (Figure 8a) rather than the set of unique signatures. We can materialize this adjusted query, calling the materialized table FileSignatures. Now, for each unique signature s, we want to 1) find the set of file URIs F_s whose signature is s, 2) find the set of triples $\{(f,p,o) \mid f \in F_s\}$, 3) sort the results by subject and property[1], and 4) perform the crosstab operation to convert the properties into attribute names in the query results. Steps 1-3 are captured by the SQL in Figure 8b. The result of the crosstab is materialized as a signature extent and is available for further querying by users. This process is repeated for each signature inferred by the system.

This approach is far more efficient than the SQL in Figure 5, since that approach requires $O(n)$ joins, where n is the number of attributes in the signature. The crosstab algorithm is linear with respect to the number of files and the number of triples. Our focus in this paper is on semantics, but our experiments have shown that the improved query is over an order of magnitude faster.

Signatures provide an overview of the data collected with the harvest mechanism. Users can check their assumptions about the metadata that is collected by reviewing the set of signatures found and which signature a particular file exhibits. For example, in our domain, users expected that all files containing parameters to the simulation would have the same signature. However, two similar but distinct signatures were found by the system, exposing the fact that that

---

[1] The single-pass crosstab algorithm used requires that the data be sorted.

a)
```
SELECT subject,
       array_accum(property)
       as signature
FROM (
  SELECT subject, property
  FROM    Triples
  ORDER BY subject, property
)
GROUP BY subject
```

b)
```
SELECT t.subject,
       t.property,
       t.object
FROM    FileSignatures fs,
        Triples t
WHERE   fs.signature = <s>
  AND   fs.subject = t.subject
ORDER BY t.subject, t.property
```

Fig. 8. Partial SQL to compute signature extents. The relation FileSignatures in (b) is the result of query (a).

parameter files created for different versions of the code had a slightly different format. A new collection script to parse the older parameter files was created.

4.3   Update Semantics

So far, we have discussed how to efficiently compute signature extents from a large set of RDF triples, but how are these data to be maintained as the RDF stream changes? New simulations result in new files being delivered with potentially new signatures. As requirements change, existing collection scripts will evolve and new collection scripts will be written. New applicability rules may also be defined, causing existing collection scripts to operate on new files. In each of these situations, there are three classes of changes that must be accommodated: new files with potentially new signatures, new properties for existing files resulting in a change of signature, or new values for existing properties of existing files. How the system reacts to these possibilities is the subject of this section.

New Files. When new files are presented to the system, they may or may not exhibit a previously encountered signature. If they do, then a new tuple may be inserted into the appropriate signature extent, and no schema changes are required. If the signature has not been previously encountered, then a new signature extent can be created and a the new tuple inserted into it.

New Properties, Existing Files. If a collection script is modified and then re-executed over existing data, two possibilities must be addressed. First, the newly modified collection script may emit different values for an existing property of an existing file. We describe this case in the sequel. Second, a collection script may emit an entirely new property for an existing file, changing the file's signature. Since we have previously computed signature extents and materialized them, we must massage the database to accommodate this new signature.

One choice is to simply drop and reload the database whenever the collection scripts are modified or another change is made, but an incremental strategy is desirable. If the file's new signature has been previously encountered, then an extent exists for it, and the tuple can be deleted from the old signature extent and inserted into the new one. If the signature has not been previously encountered, then a new signature extent must be created first.

New Values, Existing Properties, Existing Files. To support update of property values, we must modify our interpretation of RDF. The RDF data model allows a single property to be asserted more than once for a particular subject. Instead, we enforce that no two triples in a given database instance may have the same subject and property. To accommodate updates to a property's value, we interpret the assertion of a property as a command to overwrite the previous value, if one exists. This interpretation implies that there is a total order on the RDF triples, corresponding to their arrival in the system.

To define the total order, we must consider executions of the harvest program, executions of collection scripts, and the order of assertions produced by a collection script. Executions of the harvest program can be serialized naturally by the server. However, within a single execution of the harvest program, multiple collection scripts may attempt to assert the same property for the same file. To resolve this ambiguity, we defer to the order of the applicability rules. Recall that these rules specify which collection scripts to fire for which files. The latest rule that causes a duplicate assertion to be made overrides any previous rules. The applicability rules are managed by the data creators just as the collection scripts are, so changes can be made unilaterally. There is also the possibility that a single collection script may assert the same property for the same file twice in a single execution. We rely on the script author to understand that only the later value will be retained.

To minimize redundant work, we keep track of which collection scripts were executed with which execution of the harvest program. If the harvest program is re-executed over existing files, we only fire those collection scripts that are new or have been modified since the last execution. This policy reduces the amount of time required to harvest metadata and reduces the conflicts that must be resolved during loading.

Batches. The semantics we have just described can result in a great deal of data reorganization work. Very small changes to a collection script can result in many insertions, updates, and deletions, and potentially require new database tables to be created. There is a tradeoff between processing new metadata incrementally and buffering batches of metadata to process all at once.

If we enact the policies above after every triple arrives, we will obtain the correct semantics, but we will fire multiple SQL statements for every triple. The volume of data is large enough that this approach is unacceptable. Fortunately, triples generally arrive in batches, usually corresponding to an execution of the harvest program. We interpret the triples in a batch as arriving simultaneously, and only compute the new schemas once per batch. As described, there may be duplicate properties for one file asserted in a single batch. We remove these duplicates inside the harvest program, according to the semantics above, prior to the database load operation. Therefore, even though we consider each batch as a simultaneous set of updates, no ambiguity can arise.

In our application there is a natural batching strategy. For each run of the CORIE simulation code, around 20k files and around 100k triples are loaded into the system. If we consider this set a batch, we can balance the tradeoff between stale data and computing signatures that are replaced without ever being accessed.

Deletes. Deletes are more problematic. If we do not support deletes, there is no way to remove properties associated with files to support changing requirements, which prevents the correct signatures from being exhibited. But in order to support deletes, we must allow authors of collection scripts to specify that a file should no longer have a given property. (Note that we do not wish to support deletes of files themselves. The fact that a file once existed is important lineage information.)

We entertained two possible semantics for deletes: 1) Whenever a batch of metadata arrives for a file, assume the old metadata is incorrect and drop it all. These semantics agree with the update semantics already specified; new triples will still "replace" old triples since the old triples are deleted beforehand. The problem with these semantics is that collection scripts are prevented from extending the metadata associated with an existing file. They must produce all metadata for a file in every batch. Another choice is to 2) allocate a special URI "value:delete" that is interpreted as a deletion when it appears as the object of a triple. The problem (other than the inelegance of requiring a specially interpreted value) is that the collection scripts must produce "delete commands" as well as standard metadata, complicating their design and implementation. Although the collection scripts are expected to undergo refinement and change, using them as an interface to perform "one time only" database mutations is awkward. Currently, our implementation uses the second semantics.

4.4   Blank Nodes Revisited

Recall that blank nodes represent placeholders for unnamed subjects and objects in an RDF graph. Semantically, blank nodes are existentially quantified variables. In our design, collection scripts can not emit make use of blank nodes. The subject of every RDF triple represents a physical file. Collection scripts have no way of expressing triples whose subject is a blank node.

The disadvantage of this design is that collection scripts must redundantly emit the same information for many files. For example, all region information (xmin, xmax, ymin, ymax, region name) is linked directly to the file rather than linked to a blank node as in Figure 3. The concept of region is a separate entity and should be abstracted using a blank node in the RDF graph. In a relational setting, we note that region name functionally determines xmin, ymin, xmax, and ymax. Normalization procedures prescribe that we decompose a signature extent involving these properties by extracting a "region" table.

Since the collection scripts cannot express this feature of the data, we rely on tools to discover it after the data has been loaded. Several algorithms exist for discovering these functional dependencies [23]. The results of these algorithms can be used to further refine the schema. The tradeoff is twofold: First, a more complex schema may make data exploration more difficult for users unfamiliar with relational principles. Second, the processing of new RDF tuples becomes more expensive as the schema becomes more complex. The logic to transform a batch of RDF triples into a set of tuples becomes complex when considering updates, deletes, and now decomposed tables. Since some changes to collection scripts may require a significant amount of data to be corrected or reloaded, minimizing the complexity of the load operation is important.

For these reasons, we compute functional dependencies and perform prescribed decomposition only offline after a batch of data has been loaded. Further, we publish the data in terms of signatures, even though the underlying schema may be more complex. Modern RDBMS support this form of logical data independence quite well.

Performance is currently adequate considering the database represents over 6 million files and over 30 million RDF triples. After applying the techniques discussed in this paper for speeding up execution of collection scripts, identification of signatures, and population of signatures, we can re-load the entire repository, including re-harvesting the RDF triples, in a few hours. This level of performance is necessary, since there is a possibility that the majority of the database must be effectively reloaded if significant changes to collection scripts are made at one time.

5   Web Interface

Having imposed some structure on the metadata stream, we publish the data to the web for validation, exploration, and query. Generally changes to a database schema require changes to an application since applications reference table names and column names explicitly. However, an application can be designed generically by retrieving table names and column names from the catalog rather than hard-coding them. The HTML to display a table's information is generated dynamically from the catalog. We took this approach, extending source code for a free generic database interface [28]. The entry point is a list of tables in the current database.

5.1   Validation Using Signatures

The initial view in the web interface shows the signatures inferred by the system. In addition to a system generated name, the properties that make up the signature are displayed, giving an overview of how the files are organized in the database.

The list of signatures computed by the system provides immediate information about what sort of data is being captured. For example, users can see that some signatures are very similar, differing in only one property (e.g., <plottype, region, variable, animation> versus <plottype, region, variable>). This configuration suggests that the presence of the animation property is acting as a boolean. If the animation property exists, then the file type is an animated gif; if not, it is a single frame. The value of the animation property may be irrelevant. Perhaps a better configuration is for files in both signature extents to assert a GIFtype property, with either the value animation or single frame. If this configuration improves understanding, appropriate adjustments to the collection scripts can be made, and the database schema will adapt.

5.2   Query

The interface also allows users to construct simple queries via the signatures. Properties encountered in the metadata stream are shown, along with a range of values. This kind of summary information is important for validation as well as query formulation. For example, one of the parameters to the simulation, implicitness, indicates a coefficient controlling the weights of implicit and explicit methods for solving for each timestep. Those unfamiliar with the application can see the range of values found in the database before issuing a query. In fact, those unfamiliar with the term use these value ranges as clues to its meaning.

Figure 9 illustrates the query interface. To construct a query, users select signatures from the left, which populates a list of properties on the right. If a single extent is selected, then these properties simply form the SELECT clause of a SQL statement. If multiple signatures are selected, the natural join between the two is computed. Allowing only the natural join limits the expressiveness of this query interface, but has suited our purposes for the application thus far. Defining the precise query features necessary in this domain is an open problem. Selection conditions can be added at the bottom of the screen. The query can also be saved as a materialized view, which is refreshed at system-configurable intervals.

After retrieving the results of queries, the user can view the file (useful for images) or make annotate the file. Figure 10 shows the results of a query, and demonstrates how the user can click a link access the file itself.

The query interface allows us to make efficient use of the scientists' time. We can meet with them for an hour, browse through signature extents, and construct views on the fly. In several of these meetings, we have discovered anomalies in the metadata that reflected real anomalies in the source data. We receive comments such as the following:

- "Why are there only 3 salinity data products for this simulation run? I was expecting 4 thousand!"
- "Why are there two copies of the parameter file for every simulation run?"
- "The date should be divided into month and year; we should change that in the collection scripts."

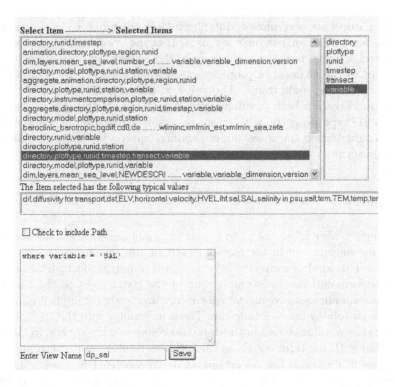

Fig. 9. To express queries and saved views, users select signatures on the left and add selection conditions at the bottom.

6   Related Work

Our base representation of RDF triples is directly related to the work of Agrawal et al. in managing E-commerce data [3]. Their system also copes with frequently changing attributes by adopting a vertical representation of data that is isomorphic to our base representation of RDF triples. The authors observe that such a representation makes queries difficult to express, as we have also argued. A horizontal view is constructed over the vertical representation of the data to ease this difficulty. The authors' notion of horizontal representation is very different from our signature extents, however. The horizontal representation is a single table that exhibits all attributes exhibited by any item in the database, acting as an implementation of the Universal Relation [22]. Null values are used to fill the table where an attribute has not been defined for an item. The resulting table may have thousands of attributes, and many of the tuples are very sparse. Our extents actually partition the data among many "horizontal" tables, each having only a handful of columns and significantly fewer tuples. Using extent tables, we can achieve interactive query performance with at least an order of magnitude more data than Agrawal et al. describe.

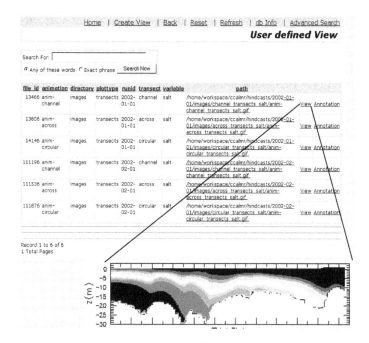

Fig. 10. Query results allow access to the file itself.

Schema extraction from semi-structured data has been studied intensely [12, 13,26]. The RDF data model provided a closer match with our desired semantics than the more general semi-structured data models. Further, semi-structured data models are oriented toward graphs with deep and complex structure. The schema information extracted with these systems would not necessarily provide guidance for query formulation in our domain.

RDF databases are gaining popularity in both research and commercial contexts [9,19,18]. These systems organize the data according to RDF Schema information provided along with the RDF data. Contrast this situation with our domain, where the schema information is not recorded explicitly and is frequently changing. Systems that allow querying of unstructured RDF [25] operate via graph matching and have not yet demonstrated scalability. Further, the users are required to "fish" for query results, since no schema structures are present to guide query formulation. Guha has done some early work on a scalable native RDF database that does not rely on RDF Schema, but thus far results are not provided [15].

More recent work by Christophides et al. advocates views over RDF databases constructed as virtual RDF classes [21], which recalls our design. However, users are charged with building the views using a specialized language. We are taking steps towards deriving appropriate views using only the base RDF data and the patterns therein.

Relational representations of XML data are also of interest. Some depend on RDF Schema information, which we do not have. Earlier work compares generic representations of XML [11]. The *edge schema* captures parent-child relationships between nodes in the XML tree, and is very similar to the common representation of RDF triples we have adopted. Binary representations involve separate tables for each element label, with results constructed via joins.

Metadata standards such as Dublin Core [1] and those produced by the Federal Geographic Data Committee (FGDC) [2] provide pre-defined schemas for metadata. These standards are usually intended to be human-readable, and are not usually amenable to structured querying. Further, the standards are often intended for large granularity datasets rather than individual files. For example, in our domain, an entire year's worth of simulations may be described by a single FGDC document.

Research on ontology models and tools has become commonplace in the last few years. The OWL languages for capturing ontological properties [6], based on RDF, have become W3C recommendations. While work on ontologies show promise for capturing complex relationships across domains, adoption has been slow due to practical issues. Usually ontology tools assume that a Ontologist, Knowledge Engineer, or Cybrarian [24] is available to model source metadata in the target system. This task is far from trivial, which is why job titles such as those mentioned have been invented. Our framework streamlines the process of converting scattered source data to machine-processable metadata. Inferring and exploiting the complex relationships supported by ontology models remains future work.

The Grid [10] community has recognized the need for a comprehensive metadata management solution in Grid environments. The MCAT metadata information catalog supports metadata processing in the context of the San Diego Super Computing Center's Storage Request Broker (SRB) [5]. More recently, the Metadata Catalog Service (MCS) [29] has been shown to perform well under heavy query workloads and large database sizes [27]. Our goals differ from these systems, however. We are working toward a system that can adapt to evolving requirements with little or no user intervention. The MCAT system is designed to process metadata queries over using specialized query structures. While the schemas providing structure to the data are not necessarily fixed, users must explicitly update the schema to reflect changing requirements. The ability for MCAT to handle frequent changes is unclear. Other features such as location transparency and replication are important and complementary to our own work.

7   Future Work

There are several research directions to follow based on this work, primarily in the area of finding and exploiting richer structures in the RDF data. Currently we infer simple groupings from the data patterns, and we discussed using functional dependencies to further refine the schema. However, views defined by users in the web interface provide very important information as to how users will access their data. Beyond simply materializing these views, the schema can be designed to make these user views efficient. Finding automatic techniques to transform the schema based on user-defined views is an interesting direction to take.

Although we acknowledge that inferred functional dependencies can lead to improved schema design, we have not applied the same analysis to other data dependencies from relational theory: join dependencies and inclusion dependencies. In fact, a rigorous interpretation of these dependencies in our domain would be useful.

We exploit patterns in the metadata stream to facilitate query expression and improve performance. However, a schema serves another purpose as well: enforcement of constraints on the data. If patterns found by the system are acknowledged by users, the system could promote the patterns into hard constraints. After this promotion, violations of the constraints in the metadata stream would be rejected outright as errors. Providing a flexible transition between reactive and proactive pattern exploitation presents interesting theoretical and practical challenges.

The query interface provided via the web supports only simple natural joins, making many useful queries impossible to express. We predict that an interface can be designed that supports all relevant queries in our scientific domain without requiring the full power of SQL.

Acknowledgements. This work was supported by NSF ITR Award No. ACI-0121475. We would like to thank the entire CORIE team for their feedback and guidance.

References

[1] Dublin Core Metadata Standard. `http://dublincore.org/index.shtml`, 1997.

[2] Content standard for digital geospatial metadata.
`http://www.fgdc.gov/metadata/metadata.html`, 2004.

[3] R. Agrawal, A. Somani, and Y. Xu. Storage and querying of e-commerce data. In *The VLDB Journal*, pages 149–158, 2001.

[4] A. Baptista, M. Wilkin, P. Pearson, P. Turner, M. C., and P. Barrett. Coastal and estuarine forecast systems: A multi-purpose infrastructure for the columbia river. *Earth System Monitor, NOAA*, 9(3), 1999.

[5] C. Baru, R. Moore, A. Rajasekar, and M. Wan. The SDSC storage resource broker. In *Proceedings of the Centers for Advanced Studies Conference*, Toronto, Canada, November 1998.

[6] S. Bechhofer, F. van Harmelen, J. Hendler, I. Horrocks, D. L. McGuinness, P. F. Patel-Schneider, and L. A. Stein. Web ontology language reference. W3C Recommendation, `http://www.w3.org/TR/2003/CR-owl-ref-20030818/`, 1999.

[7] D. Beckett and B. McBride. RDF/XML syntax specification.
http://www.w3.org/TR/rdf-syntax-grammar/, 2004.

[8] D. Brickley and R. V. Guha. RDF vocabulary description language 1.0: RDF Schema. http://www.w3.org/TR/rdf-schema/, 2004.

[9] J. Broekstra, A. Kampman, and F. van Harmelen. Sesame: A generic architecture for storing and querying rdf and rdf schema. In I. Horrocks and J. Hendler, editors, *Proceedings of the First Internation Semantic Web Conference*, number 2342 in Lecture Notes in Computer Science, pages 54–68. Springer Verlag, July 2002.

[10] A. Chervenak, I. Foster, C. Kesselman, C. Salisbury, and S. Tuecke. The data grid: Towards an architecture for the distributed management and analysis of large scientific datasets. *Journal of Network and Computer Applications*, 23:187–200, 1999.

[11] D. Florescu and D. Kossmann. Storing and querying xml data using an rdmbs. *IEEE Data Engineering Bulletin*, 22:27–34, 1999.

[12] M. Garofalakis, A. Gionis, R. Rastogi, S. Seshadri, and K. Shim. XTRACT: a system for extracting document type descriptors from XML documents. In *ACM Special Interest Group on Management of Data*, pages 165–176, 2000.

[13] R. Goldman and J. Widom. Dataguides: Enabling query formulation and optimization in semistructured databases. In M. Jarke, M. J. Carey, K. R. Dittrich, F. H. Lochovsky, P. Loucopoulos, and M. A. Jeusfeld, editors, *Proceedings of 23rd International Conference on Very Large Data Bases*, pages 436–445. Morgan Kaufmann, 1997.

[14] J. Gray, A. Bosworth, A. Layman, and H. Pirahesh. Data cube: A relational operator generalizing group-by, crosstab and sub-totals. In *ICDE*, pages 152–159, 1996.

[15] R. V. Guha. *rdfDB : An RDF Database*. http://www.guha.com/rdfdb/, 2001.

[16] P. Hayes and B. McBride. Rdf semantics. W3C Recommendation, http://www.w3.org/TR/rdf-mt/, 2003.

[17] I. A. Howes, M. C. Smiths, and G. S. Good. Understanding and deploying LDAP directory services. Technical report, 1999.

[18] G. Karvounarakis, S. Alexaki, V. Christophides, D. Plexousakis, and M. Scholl. RQL: A declarative query language for RDF. In *The Eleventh International World Wide Web Conference*.

[19] G. Karvounarakis, V. Christophides, D. Plexousakis, and S. Alexaki. Querying RDF descriptions for community web portals. In *Journees Bases de Donnees Avancees*, pages 133–144, 2001.

[20] L. V. S. Lakshmanan, F. Sadri, and S. N. Subramanian. Schemasql: An extension to SQL for multidatabase interoperability. *Database Systems*, 26(4):476–519, 2001.

[21] A. Magkanaraki, V. Tannen, V. Christophides, and D. Plexousakis. Viewing the semantic web through RVL lenses. In *Second International Semantic Web Conference*, pages 20–23, 2003.

[22] D. Maier, J. D. Ullman, and M. Y. Vardi. On the foundations of the Universal Relation Model. *ACM Transactions on Database Systems (TODS)*.

[23] H. Mannila and K.-J. Räihä. Algorithms for inferring functional dependencies from relations. *Data and Knowledge Engineering*, 12(1):83–99, 1994.

[24] D. L. McGuinness. Conceptual modeling for distributed ontology environments. In *Proceedings of The Eighth International Conference on Conceptual Structures*, 2000.

[25] L. Miller. RDF Squish query language and Java implementation. Public draft, Institute for Learning and Research Technology, 2001. http://ilrt.org/discovery/2001/02/squish/.

[26] S. Nestorov, S. Abiteboul, and R. Motwani. Extracting schema from semistructured data. In *ACM Conference on Knowledge Discovery and Data Mining*, pages 295–306, 1998.

[27] A. Rajasekar. MCAT - a meta information catalog.
http://www.npaci.edu/DICE/SRB/mcat.html.

[28] E. Robillard. GenericDB. http://www.genericdb.com/.

[29] G. Singh, S. Bharathi, A. Chervenak, E. Deelman, C. Kesselman, M. Mahohar, S. Pail, and L. Pearlman. A metadata catalog service for data intensive applications. In *Proceedings of the 2003 ACM/IEEE conference on Supercomputing*, November 2003.

[30] M. Stonebraker, L. A. Rowe, and M. Hirohama. The implementation of Postgres. *TKDE*, 2(1):125–142, 1990.

Semantic Visualization of Biochemical Databases

Esteban Zimányi and Sabri Skhiri dit Gabouje*

Department of Informatics & Networks, Faculty of Engineering CP 165/15,
Université Libre de Bruxelles,
50 av. F.D. Roosevelt, 1050 Brussels, Belgium
{sskhirid,ezimanyi}@ulb.ac.be

Abstract. Extracting and visualizing information from biochemical databases is one of the most important challenges in biochemical research. The huge quantity and high complexity of the data available force the biologist to use sophisticated tools for extracting and interpreting accurately the information extracted from the database. These tools must define a graphical semantics associated to the data semantics in accordance with biologist usages. The aim of these tools is to display complex biochemical networks in a readable and understandable way. In this paper we define the notion of *customizable representation model*, which allows the biologist to change the graphical semantics associated to the data semantics. The approach is also *generic* since our graphical semantics is common to several kinds of biochemical networks. We also defined *adaptive graph layout algorithms* taking into account the particular semantics of biochemical networks. We show how we implemented these notions in the BioMaze project[1].

1 Introduction

Data visualization is an important research area in bioinformatics. The availability of the complete sequence from more than 50 genomes of organisms ranging from bacteria to human leads to huge biochemical databases, and this critical mass of data is still rapidly increasing.

Biochemical databases typically contain information about *biochemical entities* such as compounds, genes, and polypeptides, as well as the *interactions* between them. There are two categories of interactions: (1) *transformations*, such as reactions (between compounds), expressions (of a gene that lead to synthesis of polypeptides), assembly-disassembly (between biochemical entities) and (2) *control*, like catalysis (a polypeptide catalyzes or inhibits one or more biochemical reactions), or activation-deactivation (turning on or off the biochemical function of a polypeptide).

---

* This work was partially funded by the Wallonia Region under the BioMaze project.
[1] The partners of the Biomaze project (http://cs.ulb.ac.be/research/biomaze/) are Université Libre de Bruxelles, Université Catholique de Louvain-la-neuve and Facultés Universitaires Notre-Dame de la Paix de Namur.

M. Bouzeghoub et al. (Eds.): ICSNW 2004, LNCS 3226, pp. 199–214, 2004.
© IFIP International Federation for Information Processing 2004

The term *biochemical pathway* or *biochemical network* regroups different families of networks. *Metabolic pathways* are networks of biochemical reactions catalyzed by polypeptides resulting from the expression of a gene. This expression is controlled by a set of parameters like transcription factors, activation, inhibition, etc. For this reason metabolic pathways are said to be genetically regulated. These regulatory actions are represented in *metabolic regulation networks*. Finally, *signal transduction networks* describe the information transfer from a cellular location, typically the extra cellular medium, to another, typically the cell nucleus.

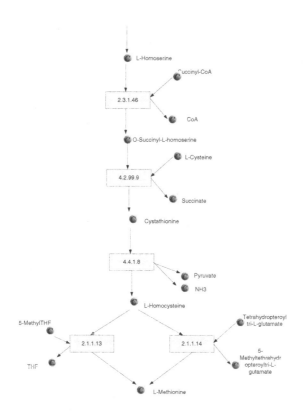

Fig. 1. Metabolic pathway of the methionine synthesis. The boxes represent the biochemical reactions and the arrows show the direction (from substrates to products).

As pointed out by [4] there is a great deal of variation in the structure of different biochemical databases, such as Swiss-Prot, GenBank, or BioCyc. We can distinguish two types of approaches: either the database aims to represent as much as possible our biological knowledge, or the contents of database is structured according to particular application objectives. As a consequence the quality of data extraction depends on the quality of the database structure.

Further, the quality of the analysis depends on the quality of the data extraction from the database. Finally, high-performance visualization tools are needed due to the huge amount of data.

Biochemical databases are used in many different research areas. For example, the pharmaceutical industry can reduce the time and the cost of design of new drugs with what is called rational design: biochemical databases can be used to identify a drug target, to find metabolites involved in a particular pathway, or to find polypeptides that catalyze a specified reaction. In toxicology, these databases can be used for simulate *in silico* the introduction of a specific biochemical compound in the metabolism, asking all pathways implied by this introduction. Biochemical databases can also be used in bacteriology: the knowledge of the complete genome and the metabolic networks of bacteria can be useful for taking advantage of it (e.g., in bio-degradation) or for fighting it.

Since visualization plays a key role in this kind of applications, it has to outline the semantics of data in a readable way. A *representation model* describes the graphical semantics associated to each element. For example, a reaction may be represented by a box having some width and height, the compound by a circle of some radius in which a particular icon is shown, etc. A representation model has to be chosen with care, because it determines the comprehension of the data semantics.

This paper focuses on the visualization problem and the solutions proposed by the BioMaze project. The objective of the project is to develop tools for the storage, analysis, and visualization of biochemical pathways, in particular (1) metabolic pathways with genetic regulation, (2) signal transduction, and (3) interaction graphs describing all possible interactions between two biochemical entities. Section 2 describes the global context of the BioMaze project. In Section 3 we review the visualization problem and its implementation in popular biochemical databases, while Section 4 describes our solution to these visualization problems. Finally, in Section 5 we summarize our work and give further perspectives.

2   The BioMaze Project

A major challenge of the post-genomic era is to determine the functions of all the genes and gene products at the genome level. In order to improve the prediction of such functions it is important to take in account the information about the different organization levels of the living cell. In particular, it is necessary to consider the set of physical and functional interactions between genes and proteins. Such interactions form networks of cellular processes, called biochemical networks, which include metabolic networks, regulatory networks for gene expression, and signal transduction.

The huge quantity of data available and its continuous growth, the need to integrate such information, as well as the necessity of sophisticated software tools for manipulating it represent true challenges for the research in bioinformatics. New tools for integrating, querying, extracting, analyzing, and visualizing biochemical databases are essential for the pharmaceutical and biotechnology industry, in particular for the design of new drugs and vaccines. Such highly sophisticated tools must be designed by multi-disciplinary teams, and require recent results in computer science in areas such as operational research (graph algorithms, constraint logic programming, automatic learning, form recognition, etc.), databases (huge schema management, object-oriented interfaces, evolution, meta-data, etc.), and visualization (multi-resolution, multi-representation, complexity management, etc.).

The aim of the BioMaze project is to develop a set of tools including:

1. an information system allowing to represent information about biochemical networks, and including functions for evolution management, generation, and documentation;
2. an open system of specialized software components to exploit biochemical data, including extraction, analysis, navigation, and visualization; and
3. a Web interface given access to the services providing by those specialized components.

2.1   The BioMaze Information System

Nowadays many companies in the pharmaceutical and biotechnology sectors use approaches at the genomic scale in the design of more specific drugs. This requires the characterization of both the function of individual genes or proteins as well as the physical and functional interactions in which they participate.

Existing general databases, such as Swiss-Prot [2] and GenBank [1], may be used to certain extent for determining if a group of genes is implied in a particular cellular process (e.g., in a metabolic pathway). This approach is limited since the information contained in most databases is not appropriate for establishing functional relations between genes and their products. Further, these databases store their information mostly in text form, making difficult its computer analysis. For this reason, more specialized databases representing information on cellular processes and interactions were developed (e.g., EcoCyc [7]). However, most of these databases cope with only one type of biochemical networks (either protein-protein interactions, gene regulations, or signal transduction) and offer very restrictive analysis tools.

The goal of the aMaze database [9], which underlies the BioMaze project, is to provide a rich source of information about different protein functions and cellular processes. In particular, aMaze allows to associate individual biological entities and interactions into large complex networks describing different types of cellular processes.

The aMaze data model [13,14] comprises three basic classes of objects: *Biochemical Entity*, *Biochemical Interaction*, and *Process*. A *Biochemical Entity* represents physical entities (such as protein, gene, compound, etc.) and their structural properties (e.g., gene position on the chromosome). A *Biochemical Interaction* represents molecular activities, which can be of several types. *Entity Processing* has Biochemical Entities as input and as output (such as chemical reaction, and protein-protein interaction). On the other hand, *Control* has a Biochemical Entity as input and another Biochemical Interaction as output (e.g., a catalysis is an interaction between a protein and a reaction). Finally, *Process* represents a collection of interconnected elements. It allows to build graphs of biochemical pathways at various levels. They can be built at the enzyme and metabolite level by considering the chemical reactions as nodes and linking them through their inputs and outputs, or at the pathway level by considering whole pathways as nodes and linking those via common key metabolites.

The aMaze model covers a large variety of activities (transcriptional regulation, attenuation, macromolecule processing, transport, etc.) and processes (metabolic regulation, signal transduction) and deals with spatial locations and compartments. These last two aspects are important for interactions, for example a transduction by phosphorylation in the nucleus cell can be differentiated from the same interaction in cytoplasmic medium.

The aMaze database provides a rich description of the current state of our knowledge about biology and biochemical processes. However, since this knowledge evolves as new results from biological research become available, the database schema must also evolve for reflecting this knowledge. It is well-known that database evolution is a labor-intensive activity, since a modification of the database schema implies modifications of all related database components both at the schema level (e.g., tables, constraints, programs, forms, Web interfaces, etc.) and at the data level (e.g., migrating data from old structures to new structures). Thus, CASE tools are needed for ensuring the coherence of all such modifications.

The BioMaze project uses DB-Main [5], a powerful CASE tool allowing forward and reverse engineering. The aMaze database is described in DB-Main using a generalized entity-relationship conceptual schema with inheritance, aggregation, etc. From this conceptual schema the logical and physical schemas of the database are generated. DB-Main copes with many logical models including relational, object-relational, and semi-structured (XML) models, as well as the physical models of many available DBMSs, in particular PostgreSQL on which the aMaze database is currently implemented.

One of the objectives of the BioMaze project is to extend the DB-Main tool with sophisticated services for schema evolution. Such services include: (1) automatic documentation of the database addressed for both users and developpers of other tools, (2) code generation, allowing to produce schema definition (in SQL, Java, and XML) and mappings between these schemas, (3) management of the evolution, coping with the propagation of semantic modifications to the different schemas and mappings, and isolating the applicative components from such modifications. However, as we will se later, the other components of the BioMaze tool that manage annotation, retrieval, and visualization must also deal with the evolution of the underlying database.

2.2   Analysis Tools

In order to allow an efficient exploitation of biochemical databases, sophisticated analysis tools are needed. Such tools allow the user to select, search, and navigate complex biochemical networks. A common requirement is the search of specific paths into a particular network, for example (1) finding all processes transforming the compound A into B in less than X steps, where the term transform refers to a biochemical reaction or to a gene expression, or (2) finding all reactions catalyzed by a set of genes (sub-graph extraction).

The search of similarities is another important requirement when analyzing biochemical networks. For example, it is necessary to compare the metabolic pathways of different organisms (in designing specific drugs) or of different tissues (in understanding diseases and treatment design). It is also necessary to determine common characteristics as well as differences between networks, and to predict missing elements.

In the context of the project we are developing tools for discovering recurring topological patterns among biochemical networks, at different resolution levels. Such tools also allow to discover similarities and differences between such networks. These tools are developed using constraint logic programming on the Oz-Mozart platform [15]. They are based on methods coming from operational research and algorithmics, including artificial learning and statistical methods.

3   Visualization Issues

We describe next the problems raised by the visualization of biochemical networks. In this paper we consider that such networks are represented by bipartite graphs whose nodes are either biochemical entities or interactions.

3.1   Representation Model

We call *representation model* the graphical semantics used to represent the data stored in a biochemical database, in particular the biochemical networks. Choosing a representation model is of paramount importance because it has to convey the semantics represented by the data.

Although researchers in bioinformatics do not agree about which representation model to use, two schools emerge: one represents metabolic pathways as usual in biochemistry books, as in BioCyc [7], while the second one proposes more expressive models for such pathways, like the Khon model [8], the Cook model [3] or the Maimon and Broming model [10]. An example of the Kohn representation model is given in Figure 2.

The problem with simple models is that they are sometimes ambiguous: e.g., an arrow in the Kegg model is used both for representing the input/output of a reaction but also in phosphorylation (i.e., the addition of a phosphate group), or in other cellular transport interactions. On the other hand, although the expressive models convey a rich semantics, the problem is that they are difficult to understand and to read.

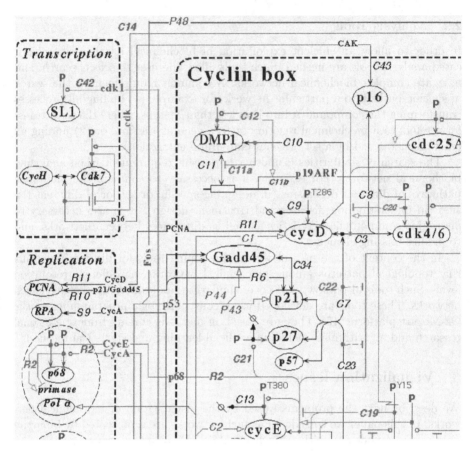

Fig. 2. The Kohn representation model. This model represents the data semantics precisely but, sometimes, it is hard to read.

3.2   Database Evolution and Dynamic Diagram Generation

As already said, the database underlying BioMaze frequently evolves to reflect new knowledge resulting from research in cellular biology. Since the visualization tools have to deal with this evolution of data semantics, the diagrams must be generated dynamically, i.e., they are displayed upon user request. This contrasts with some biochemical representation tools, like Kegg [6], in which diagrams are realized manually.

Therefore, given a graph representing a biochemical network, the visualization tools must compute the position of each graphical element and draw it without overlapping and minimizing edge crossing. This is a traditional problem of graph layout. In addition, the tool have to deal with the fact that the visualization of metabolic pathways differs from the visualization of interaction graphs. Metabolic pathways follow a main direction outlining the process, while interaction graphs do not. In [13] is suggested to represent metabolic pathways horizontally (see Figure 1) and regulatory actions vertically. To resolve this problem we must introduce *graphical constraints* associated to particular subgraphs.

3.3   Signal Transduction Graphs

Signal transduction graphs represent the processes of information transfer from a cellular location to another, typically from the exterior of the cell to its nucleus. From the visualization point of view, signal transduction graphs must be understood as a particular case of general metabolic pathways in which the interactions are of specific type.

One issue is to ensure that the graphical semantics stays coherent with the semantics used for metabolic pathways, unlike some biochemical tools. Another issue is to represent the cellular context (i.e., cellular locations and compartments) in which the interactions take place.

3.4   Interaction Graphs

An interaction graph represents all possible interactions between two entities of the same type (e.g., polypeptide-polypeptide or gene-gene) or of different type (e.g., gene-polypeptide). This kind of graph can contain up to 3000 nodes but, in general, the interesting interactions to visualize do not exceed 500 nodes. Such graphs are not visualized like metabolic pathways, since particular graphical constraints have to be adopted.

Here we have two important issues: (1) how to display in a readable way huge graphs of many thousand nodes and (2) devising efficient mechanisms for filtering the graph and for allowing users to find set of interactions in which they are interested.

3.5   Navigation

An important visualization issue is the ability to navigate into the database from a graphical selection. Two types of navigation exist: (1) basic navigation allowing the user to obtain textual information about a graphical element, for example the name and other characteristics of a compound, and (2) an advanced navigation allowing to user to create queries from graphical selection, for example finding all pathways where two selected compounds are involved.

4   The Visual BioMaze Approach

This section describes our approach to the problem of visualizing biochemical networks. This approach has been implemented in the the BioMaze visualization module, called Visual BioMaze, resulting into an efficient and flexible visualization tool.

4.1 Customizable and Generic Representation Models

An innovative aspect of our approach is the definition of representation models that are both *customizable* and *generic*. These two aspects are explained next.

As we have seen in Section 3.1, biologists do not agree on the representation model used for visualizing biochemical networks. Therefore, each tool implements a particular representation model. In order to provide a flexible visualization tool, instead of choosing a particular model we introduced the notion of *customizable representation model*. This means that the same biochemical network can be visualized with different representation models. The tool provides several predefined models but the users can also customize such models according to their research needs. Further, users may explore alternative representation models over the same biochemical network.

As a consequence, this approach allows two new interesting possibilities: (1) users can devise or adapt a model to highlight particular aspects in which they are interested (2) if the database schema evolves and if the information about which entities has evolved is known, a new representation model expanded with these new entities can be (semi-)automatically generated. This latter feature provides an elegant solution for the problem of visualizing an evolving database.

On the other hand, the Visual BioMaze tool aims at representing three types of networks: metabolic pathways, signal transduction networks, and interaction networks. The three types of networks are represented as graphs, where the nodes are either biochemical entities (compound, gene, polypeptide) or interactions (reaction, control, signal). Our approach to represent the three types of graphs in an integrated visualization tool is to define a *general representation model*. This model describes the graphical semantics associated to each entity and interaction node, regardless of the graph type.

As a consequence, we can cope with graphs having mixed types. An example of a network composed of a signal transduction part and a metabolic part arrives when a liver's cell receives the signal that the sugar rate increases in the blood (transduction) and its response in which the insulin acts (metabolic pathway). Since we allow typed subgraphs, the visualization module can recognize the different subgraphs and apply specific graphical constraints according to the subgraph type.

4.2 Implementation

We use XML for implementing representation models. Such models are based on an XML Schema definition that prescribes the correctness of the model and provides validation features.

The current representation model defines two objects types, `Element` and `Link` corresponding, respectively, to nodes and edges of biochemical graphs. An element defines the graphical semantics associated to each possible interaction, control, and biochemical compound, while a link defines the graphical semantics for the edges between such elements. The code below, extracted from the Visual BioMaze default representation model, represents compounds by a circle

of radius 15 in which an icon `compound.bmp` is displayed; the identifier of the
compound is shown outside the circle (see Figure 3).

```
<Element>
  <Type>Compound</Type>
  <Glyph>
    <Shape>
      <Circle>
        <Radius>15</Radius>
      </Circle>
    </Shape>
    <BorderColor>None</BorderColor>
    <FillColor>None</FillColor>
    <Text>
      <Present>true</Present>
      <Content>?ID</Content>
      <Position>Out</Position>
    </Text>
    <Icon>
      <Present>true</Present>
      <Location>/image/compound.bmp</Location>
    </Icon>
    <BorderVisibility>true</BorderVisibility>
  </Glyph>
</Element>
```

The different tags are as follows. `Type` defines the node type. `Glyph` defines
the associated graphical semantics and is composed of the following elements.

1. `Shape`, defining the shape associated to the element, that can be `Box`, `Circle`,
   `Ellipse`, `Arrow`, and `Tshape`. The allowed shapes and their particular attributes are defined using XML Schema.
2. `Text`, defining the text associated to the element. As shown in Figure 3,
   the text associated to elements can be displayed outside the shapes (e.g.,
   for compounds) or inside them (e.g., for reactions). This is defined by the
   `Position` tag. Further, the text can be either a generic text or a particular
   attribute of the represented object (e.g., its identifier). This is expressed by
   introducing a ? character (e.g., ?ID in the above example).
3. `BorderColor` and `FillColor` defining the colors of the border and the inte-
   rior of the shape.
4. `Icon`, defining if an image must be shown in the shape.
5. `BorderVisibility`, defining if the shape border is visible. This provides an
   easy way to introduce new shapes to characterize an interaction. Indeed, if an
   interaction must be represented by a complex form that does not correspond
   to the predefined shapes, the user can introduce it as an icon and set the
   border visibility to false.

| 1.2.1.11 | ●-Aspartate 4-semialdehyde |

Fig. 3. a) A compound is represented by a circle in which an icon is inserted, and b) A biochemical reaction is represented by a box.

The XML Schema code below defines the possible values for the `Type` tag of `Element`. If the database evolves and a new kind of element (i.e., interaction) appears, we can add it to the possible elements and define its link to the other types.

```
<xs:simpleType name="ElementType">
   <xs:restriction base="xs:string">
   <xs:enumeration value="Reaction"/>
   <xs:enumeration value="Compound"/>
   <xs:enumeration value="Catalysis"/>
   <xs:enumeration value="Expression"/>
   <xs:enumeration value="InhibitionNode"/>
   <xs:enumeration value="Gene"/>
   <xs:enumeration value="Polypeptide"/>
</xs:restriction>
```

The `Link` tag defines the graphical semantics associated to the edges between interaction types. The example below represents the links from catalysis to reactions by a line whose head is a circle of radius 18 in which is displayed the icon `catalyze.jpg` and the text +, and without tail (see Figure 4).

```
<Link>
  <Between>
    <From>Catalysis</From>
    <To>Reaction</To>
  </Between>
  <Effect>Continuous</Effect>
  <Color>Black</Color>
  <Head>
    <Present>true</Present>
    <Glyph>
      <Shape>
        <Circle>
          <radius>18</radius>
        </Circle>
      </Shape>
      <BorderColor>Black</BorderColor>
      <FillColor>None</FillColor>
      <Text>
        <Present>true</Present>
```

```
      <Content>+</Content>
      <Position>In</Position>
    </Text>
    <Icon>
      <Present>true</Present>
      <Location>/images/catalysis/catalyze.jpg</Location>
    </Icon>
    <BorderVisibility>true</BorderVisibility>
  </Glyph>
</Head>
<Tail>
  <Present>false</Present>
</Tail>
<width>4</width>
</Link>
```

The different tags are defined as follows:

1. **Between**: defines the interactions for which the edge is defined.
2. **Effect**: describes the line style.
3. **Head** and **Tail**: defining the glyphs for the extremities. These glyphs can not be defined if the **Present** tag is set to **false**. The head and tail glyphs are important in biochemical network visualization, since some interactions such as inhibition or catalysis are represented by a specific form at the edge extremities.

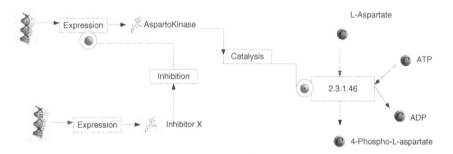

Fig. 4. Example of a representation model. When representing links (e.g., from a catalysis to a reaction), graphical elements such as the head glyph, the line effect, the color, etc., are customizable by the representation model.

4.3   The Visual BioMaze Graph Layout Algorithm

Many research efforts have been realized for many years in the area of graph layout and efficient graph layout algorithms have been developed. However, such algorithms are devised for general graphs and do not take into account semantic issues. These algorithms are inadequate for biochemical networks since these networks have associated particular semantics.

For example, a metabolic pathway follows a main direction that the visualization has to outline to represent it efficiently; further the regulatory pathway associated to it cannot be distributed around the pathway but also follows a specific direction. The same observation can be made about transduction signal graphs where the visualization has to outline the message direction.

Graph layout algorithms taking into account data semantics are currently a research domain, and there exists commercial tools that provide proprietary solutions. Our approach is to define a graph layout algorithm that is *adaptive*, adjusting itself to particular subgraph motifs. We are currently developing an algorithm capable of finding linear, cyclic, or hierarchical subgraphs, and locally applying a specialized graph layout. Further, we also provide *interchangeable* graph layout, giving the user the possibility to choose an existing algorithm, or to define his own.

4.4   The Visual BioMaze Prototype

BioMaze and aMaze are developed in Java under Eclipse [12], a powerful and extensible platform provided by IBM. Under this framework, BioMaze and the BioMaze visualization module, Visual BioMaze, are developed as plug-ins.

Figure 5 shows a snapshot of the first Visual BioMaze prototype. It provides the following functions:

1. dynamic generation of a metabolic pathway with a simple graph layout algorithm,
2. the user can apply and define different representation models to the graph to be displayed (the default model is that described by van Helden in [13]), and
3. the user can implement his own graph layout algorithm and load it by the Visual BioMaze tool.

The visualization module takes advantage of the extensibility features provided by Eclipse, thus allowing users to customize and extend it. For example, if the user wants to define his own graph layout algorithm, he can create a new plug-in that implements a predefined interface. When the user copies it into the plug-in Eclipse directory the new graph layout algorithm is available in the Visual BioMaze preference pages. If the user wants to distribute it, he only needs to provide the plug-in. In the current version, the user must write the whole graph layout algorithm, but a future version will modularize the different steps of the algorithm allowing the user to define individual steps of it.

The following features will be addressed in the next version of the prototype:

1. Expand the representation model for *signal transduction*. Indeed, the current XML Schema definition cannot specify the graphical semantics associated to an interaction in a particular cellular location.

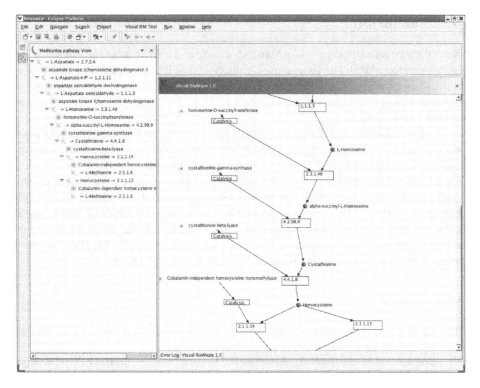

Fig. 5. The first Visual BioMaze prototype under the Eclipse platform.

2. Introduction of *graphical constraints*: e.g., in a metabolic pathway the main direction has to be outlined vertically and the regulation path horizontally. Graphical constraints will force the graph layout algorithm to consider these directions. The challenge is to find a trade-off between the expressivity of these constraints and their efficient implementation.

3. To implement a *legend editor* that provides a user-friendly interface for defining and customizing representation models. Instead of manipulating XML files, the user visually defines the representation model with appropriate dialog boxes. The editor will then automatically generate the corresponding XML file.

4. To implement an advanced *navigation system* allowing users to formulate queries when clicking on graphical elements.

5. Introduction of the concepts of *multi-resolution* and *multi-representation*. Multi-resolution provides the mechanisms for displaying the graph at different levels of detail. Multi-representation provides the mechanisms for considering a particular fact from different viewpoints. In the context of Geographical Information Systems, we have explored these two concepts in the project MurMur [11].

6. Definition of *filters* for interaction networks to provide the user a mechanism for selecting the interactions in which he is interested.

5   Conclusion

Nowadays, visualization of biochemical networks is an important challenge in bioinformatics. With the increasing quantity of available information it is essential to use powerful tools for retrieving accurate information from biochemical databases and for visualizing it efficiently. The BioMaze project attempts to answer these needs.

In this paper we described the overall objectives of the BioMaze project. Then we presented our approach for visualizing biochemical networks. It consists in defining customizable and generic representation models that provide a general framework where the user can define and apply any representation model on the graph to be visualized. Similarly, we defined adaptive and interchangeable graph layout algorithms taking into account the particular semantics of biochemical networks and allowing the user to define his own algorithm. We described how we implemented these notions in the first prototype of the Visual BioMaze tool using XML and the facilities provided by the Eclipse platform.

References

[1]   Benson D.A., Karsch-Mizrachi I., Lipman D.J., Ostell J., Wheeler D.L.: GenBank, *Nucleic Acids Research*, 31(1):23-27, 2003.

[2]   Boeckmann B., Bairoch A., Apweiler R., Blatter M.-C., Estreicher A., Gasteiger E., Martin L.J., Michoud K., O'Donovan C., Phan I., Pilbout S., Schneider M.: The Swiss-Prot protein sequence database and its supplement TrEMBL. *Nucleic Acids Research*, 31, 365–370, 2003.

[3]   Cook D.L., Farley J.F., Tapscott S.J.: A basis for visual language for describing, archiving and analyzing functional models of complex biochemical systems, *Genome Biology*, 2(4), research0012, 2001.

[4]   Deville Y., Gilbert D., van Helden J., Wodak S.: An overview of data models for the analysis of biochemical pathways, *Briefings in Bioinformatics*, 4(3): 246–259, 2003.

[5]   Englebert V., Hainaut J.-L.: DB-Main: A next generation meta-case, *Information Systems*, 24(2): 99–112, April 1999.

[6]   Kanehisa M., Goto S., Kawashima S., Nakaya A.: The Kegg database at GenomeNet, *Nucleic acid research*, 4(3): 246-259, 2003.

[7]   Karp P., Paley S., Romero P.: The pathway tools software, *Bioinformatics*, Vol. 18., Suppl. 1, pp. S225-S232, 2002.

[8]   Kohn K.W.: Molecular interaction Map of the Mammalian Cell Cycle Control and DNA Repair Systems, *Molecular Biology of the Cell*, Vol. 10, pp. 2703–2734, 1999.

[9]   Lemer C., Antezana E., Couche F., Fays F., Santolaria X., Janky R., Deville Y., Richelle J., Wodak S.J.: The aMAZE LightBench: a web interface to a relational database of cellular processes, *Nucleic Acids Research*, 32, D443-D44.

[10]   Maimon R., Browning S.: Diagrammatic Notation and Computational Structure of Gene Network. In *Proc. of the 2nd Int. Conf. on Systems Biology*, 2001.

[11]   Parent C., Spaccapietra S., Zimányi E.: Murmur: Database management of multiple representations In *Proc. of the AAAI-2000 Workshop on Spatial and Temporal Granularity*, pp. 83-86, 2000.

[12] Shavor S., D'Anjou J., Fairbrother S., Kehn D., Kellerman J., McCarthy P., *The Java Developer's Guide to Eclipse*, Addison-Wesley, 2003.

[13] van Helden J., Naim A., Mancuso R., Eldridge M., Wernish L., Glibert D., Wodak S.: Representing and analysing molecular and cellular function in computer. *Biol. Chem.*, 381(9–10):921–935. 2000.

[14] van Helden, J., Naim, A., Lemer, C., Mancuso, R., Eldridge, M., Wodak, S.: From molecular activities and processes to biological function. *Briefings in Bioinformatics*, 2(1): 81-93, 2001.

[15] Van Roy P., Brand P., Duchier D., Haridi S., Henz M., Schulte, C.: Logic programming in the context of multiparadigm programming: The Oz experience, *Theory and Practice of Logic Programming*, 3(6):717–763, 2003.

Semantic Information Interoperability in Open Networked Systems[*]

Silvana Castano, Alfio Ferrara, Stefano Montanelli, and Gianpaolo Racca

Università degli Studi di Milano
DICo - Via Comelico, 39, 20135 Milano - Italy
{castano,ferrara,montanelli,racca}@dico.unimi.it

Abstract. In open networked systems, each node shares part of its informational resources on the network and is responsible of providing an ontological description for them. To enable semantic information interoperability in networked contexts with a multitude of autonomous ontologies, appropriate matching techniques are required to determine semantic mappings between concepts of different ontologies. In this paper, we describe H-MATCH, an algorithm for dynamically performing ontology matching in open networked contexts. H-MATCH provides several matching models and metrics to work at different levels of depth, with different degrees of flexibility and accuracy, thus supporting semantic interoperability in a flexible way.

1 Introduction

In open networked systems like Peer-to-Peer and Grid, informational resources (e.g., datasets, documents) are provided by many different nodes generally spanned across multiple organizations. Open networked systems provide significant advantages in terms of flexibility, fault tolerance, and extensibility, but, in order to allow resource sharing, they introduce the problem of coping with the intrinsic dynamics of the system and with the need of a semantic description of resources [1,2,3]. Ontologies are generally recognized as an essential tool for describing resources in order to allow communication and knowledge sharing among distributed users and applications, by providing a common understanding of a domain of interest [4]. However, in open networked systems, where nodes are autonomous in terms of capabilities and resource management, information resource sharing can not be based on a global ontology. In fact, each node shares part of its resources on the network and is responsible of providing their ontological description. To enable resource sharing and semantic information interoperability in networked contexts with a multitude of autonomous ontologies, appropriate ontology matching techniques are thus required to determine semantic mappings between concepts of different ontologies that are semantically

[*] This paper has been partially funded by "Wide-scalE, Broadband, MIddleware for Network Distributed Services (WEB-MINDS)" FIRB Project funded by the Italian Ministry of Education, University, and Research, and by NoE INTEROP, IST Project n. 508011 - 6th EU Framework Programme.

M. Bouzeghoub et al. (Eds.): ICSNW 2004, LNCS 3226, pp. 215–230, 2004.
© IFIP International Federation for Information Processing 2004

related [5,6,7]. In this paper, we describe H-MATCH, an algorithm for dynamically performing ontology matching at different levels of depth, with different degrees of flexibility and accuracy. H-MATCH performs the matching of two ontologies, and provides, for each concept of one ontology, a ranking of similarity of the concepts in the other ontology. H-MATCH takes into account different levels of richness in resource descriptions, and allows one to consider various metadata elements of ontology descriptions separately or in combination. H-MATCH has been developed in the framework of the HELIOS project, whose aim is to support dynamic knowledge sharing and ontology-addressable content retrieval in peer-based systems [8].

The paper is organized as follows. In Section 2, we present the foundations of our approach for ontology matching. In Section 3, we describe the matching process. In Section 4, we discuss applicability issues in open networked contexts. In Section 5, we discuss related work on ontology matching. Finally, in Section 6, we give our concluding remarks.

2   Foundations for Semantic Information Interoperability

The problem of matching ontologies in multi-ontology contexts of open networked systems introduces a number of challenging issues to be addressed for semantic information interoperability. In this paper, we focus on three major requirements:

- The advent of the Semantic Web has produced a large body of research around ontology languages, and many standard proposals that can be used for resource description in open networked systems have emerged (e.g., RDF, DAML+OIL, OWL). Different ontologies can describe the same domain using different descriptions of the same resources, also using the same language. An important requirement of ontology matching techniques is to capture the elements that are relevant for matching purposes in ontology resource descriptions in a language-independent manner, to be applicable in many contexts. H-MATCH addresses this requirement by exploiting a reference ontology model (see Section 2.1).
- The meaning of ontology concepts depends basically on the names chosen for their definition and on their contexts, namely on their properties and on the relations they have with other concepts in the ontology. We are interested in addressing the fact that these two features can have a different impact in different ontology structures and can play a different relevance in the matching process. In order to address this requirement, H-MATCH computes a comprehensive value of matching of two concepts, by combining both their linguistic and their contextual features. Furthermore, H-MATCH allows one to set the relevance of the linguistic and contextual features in the matching process.
- A key requirement of dynamic matching is the capability of coping with different levels of detail and structuring in describing the resources of interest, by considering various ontology elements separately or in combination.

In the remainder of the paper, we will show how H-MATCH addresses this requirement by providing four different matching models for dealing with different levels of depth and different degrees of flexibility and accuracy of results. These matching models are used for dynamically suiting the matching process to different levels of richness in ontology descriptions.

2.1   A Reference Ontology Model

H-MATCH is based on a reference ontology model, called H-MODEL, capable of representing the ontology features that are relevant for matching purposes in a language independent way, in terms of concepts, properties, and semantic relations. To describe H-MODEL, in the following we focus on the OWL language, which provides three increasingly expressive sublanguages designed for use by specific communities of implementers and users, with different needs in terms of resource description accuracy [9]. Hereafter, we describe the constructs of H-MODEL, by showing the correspondent elements of OWL that can be mapped on them.

Concept. A concept c in H-MODEL is defined as a pair of the form $c = (n_c, P_c)$, where n_c is the concept name, and P_c is a set, possibly empty, of properties of c. Each concept c in H-MODEL represents a class declaration in OWL. The concept name n_c is set by referring to the RDF ID associated with the class declaration in OWL.

Property. A property p in H-MODEL is defined as a pair of the form $p = (n_p, PC_p)$, where n_p is the property name, and PC_p is a set of property constraints. Each property constraint associates a property p with a concept c, by specifying the minimal cardinality and the property value v_p of p in c. A property constraint $pc_p \in PC_p$ is a 3-tuple of the form $pc_p = (c, k_p, v_p)$, where c is a concept, $k \in \{0, 1\}$ is the minimal cardinality associated with p when applied to c, and v_p is the value associated with p when applied to c, and can be a datatype dt_p or a reference name. We call strong properties the properties with $k = 1$, and weak properties the ones with $k = 0$. Each property p represents a property declaration in OWL. The property name n_p is set by referring to the RDF ID associated with the property declaration. The property cardinality k_p as well as the property value v_p are enforced by exploiting OWL property restrictions. In particular, OWL cardinality restrictions are exploited for setting the cardinality of the property, while the AllValuesFrom, SomeValuesFrom, and has-Value OWL clauses are exploited for setting the value of the property, that can be a datatype, or a reference name representing the name of a concept or an individual in OWL.

Semantic relations. A semantic relation sr in H-MODEL is defined as a binary relation of the form $sr(c, c')$, where c and c' are concepts and sr is the relation holding between them. H-MODEL provides same-as, kind-of, and part-of semantic relations. In particular, the same-as and the kind-of relations represent the equiva-lentClass and the subClassOf relations in OWL, respectively. Moreover, the kind-of relation is exploited for the representation of the intersectionOf, and the unionOf OWL operators. For an intersection clause of the form $A \equiv B \sqcap C$ we set two kind-of relations of the form A kind $-$ of B and A kind $-$ of C. For a union clause of the form $A \equiv B \sqcup C$ we set a two kind-of relations of the form B kind $-$ of A and C kind $-$ of A. Finally, the part-of relation is used for representing an enumerated class defined as a collection by means of the oneOf OWL clause. In particular, we set a part-of relation between each H-MODEL element representing a component of the collection and the H-MODEL concept representing the enumerated class. A H-MODEL graphical representation of OWL ontologies is shown in Figure 1 (see Section 3).

2.2   Linguistic Features

Linguistic features refer to names of ontology elements and their meaning. To capture the meaning of names in an ontology in the matching process, we refer to a thesaurus Th of terms and terminological relationships among them. Th is automatically derived from the lexical system WordNet [10]. For the thesaurus construction, we note that in real ontologies, like OWL ontologies, ontology element names can be composed by one or more terms. Terms and terminological relationships to be stored in Th are selected as follows.

Basic terms. Given the set T of terms used as names of ontology elements, a term $t \in T$ is a basic term, denoted as bt, if an entry for bt exists in WordNet. In the thesaurus construction, an entry is defined for each basic term $bt_i \in T$.

Compound terms. Given the set T of terms used as names of ontology elements, a term $t \in T$ is a compound term, denoted as $ct =< bt_1, bt_2, \ldots, bt_n >$, if ct is composed by more than one basic term bt_i and an entry for ct does not exists in WordNet. For managing compound terms and their terminological re-lationships, we follow an approach similar to [11]. In a typical compound term ct, one of its constituent basic terms denotes the central concept represented by ct, while the remaining basic terms denote a specification of such a central concept. In particular in English, the basic terms appearing on the left side of ct denote the specification of the meaning of term appearing on the right side. Our thesaurus organization makes explicit these considerations for compound terms, by introducing appropriate terms and terminological relationships entries in Th necessary to: i) correctly capture the meaning of a compound term and ii) to represent all terminological relationships of interest with other terms in Th. Given a compound term $ct =< bt_1, bt_2, \ldots, bt_n >$, an entry is defined in Th for ct and for each constituent basic term $bt_i, i = 1, 2, \ldots, n$.

Terminological relationships. Terminological relationships in Th are defined by considering terminological relationships among synsets provided by WordNet.

Terminological relationships considered in Th together with their corresponding relationships in WordNet is shown in Table 1. In the thesaurus construction, for each basic term entry $bt_i \in Th$, a terminological relationship entry is defined in Th (i.e., SYN, BT/NT, or RT) if bt_i belongs to one of the WordNet synsets associated with the other basic term entries bt_j by a terminological relationship, according to the correspondences reported in Table 1. For each compound term entry $ct_i =< bt_{i_1}, bt_{i_2}, \ldots, bt_{i_n} >\in Th$, we define a terminological relationship BT/NT between ct_i and bt_{i_n}, to capture the fact that ct_i is a specification of bt_{i_n}. Furthermore, a RT terminological relationship between ct_i and each remaining basic term $bt_{i_j}, j = 1, 2, \ldots, n - 1$ is also defined in Th, for capturing the fact that these terms qualify ct_i.

Table 1. Terminological relationships for ontology matching

Terminological relationship in Th	Relationship in WordNet
SYN (synonymy)	synonymy
BT/NT (broader/narrower terms)	hyponymy hypernymy
RT (related terms)	meronymy coordinate terms

Weighting terminological relationships. In H-MATCH, a weight W_{tr} is associated with each terminological relationship $tr \in \{\mathsf{SYN}, \mathsf{BT/NT}, \mathsf{RT}\}$ in Th in order to express its implication for semantic affinity. Different types of relationships have different implications for semantic affinity. In particular, we set $W_{\mathsf{SYN}} \geq W_{\mathsf{BT/NT}} \geq W_{\mathsf{RT}}$. Synonymy is generally considered a more precise indicator of affinity than other relationships, consequently $W_{\mathsf{SYN}} \geq W_{\mathsf{BT/NT}}$. The lowest weight is associated with RT since it denotes a more generic relationship than BT/NT. Weights for terminological relationships are defined as shown in Table 2.

Table 2. Weights associated with terminological relationships

Terminological relationship	Weight
SYN	1.0
BT/NT	0.8
RT	0.5

2.3 Contextual Features

Contextual features refer to the properties and concepts directly related to a given concept in an ontology. The importance of considering contexts when matching heterogeneous information is well-known [12]. In particular, the approach used for detecting the context of concepts influences the matching results.

For ontology matching, a notion of context is essential, since semantic relations and properties play a key role in ontology specification. Given a concept c, we denote by $P(c)$ the set of properties of c, and by $C(c)$ the set of concepts that participate in a semantic relation with c (in the following referred to as *adjacents*), respectively. The context of a concept in H-MATCH is defined as the union of the properties and of the adjacents of c, that is, $Ctx(c) = P(c) \cup C(c)$.

Weighting contextual features. In H-MATCH, a weight W_{sr} is associated with each semantic relation to denote the strength of the connection expressed by the relation on the involved concepts for semantic affinity evaluation purposes. The greater the weight associated with a semantic relation, the higher the strength of the semantic connection between concepts. Furthermore, we associate a weight W_{sp} to strong properties, and a weight W_{wp} to weak properties, respectively, with $W_{sp} \geq W_{wp}$ to capture the importance of the property in characterizing the concept for matching. In fact, strong properties are mandatory related to a concept and are relevant to give its structural description. Weak properties are optional for the concept in describing its structure, and, as such, are less important in featuring the concept than strong properties. Weights considered in H-MATCH for properties and semantic relations are summarized in Table 3 [1].

Table 3. Weights associated with contextual features

Context element	Weight
same_as relation	1.0
kind_of relation	0.8
part_of relation	0.5
strong_property	1.0
weak_property	0.5

2.4   Basic Matching Functions

Term affinity function. The aim of the term affinity function $\mathcal{A}(t, t') \rightarrow [0, 1]$ is to evaluate the affinity between two terms t and t' with respect to Th. $\mathcal{A}(t, t')$ of two terms t and t' is equal to the value of the highest-strength path of terminological relationships between them in Th if at least one path exists, and is zero otherwise. A path strength is computed by multiplying the weights associated with each terminological relationship involved in the path, that is:

---

[1] Weight definition relies on our previous experience in developing schema matching techniques. In particular, terminological relationships weights have been extensively experimented in the ARTEMIS integration system [13]. Following similar considerations, we have defined weights for contextual features, which have been tested on a number of real ontologies, with satisfactory results. The matching support tool under development allows the designer to modify such default values, by choosing interactively different parameter setting, if necessary.

$$\mathcal{A}(t,t') = \begin{cases} \max_{i=1...k} \{W_{t \to_i^n t'}\} & \text{if } k \geq 1 \\ 0 & \text{otherwise} \end{cases} \tag{1}$$

where: k is the number of paths between t and t' in Th; $t \to_i^n t'$ denotes the ith path of length $n \geq 1$; $W_{t \to_i^n t'} = W_{1_{tr}} \cdot W_{2_{tr}} \cdot \ldots \cdot W_{n_{tr}}$ is the weight associated with the ith path, where $W_{j_{tr}} \mid j = 1, 2, \ldots, n$ denotes the weight associated with the jth terminological relationship in the path.

Datatype compatibility function. A datatype compatibility function is defined to evaluate the compatibility of data types of two properties according to a pre-defined set CR of compatibility rules. The datatype compatibility function $\mathcal{T}(dt, dt') \to \{0, 1\}$ of two data types dt and dt' returns 1 if dt and dt' are compatible according to CR, and 0 otherwise, that is:

$$\mathcal{T}(dt, dt') = \begin{cases} 1 & \text{iff } \exists \text{ a compatibility rule for } dt, dt' \text{ in } CR \\ 0 & \text{otherwise} \end{cases} \tag{2}$$

For instance, with reference to XML Schema datatypes (which are relevant for OWL ontology matching), examples of compatibility rules that hold are: xsd:integer $\Leftrightarrow$ xsd:int, xsd:integer $\Leftrightarrow$ xsd:float, xsd:decimal $\Leftrightarrow$ xsd:float, xsd:short $\Leftrightarrow$ xsd:int.

Property and semantic relation closeness function. A closeness function $\mathcal{C}(e, e') \to [0, 1]$ calculates a measure of the distance between two elements of concept contexts (i.e., two properties, two semantic relations, or a semantic relation and a property, respectively). $\mathcal{C}(e, e')$ exploits the weights associated with context elements and returns a value in the range [0,1] proportional to the absolute value of the complement of the difference between the weights associated with the elements, that is:

$$\mathcal{C}(e, e') = 1 - \mid W_e - W_{e'} \mid \tag{3}$$

where W_e and $W_{e'}$ are the weights associated with e and e', respectively. For any pairs of elements e and e', the highest value (i.e., 1.0) is obtained when weights of e and e' coincide. The higher the difference between W_e and $W_{e'}$ the lower the closeness value of e and e'. We note that the closeness of a property and a semantic relation can be evaluated in order to capture the structural heterogeneity among different ontological descriptions.

3 Ontology Matching with H-MATCH

The general goal of ontology matching techniques is to find concepts that have a semantic affinity with a target concept, by producing a measure of their affinity. To satisfy the main requirements for ontology matching described in the introduction, we have defined four matching models for H-MATCH, by exploiting the basic matching functions of Section 2.4. The matching models have been conceived to span from surface to intensive matching, with the goal of providing a wide spectrum of metrics suited for dealing with many different matching scenarios that can be encountered in comparing real ontologies (e.g., OWL ontologies). Each model calculates a semantic affinity value $SA_{c,c'}$ of two concepts c and c' which expresses their level of matching. $SA_{c,c'}$ is produced by considering linguistic and/or contextual features of concept descriptions. In a matching model, the relevance of the linguistic and the contextual features of c and c' in the matching process can be established, by properly setting the linguistic affinity weight $W_{la} \in [0, 1]$ in the semantic affinity evaluation process.

3.1   Surface Matching

The surface matching is defined to take into account only the linguistic features of concept descriptions. Surface matching addresses the requirement of dealing with high-level, poorly structured ontological descriptions. Given two concepts c and c', surface matching provides a measure $SA_{c,c'}$ of their semantic affinity by exploiting the terminological affinity function (1), that is:

$$SA_{c,c'} = A(n_c, n_{c'}) \tag{4}$$

where n_c and $n_{c'}$ are the names of c and c', respectively.

3.2   Shallow Matching

The shallow matching is defined to take into account both concept names and concept properties. With this model, we want a more accurate level of matching, by taking into account not only the linguistic features but also information about the presence of properties and about their cardinality constraints. For property comparison, each property $p_i \in P(c)$ is matched against all properties $p_j \in P(c')$ using (1) and (3), and the best matching value $m(p_i)$ is considered for the evaluation of $SA_{c,c'}$, as follows:

$$m(p_i) = \max\{A(n_{p_i}, n_{p_j}) \cdot C(p_i, p_j)\}, \forall p_j \in P(c') \tag{5}$$

where n_{p_i} and n_{p_j} denote the names of p_i and p_j, respectively. $SA_{c,c'}$ is evaluated by the shallow matching as the weighted sum of the linguistic affinity of c and c', calculated using (1), and of their contextual affinity, calculated as the average of the property best matching values computed using (5), that is:

$$SA_{c,c'} = W_{la} \cdot A(n_c, n_{c'}) + (1 - W_{la}) \cdot \frac{\sum_{i=1}^{|P(c)|} m(p_i)}{|P(c)|} \tag{6}$$

3.3   Deep Matching

The deep matching model is defined to take into account concept names and the whole context of concepts, in terms of properties and semantic relations. Each element $e_i \in Ctx(c)$ is compared against all elements $e_j \in Ctx(c')$ using (1) and

(3) and the best matching value $m(e_i)$ is considered for the evaluation of $SA_{c,c'}$, as follows:

$$m(e_i) = \max\{\mathcal{A}(n_{e_i}, n_{e_j}) \cdot \mathcal{C}(e_i, e_j)\}, \forall e_j \in Ctx(c') \qquad (7)$$

where n_{e_i} and n_{e_j} denote the names of e_i and of e_j, namely the names of a property or of an adjacent, respectively. $SA_{c,c'}$ is evaluated by the deep matching as the weighted sum of the linguistic affinity of c and c', calculated using (1), and of their contextual affinity, calculated as the average of the matching values for the elements of the context of c using (7), that is:

$$SA_{c,c'} = W_{la} \cdot \mathcal{A}(n_c, n_{c'}) + (1 - W_{la}) \cdot \frac{\sum_{i=1}^{|Ctx(c)|} m(e_i)}{|Ctx(c)|} \qquad (8)$$

3.4 Intensive Matching

The intensive matching model is defined to take into account concept names, the whole context of concepts, and also property values, for the sake of a highest accuracy in semantic affinity evaluation. In fact, by adopting the intensive model not only the presence and cardinality of properties, but also their values have an impact on the resulting semantic affinity value. Given two concepts c and c', the intensive matching calculates a comprehensive matching value for the elements of the context of c such as in (7) and, moreover, calculates a matching value $v(p_i)$ for each property $p_i \in P(c)$. The matching value $v(p_i)$ is calculated as the highest value obtained by composing the affinity of the name n_{p_i} and the value v_{p_i} of p_i with the name n_{p_j} and the value v_{p_j} of each property $p_j \in P(c')$, respectively. For property values comparison, we exploit the terminological affinity function (1) in case of object properties, and the datatype compatibility function (2) in case of datatype properties, that is:

$$v(p_i) = \begin{cases} \max\{\mathcal{A}(n_{p_i}, n_{p_j}) \cdot \mathcal{A}(v_{p_i}, v_{p_j})\}, \forall p_j \in P(c') \text{ iff } v_{p_i} \text{ is a reference name} \\ \max\{\mathcal{A}(n_{p_i}, n_{p_j}) \cdot \mathcal{T}(v_{p_i}, v_{p_j})\}, \forall p_j \in P(c') \text{ iff } v_{p_i} \text{ is a datatype} \end{cases}$$
$$(9)$$

$SA_{c,c'}$ is evaluated by the intensive matching as the weighted sum of the linguistic affinity of c and c', calculated using (1), and of their contextual affinity, calculated as the average of the matching values for the elements of the context of c using (7) and for the property values calculated using (9), that is:

$$SA_{c,c'} = W_{la} \cdot \mathcal{A}(n_c, n_{c'}) + (1 - W_{la}) \cdot \frac{\sum_{i=1}^{|Ctx(c)|} m(e_i) + \sum_{j=1}^{|P(c)|} v(p_j)}{|Ctx(c)| + |P(c)|} \qquad (10)$$

3.5 Example of Matching Two OWL Ontologies

As an example of the ontology matching problem, we consider two real OWL ontologies describing the publications domain in different ways. In particular, the first ontology (Ka) describes publications in the context of research projects, while the second ontology (Portal) describes publications in the context of a Web

Table 4. Features of the Ka and Portal ontologies

	Ka	Portal
Language	OWL Lite	OWL Full
# of concepts	251	291
# of properties	154	204
Average # of properties per concept	13	4
Average # of relations per concept	2	2

Table 5. Example of matching results with H-MATCH

Matching model	$SA_{Special\_Issue\_Publication,Publication}$	$SA_{Article\_In\_Book,Book}$
Surface	0.8	0.8
Shallow	0.6357	0.6435
Deep	0.6527	0.6435
Intensive	0.6175	0.6262

portal. These ontologies are heterogeneous in terms of language specification (i.e., OWL Lite and OWL Full, respectively) as well as in terms of contents, although both of them provide a subset on concepts related to publications. Small portions of Ka and Portal describing publications are shown in Figure 1(a) and Figure 1(b), respectively. We show the H-MODEL representation of the OWL elements which are relevant for H-MATCH by means of a graphical representation. In particular in Figure 1, white ovals represent concepts, grey ovals represent properties, and boxes represent datatypes. Arrows are used for representing kind-of relations, double-stricken and stricken lines for representing strong and weak property respectively, and dashed lines for representing property values. The main features of Ka and portal are summarized in Table 4. We exploit H-MATCH for matching Ka against Portal in order to automatically discover the affinity between the concepts that describe publications, in spite of concept heterogeneity in the two ontology descriptions. Moreover, we use H-MATCH also for providing, for each concept of Ka, a measure of semantic affinity with the concepts of Portal. In Table 5, we show the best results obtained from matching two concepts of Ka (i.e., Special_Issue_Publication and Article_In_Book) against Portal using our four matching models, with $W_{la} = 0.6$.

In our first example, the term Special_Issue_Publication is a specification of the term Publication (i.e., a BT/NT relationship is defined between them in Th). The semantic affinity value calculated using the surface matching model is due to this terminological relationship. Using other matching models, this affinity value based only on linguistic features is revised, by exploiting also contextual features. In particular, the shallow and intensive matching results are lower than the deep one, due to the fact that in Ka Special_Issue_Publication has a large number of properties which are different from the properties of Publication in Portal. Using the deep matching model, the kind-of relation between Special_Issue_Publication and Journal, which is a Publication in Portal has an important role in determining the

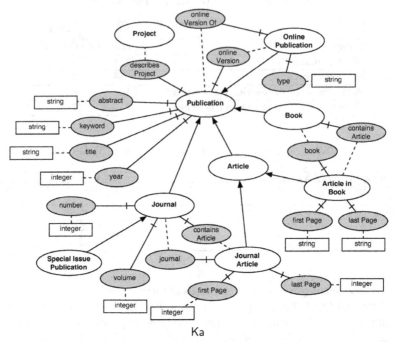

Ka

http://protege.stanford.edu/plugins/owl/owl-library/ka.owl

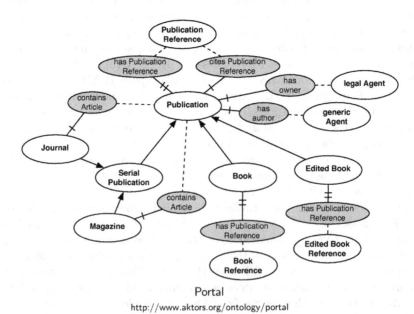

Portal

http://www.aktors.org/ontology/portal

Fig. 1. Ka and Portal ontology portions

semantic affinity value. On the opposite, in our second example, Article_in_Book does not have any semantic relation with Book in Ka. For this reason, we obtain the same semantic affinity value with the shallow and the deep model. In this case, the intensive model is more accurate, because property values are considered in the semantic affinity evaluation.

3.6   Considerations

The four different models are exploited for suiting ontology matching to different application scenarios. The main features of the matching models and their corresponding suggested scenarios with respect to OWL ontologies are summarized in Table 6.

The choice of the appropriate matching model depends on the level of detail of the ontology description as well as on the expected degree of precision of the results. The shallow model is useful when only concept names are to be considered. It requires few computational resources since neither concept properties nor semantic relations are considered. This model is well suited, for example, to perform an initial ontology comparison to decide wether it is worth to perform a deeper analysis. If the ontology is constituted mainly by concepts with a few number of properties and hierarchical relation among concepts, the shallow and deep model allow a good degree of precision without requiring great amount of computational resources. In presence of an articulated ontology, with rich resource descriptions and where relations among concepts are described through property values, the intensive model guarantees the most accurate results, although being the most expensive in term of computation.

Table 6. Applicability of the matching models

	Surface	Shallow/Deep	Intensive
OWL sub-language	Lite/DL/Full	Lite/DL/Full	Lite/DL/Full
Ontological description	Poorly structured ontologies with very simple resource description	Schematic ontologies with taxonomic resource description	Articulated ontologies with rich resource description
Suggested for	Linguistic-driven matching	Linguistic and context-driven matching	Linguistic, value, and context-driven matching
Advantages	Less computation	More accurate characterization of matching concepts	Finest characterization of matching concepts

4 Applicability to Semantic Information Interoperability in Open Networked Systems

In this section, we discuss the main applicability issues of our ontology matching techniques for semantic information interoperability in open networked systems based on the Peer-to-Peer (P2P) paradigm.

4.1 Resource Discovery

In schema-based P2P networks, where resources are described by means of an ontology rather than being identified only by file names, H-MATCH can be exploited to find out resources semantically related to a given target request. In a Grid environment, where different nodes expose different kind of services, H-MATCH can be used to overcome the lack of agreement on the way resources are described, and to help a node in finding nodes which have compatible resource descriptions. In general, a resource request is represented as a H-MODEL description of the target concept(s) of interest. When a node receives an incoming request, this is compared against the node ontology, by applying the H-MATCH algorithm. The matching evaluation depends on the expressiveness of the ontological description contained in the request and on the desired level of accuracy (i.e., surface, shallow, deep, or intensive matching). H-MATCH provides a ranking of concepts, ordered by their semantic affinity value with the target. A threshold-based mechanism is used for filtering the concepts to be returned to the requesting node. A deeper description of ontology-based content retrieval in P2P systems is described in [14].

4.2 Query Routing

In P2P networks, the query routing policy is one of the main factors that affect the load of the entire network and the effectiveness of the query answers. A semantic routing algorithm can be an alternative to the broadcasting of queries and can reduce the need of a more or less centralized index of the resources present in the network. H-MATCH results can be used to find the most relevant peers with respect to a given resource. A peer can exploit these associations among resources and peers to find the best recipients for future queries and to forward appropriately incoming queries to other peers. This semantic routing reduces both the network and the peers load, thus providing a greater scalability than routing techniques based on the topology of the network. We are working on the development of a semantic routing protocol which exploits H-MATCH results in the framework of the FIRB WEB-MINDS project, and some initial results on such topic are described in [15].

4.3 Semantic Communities

H-MATCH can be adopted to discover semantic mappings among nodes storing similar concepts in a networked system. The ability to define such semantic mappings among independent nodes, allows us to introduce the idea of *semantic communities* of nodes on predefined topic of interests described by means of one or more key-concepts. Given a topic of interest, each node applies H-MATCH to its ontology searching for relevant concepts and semantic mappings to nodes storing concepts semantically related to the topic (*semantic neighbors*). Exploiting semantic neighbors ontologies, further mappings can be discovered. Following the chain of mappings, a set of nodes constituting the semantic community on the considered topic of interest is identified. Because of the absence of a centralized organization which provides a complete list of semantic mappings between each pair of nodes, the community definition is a spontaneous process. As a consequence more than one semantic community on the same topic of interest can coexist, especially in large networks.

5   Related Work

Work related to ontology matching for multi-ontology networked systems can be grouped into two main families of ontology matching approaches, namely model-based and logic-based approaches. The model-based approach is based on the idea of exploiting the ontology metadata model for working on the ontology structure through a set of techniques of analysis, matching and learning. As an example, the Glue [7] approach exploits machine learning techniques to find semantic mappings between concepts stored in distinct and autonomous ontologies. Given two distinct ontologies, the mapping discovery process between their concepts is based on the measure of similarity which is defined through the joint probability distribution. The measure of similarity between two concepts is computed as the likelihood that an instance belongs to both the concepts. Another approach for model-based metadata matching in described in [16], where the choice of metadata for classifying data sources according to the requirements of a given application or task is discussed. In this approach, metadata information is organized as a set of categories and concepts, and the matching is enforced through fuzzy metrics.

The logic-based approach is based on the idea of exploiting the semantics associated with ontological descriptions for defining and analyzing mappings through automatic reasoning techniques. In particular, mapping discovering is reduced to the problem of checking a set of logical relations. For instance, in [6] the Ctx-Match algorithm is defined in order to point out semantic mapping between concepts stored in distinct peers of a Peer-to-Peer system. This algorithm compares the knowledge contained in different contexts looking for semantic mappings denoting peers interested in similar concepts. Ctx-Match is based on a semantic explication phase where concepts are associated with the correct meaning with respect to their context, and on a semantic comparison phase where concepts are translated in logical axioms and matched. As another example, in [17] the meaning of mappings is formally defined. The semantics provides a basis for reasoning about mappings (e.g., determining whether two mappings are equivalent or if a certain mapping formula is entailed by a mapping), combining evidence to propose likely mappings, and learning mappings. In particular, the reasoning is used for determining whether two mappings are equivalent, and whether a mapping is minimal (i.e., removing any formula from the mapping loses information).

With respect to these approaches, a main advantage of H-MATCH is the capability of dealing with different levels of accuracy in ontological descriptions by considering both the linguistic and the contextual features of ontology concepts. H-MATCH is suitable for dynamic scenarios like Peer-to-Peer and Grid, where ontologies evolves quickly and are characterized by different levels of accuracy in resource description.

6   Concluding Remarks

In this paper, we have presented the H-MATCH approach to the problem of ontology matching in multi-ontology contexts such as in open networked systems. H-MATCH has been implemented in the framework of the HELIOS project for supporting dynamic knowledge sharing and ontology-addressable content retrieval in peer-based systems [8]. Our future work will be devoted to the intensive experimentation on H-MATCH on real ontology matching cases in order to address the following issues: i) extensively testing the approach actually adopted for compound term management in the thesaurus; ii) optimizing the matching process, by further reducing the number of matches performed in the deep and intensive model; iii) revising the notion of concept context, by detecting concept contexts in a dynamic fashion. In particular, a promising research direction can consider the so-called *focus + context* or *fisheye* techniques for context detection in the ontology matching process. These techniques allow context detection by dynamically distorting the information structure according to the varying interests levels of its parts. The fisheye techniques have been developed originally for addressing the problem of displaying large information structures [18], and have been applied more recently to a large set of context detection problems, such as the node neighborhood detection in the World Wide Web [19].

References

1. Broekstra, J., et al.: A Metadata Model for Semantics-Based Peer-to-Peer Systems. In: Proc. of the 1st WWW Int. Workshop on Semantics in Peer-to-Peer and Grid Computing (SemPGRID 2003), Budapest, Hungary (2003)
2. Nejdl, W., et al.: EDUTELLA: a P2P Networking Infrastructure Based on RDF. In: Proc. of the 11th Int. World Wide Web Conference (WWW 2002), Honolulu, Hawaii, USA (2002)
3. Halevy, A., Ives, Z., Suciu, D., Tatarinov, I.: Schema Mediation in Peer Data Management Systems. In: Proc. of the 19th Int. Conference on Data Engineering (ICDE 2003), Bangalore, India, IEEE Computer Society (2003)
4. Berners-Lee, T., Hendler, J., Lassila, O.: The Semantic Web. Scientific American (2001)

5. Motik, B., Maedche, A., Volz, R.: A Conceptual Modeling Approach for Semantics-Driven Enterprise Applications. In Springer, ed.: Proc. of Confederated Int. Conferences DOA, CoopIS and ODBASE 2002, Irvine, California, USA (2002) 1082–1099
6. Bouquet, P., Magnini, B., Serafini, L., Zanobini, S.: A SAT-based Algorithm for Context Matching. In: Proc. of the 4th Int. and Interdisciplinary Conference on Modeling and Using Context (CONTEXT 2003), Stanford, CA, USA, Springer Verlag (2003) 66–79
7. Doan, A., Madhavan, J., Domingos, P., Halevy, A.: Learning to Map between Ontologies on the Semantic Web. In: Proc. of the 11th Int. World Wide Web Conference (WWW 2002), Honolulu, Hawaii, USA (2002) 662–673
8. Castano, S., Ferrara, A., Montanelli, S., Zucchelli, D.: HELIOS: a General Framework for Ontology-based Knowledge Sharing and Evolution in P2P Systems. In: Proc. of the 2nd DEXA Int. Workshop on Web Semantics (WEBS 2003), Prague, Czech Republic, IEEE Computer Society (2003)
9. Smith, M.K., Welty, C., McGuinness, D.L., (Eds.): OWL Web Ontology Language Guide (2004)
10. Miller, G.A.: WordNet: A Lexical Database for English. Communications of the ACM (CACM) **38(11)** (1995) 39–41
11. Lauer, M.: Designing Statistical Language Learners: Experiments on Noun Compounds. PhD thesis, Macquaire University, Australia (1995)
12. Ouksel, A.M., Naiman, C.F.: Coordinating Context Building in Heterogeneous Information Systems. Journal of Intelligent Information Systems **3** (1994) 151–183
13. Castano, S., De Antonellis, V., De Capitani Di Vimercati, S.: Global Viewing of Heterogeneous Data Sources. IEEE Transactions on Knowledge and Data Engineering **13** (2001) 277–297
14. Castano, S., Ferrara, A., Montanelli, S., Racca, G.: Matching Techniques for Resource Discovery in Distributed Systems Using Heterogeneous Ontology Descriptions. In: Proc. of the Int. Conference on Coding and Computing (ITCC 2004), Las Vegas, Nevada, USA, IEEE Computer Society (2004)
15. Castano, S., Ferrara, A., Montanelli, S., Pagani, E., Rossi, G.P., Tebaldi, S.: On Combining a Semantic Engine and Flexible Network Policies for P2P Knowledge Sharing Networks. In: Proc of the 1st DEXA Workshop on Grid and Peer-to-Peer Computing Impacts on Large Scale Heterogeneous Distributed Database Systems (GLOBE 2004). (2004)
16. Madhavan, J., A. Bernstein, P., Rahm, E.: Generic Schema Matching with Cupid. In: Proc. of the 27th Int. Conference on Very Large Data Bases (VLDB 2001), Rome, Italy (2001) 49–58
17. Jayant Madhavan, Philip A. Bernstein, P.D., Y. Halevy, A.: Representing and Reasoning about Mappings between Domain Models. In: Proc. of the 18th National Conference on Artificial Intelligence and 14th Conference on Innovative Applications of Artificial Intelligence, Edmonton, Alberta, Canada, AAAI Press (2002) 80–86
18. Furnas, G.W.: Generalized fisheye views. In: Proc. of the SIGCHI conference on Human factors in computing systems, Boston, Massachusetts, United States, ACM Press (1986) 16–23
19. Mukherjea, S., Hara, Y.: Focus+context views of world-wide web nodes. In: Proc. of the eighth ACM conference on Hypertext, Southampton, United Kingdom, ACM Press (1997) 187–196

A New Mechanism for the Interoperability of Data Systems

Miren I. Bagüés*, Jesús Bermúdez, Arantza Illarramendi, Alberto Tablado, and Alfredo Goñi**

University of the Basque Country, Donostia, Spain

Abstract. New advances in the areas of Internet and network communications have facilitated in some way the work with distinct data systems located at different places. However, what it is still missing is the possibility of a real and efficient interoperation among those systems. In this paper we present a new mechanism that favors the interoperability of agent based data systems. That mechanism permits an agent of a system 1) to send suitable messages to agents of another system without requiring the establishment of a common communication pattern in advance; and 2) to understand, completely or partially, the messages that are sent by agents of other systems. Moreover, the mechanism also allows the communication among agents that follow different standard languages such as FIPA-ACL and KQML. The main support of the proposed mechanism is an ontology that is divided into three interrelated layers and four different categories.

1 Introduction

The new advances in the areas of Internet and network communications facilitate in some way the work with distinct data systems. However, what it is still missing is the possibility of a real and efficient interoperation among these systems due to their heterogeneity. Besides, nowadays it is increasing the need of the interoperability of these systems in order to interchange information and services.

By data system we mean those systems that must deal with data coming from different sources, that use data management systems and other techniques to work with them and, that provide information to users and other systems. Nowadays there exists a tendency of using agents in data systems because agent technology is broadly recognized as an appropriate technology for approaching problems showing highly distributed nature that need flexible and adaptable

---

* This work is supported by a grant of the Basque Government.
** All authors are members of the Interoperable DataBases Group, online at http://siul02.si.ehu.es. This group is part of the Department of Computer Languages and Systems, at the University of the Basque Country in Spain. This work is mainly supported by the University of the Basque Country, Diputación Foral de Gipuzkoa (cosupported by the European Social Fund) and CICYT [TIN2004-07999-C02-00].

M. Bouzeghoub et al. (Eds.): ICSNW 2004, LNCS 3226, pp. 231–249, 2004.
© IFIP International Federation for Information Processing 2004

solutions [1]. In this paper we concentrate on these kinds of agent based data systems.

Moreover, currently the communication among agents is, in general, based on the interchange of messages. Agents must be aware in advance of the structure, language and the meaning of the messages in order to deal with them. Although this kind of communication is useful it is also true that it is somehow *limited* because it forces agents to share the same communication pattern. Therefore, the interoperation of agents from different systems is difficult in this scenario. Things get even worse when the agents follow distinct standard communication languages.

In order to allow *communication at a semantic level* among agents that favors the interoperability of data systems we have defined a new mechanism based on the use of an ontology which contains terms related to the communication acts among agents. While messages are the medium through which agents interact they can also be considered as utterances of communication languages. Throughout this paper we use the words "message" and "communication act" as synonyms.

The designed ontology is divided into three interrelated layers and four different categories: *actors* that interact among them using different kinds of messages; *messages* that have different purposes and deal with different kinds of contents; *contents* are the sentences included in the messages; and *subjects* that represent the topic of the messages. Axioms exist in the ontology that describe the interrelationships among these categories.

In the top layer of the ontology, the messages category `Communication Act`, includes terms that describe general communication acts with the aim of being valid in any communication framework. We suggest a conceptualization based on Searle's classes of *illocutionary acts* [2,3]: `Assertive`, `Directive`, `Commissive`, `Expressive`, and `Declarative`. Moreover, some specialization of those classes are also appropriate. For example, `Request` and `Inquiry` as different kinds of `Directive`. Of course, the point of this top level conceptualization is a general agreement to serve as a universal reference; therefore, we take it as a work in progress and not as a definitive specification. The `Actor` category represents those entities that send or receive messages. The `Subject` category represents domain specific terms describing the topics of the message. And finally, the `Content` category represents the kind of sentence included in the message.

The middle layer of the ontology is devoted to general purpose communication languages. Specified as subterms of the top layer terms, in the messages category appear terms that two standards, FIPA-ACL [4] and KQML [5], have defined to use as communication acts (e.g. `FIPA-Inform` term for FIPA-ACL and `KQML-Tell` term for KQML are subterms of `Assertive`).

In the bottom layer all the terms described are directly related to a concrete data system that has been considered. Therefore, the first two layers are valid for all data systems. Only the bottom layer must be defined for each data system.

We describe the ontology of communication acts using OWL(Web Ontology Language) [6], a well founded formalism developed by the Web Ontology Working Group [7] under the auspices of the W3C (World Wide Web Consortium) [8]. In our context, messages are OWL documents. Therefore, messages among agents that use the proposed ontology in this paper have an abstract representation as individuals of a shared universal class of messages. Some researchers have pointed out [9,10] the benefits of an XML encoding of messages. We believe that an OWL encoding of messages is even more advantageous because it incorporates semantics to the XML syntax. Parsers for OWL documents can be constructed with off-the-shelf tools. The use of OWL technology facilitates software engineering of agents by incorporating the new trends in the Semantic Web [11] technology. Moreover, Semantic Web technologies help in the standardization of the operational semantics of communication acts and offer a well defined infrastructure for sharing ontologies (domain ontologies, device ontologies or whatever).

Furthermore, we claim that the whole communication acts ontology provides interoperability support due to the recognition of communication acts from one language as instances of communication acts in other language. Sometimes the "translation" will not be complete, but partial comprehension of the communication may be useful and preferable to the "not understood" answer given nowadays. Reasoning support provided by the chosen formalism (OWL) may help during the interaction process, as will be explained in section 3.4.

The proposed mechanism, based on the use of the ontology provides the following advantages:

- *Discovering.* An agent that needs to send a message to an agent of another data system can discover the structure of the message that it must send by following a reasoning process with the ontology.
- *Understanding.* An agent can understand, completely or partially, the message sent by an agent of another data system by following a reasoning process with the ontology.
- *Multilanguage.* Two agents that use different communication languages can communicate, although in some situations the communication may be limited. In the current state of the ontology only FIPA-ACL and KQML standards are considered but new ones can be incorporated when necessary.
- *Evolution.* Modifications of the communication terms, at any layer, do not affect agent communications, only the ontology must be fitted.

In the rest of this paper we present first, in section 2, some principles that maintain the proposed mechanism for interoperability. In section 3 we highlight the three layers of our communication acts ontology. Next, in section 4, we show two examples of the use of the interoperability mechanism. Then, in section 5 we comment upon some related works and we finish with the conclusions in section 6.

2 Underlying Principles

The main goal of the present paper is to stress the benefits of achieving an ontological commitment about communication acts performed by cooperating agents.

This is complementary to the development of standards for agent communication languages like KQML or FIPA-ACL. These standards look for general homogeneity through compliance to the standard but are still unable to permit interoperability of agents using different standards, or even the same standard, as is the case with KQML dialects.

Every ontology is defined with a specific purpose. The goal of our ontology is to achieve the interoperability of agent based systems, more particularly interoperability among the agents (of those data systems), that use messages to communicate with each other. We assume agents are committed to cooperate, that is, all agents try to perform the actions that are requested of them. We do not pretend in this paper to present our ontology as the reference ontology (with a definitively established set of terms and relationships among them) for communication among agents. Our purpose is to present it as a proposal because we believe that an accorded ontology for communication is a must. That pragmatic effort should be pointed towards the desired interoperability of agents.

We are conscious of the many possible different approaches to the leading guideline for defining the terms and relationships in the communication acts ontology so, first of all we are going to explain our point of view. It is widely accepted that formalizing the semantics of communication acts avoids ambiguity and establishes a firm ground for implementation purposes. Nevertheless, the multimodal logics [1] used nowadays to express the semantics are often non-computable and it is recognized that the task of validating the implementation based on that logic semantics is very hard. Even, the implementer's intuitive understanding of the communication acts often prevail over the concise semantic definitions [9]. Furthermore, the use of different models and modalities to formalize the semantics of different languages (e.g. KQML and FIPA-ACL) makes them impossible to compare with respect to their formal definition. In this situation, we have adopted a more pragmatic view, we give up some formal properties and modal knowledge. We describe communication acts as somehow more primitive concepts. However, the deep semantics of the communication acts in KQML and FIPA-ACL could be maintained, as in their original specifications, for those agent systems that implement modalities (such as belief, desire, intention).

However, we do not give up on formality, we describe communication acts using OWL that provides suitable computational properties due to its foundations on description logics [16]. Notice that our aim is interoperability, we are not devoted to prove properties of the agent systems, thus we do not need such complex logics mentioned above. The ontology that we propose is a lattice of terms of communication acts and the reasoning system will allow one to compute subsumption between terms and recognition of individuals belonging to

---

[1] The multimodal logics referred here are a family of first order logics with various modal operators. Particularly modalities for expresing *beliefs*, *desires* and *intentions* of agents perfoming communication acts. FIPA-ACL uses SL (Semantic language) [4] which is based on [12,13] and, [14] reports on the modal operators used in KQML. See [15] for more detais.

these terms. Finally, the ontology is basically designed for software agents communication but it may also be used for the communication among human and software agents.

3   The Communication Acts Ontology

In this section we present our proposal for the ontology used for communicating among agents, COMMONT (hereafter COMMunication Acts ONTology) . Firstly, we introduce terms and properties for the top layer. Secondly, we quickly review some of the similarities and differences of KQML and FIPA-ACL with respect to the terms appearing in COMMONT. Finally, we focus on the communication acts appearing in the bottom layer of the ontology that are related to a real data system. We explain the design decisions and illustrate the possibilities of the formalism for helping in the management of the interoperation.

3.1   The Top Layer of the Ontology

Through this subsection we show the terms corresponding to the four categories from the ontology in the following order: first those corresponding to `Communication Acts` and then those corresponding to `Content`, `Subject` and `Actor` respectively.

A. Communication Acts

This top layer conceptualization about communication acts should be considered as a framework agreement.

The most general term of this layer is the `CommunicationAct` term. Its individuals are communication acts that may have a sender and a receiver, and depending on its kind they may have a content and a subject. Let us specify it using an abstract syntax in the following manner:

$$\texttt{CommunicationAct} \sqsubseteq \forall \texttt{has-sender.Actor} \sqcap\ \leq 1\ \texttt{has-sender} \sqcap$$
$$\forall \texttt{has-receiver.Actor} \sqcap$$
$$\forall \texttt{has-content.Content} \sqcap$$
$$\forall \texttt{has-subject.Subject}$$

For the presentation we prefer this logic notation[2] instead of the more verbose XML-like notation of OWL. The sentence means that `has-sender`, `has-receiver`, `has-content` and `has-subject` are properties that may be applied to communication acts. Every sender and receiver of an individual in `CommunicationAct` must be an individual of the class `Actor` and there is at most one `has-sender`. Moreover, every content and subject must be an individual of class `Content` and `Subject` respectively. But it does not mean that

---

[2] This notation is common in the description logics field. See [16] for a full explanation. Furthermore, take this statement as a proposal not as a definitive conceptualization.

necessarily every communication act has a sender, a receiver, a content and a subject (that is a different sentence that should be expressed using a different operator i. e. $\exists$ `has-sender`).

Speech acts theory [2] has been used as a source of inspiration for designing agent communication languages and particularly Searle's classification of *illocutionary acts* [17]. Following this tradition we split up the communication acts into Searle's five classes. `Assertive` is the class of communication acts which commit the sender to the truth of an expressed proposition, `Directive` are those communications which involve getting the receiver to do something, `Commissive` are those which involve committing the sender to some course of action, `Expressive` are those which convey a psychological state of the sender, and `Declarative` are those which bring about the correspondence of the world to the words declared. Some constraints are required for communication acts in those classes. For instance, the content of an assertive must be a proposition, the content of a commissive must be a commitment and the content of a directive must be an action.

$$\text{Assertive} \sqsubseteq \text{CommunicationAct} \sqcap$$
$$\forall \text{has-content.Proposition}$$
$$\text{Directive} \sqsubseteq \text{CommunicationAct} \sqcap$$
$$\forall \text{has-content.Action}$$

Moreover, it is reasonable to specify particularizations of those classes. Notice that software agents in our context are not prepared to interpret arbitrary communication acts (as is the case in natural language communication), they only recognize individuals on the basis of the values of their properties. Therefore, we want to distinguish a directive asking for information (`Inquiry`), from a directive requesting to perform another kind of action (`Request`); we want to distinguish an assertive informing in response to another message (`Reply-Assertive`), from an assertive that informs autonomously (`Inform`). More specialization should be included if necessary, and notice that disjointness of classes is not assumed unless stated explicitly or logically deduced from statements.

$$\text{Request} \sqsubseteq \text{Directive} \sqcap$$
$$\exists \text{has-content.Demmand}$$
$$\text{Inquiry} \sqsubseteq \text{Directive} \sqcap$$
$$\exists \text{has-content.Query}$$
$$\text{Inform} \sqsubseteq \text{Assertive}$$
$$\text{Reply-Assertive} \sqsubseteq \text{Assertive} \sqcap$$
$$\exists \text{in-reply-to.CommunicationAct}$$

B. Content, Subject, and Actor

Communication acts in general may be broken down into the type of action (assert, request, inform, etc.) and the propositional content which specifies details of the action. So the top layer ontology includes a conceptualization of

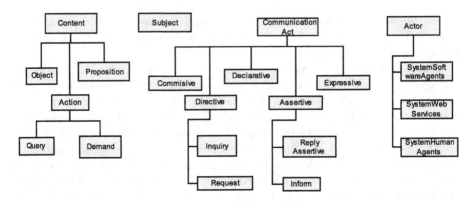

Fig. 1. Top layer of the COMMONT ontology.

classes of contents. So far, the class **Content** has subclasses **Object**, **Action** and **Proposition** that should be properly conceptualized and subdivided into more specialized classes in the future. For instance, **Query** and **Demmand** for the subclass **Action**.

Moreover, every communication act may refer to a topic that we name as its subject. The top layer class **Subject** will be specialized by domain ontologies (e.g. sanitary domain ontology, financial domain ontology,...).

In the context of COMMONT, by actors we mean those entities sending or receiving messages. We have divided the category of actors into three subcategories: **SystemWebServices**, **SystemSoftwareAgents** and **SystemHumanAgents**. Those terms respectively describe the general features of the web services defined in the system, the different type of agents that take part in the system and the different human users that are going to interact with the system.

In figure 1 can be seen the top layer of the ontology described in this subsection.

3.2 The Middle Layer of the Ontology

The top layer ontology can be extended with specific terms that belong to general purpose agent communication languages, like those from KQML or FIPA-ACL. In the case of FIPA-ACL, classes of messages of this language are specified as subterms of top layer terms according to their semantics. For example,

$$\text{FIPA-Inform} \sqsubseteq \text{Assertive}$$
$$\text{FIPA-Inform-If} \sqsubseteq \text{Inform} \sqcap \text{FIPA-Inform}$$
$$\text{FIPA-Inform-Ref} \sqsubseteq \text{Inform} \sqcap \text{FIPA-Inform}$$
$$\text{FIPA-Agree} \sqsubseteq \text{Reply-Assertive} \sqcap \text{FIPA-Inform}$$
$$\text{FIPA-Request} \sqsubseteq \text{Directive}$$
$$\text{FIPA-Query-If} \sqsubseteq \text{Inquiry} \sqcap \text{FIPA-Request}$$
$$\text{FIPA-Query-Ref} \sqsubseteq \text{Inquiry} \sqcap \text{FIPA-Request}$$

In the same way, classes of messages of KQML are specified. For example,

$$\text{KQML-Tell} \sqsubseteq \text{Assertive}$$
$$\text{KQML-Ask-If} \sqsubseteq \text{Inquiry}$$

It is of vital relevance for the interoperability aim of the ontology to be able to specify ontological relationships among classes of different standards. For instance, the following axioms represent that KQML-Ask-If is equivalent to FIPA-Query-If and that KQML-Achieve is a subclass of FIPA-Request, and KQML-Tell is a subclass of FIPA-Inform.

$$\text{KQML-Ask-If} \equiv \text{FIPA-Query-If}$$
$$\text{KQML-Achieve} \sqsubseteq \text{FIPA-Request}$$
$$\text{KQML-Tell} \sqsubseteq \text{FIPA-Inform}$$

Nevertheless, KQML and FIPA-ACL differ substantially in their semantic framework [18] to the point that, in general, a complete and accurate translation between them is not possible. But it is also true that they share basic concepts and principles to such an extent that we can define ontological relationships in the context of the interoperability of data systems.

Conceptually KQML and FIPA-ACL consider two components in a message: the message class component and the message content component. Both also claim to be independent of the content language and promote the message class component as being responsible for determining the kinds of communication acts they consider. Nevertheless, a more in-depth study of both languages reveals some disagreement with respect to the limits of what to include in the message class component or in the message content component. In fact, the boundaries of the two components are not clearly cut. For example, when a FIPA agent wants to tell another agent to achieve one goal G, the agent will send a message of class FIPA-Request, with a content expression referring to an action achieve (from an ontology of actions) and with the goal G as a parameter. Instead, a KQML agent trying to communicate the same thing will send a message of class KQML-Achieve with the goal G in the content expression. Luckily, that relationship can be expressed in the COMMONT ontology using the following sentence:

$$\text{KQML-Achieve} \equiv \text{FIPA-Request} \sqcap$$
$$\exists \text{has-content}.\{\text{achieve}\}$$

We think that the decision of what to include in the message class component and what to include in the content component is biassed by the purpose of the language. General purpose languages tend to design more general classes of messages shifting to the content component the responsibility of expressing more concrete things. In KQML design, the repertoire of classes of messages is consciously not closed in order to cope freely with this situation. But experience has shown that various KQML dialects have emerged, and unfortunately they are not interoperable with the genuine KQML. This lack of interoperability is another reason that guarantees the interest of the CommOnt ontology we are proposing. On the other side, typical agent based data systems usually deal with a limited collection of kinds of messages. Shifting the responsibility of interpreting those messages to the content component may not be the most appropriate decision. Taking that in mind we have designed the bottom layer of the ontology.

3.3   The Bottom Layer of the Ontology

It is often the case that every single agent based system uses a limited collection of communication acts that constitute its particular communication language. Some of those communication acts can be defined as particularizations of existing standards in the middle layer and maybe some others as particularizations of top layer terms. Nevertheless their specification in our communication ontology will favor the interoperability with related agent based systems.

We are going to present the terms for this layer using a concrete data system, AINGERU[3]: an agent based data system for a new way of tele-assistance for elderly people. The AINGERU system, apart from supporting the functionalities provided by current tele-assistance services, also offers: an active assistance by using agents that behave in the face of anomalous situations without a direct intervention of the user; an anywhere and anytime assistance by using wireless communications and PDAs (Personal Digital Assistant); and the monitoring of personal vital signs by using sensors that capture the values of those signs and feed a decision support system that analyzes them and generates an alarm when necessary.

After completing the requirements analysis of the system, three major classes of messages were identified (among others that we do not explain here so as not to include too much detail): A-Request[4], A-QueryRef and A-InformResult.

- A-Request includes the messages demanding the receiver to perform an action
- A-QueryRef includes the messages asking the receiver for some information
- A-InformResult includes the messages sending results in reply to some request.

More specifically, the value of the property has-content for every message in the class A-Request is an action from the class Demmand named do. The value of has-content for a message in A-QueryRef is an action from the class Query named give-me; and, respectively, the value of has-content for a message in A-InformResult is a content named collection.

---

[3] AINGERU is the word in the Basque language for expressing the notion of a guardian angel.

[4] A-Request means Aingeru-Request and analogously for all the A- prefixes.

$$\text{A-Request} \sqsubseteq \text{Request} \sqcap$$
$$\exists\text{has-content.}\{\text{do}\}\sqcap \leq 1 \text{ has-content} \sqcap$$
$$\exists\text{has-subject.Subject}\sqcap \leq 1 \text{ has-subject}$$
$$\text{A-QueryRef} \sqsubseteq \text{Inquiry} \sqcap$$
$$\exists\text{has-content.}\{\text{give-me}\}\sqcap \leq 1 \text{ has-content} \sqcap$$
$$\exists\text{has-subject.Subject}\sqcap \leq 1 \text{ has-subject}$$
$$\text{A-InformResult} \sqsubseteq \text{Reply-Assertive} \sqcap$$
$$\exists\text{has-content.}\{\text{collection}\}\sqcap \leq 1 \text{ has-content} \sqcap$$
$$\exists\text{has-subject.Subject}\sqcap \leq 1 \text{ has-subject}$$

Notice that now the interpretation of a message from A-Request (respectively from the other two classes) depends entirely on its subject.

Moreover, considering two components in a message (as FIPA-ACL and KQML would consider them) we have advocated for including in the message class component the explicit representation of the specific type of communication act, depending on the kind of the subject of the message. Therefore, each of the previous major classes are subdivided into different subclasses (see figure 2 for a fragment of the ontology and [19] for a broader explanation). For instance,

$$\text{MedicineModify} \sqsubseteq \text{A-Request} \sqcap$$
$$\exists\text{has-subject.Medicine}$$
$$\text{LocationQuery} \sqsubseteq \text{A-QueryRef} \sqcap$$
$$\exists\text{has-subject.Location}$$
$$\text{VitalSignInform} \sqsubseteq \text{A-InformResult} \sqcap$$
$$\exists\text{has-subject.VitalSign}$$

A MedicineModify message is used to request a change in the medicines prescription, a LocationQuery message asks for the coordinates of the physical location of a user, and a VitalSignInform message informs about the values of the vital signs of a person. This type of representation facilitates the interpretation of messages by the agents. In the subsection 3.4 we explain in more detail the advantages of this approach.

In this bottom layer of the ontology also appear terms related with the subject category and actor category. Concerning subject category, in figure 3 can be observed an example of a fragment of the ontology of subjects in AINGERU. Agent based data systems developed on different domains will use different ontologies of subjects, but those developed on the same domain should share some concepts in the ontology of subjects if they want to interoperate.

With respect to the category of actors in our application scenario (see figure 3), HumanAgents includes subclasses for users of the AINGERU system as well as for those people concerned with the user assistance, from sanitary people to relatives. SoftwareAgents includes specialized classes for agents described taking into account their location and goals (for example, whether they work

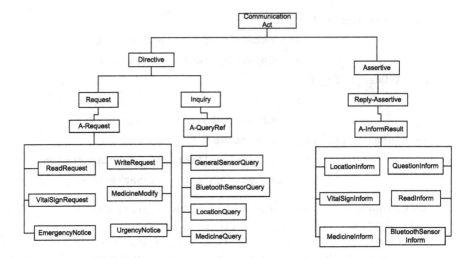

Fig. 2. Fragment of the message category of COMMONT.

in a PDA or in a computer, are they attending a sensor or interacting with an ontology, and so on). `AingeruWebServices` is a subclass of `SystemWebServices` that describes the web services exported by AINGERU. For example, the web service `WebLocation` permits one to obtain the location of the user of the PDA. Every service in `AingeruWebServices` has a property `provideService` whose value is an DAML-S description of the Web Service that these agents provide.

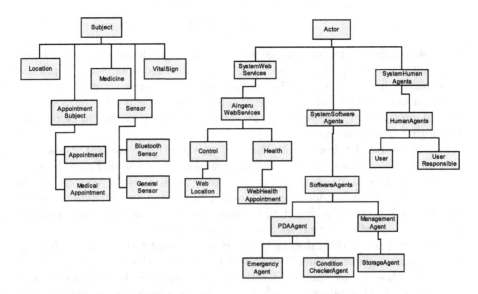

Fig. 3. Fragment of the Subject and Actor categories of COMMONT.

Having web services as a part of our ontology permit us to describe them at a semantic level independently of the language in which they are expressed. Due to this it is easier to find the adequate service in each case. If an external agent wants to use one of the services that the system exports as web services, it has two different ways of doing it: describing semantically what it wants to do (the reasoning mechanism of the ontology will infer which is the web service it has to use and which are the attributes it needs); or, using the standards for Web Services.

3.4   Benefits of the Explicit Representation of Messages Using OWL

Now we want to show some more benefits of representing explicitly the messages as individuals of OWL classes. The description of classes can include necessary constraints for the individuals in a class as well as sufficient conditions for individuals to be recognized as members of a particular class. All the logic sentences stated so far (except those with the equivalence $\equiv$ symbol) express necessary constraints for the individuals in the class named to the left of the $\sqsubseteq$ symbol. Moreover, it is possible to take advantage of the formalism to state axioms that specify minimal sufficient conditions to recognize that an individual belongs to a certain class. For instance:

$$\texttt{Inquiry} \sqcap \exists\texttt{has-subject.Location} \sqsubseteq \texttt{LocationQuery}$$
$$\texttt{Reply-Assertive} \sqcap \exists\texttt{has-subject.Medicine} \sqsubseteq \texttt{MedicineInform}$$

Using this capability of expressiveness of the OWL formalism and the supported reasoning capability, it is possible to discover the most specific class of a message and the collection of properties that are applicable to it. That information can be used by an external agent for the construction of a message that must be sent to an agent of a different system. Basically, the external agent only needs to know the top layer class of the message it wants to send in addition to the subject that it is about. Examples that illustrate this task are presented in section 4. Notice that this process is done at runtime, allowing an agent to interoperate with a different kind of agent without being previously aware of how to do it. Sometimes the message built may be partially understood. But this gives the agents the opportunity to react, which is hopefully better than receiving a "non understood message" response.

4   Examples of the Use of the CommOnt Ontology

We show in this section two different scenarios in which the agents of different systems interoperate between them. The main goal of the section is to show through two examples how our proposal helps in the task of the interoperation among agents.

4.1   Interoperation of an External Agent with Aingeru

The external agent belongs to an information system of a hospital and its task is to know where the user is because an alarm has been received from the EmergencyAgent in the PDA of the user.

There are two main steps that the external agent must do to accomplish its goal: i) to discover how to communicate with AINGERU agents and ii) to contact the adequate AINGERU agent. In the first step the ontology plays an important role. The external agent knows *what it wants* to communicate but it does not know *how* to interchange messages with AINGERU agents. Therefore, it uses the COMMONT ontology to obtain the properties that an AINGERU message must have. In this step, we can observe how our mechanism favors the interoperability with external agents. The external agent asserts the following statements to create a new message[5] m1 that asks for the location of a user:

```
m1   <type> Inquiry
m1   <has-subject> loc1
loc1 <type> Location
```

Then the reasoning system will infer that m1 is an instance of the LocationQuery class.

```
m1 <type> LocationQuery
```

Next the external agent asks the ontology for the attributes associated to LocationQuery. It will receive the following list of attributes: ident, has-sender, has-receiver, has-subject, has-content.

In the second step, the external agent needs to discover which and where the specialist AINGERU agent is. That agent is to whom the external agent must send the message obtained at step 1. There are several agencies in AINGERU that offer facilities to discover which agent offers a certain service. They are called Service Discovery facilities and are based on the DAML-S [20] Web Services Description Language. In our example, the external agent asks (to the Service Discovery) for the particular agent that is in charge of knowing the location of the user.

In this step we can see the flexibility that AINGERU offers to deal with different agents. With the information obtained in both steps the external agent can create the LocationQuery message that must be sent (see figure 4).

Once the message is created and the external agent knows to which agent needs to send its request, it establishes the communication and waits for the response. When the external agent receives a reply message it asserts the statements within that message in order to understand it. Then the reasoning system will infer that the message is an instance of the LocationInform class.

```
m2 <type> LocationInform
```

---

[5] We use an abstract syntax.

244 M.I. Bagüés et al.

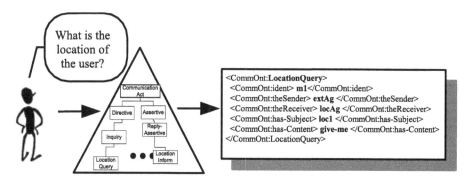

Fig. 4. Using the ontology to build the message.

Next the external agent asks the ontology for the values of the properties associated to m2. It will receive the following pairs of attribute-value:

```
ident:m2
has-sender:locAg
has-receiver:extAg
has-content:collection
has-subject:loc1
loc1.theLocation:43°18′26″, −2°0′41″
```

With this information the external agent can understand the message that it has received, which is: The user location is $43°18′26″$, $−2°0′41″$(see figure 5).

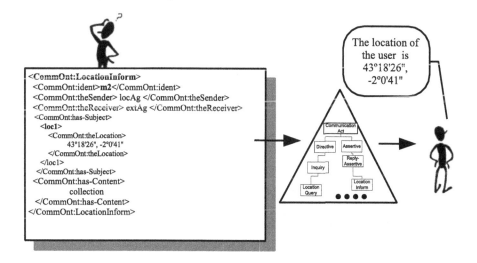

Fig. 5. Using the ontology to understand the result.

4.2   Interoperation Between an Agent That Uses FIPA-ACL Messages and Another That Uses KQML Messages

In this example we want to show how interoperation using messages from different languages can be achieved through our COMMONT ontology. Let us suppose an agent F, that uses FIPA-ACL messages, requests to an agent K, that uses KQML messages, to achieve a temperature of 21 degrees in a room. F will send the following FIPA-ACL message mF1:

```
(request
   : sender (agent-identifier : name F)
   : receiver (set (agent-identifier : name K))
   : content ''achieve = (temperatureRoom,21)'')
```

The abstract representation of that message using COMMONT involves the following statements:

```
mF1 <type> FIPA-Request
mF1 <has-sender> F
mF1 <has-receiver> K
mF1 <has-content> achieve
mF1 <has-subject> (temperatureRoom,21)
```

Then, due to the axiom

$$\text{KQML-Achieve} \equiv \text{FIPA-Request} \sqcap \exists \text{ has. content.} \{\text{achieve}\}, \text{mF1}$$

is recognized as a message in KQML-Achieve, and the agent K understands it completely and is able to process it.

Let us suppose now that agent F sends to agent K the following FIPA-ACL message mF2:

```
(request
   : sender (agent-identifier : name F)
   : receiver (set (agent-identifier : name K))
   : content
      ''((action (agent-identifier : name K)
        (inform-if
          : sender (agent-identifier : name K)
          : receiver (set (agent-identifier : name F))
          : content ''empty mailbox''))'')
```

Then the abstract representation includes, among others, the following statements:

```
mF2 <type> FIPA-Request
mF2 <has-content> action
```

In this case there is not enough information for recognizing mF2 as a message in any KQML class. The most likely continuation of this conversation in nowadays agent systems would be a "not understood" message and the end of the conversation. But due to the axiom `FIPA-Request` $\sqsubseteq$ `Directive` in COMMONT ontology, `mF2 <type> Directive` is deduced.

Since every agent using COMMONT know the terms in the top layer of the ontology, agent K understands `mF2` only partially (K understands that `mF2` is a `Directive`, but no more). Trying to cooperate, agent K sends to agent F a `KQML-Tell` message informing about its own capabilities on performing directives. Due to `KQML-Tell` $\sqsubseteq$ `FIPA-Inform`, agent F is able to completely understand the reply from K, and to discover that `empty` is a predicate about which agent K can be asked. Therefore, agent F decides to deliver to agent K a message from another class, like the following `mF3`:

```
(query-if
    : sender (agent-identifier : name F)
    : receiver (set (agent-identifier : name K))
    : content ''empty mailbox'')
```

Now the abstract representation includes the following statements:

```
mF3 <type> FIPA-Query-If
mF3 <has-content> empty
mF3 <has-subject> mailbox
```

Since the axiom `KQML-Ask-If` $\equiv$ `FIPA-Query-If` is in COMMONT, `mF3 <type> KQML-Ask-if` is deduced and, therefore, agent K is able to understand `mF3` completely and to process it satisfactorily.

5   Related Works

Our work is complementary to the development of standards for agent communication languages like KQML or FIPA-ACL (well summarized in [9]). These standards look for general homogeneity through compliance to the standard. In the following we mention some other related works. In [21] a formal framework is presented for agents to negotiate the semantics of their ACL at runtime. A *semantic space* provides a means to systematically analyze inter-agent communication. A point in this space can be identified with a particular communication act. They advocate for the specification of message semantics in a common formalism. We view our COMMONT ontology as a complementary effort. Any interesting relationship between classes of messages discovered within their analysis method can be explicitly encoded in COMMONT. Therefore, our proposal framework acts as a compiled representation of messages classification.

The following two papers [22,23] present a semantic communication stack that includes the message class component and the content component among others. They emphasize in the need for agreements on the formalisms used for each component and in the need to manage the dependencies between components. They also point out that one of the major challenges is to find out the right trade-off between implicit versus explicit semantics describing abstractions

in each component. In our case the content component and the message component can be described using the same formalism. Moreover, in [24] they propose
an abstract ontology representation (AOR) for capturing abstract models of
communication related knowledge (domain models, agent communication languages, content languages and models of how these interact). Our COMMONT
ontology can be considered as part of that AOR.

A different approach for interoperability, based on the inclusion of prefor-
matted message templates within the advertised capability description of agents
is presented in [25]. The shallow-parsing template approach presented in that
paper relaxes the constraint that agents share a common language for describing the content and format of messages. One main difference of that approach
with respect to ours is their major emphasis on syntactic aspects.

Furthermore, experience reported in [26] suggests that there is a strong overlap in the communication acts required by many agent systems and therefore
they claim that a small comprehensive set would be sufficient for many multi-
agent systems. We agree with them and furthermore, the COMMONT ontology
permits the description of different communication acts whilst maintaining the
relevant relationships. Finally, in [26] it is noticed that the question of how much
content information should be pushed to the message component is an important
research issue. Our work goes in that direction.

6   Conclusions

The heterogeneous data systems interoperability is a need that is manifested
each time with a greater intensity in different fields. However, currently the
interoperation is very restricted and there is a long way to traverse until a real
and efficient interoperation is possible.

In this paper we have presented one mechanism that takes us one step closer
to achieving that interoperability by allowing the communication among agents
of different data systems.

The mechanism is based on one ontology that describes the communication
acts among agents of different data systems. That ontology is made up of three
layers that try to collect communication acts at different levels of abstraction.
The terms of the top layer should be defined by experts in the agents communication area and they should be considered as reference terms for communication.
The elements of the middle layer reflect the terms that different standard communication languages have defined.

Finally, in the bottom layer, we advocate for defining terms that describe
messages used in each concrete data system. This type of message descriptions
facilitates their interpretation because it is possible to reason with them.

References

1. Jennings, N.R.: An agent-based approach for building complex software systems.
   Commun. ACM **44** (2001) 35–41

2. Searle, J.R.: Speech acts. Cambridge University Press (1969) New York.

3. Traum, D.R.: Speech acts for dialogue agents. In Wooldridge, M., Rao, A., eds.: Foundations of Rational Agency. Kluwer Academic Publishers (1999) 169–201

4. Foundation For Intelligent Physical Agents: FIPA Communicative Act Library Specification. (2002) http://www.fipa.org/specs/fipa00037/SC00037J.html.

5. Finin, T., Labrou, Y., Mayfield, J.: KQML as an agent communication language. In Bradshaw, J., ed.: Software Agents. MIT Press (1997)

6. World Wide Web Consortium: OWL Web Ontology Language Reference. (2003) http://www.w3.org/TR/owl-ref.

7. Web-Ontology (WebOnt) Working Group: (2004) http://www.w3.org/2001/sw/WebOnt/.

8. World Wide Web Consortium: (2004) http://www.w3.org.

9. Labrou, Y.: Standardizing agent communication. In Marik, V., Stepankova, O., eds.: Multi-Agent Systems & Applications. Advanced Course on Artificial Intelligence (ACAI-01), Springer-Verlag (2001) 74–97

10. Grosof, B., Labrou, Y.: An approach to using xml and a rule-based content language with an agent communication language. In Dignum, F., Greaves, M., eds.: Issues in Agent Communication. Lecture Notes in Artificial Intelligence. Springer-Verlag (2000) 96–117

11. Berners-Lee, T., Hendler, J., Lassila, O.: The semantic web. Scientific American **284(5)** (2001) 34–43

12. Cohen, P., Levesque, H.: Intentions is choice with commitment. Artificial Intelligence **42** (1990) 213–231

13. Bretier, P., Sadek, M.D.: A rational agent as the kernel of a cooperative spoken dialogue system: implementing a logical theory of interaction. In Müller, J., Wooldridge, M., Jennings, N., eds.: Intelligent Agents III. Volume 1193. Springer-Verlag, Berlin, Germany (1997) 189–204

14. Labrou, Y., Finin, T.: Semantics and conversations for an agent communication language. In: Proceedings of the 15th International Joint Conference on Artificial Intelligence (IJCAI-97), Nagoya, Japan (1997) 584–591

15. Wooldridge, M.: Reasoning about Rational Agents. MIT Press (2000)

16. Baader, F., Calvanese, D., McGuinness, D., Nardi, D., Patel-Schneider, P.: The Description Logic Handbook. Theory, Implementation and Applications. Cambridge University Press (2003)

17. Searle, J.R.: A classification of illocutionary acts. Language in Society **5** (1976) 1–23

18. Labrou, Y., Finin, T., Peng, Y.: Agent communication languages: the current landscape. IEEE Intelligent Systems **14** (1999) 45–52

19. Bagüés, M.I., Bermúdez, J., Illarramendi, A., Tablado, A., Goñi, A.: Using ontologies in the development of an innovating system for elderly people tele-assistance. In: Proceedings of the International Conference on Ontologies, Databases and Applications of SEmantics. Volume 2888 of Lecture Notes on Computer Science., Springer-Verlag (2003) 889–905 Sicily, Italy.

20. DAML Services: (2004) http://www.daml.org/services.

21. Reed, C., Norman, T.J., Jennings, N.R.: Negotiating the semantics of agent communication languages. Computational Intelligence **18** (2002) 229–252

22. Willmott, S., Dale, J., Charlton, P.: Agent Communication Semantics for Open Environments. Foundation for Intelligent Physical Agents. (2002) Input document f-in-00066. http://www.fipa.org/docs/input/f-in-00066/.

23. Calisti, M.: Abstracting communication in distributed agent-based systems. In: Proceedings of the 16th European Conference on Object-Oriented Programming, Malaga, Spain (2002)
24. Willmott, S., Constantinescu, I., Calisti, M.: Multilingual agents: Ontologies, languages and abstractions. In: Proceedings of First International Workshop on Ontologies in Agent Systems, Montreal, Canada (2001)
25. Payne, T., Singh, R., Sycara, K.: Communicating agents in open multi-agent systems. In: First GSFC/JPL Workshop on Radical Agent Concepts (WRAC), McLean, VA, USA (2002)
26. Nodine, M.H., Unruh, A.: Facilitating open communication in agent systems: The InfoSleuth infrastructure. In: Proceedings of the 4th International Workshop on Intelligent Agents IV, Agent Theories, Architectures, and Languages. (1997) 281–295

An Architecture for Recommendation Based Service Mediation

Bhaskar Mehta, Claudia Niederée, Avare Stewart, Claudio Muscogiuri, and
Erich J. Neuhold

Fraunhofer IPSI, Damstadt 64293, Germany

Abstract. Resource brokering is a crucial activity in Grid infrastructures and other environments with dynamic resource selection. The mediation between resource requirements and available resources relies on adequate resource description, which becomes a special challenge when the resources are (Grid) services.

In addition to the description of service semantics, service quality is another useful selection criteria in effective service mediation. Inspired by the success of community- and usage-pattern-based filtering and recommendation systems for targeted information access, this paper discusses automatic and manual service rating as an option for judging service quality. Such ratings can contribute to targeted service selection and complement the mediation based on service semantics.

1 Introduction

The challenge of mediating between the need for a resource and an adequate resource like e.g. a Grid service is comparable to the challenge of mediating between individual information needs and relevant information objects in an information space. In both cases

- a need for a specific type of resources exists and in reply to this request one or more resources are identified that fulfill the need as well as possible.
- descriptive metadata are a crucial building block for effectively mediating between resource needs and available resources;

However, there are some important differences. The amount of resources available in the global information space is several orders of magnitudes larger than the amount of Grid resources available today. Furthermore, information objects, especially text documents can be analyzed by automatic methods to extract at least part of their semantics (meta-data) whereas services have to be annotated manually with meta-data describing their semantics. It is not possible to extracted this information automatically. The users of services are not (only) humans but also applications and other services, which requires more explicit semantics and formalization in resource description.

Basic syntactic information for consistent service invocation is given by providing information like service names, addresses, and parameters, using service

M. Bouzeghoub et al. (Eds.): ICSNW 2004, LNCS 3226, pp. 250–262, 2004.
© IFIP International Federation for Information Processing 2004

description languages like e.g. Web Service Definition Language or WSDL [7]. For targeted (semi-)automatic service selection more information is required. The most important kind of service annotation for this purpose is metadata that describes service semantic i.e. the functionality provided by the service [23]. A further service selection criterion is provided by service quality that includes parameters like availability of the service, performance, etc. Services, thus, have to be described along different complementing dimensions that together give a picture of the usefulness of a service in a specific scenario for its application.

The similarity of service mediation with the mediation of information objects suggests that some of the well-established methods of information mediation can also be exploited for improving service mediation. This paper discusses metadata based on explicate user rating and on the evaluation of usage pattern, as they are traditionally used for personalization approaches, as an additional source of information for describing service quality. This may result in information like "applications, which used service X also used service Y" or "service X and Y are the most prominent printing services".

The rest of the paper is structured as follows: Section 2 summarizes state of the art and related work in the area of syntactic and semantic services description, as well as rating and usage-pattern based information filtering approaches. Section 3 discusses dimensions of service descriptions and introduces Quality of service and Usage patterns as a complementary dimension. Starting from the idea of content rating, section 4 discusses and architecture for realizing recommendation-based service mediation. The paper concludes with a summary and some ideas for future work.

2   State of the Art and Related Work

2.1   Web Services Description and Selection

The need to support the dynamic discovery and composition of services in heterogeneous environments necessitates mechanisms for registering and discovering interface definitions and endpoint implementation descriptions and for dynamically generating proxies based on (potentially multiple) bindings for specific interfaces. The language for Web Service description WSDL [7] supports this requirement by providing a standard mechanism for defining interface definitions separately from their embodiment within a particular binding.

Web service selection can be performed from two perspectives: bottom-up and top-down. Top-down selection of web services starts from the business processes. The bottom-up perspective, on the other hand, starts from the available web services, and tries to select those that fit best. In practice, both selection approaches are often combined. This phase can, for instance, be supported with the Universal Description, Discovery and Integration (UDDI)[8] standard that provides rules for building service directories and facilitates top-down querying capabilities [13]. Nevertheless, WSDL provides service descriptions that are syntactic in nature, thus fundamentally comprising a description of the service's provided methods, like APIs, but with no semantics, besides additional full text description of non-functional service's properties such as the geographical location of the service provider, performance, its price, and so on. Therefore, most of the search engines of WSDL/UDDI repository implement keyword-based search algorithms on table-based models of services' interface descriptions, with search results of consequently low precision (i.e. services with same interface provide different behaviors) [1].

2.2   Role of Web Services in the Grid

The Open Grid Services Architecture (OGSA)[14] defines a Grid service as follows [14]: a Web service that provides a set of well-defined interfaces and that follows specific conventions. The interfaces address discovery, dynamic service creation, lifetime management, notification, and manageability; the conventions address naming and upgrading. The Web services framework and its adopted Web Service Definition Language (WSDL) offer the Grid scenario a standard mechanism for defining both services interfaces and services binding (transport protocol and data encoding format). Furthermore, the widespread adoption of Web services mechanisms means that a framework based on Web services can exploit numerous tools and extant services, such as WSDL processors that can generate language bindings for a variety of languages.

The Open Grid Services Infrastructure specification version 1.0 [14] defines a set of conventions and extensions on the use of WSDL and XML Schema [2] to enable stateful Web services. In parallel with and subsequent to this OGSI work, the Web services architecture has evolved, with for example the definition of WSDL 2.0 [7] progressing and the release of new draft specifications such as WS-Addressing [3].OGSI exploit functionality provided by other specifications (in particular, WS-Addressing) and to align OGSI functions with the emerging consensus on Web services architecture.

Additional efforts aiming at refactoring OGSI interfaces to incorporate the new developments to produce Web Service standards have produced five specifications,which are collectively named the WS-Resource Framework (WSRF) [11]. WSRF specifications retain all of the essential functional capabilities present in OGSI, while changing some of the syntax (e.g., to exploit WS-Addressing) and adopting a different terminology in its presentation. In addition, the specifications partition OGSI functionality into distinct functionality that allows flexible composition in a mix-and match manner. The factoring, composition capability and greater reliance on broadly accepted Web service concepts provide a simpler, more familiar and incremental path for developers wishing to exploit OGSI functionality.

2.3   Semantic Web Services

Semantic Web technologies allow for the development of ontology systems to support the exchange of knowledge on the Web. Ontologies description languages have been developed for this purpose, like the Resource Description Framework

(RDF) [21], and its more powerful (in term of ontology modeling primitives) successor, the Web Ontology Language (OWL)[22]. A legitimate approach is to take advantage of OWL capabilities to leverage the notion of web services by enriching their signature with semantic information. The OWL Service Coalition has been recently developing a Semantic Markup language for Web Services (OWL-S)[10], with the declared goal of developing ontologies of services and resources on the Web. OWL-S approach is to put a semantic layer on top of the syntactic layer already provided by WSDL: service resources are described by Services Profiles written in ad-hoc OWL ontologies, that use OWL classes as abstract types of WSDL messages, and refer to WSDL binding to specify the actual service interface [9]. To specify semantic of services, a Service Profile can link to a Service (process) Model profile to specify inputs, outputs, post and pre-conditions.

As a complement to the semantic expressed in the Service Model, a Service Profile can link to custom ontologies in order to specify additional properties of the service resource being advertised, like service taxonomies, quality ratings and quality of service; the OWL-S specification does not dictate specific ontologies for these features, but rather it provides a semantic model to integrate them. In practice, custom ontologies can be developed to formalize dimensions of service description like quality ratings and quality of service; the design of such dimensions will be effecting, and is effected by the design of the service brokering algorithm. The approach of this paper is to infer some of those dimensions from the lessons learned in the recommender systems and collaborative filtering areas.

2.4   Recommender Systems/Collaborative Filtering

The similarity of service mediation with the mediation of information objects suggests that some of the well-established methods for information mediation can also be exploited for improving service mediation. In this section we consider the approaches used in Recommender Systems for information mediation and filtering and from these approaches identify those that can be exploited for improving service mediation in grid environments.

Recommender System can be defined as system that learns about a person's needs and, based on this knowledge, has the effect of guiding the user in a personalized way to useful objects in a large space of possible options. Several classes of recommender systems can be distinguished [6]. The first, content-based recommender systems (or item-to-item correlation), (e.g. [19], [24]), make recommendations for users based on a profile built by analyzing the similarity between the content of information objects the user has seen and rated in the past and new information object. Second, in the demographic-based systems (see e.g. [18], [20], a user is categorized into demographic classes based on personal attributes and a recommendation is made based on belonging to similar a class. Third, collaborative recommenders (or people-to-people correlation) use the similarity between users, as determined by their similar rating of information object, as the basis of a recommendation. (see e.g. [4],[17]. Fourth, knowledge-based recommenders suggest items based on: functional knowledge of users needs; how items can satisfy those needs; and the use of the so called similarity metrics - which describes, for a given criteria such as price or location, what accounts for similar when two items are deemed substitutable [6] [26]. Finally, the utility-based approach (e.g. [6] [16]) determines a match between a user's need and a set of available options by using a utility function. The utility function is created by allowing users to specify constraints (e.g. warranty, delivery time, service contract) on features of the items under consideration. Such systems support recommendations by using constraint satisfaction techniques to produce a rank ordered list of items which satisfy the imposed constraints.

Knowledge about users needs in recommender systems are typically represented in profiles of the user. The data in such profiles are either collected explicitly or implicitly. Using explicit collection methods, the user directly provides the system with information about his preferences by selecting relevant topics, e.g. from a topic list, or by rating content (see e.g. [15], [12]). In implicit methods, the users preferences are inferred by observing their usage data or behavior and interaction with the system [25]. Example usage data include: page access, length of time viewing, site files, access logs, registration or remote agent observations, access sequences, transactional information, the contents of hotlists, or navigation history.

Taking into account the established techniques existing in recommender systems, we consider those that can support our goals and play a beneficial role in the identification of quality grid services are collaborative-based, utility and knowledge based recommender systems. The benefit of incorporating utility based recommenders is that quality measures such as speed, reliability, product availability, can be considered making it possible for example to trade off price against delivery schedule for users or applications with varying service needs. The benefit of incorporating collaborative recommender systems into the grid is that quality measures as experienced by other users can be taken into account. In knowledge-based systems, the functional knowledge can be justified by the existence of an ontological description of the resources in the grid domain [5] or additionally by system usage model based on agent observations such as: temporal usage, frequency of use, patterns of use, situation-to-situation-correlation between type of application and selected resources. Knowledge based systems can lend themselves to supporting recommendations in a grid by supporting the decision making about the substitutability between items in a set which have all been deemed semantically relevant for a given category and capable of satisfying a user's needs.

3   Quality and Usage Pattern as Dimensions for Service Description

In a Grid infrastructure, different nodes may provide competing services. Moreover, the resources may change over time. Semantics and syntax are not suffi-

cient to choose the best available resource in such an environment. The quality
of resources as well as best practices of service combination reflected by usage
pattern are also important factors for making adequate service choices. For example, knowing how and which process a service is going to implement when
invoked, and that the process model advertised by the service offer is matching the model of the service need does not guarantee how well the service will
perform. For a more complete description of services the associated metadata,
thus, should cover QoS information as well as usage pattern in addition to the
syntactic and the semantic dimension (see figure 3).

In order to take into account the two additional service description dimensions (QoS and usage pattern) and the combination of the dimensions, we need
to consider the following three questions for each of the four dimensions.

1. What metadata is needed?
2. How can this metadata be collected in a systematic way?
3. How can this metadata can be used for service selection and mediation?

In Sections 3.2 and 3.3, we shall discuss the first two questions along the
dimensions of Quality of service and Usage Patterns. In Section 4, we discuss
the third question and outline an architecture for service selection and recommendation.

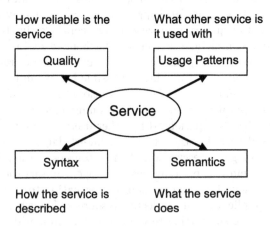

Fig. 1. Dimensions of Service Description

3.1   The Quality of Service Dimension

Besides the functionality (semantics of a service the quality of a service is considered another important factor for service selection (see related work section).
Quality statements for services are especially challenging, since service quality

may vary over time. The following list represents examples of parameters for describing service quality and are thus (partly) answering the first question:

1. *Operation Time* - This refers to the typical operation times for the service, which need not be 24x7. Services which are available for a longer time are likely to be more reliable and have more up time.
2. *Availability* - This can reflect how busy the service is, or how much usage can the service handle, or how much up time and downtime this service has. If there is a long queue or waiting time for a service on an average, other similar services could be preferred in comparison to this one.
3. *Performance* - If two nodes in a grid offer the same service, the node which is faster should be preferred. This parameter depends on how powerful a service provider is. This gives us an idea about if the service is likely to be faster in comparison to another competing node. A challenge to be solved is how performance can be described in a comparable way.
4. *Efficiency* - In a grid based environment, the efficiency depends not only on the workload of the service, but also on the network traffic, as properties like response time are unpredictable. Use of common benchmarks may increase the comparability of data.

Further metadata can be used to describe service quality. In addition to the above generic parameters for describing QoS, one might also use parameters that are characteristic for describing the quality of specific classes of services.

The next question is how to get this data. As in the case of recommendation systems, there are two basic ways of collecting the required metadata about services: explicit and implicit collection. Explicit collection contains:

Information from the service provider: Metadata about service quality can be created by the service provider as part of publishing his service.

User rating: The user is likely to be in a position to give feedback after a using the service by rating it. One possible way of collecting data from the usage will be to contact the user after the application has consumed a service for a fixed number of times (say 5). The user is then required to rate the service e.g. on a numeric sale of 1-5 for a selection of service quality parameters.

Implicit collection of QoS data can be done in different ways and depends on the quality of service parameter to be considered. Examples are:

Operation time: Since every service provider is required to register its services with the service registry, the time since which a service has been made available is known. The service can be pinged by the service registry after a fixed time repeatedly to find if the service is still alive.

Availability: This QoS parameter can also be judged by pinging the service periodically. Availability is measured as a percentage of number of successful pings against total number of pings. It is assumed that a service does not respond to a ping when it is overloaded.

Performance and efficiency: These two parameters are more difficult to assess. They would require systematic testing using e.g. agreed upon benchmarks for an entire service category.

Another indirect source on learning about service quality is analysing the frequency of use of a specific service. This aspect is covered in the next section in the context of the Usage Pattern dimension.

3.2   The Usage Pattern Dimension

For the purposes of making recommendations, **Usage Patterns** can greatly assist a new user/application in finding out which services have been used by applications with similar requirements. This can be considered as taking into account some form of best practice in combining service groups. This idea is inspired by the approach used in collaborative filtering: The assumption there is that people will tend to agree with the evaluation of a certain information item, if they have displayed similarity in the pattern of past judgements of information items. A recommendation system based on collaborative filtering makes use of the opinions of people who have already seen a piece of information to give recommendation to people who have not yet seen it.

In the grid, applications are the typical users of a data. Assuming that an application needs to authenticate itself before using a service registry usage data can be collected about an application, recording which service have been used by an application. If there is no manual rating of service available usage of a service, repetitive usage of a service can be interpreted as a sign of a positive rating of a specific service. This is comparable to tracking user behavior in a personalization system and interpret it for finding out the user's preferences (see also related work). Ratings gained by interpretation of usage pattern as well as by explicit ratings can be used to compute pairwise correlation coefficients among existing users/applications. The correlation coefficient is a measure for how similar two applications are. The system can make predictions or recommendations for services to be used next based on the degree of correlation.

Moreover the evaluation of usage patterns may also be used to determine information of the following kinds, that can contribute to improved service selection, mediation, and recommendation:

 – Services frequently used together (Co-Usage)
 – Most frequently used service in a category

In order to get this data, the transactions between applications and the service registry will have to be logged. Assuming every application can be uniquely identified, interactions like the services requested by an application can be tracked (this aspect is discussed in more detail in the next section). *Co-Usage* can be measured using data mining techniques on the available data. Association rules mined from the data can be used to recommend services which are normally used together with services already consumed by the user.

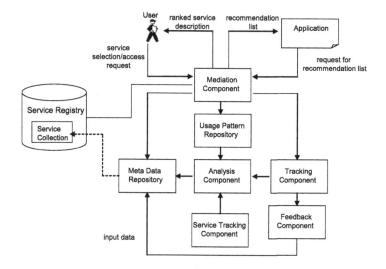

Fig. 2. Architecture for Service Mediation

4   Architecture for Service Mediation

The architecture for service recommendation and selection (see figure 2) proposed in this paper is built on the top of a preexisting *service registry* like a UDDI registry, which houses the service descriptions. As the current service registry technologies support syntactic description only, there is only basic metadata managed within the registry. All the additional metadata is managed in a *metadata repository* containing semantic information about service functionality, as well as information about quality of service and usage patterns-based metadata.

In order to fill the metadata repository with metadata for QoS and Usage patterns, data has to be collected and analyzed. For the Quality of service metadata, there is a *Service tracking component* which monitors the services registered in the registered periodically in order to collect and validate data on QoS. As discussed in the previous section individual QoS parameters require different methods to be validated. The results of monitoring the services are used to update the respective QoS metadata within the metadata repository, like e.g. data about the availability of a service or about its operation time.

In this architecture, applications and users with service requests do not directly interact with the service registry, but with the mediation component. This enables the *tracking component*, which is a further source for service description metadata, to log which services are being used by which applications.

The *analysis component* has manifold purposes: it analyzes the data collected by the tracking component periodically. The analysis results are stored in the Usage Pattern repository as metadata for individual applications and they are also used to update metadata for individual services that are based on usage pattern (e.g. frequency of usage). Furthermore, the analysis components mines this data to find association rules and co usage patterns applying data mining methods. The analysis results are again stored in the usage pattern repository for later use in service recommendation. Moreover, it collects data from the service tracking component and put in metadata for QoS parameters like availability and operation time.

In order to collect user ratings, there is a *feedback component* which contacts the user after an application running on the behalf of the user has consumed a service for a specific number of times (e.g. 5). User ratings are collected and combined by the Analysis component to add User rating metadata to the meta data repository.

Relying on this architecture the service selection and mediation process consists of the following steps:

1. An application or user contacts the mediation component. It identifies itself and presents its request for a service for fulfilling a task. The request describes the service along (part of the) dimensions discussed in section 3. In addition the request may also contain an application profile (comparable to a user profile in personalization approaches) that describes preferences of the application/user with respect to the service. The application may e.g. put more focus on reliable than on very fast services. Such profiles can be used to fine tune the mediation process.
2. The mediation component uses a match making algorithm and the data available in the metadata repository to create a ranked list of service candidates. For this purpose metadata on service semantics are combined with metadata on QoS and usage pattern according to the strategy of the match-making. Given the current trend in research towards semantic enrichment, it is foreseen that the description of service semantics will be in the focus of the match making algorithm. However, QoS and the Usage Patterns will play an important role in service ranking, like e.g.
   a) Services with higher availability and operation time can be ranked higher.
   b) The service with the best user ratings in its service category can be ranked higher.
3. For the top ranked services the mediation component contacts the service registry in order to fetch the syntactic descriptions of the respective services, that are required for service activation.
4. The ranked service list together with the syntactic information will be returned to the requesting application/user.

The recommendation process works as follows:

1. An application or user contacts the mediation component. It identifies itself and presents its request for service recommendation.
2. The mediation component gets the usage pattern of this application from the Usage pattern repository. The application's/user's preferences are inferred by observing their usage data or behavior and interaction with the system.

Example usage data include: service access, , access logs, registration or remote agent observations, access sequences, transactional information, or navigation history.

3. The usage pattern component finds applications with a similar usage pattern to the application making the request and then returns a recommendation list containing the services used by such applications. This computation takes ideas from the collaborative recommender systems as discussed in Section 2.4. The benefit of incorporating collaborative recommender systems into the grid is that quality measures as experienced by other users can be taken into account. In knowledge-based systems, the functional knowledge can be justified by the existence of an ontological description of the resources in the grid domain [5] or additionally by system usage model based on agent observations such as: temporal usage, frequency of use, patterns of use, situation-to-situation-correlation between type of application and selected resources. Knowledge based systems can lend themselves to supporting recommendations in a grid by supporting the decision making about the substitutability between items in a set which have all been deemed semantically relevant for a given category and capable of satisfying a user's/application's needs.

5   Conclusions and Future Work

In this paper we presented additional dimensions of service description that complement the syntactic and semantic metadata dimension and contribute to improved service mediation. As a starting point and in order to embed our ideas in the broader context we discussed the different dimensions of service descriptions for service selection and mediation. The additional dimensions, usage pattern and quality of service, are used for service mediation and service recommendation and are based on usage-pattern like co-usage of services, service rating and quality of service parameters. For both dimensions we discussed what meta data is required to capture the respective dimension and how this meta data can be collected for specific services. Furthermore, we discussed some use cases in the context of service mediation and service recommendation that exploit a combination of metadata from different service description dimensions showcasing possible applications of our approach. Finally, taking a traditional (UDDI-based) service registry as a starting point, we proposed a first component architecture for a system supporting service mediation and recommendation exploiting the four service description dimensions.

As in the case of semantic service description, this work is still in an early state and their is still a lot of research and development work to be done in this area, like e.g.:

- Methods used in data mining and recommender systems have to be validated and adapted for application in the service mediation context.
- A prototypical implementation of the proposed service mediation architecture will help to further develop the approach and will result in insights with respect to aspects like e.g. user acceptance of the service rating, i.e, is the

user ready to invest time in service rating in order to gain improved service
mediation.

- Evaluation of the proposed methods will be required to validate the approach and, especially, to fine tune the combination of the metadata from the different dimension for successful service mediation. .
- Furthermore, it is an important issue to examine in more detail the dependencies between the different dimensions of service description.

References

1. A. Bernstein and M. Klein. High Precision Service Retrieval. In *Proceedings of the First International Semantic Web Conference (ISWC'02), Sardinia, Italy (to appear)*. Springer-Verlag, 2002.
2. Paul V. Biron and Ashok Malhotra. XML Schema Part 2: Datatypes - W3C Recommendation, 02 May 2001, http://www.w3.org/TR/xmlschema-2/, May 2001.
3. A. Bosworth, D. Box, E. Christensen, F. Curbera, D. Ferguson, J. Frey, C. Kaler, D. Langworthy, F. Leymann, B. Lovering, S. Lucco, S. Millet, N. Mukhi, M. Nottingham, D. Orchard, J. Shewchuk, T. Storey, and S. Weerawarana. Web Services Addressing. ftp://www6.software.ibm.com/software/developer/ library/ws-add200403.pdf, March 2004.
4. V. Bouthors and O Dedieu. Pharos, a Collaborative Infrastructure for Web Knowledge Sharing. *In Serge Abiteboul and Anne-Marie Vercoustre, editors, Research and Advanced Technology for Digital Libraries, Proceedings of the Third European Conference, ECDL'99, Paris, France: LNCS*, 1999.
5. J. Brooke, K. Fellows, K. Garwood, and C. Goble. Semantic Matching of Grid Resource Descriptions. *Proceedings of The Second European Across Grids Conference, Nicosia, Cyprus*, 2004.
6. R. Burke. Hybrid Recommender Systems: Survey and Experiments. *User Modeling and User-Adapted Interaction*, 12(4):331–370, ?? 2002.
7. E. Christensen, F. Curbera, G. Meredith, and S. Weerawarana. Web Services Description Language (WSDL) 1.1 - W3C Note 15 March 2001. http://www.w3.org/TR/wsdl, March 2001.
8. Erik Christensen, Francisco Curbera, Greg Meredith, and Sanjiva Weerawarana. UDDI Version 2.0 Data Structure Reference - UDDI Open Draft Specification 8 June 2001. http://www.uddi.org/pubs/DataStructure-V2.00-Open-20010608.pdf, June 2001.
9. The OWL Services Coalition. OWL-S: Semantic Markup for Web Services. http://www.daml.org/services/owl-s/1.0/owl-s.html.
10. The OWL Services Coalition. OWL-based Web Service Ontology OWL-S 1.1 DRAFT. http://www.daml.org/services/owl-s/1.0/, January 2004.
11. Karl Czajkowski, Donald F Ferguson, Ian Foster, Jeffrey Frey, Steve Graham, Sedukhin, David Snelling, Steve Tuecke, and William Vambenepe. The WS-Resource Framework. http://www-106.ibm.com/developerworks/library/ws-resource/ws-wsrf.pdf, March 2004.
12. J. Davies, R. Weeks, and M. Revett. Information Agents for the World Wide Web. *BT Technology Journal*, 14(4):105–114, 1996.
13. Aldo de Moor and Willem-Jan van den Heuvel. Web Service Selection in Virtual Communities. February 2004.

14. I. Foster, C. Kesselman, J. Nick, and S. Tuecke. The Physiology of the Grid: An Open Grid Services Architecture for Distributed Systems Integration. *http://www.globus.org/research/papers.html*, 2002.
15. V. Goldmann, A. Langer, and Rosenschein. S. Musag: An Agent that Learns what you Mean. In *Proceedings of the First International Conference on Practical Applications of Intelligent Agents and Multi-Agents Technology (PAAM96)*, pages 311–329, 1996.
16. H. Guttman, A. Moukas, and P. Maes. Agent-mediated Electronic Commerce: A Survey. *Knowledge Engineering Review*, 13(2):147–159, 1998.
17. J.A. Konstan, B.N. Miller, D. Herlocker Maltz, J.L. Gordon, and Reidl L.R. Applying Collaborative Filtering to Usenet News. *Communications of the ACM*, 40(4):77–87, 1997.
18. B. Krulwich. Lifestlye Finder: Intelligent User Profiling Using Large-Scale Demographic Data. *Artificial Intelligence Magazine*, 2(18):37–45, 1997.
19. K. Lang. NewsWeedweeder: Learning to Filter News. *In Proc. ICML 95,*, pages 331–336, 1995.
20. Pazzani M. A framework for Collaborative, Content-based and Demographic Filtering. *Artificial Intelligence Review*, 5-6(13):393–408, 1999.
21. F. Manola and E. Miller. RDF Primer W3C Recommendation 10 February 2004. http://www.w3.org/TR/rdf-primer/.
22. D. McGuinness and F. Dvan Harmelen. OWL Web Ontology LanguageOverview, W3C Recommendation 10 February 2004. http://www.w3.org/TR/2004/REC-owl-features-20040210/, February 2004.
23. S. A. McIlraith, T. C. Son, and H. Zeng. Semantic Web Services. *IEEE Intelligent Systems*, 16(2):46 – 53, March/April 2001.
24. R.J. Mooney and L. Roy. Content-Based Book Recommending Using Learning for Text Categorization. *Proceedings of the Fifth ACM Conference on Digital Libraries San Antonio, TX, June (2000)*, pages 195–204, June 2000.
25. A. Pretschner and S. Gauch. Personalization on the Web Technical Report, ITTC-FY2000-TR-13591-01. Technical report, The University of Kansas, Lawrence, KS, December 1999.
26. B. Towle and C.N. Quinn. Knowledge Based Recommender Systems Using Explicit User Models. *Knowledge-Based Electronic Markets Workshop at AAAI 2000, Austin, TX.*, 2000.

Static–Dynamic Integration of External Services into Generic Business Processes

Günter Preuner[1], Christian Eichinger[1], and Michael Schrefl[2*]

[1] Institut für Wirtschaftsinformatik – Data & Knowledge Engineering,
Johannes Kepler Universität Linz, A-4040 Linz, Austria
[2] Avanced Computing Research Center, University of South Australia,
Mawson Lakes SA 5095, Australia

Abstract. Organizations usually handle their business cases by requesting external services that are integrated with internal procedures to a composite business process. External services may be atomic activities or, more often, arbitrarily complex processes.

In the simplest case, all business cases of a particular kind follow the same external services and internal procedures. Then, a composite service can be statically predefined without regarding peculiarities and requirements of single business cases. Such compositions ensure that processing business cases follows exact specifications. Yet in a highly dynamic environment, the actual processing may involve different services for each business case depending on its properties, such that appropriate services must be selected during runtime.

In this paper, the requirements of static and dynamic environments are naturally combined: Those parts of processing that are known in advance form the "frame" of processing. This frame comprises services that must be used in any case and comprises semantic rules that specify which requirements must be fulfilled by the services that are selected dynamically during processing. Correctness criteria define how static and dynamic composition can be appropriately integrated.

1 Introduction

Organizations perform their business cases not completely autonomously but use external services, which are provided by other organizations, together with intra-organizational procedures. External services may be atomic activities or — in the general case — complex processes.

An organization that requests services (referred to as *service requester*) from another organiation (the *service provider*) may process business cases in different ways: First, processes can be defined *statically,* i.e., completely in advance, which is suitable only if all parts of processing are known in advance. Second, a business process may not be defined at all in advance, but all activities may be selected for a business case *dynamically* during processing. Yet dynamic composition has

---

* Research performed at both universities within ARC Discovery Project DP0210654.

severe drawbacks since there is no possibility to pre-define processes in order to achieve that similar business cases are handled uniformly.

In this work, static and dynamic process definitions are combined to a "static–dynamic" approach: All parts of processing that are known in advance are integrated into a business process. Each part of processing that is not specified in advance is represented by a generic activity, which serves as a "place holder" for the dynamically selected service. Selection of a service during processing is considered as a work task of its own (which might be an arbitrarily complex process, again, e.g., a tendering procedure for the purchase of technical equipment). Such work tasks will be referred to as *build activities* and *build processes*.

For each generic activity, the pre-defined business process may specify by semantic rules (1) which kind of service is required to implement the generic activity (e.g., delivery of a computer system with hardware and software), (2) whether one service must be selected or services from different providers can be combined (hardware and software may be purchased from different suppliers), and (3) which case-specific constraints influence the selection of services (e.g., the system must be bought from a supplier who delivers within twelve months).

Static composition has been treated in detail in [1,2]. In [5], an overall process is defined first; this process is split in a top-down fashion into several fragments, each one being assigned to a particular organization, which defines a more detailed private implementation for the assigned fragment. Similarly, [6] distinguishes public and private specifications, yet on a more technical level. In [7], global applications are defined with state-charts, comprising a set of activities, which are refined by (legacy) applications. Composition of independent services in a bottom-up fashion has been discussed in [8,9,10].

Dynamic specification of processes has been discussed in general in the realm of dynamic change of workflows, e.g., [3], and, recently, in the health-care domain [4] where generic processes are made concrete during processing by build activities. Although our work deals with the dynamic specification in an ontology-based, inter-organizational setting, concepts of build activities for generic processes are appropriate for our approach, as well. In [11,12], a very dynamic approach of composition is introduced, where composition is guided by formal rules, yet without considering static composition aspects.

Our work goes beyond these approaches in that we combine static and dynamic composition to a static-dynamic approach as motivated above with precise correctness criteria. Build activities are first-class activities that select services according to the given semantic rules. Requested services distinguish activities (1) that are invoked by the requester and those (2) that are invoked by the provider, where execution can be observed by the requester.

Services are represented by ontologies, which appear to comprise the most adequate techniques for semantic composition of web services; cf., e.g., [13]. In addition, rules expressed upon these ontologies support the selection of services. Semantic matching of services has been discussed in detail in recent research [14,15,16]. We will build upon existing work and restrict our discussion to how ontologies can support our approach of composition. Hence, we neither enforce the use of a particular ontology nor introduce "yet another" ontology language; instead, any ontology that allows to classify services may be used.

We use *Object/Behavior Diagrams (OBDs)* [17] for the design of business processes. OBDs are considered appropriate for our approach since they have a proper formal semantics based on Petri Nets and their concept of behavior-consistent specialization [18] proved to be an adequate foundation for composition. Nevertheless, our approach can be applied to other models that support specialization, as well, like UML [19] with specialization as proposed in [20].

The remainder of this paper is structured as follows: Section 2 briefly introduces OBDs. Section 3 presents the service architecture for static-dynamic composition. Section 4 explains how ontologies and semantic rules support the dynamic selection of services. Correctness and construction of composed processes are presented in Sect. 5. Finally, the work is concluded in Sect. 6.

2   Modeling Services with OBDs

Object/Behavior Diagrams (OBDs) were introduced as a conceptual object-oriented design notation, where processes are represented by Behavior Diagrams [18]. Each Behavior Diagram is associated with an object class and defines the behavior of all instances of this class.

Behavior Diagrams consist of a set of *activities,* i.e., atomic units of work, a set of *states* in which objects may reside, and a set of *arcs,* which connect activities with states. Each activity has at least one pre-state and one post-state. *Initial* states have no incoming arcs and represent the virtual processing state of an object before its creation. Analogously, a state is *final* if no activity consumes from it. Further, Behavior Diagrams comprise labels in order to distinguish different aspects of processing. Labels are motivated by the analogy of copies of a paper form in traditional paper work, where different copies "flow" in a different way through the workflow. Analogously, *labeling properties* ensure that every label has one initial state, at least one final state, and resides in exactly one state or activity state at each point of time. For brevity, activities, states, and labels are commonly referred to as *elements.*

Example 1. Figure 1 shows LBD MOrder *(music order)*, which comprises activities, e.g., selectCDs, and states, e.g., ordered. Initial state α is depicted by dashed lines and is usually omitted in the graphical representation. Labels o and r represent the handling of the order and registering the CDs. Please ignore state symbol toOrder depicted with dashed borders for the moment.

The *life-cycle state (LCS)* of an object specifies which of its labels reside in which states. An activity can be invoked on an object if this object resides in all pre-states of the activity. After an activity has been completed, the object resides in all post-states of the activity. Different from Petri Nets, an activity does not "fire" automatically, but must be explicitly invoked. Further, we assume that the execution of activities takes time and distinguish *starting* and *completing* an activity. Between starting and completing an activity on an object, the object

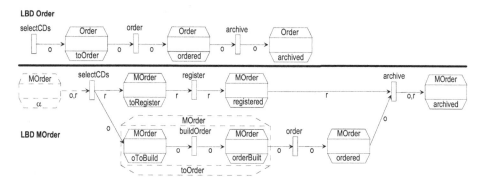

Fig. 1. LBDs Order and MOrder

resides in an implicit activity state named after the activity. A sequence of LCSs is called a *life-cycle occurrence (LCO)*.

Example 2. Consider LBD MOrder: Each object resides initially in LCS {(α, o), (α, r)}. Starting activity selectCDs leads to LCS {(selectCDs, o), (selectCDs, r)} and completing this activity leads to LCS {(oToBuild, o), (toRegister, r)}.

Specialization of LBDs was presented in [18], distinguishing *refinement*, i.e., elements of B are refined in B', and *extension*, i.e., additional elements are introduced in B' with new labels. One kind of specialization, namely *observation-consistent specialization*, means that the processing of an object in B' must be observable as a correct processing in B in that every possible LCO in B' must be a valid LCO in B if refined elements are considered unrefined and elements added by extension are ignored.

Example 3. LBD MOrder is an observation-consistent specialization of LBD Order (cf. Fig. 1): MOrder *refines* Order in that state toOrder is refined to oToBuild, buildOrder, and orderBuilt. Further, MOrder *extends* Order by the aspect of registering, represented by label r and several activities and states labeled with r. The generalization of LCS {(buildOrder, o), (toRegister, r)} in MOrder to {{(toOrder, o)}} is a valid LCS in Order.

3   Service Architecture for Static-Dynamic Composition

The composition approach is characterized by the following service architecture, summarized in Fig. 2. Schemes of services and ontological rules are depicted as rectangles, whereas arrows depict which schemes are derived from others.

Generic service. First, the *generic service* is defined, which comprises all aspects of processing that are independent of the properties of business cases being processed. Further, it specifies at which points of processing another service or combination of services can be dynamically introduced. The generic service is an LBD that comprises three kinds of activities:

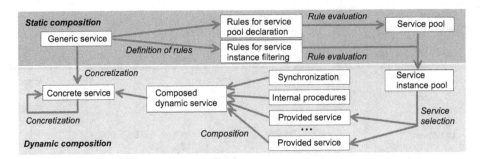

Fig. 2. Static-dynamic composition

1. *Regular activities* represent work tasks that are performed on business cases. They are either observable or invocable: *Observable activities* are executed by the provider, who allows the requester to *observe* their execution. *Invocable activities* are defined by the provider, but their invocation is delegated to the requester. Activities from internal procedures and synchronization activities (see below) are invocable since they must be invoked by the requester.
2. *Generic activities* cannot be executed but are "place holders" for services that are dynamically selected for a business case during processing.
3. *Build activities* are invoked by the service requester to replace generic activities by actual services. They are included in the process as first-class activities in order to enable the modeler of a process to predefine at which point of processing a service must be selected for a generic activity.

The generic service may be defined from scratch by the service requester or may result from integrating several external services with internal procedures. Such a static integration is useful if a particular set of services must be used for every business case and, thus, is not case-specific. For example, the service of a music trader could be integrated into the generic service if a library must buy all its CDs from this trader. The definition of a generic service by integrating services makes use of the approach presented in [1,2]. Since the way how the generic service has been defined does not influence static-dynamic composition as presented in this paper, we will take the generic service as given.

Example 4. Suppose that a music library frequently buys music CDs from different music traders. Therefore it defines a (very simple) service that comprises activities that are executed internally (like selecting and registering music CDs) and a generic activity for ordering. The process is depicted by LBD MOrder in Fig. 3. Regular invocable activities are marked with tag *Inv*, the generic activity order is represented by a shaded activity symbol and is marked with tag *G*, activity buildOrder for building a concrete service for order is marked with *B* and annotated with the generic activity to be built.

Composed dynamic service. The composed dynamic service is a service that can be used to replace a particular generic activity. In the following, we use the

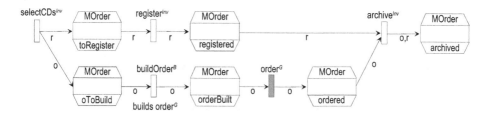

Fig. 3. Generic service of a library

phrase that a service or a combination of services *fulfills* a generic activity if the service or the combination of services provides all the functionality that is needed to realize the work task that the generic activity stands for. There are three possibilities of replacement, each one requiring a different set of services:

1. *Single service replacement:* There is one service selected that fulfills a particular generic activity.
2. *Coordinated service replacement:* There is a set of independent services that, when combined, fulfill the generic activity. The service requester coordinates the services by introducing synchronization elements, i.e., further activities, states, and labels.
3. *Coordinated service replacement with internal processing:* The service requester might complement external services with internal procedures if the former do not fully fulfill the generic activity since particular aspects of processing are missing. Synchronization elements coordinate the external services and the internal processes. Internal processes may include generic and build activities again, such that replacement can be performed recursively.

Figure 2 depicts the (most complex) third case. For more details on composing external services with internal processes, see Sect. 5. The build activity searches adequate services, decides on which kind of replacement is used, which services are selected, and — if necessary — coordinates the set of services with or without further internal processing.

Example 5. Suppose that the service of a music trader MT1-Order shown in Fig. 4 is selected for generic activity order: The music trader's service performs both payment and delivery. Hence, it fulfills generic activity order without any need for internal processing or synchronization.

Alternatively, another music trader with process MT2-Order could be selected whose service offers creation of an order and delivery. The service requester has to combine this service with a bank's service BT1-Transfer for money transfers. The services and their composition with internal activities are depicted in the bottom section of Fig. 4.

Concrete service. The *concrete service* is defined by replacing a generic activity by the dynamic service that has been defined by the build activity. Making services concrete is an iterative procedure since a composed service may include

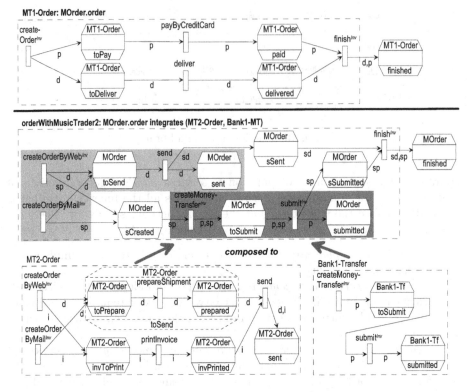

Fig. 4. LBDs MT1-Order and orderWithMusicTrader2

an arbitrary number of generic activities, which are not made concrete at the same time, and since a selected service may include generic activities again. For details on concretization see Sect. 5.

Rules for service pool declaration and service instance filtering. These rules refer to an ontology of services and define which functionality must be offered by the service to be selected dynamically and how a service is actually selected by matching the services' properties and the business cases' requirements. Semantic rules are defined for each generic activity in a twofold manner: Services that fulfill a generic activity fully or partially are determined by *rules for service pool declaration* and are stored in a *service pool*. Given a set of services in a service pool, *rules for service instance filtering* specify how all services or combinations of services are determined that comply with a business case's requirements. The appropriate services or combinations thereof are stored in the *service instance pool*. From there, one service or service combination is actually selected for replacing the generic activity. See Sect. 4 for details.

4   Semantic Service Discovery

Service instances capable of fulfilling a generic activity are identified in a two-step approach consisting of (1) *Service Pool Declaration* and (2) *Service Instance Filtering* which are backed by ontologies as described in this sections.

4.1   Service Pool Declaration

The *service pool ontology* underlying the service pool declaration classifies all external services needed to fulfill generic activities and specifies service-specific properties, the *service profile*. Furthermore, each service is described by an OBD. As ontology integration is not within the scope of this paper, we refer to existing approaches in the fields of ontology integration, ontology matching and service integration [14,21,15]. In our ontology, services are represented as instances of service classes and will be referred to as *service instances*.

Example 6. Figure 5 depicts the service pool ontology for services needed in our running example. For the sake of simplicity, the example ontology shows only service providers and omits the specification of products and services, which is usually part of any real world ontology. Furthermore, the range of properties has been omitted. Service instances are identified by a grey header.

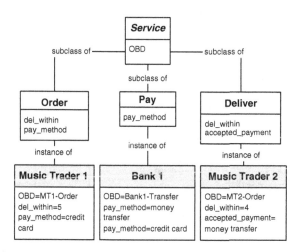

Fig. 5. Sample service pool ontology

Three different service pools are distinguished with respect to their contribution to the fulfillment of a generic activity:

1. *Full service pool:* The full service pool comprises service instances that fulfill the generic activity as a whole. These instances are candidates for a single service replacement.

2. *Partial service pool:* The partial service pool comprises service instances capable of fulfilling a specific part of the generic activity. These instances are candidates for a coordinated service replacement with internal processing.
3. *Compound service pool:* The compound service pool specifies combinations of service instances which are capable of fulfilling the generic activity as a whole. These instances are candidates for a coordinated service replacement.

Service pool members are specified by queries over the service pool ontology. These queries are attached to generic activities; their results are instances of the service pool ontology.

Executing queries over the service pool ontology requires an inference mechanism over ontologies. [22] gives an overview of ontology tools supporting inferencing and ontology building. But, as the definition of selection criteria for inferencing tools is not within the scope of this paper, we use Prolog syntax for describing rules and assume that service pool instances are expressed as facts, e.g. the rule order(X) specifies all instances of class Order and the rule del_within(X,Y) returns in Y the value of property "del_within" of instance X.

Example 7. Figure 6 extends the generic activity order introduced in Fig. 3 with service pool declarations. The service pools *full, partial* and *compound* are expressed as rules over the service pool ontology: full(X) retrieves all order services, partial(X) retrieves services that provide delivery or payment, and compound(X,Y) retrieves combinations of order and payment services where the payment service is accepted by the delivery service. The execution of the service pool computation is ordered as follows: (1) the full service pool, (2) the partial service pool, and (3) the compound service pool.

Applied to our example, these rules would return "Music Trader 1" as member of the full service pool, "Music Trader 2" and "Bank 1" as members of the partial service pool and "Music Trader 2, Bank 1" as member of the compound service pool as their payment methods match.

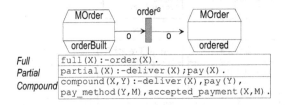

Full	`full(X):-order(X).`
Partial	`partial(X):-deliver(X);pay(X).`
Compound	`compound(X,Y):-deliver(X),pay(Y),` `pay_method(Y,M),accepted_payment(X,M).`

Fig. 6. Service pool declaration for generic activity order

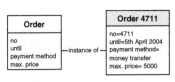

Fig. 7. Sample process instance ontology

4.2 Service Instance Filtering

The service pool instances for building a concrete service of a generic activity are filtered according to business case's requirements. The requirements of a case are again captured by an ontology, the *process instance ontology.* Figure 7 shows the process instance ontology for our example order service.

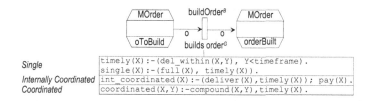

Fig. 8. Service instance filtering for generic activity order

Specific requirements are passed as parameters to parameterized queries operating on the service pools. These queries are attached to the build activities of the respective generic activity. Upon rule evaluation, the parameters are substituted with property values of the actual business case. These rules are again divided into three pools, which comply with the replacement alternatives of composed dynamic services: *single instance pool* for single service replacement, *coordinated instance pool* for coordinated service replacement and *internally coordinated instance pool* for the coordinated service replacement with internal processing.

Example 8. Figure 8 visualizes the filtering rules that specify service instance pools for generic activity order (which has been introduced in Fig. 3). Rule single(X) retrieves all order services that can deliver in time, i.e., whose property "del_within" is less than the number of days left until "5th April 2004". Rule int_coordinated(X) retrieves all payment services as well as all delivery services that satisfy the time constraint. Finally, coordinated(X,Y) retrieves all service combinations where the delivery service can deliver in time.

The evaluation of these rules on 2nd April 2004 would return the following service instance pools: single(X) containing no members as service "Music Trader 1" cannot fulfill the time constraint imposed by "Order 4711", int_coordinated(X) containing "Bank 1" as it is member of class pay and "Music Trader 2" as it can fulfill the time constraint, and coordinated(X,Y) containing "Music Trader 2, Bank 1".

When a build activity is activated for a particular business case, rules for service instance filtering are evaluated. The user then builds a sub-process fulfilling the generic activity for this business case with some or all of the returned service instances as described in the next section.

5   Correctness and Construction of Composed Services

This section presents the correctness criteria for composed dynamic services and concrete services (cf. Sect. 5.1). The construction of correct services is presented in Sect. 5.2. Hence, this section covers two steps in our architecture:

1. *Composition:* The definition of the composed dynamic service depends on the replacement strategy: There is no composition necessary for single ser-

vice replacement. For coordinated service replacement, a set of external services must be composed; for coordinated service replacement with internal processing, external services and internal procedures must be integrated. Composition follows the approach of [2].

Example 9. For fulfilling generic activity order, services MT2-Order from "Music Trader 2" and Bank1-Transfer from "Bank 1" are composed to service orderWithMusicTrader2 (cf. Example 8).

2. *Concretization:* Concretization of a service C to C' is considered a special case of composition: C resulted from an internal procedure and, possibly, a set of external service that have been statically integrated or integrated in previous concretization steps. During concretization from C to C', another service S is integrated with the services that have been integrated to C before. Hence, the concrete service is a composition of all services that are represented by C and S and the correctness criteria from [2] should hold again. Yet construction is different than in the first case since services are not composed in one step, but continuously during concretization.

Example 10. In the running example, the generic service MOrder must be made concrete by integrating service orderWithMusicTrader2.

5.1   Correctness Criteria for Composition

During static composition, external services are composed together with internal procedures. Synchronization elements (i.e., activities, states, and labels) reflect data and control dependencies between activities from different services. In order to condense the presentation, the correctness criteria will be presented here in a simplified form; for details, the reader is referred to [2].

The composite service shall include all information that is — from the viewpoint of the requester — necessary for successful processing. Hence, all invocable activities are included, whereas observable details may be abstracted in order to reduce the complexity of the composite service. The composite service must obey the following correctness criteria with respect to the services:

1. *Well-formed synchronization and internal service:* Internal procedures and synchronization elements that are embedded in the composite service are conceptually considered as a "service", as well, which is embedded in the composite service with new, internal labels. Synchronization and internal services are well-formed if the restriction of the composite service to internal labels and all elements with at least one internal label is a correct LBD.
2. *Observability and invocability compliance:* An activity is invocable (observable) in the composite service if the related activities in the services are invocable (or observable, respectively). Invocable activities are neither abstracted nor omitted in the composite service.
3. *Observability consistency:* The processing of business cases in the services should be observable as a correct processing according to the composite service.

4. *Invocability consistency:* Invocability consistency requires that at any time when an invocable activity can be started in the composite service, i.e., whenever a business case resides in all pre-states of this activity, it must be possible to start the related activities in the external services, as well.

Example 11. Consider the services depicted in Fig. 4: Services MT2-Order and Bank1-Transfer define the processing of orders and of money transfers, respectively. These services are integrated to a composite service orderWithMusic-Trader2, which comprises all aspects of order processing. Elements in the composite service that are related to elements in the services are indicated by a grey background shading. All activities and states in orderWithMusicTrader2 that are labeled with sd or sp have been introduced as synchronization elements. They constitute a correct LBD. Elements toPrepare, prepareShipment, and prepared have been abstracted to state toSend (as indicated by the state symbol with dotted borders); the aspect of invoicing (cf. label i), has been omitted.

5.2   Construction of Correct Composite Services

The definition of a composed dynamic service from services in a bottom-up fashion is summarized first; then, construction of concrete services is introduced.

Construction of Composed Dynamic Services. Construction follows the correctness criteria presented in Sect. 5.1. While conditions 1 and 2 are easy to check, checking criteria were introduced in [2] for conditions 3 and 4. Briefly, observability consistency is checked by the concept of observation-consistent specialization (cf. Sect. 2): Each external service must be an observation-consistent specialization of the composite service, when the latter is restricted to labels that correspond to labels of the external service. Further, no additional pre-states must be introduced for observable activities in the composite service since these pre-states are not considered by the service provider who starts the corresponding activities in his/her service. Invocability consistency is fulfilled if all pre-states of an invocable activity in an external service are represented as pre-states of this activity in the composite service.

Example 12. Consider once more the example in Fig. 4: Service MT2-Order is an observation-consistent specialization of orderWithMusicTrader2 if the latter is restricted to label d. orderWithMusicTrader2 introduces no new pre-states for observable activities and comprises all pre-states of invocable activities.

Construction of Concrete Services. During concretization, a generic activity is replaced by a composed dynamic service. This replacement should not have any side effects, i.e., the behavior "outside" the generic activity should not be affected by the replacement. The concrete service C_{new} is constructed from a generic or another concrete service C_{old} as follows: Begin and end activities are determined in the composed dynamic service S. Begin activities are executed as the first activities in S, i.e., no other activity therein is executed before; analogously, end activities are executed last in S. A composed dynamic service S replaces a generic activity in that the begin and end activities are synchronized with C_{old}. The construction comprises the following steps:

1. *Determination of begin and end activities:* An activity of the composed dynamic service S is called a *begin activity* if all its pre-states are initial states. Analogously, an activity is an *end activity* if all its post-states are final states. Begin and end activities must be invocable since the requester must invoke them in order to initiate and finish a selected service.

   Example 13. Service orderWithMusicTrader2 in Fig. 4 comprises begin activities createOrderByWeb and createOrderByMail and end activity finish.

2. *Local refinement of generic activity:* The generic activity in C_{old} is refined (1) to one alternative generic begin (or end) activity for each begin (or end, respectively) activity from the composed dynamic service and (2) to one state, which is post-state of all generic begin activities and pre-state of all generic end activities. The resulting LBD is an observation-consistent refinement of the original one by mapping the new activities and state to the original generic activity. The resulting service is referred to as C_{oldRef}.

   Example 14. The local refinement of the generic activity order is depicted in Fig. 9 with two alternative generic begin activities, one generic end activity, and a state in between. Generic begin and end activities carry the same name as the respective activities in orderWithMusicTrader2.

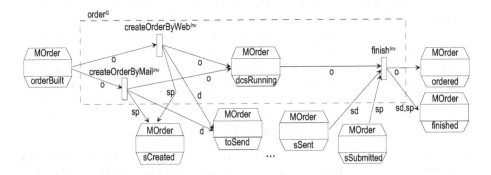

Fig. 9. Replacement of order

3. *Embedding of composed dynamic service:* The concrete service C_{new} results from C_{oldRef} and S in that each begin and end activity of S is synchronized with the corresponding generic begin and end activity of C_{oldRef}. Pairs of synchronized activities are represented by the same activity in C_{new}. All other elements of S are added in C_{new}. The set of labels of S is considered disjoint with the labels in C_{oldRef}.

Example 15. Fig. 9 depicts the refinement of order for embedding service orderWithMusicTrader2. The embedded service is not depicted in detail as the figure spots on the begin and end activities.

The resulting concrete service C_{new} is an observation-consistent specialization of C_{oldRef} and fulfills the correctness criteria for composition (cf. Sect. 5.1): Assume that C_{old} and S are correct LBDs and are correctly combined, then internal aspects of processing and synchronization elements form correct LBDs in C_{new}. Observability and invocability compliance are fulfilled since invocability of activities is not changed. Observability consistency is fulfilled since S is embedded without change (which is a special case of specialization) and no new pre-states are introduced for observable activities. Invocability consistency is fulfilled since all pre-states of invocable activities are integrated.

6   Conclusion

We presented static-dynamic integration of services that naturally combines and extends existing approaches on service integration. The distinction between static and dynamic aspects both leaves enough flexibility for selecting appropriate services for a particular business case in a dynamic environment and guarantees at the same time that behavioral aspects known in advance are explicitly specified and are obeyed for each case. The distinction of static and dynamic aspects is appropriately complemented by semantic rules for service pool declaration and service instance filtering.

Future work will extend the approach in that generic *processes* may be introduced instead of generic activities. These generic processes might specify a frame for actual processing, which the actually selected service must fit into. For example, a generic process may specify that a music trader must deliver before it requests payment. This constraint can be specified by a generic activity for delivery followed by a generic activity for payment.

References

1. Preuner, G., Schrefl, M.: Behavior-Consistent Composition of Business Processes From Internal and External Services. In Proc. ER 2002 Workshops, Revised Papers. Springer LNCS 2784 (2003)
2. Preuner, G., Schrefl, M.: Requester-centered Composition of Business Processes from Internal and External Services. To appear in: Data & Knowledge Engineering (2004)
3. van der Aalst, W.: Generic Workflow Models: How to Handle Dynamic Change and Capture Management Information? In: Proc. 4th IFCIS Int. Conf. on Cooperative Information Systems (CoopIS), IEEE Computer Society Press (1999)
4. Browne, E., Schrefl, M., Warren, J.: Goal-Focused Self-Modifying Workflow in the Healthcare Domain. In: Proc. 37th Hawaii Int. Conf. on System Sciences (HICSS) – Track 6, IEEE Computer Society (2004)

5. van der Aalst, W.: Inheritance of interorganizational workflows to enable business-to-business e-commerce. Electronic Commerce Research **2** (2002) 195–231
6. Bussler, C.: The Application of Workflow Technology in Semantic B2B Integration. Distributed and Parallel Databases **12** (2002) 163–191
7. Eyal, A., Milo, T.: Integrating and customizing heterogeneous e-commerce applications. VLDB Journal **10** (2001) 16–38
8. Chiu, D., Karlapalem, K., Li, Q., Kafeza, E.: Workflow View Based E-Contracts in a Cross-Organizational E-Services Environment. Distributed and Parallel Databases **12** (2002) 193–216
9. Hull, R., Benedikt, M., Christophides, V., Su, J.: E-Services: A Look Behind the Curtain. In: Proc. 22nd ACM SIGACT-SIGMOD-SIGART Symposium on Principles of Database Systems (PODS), ACM Press (2003)
10. Kafeza, E., Chiu, D., Kafeza, I.: View-based Contracts in an E-service Cross-Organizational Workflow Environment. In Proc. 2nd Int. Workshop on Technologies for E-Services (TES). Springer LNCS 2193 (2001)
11. Medjahed, B., Bouguettaya, A., Elmagarmid, A.: Composing Web services on the Semantic Web. VLDB Journal **12** (2003) 333–351
12. Zeng, L., Flaxer, D., Chang, H., Jeng, J.J.: PLM$_{flow}$ — Dynamic Business Process Composition and Execution by Rule Inference. In Proc. 3rd Int. Workshop on Technologies for E-Services (TES). Springer LNCS 2444 (2002)
13. Fensel, D., Hendler, J., Lieberman, H., Wahlster, W., eds.: Spinning the Semantic Web: Bringing the World Wide Web to Its Full Potential. MIT Press (2003)
14. Cardoso, J., Sheth, A.: Semantic E-Workflow Composition. Journal of Intelligent Information Systems **21** (2003) 191–225
15. Paolucci, M., Kawamura, T., Payne, T., Sycara, K.: Semantic Matching of Web Services Capabilities. In Proc. 1st Int. Semantic Web Conf. (ISWA). Springer LNCS 2342 (2002)
16. Sheshagiri, M., des Jardins, M., Finin, T.: A Planner for Composing Services Describes in DAML-S. In: Proc. Workshop on Web Services and Agent-based Engineering (WSABE). (2003)
17. Kappel, G., Schrefl, M.: Object/Behavior Diagrams. In: Proc. 7th Int. Conf. on Data Engineering (ICDE). (1991)
18. Schrefl, M., Stumptner, M.: Behavior Consistent Specialization of Object Life Cycles. ACM Trans. Software Engineering and Methodology **11** (2002) 92–148
19. Rumbaugh, J., Jacobson, I., Booch, G.: The Unified Modeling Language Reference Manual. Addison-Wesley Object Technology Series. Addison Wesley (1999)
20. Stumptner, M., Schrefl, M.: Behavior Consistent Inheritance in UML. In Proc. 19th Int. Conf. on Conceptual Modeling (ER). Springer LNCS 1920 (2000)
21. Doan, A., Madhavan, J., Dhamankar, R., Domingos, P., Halevy, A.: Learning to match ontologies on the Semantic Web. VLDB Journal **12** (2003) 303–319
22. Corcho, O., Fernáandez-López, M., Gómez-Pérez, A.: Methodologies, tools and languages for building ontologies. Where is their meeting point? Data & Knowledge Engineering **46** (2003) 41–64

Knowledge Sifter: Agent-Based Ontology-Driven Search over Heterogeneous Databases Using Semantic Web Services

Larry Kerschberg, Mizan Chowdhury, Alberto Damiano, Hanjo Jeong,
Scott Mitchell, Jingwei Si, and Stephen Smith

E-Center for E-Business, George Mason University, Fairfax, VA, USA
{kersch,mchowdh1,adamiano,hjeong,smitche2,jsi,ssmith7}@gmu.edu
http://eceb.gmu.edu

Abstract. Knowledge Sifter is a scaleable agent-based system that supports access to heterogeneous information sources such as the Web, open-source repositories, XML-databases and the emerging Semantic Web. User query specification is supported by a user agent that accesses multiple ontologies using an integrated conceptual model expressed in the Web Ontology Language (OWL). A collection of cooperating agents supports interactive query specification and refinement, query decomposition, query processing, as well as result ranking and presentation. The Knowledge Sifter architecture is general and modular so that ontologies and information sources can be easily incorporated. A proof-of-concept implementation shows how Knowledge Sifter can search geo-spatial ontology services such as the USGS Geographic Names Information System (GNIS) and Princeton University's WordNet as well as image databases including Lycos and TerraServer. Each Agent is implemented as a Web Service and the external sources are also accessed via Web Service Technology.

1 Introduction

One important problem faced by the Scientific Database Community is the *integration* of data and knowledge from multiple heterogeneous sources. Examples can be found in diverse application domains such as Earth Science, Bioinformatics, and Space Science. The federated approach [18, 28, 29, 31, 49, 52, 53] is used to allow scientists to maintain control of their data, while sharing it within the community. Many of the sharing protocols are ad hoc, and our goal is to provide a framework and architecture by which search and sharing can be easily implemented using standard protocols.

The Knowledge Sifter project, underway at George Mason University, has as its primary goals: 1) to allow users to perform ontology-guided semantic searches for relevant information, both organic and open-source, 2) to refine searches based on user feedback, and 3) to access heterogeneous data sources via agent-based knowledge services. Increasingly, users seek information outside of their own communities to open sources such as the Web, XML-databases, and the emerging Semantic Web.

The Knowledge Sifter project also wishes to use open standards for both ontology construction and for searching heterogeneous data sources. For this reason we have

M. Bouzeghoub et al. (Eds.): ICSNW 2004, LNCS 3226, pp. 278–295, 2004.
© IFIP International Federation for Information Processing 2004

chosen to implement our specifications and data interchange using the Web Ontology Language (OWL), and Web Services for communication among agents and information sources.

This paper presents the Knowledge Sifter framework as applied to searching and ranking image data from several sources.

2 Related Work

2.1 Semantic Search

Current search technology is keyword-based, while many users may prefer to formulate queries in terms of high-level semantic concepts that are more in tune with standard nomenclature and his tacit knowledge. Moreover, current search engines use proprietary indexing and rating algorithms, so one cannot analyze the search result rankings. In many cases the results returned by search engines are completely irrelevant. In our research on WebSifter, we have identified a *semantic gap* [32, 33] between the way users think and conceptualize a problem, and the primitive way they must pose queries to search engines. We have published our search-result ranking algorithms, introduced learning mechanisms to evolve user preferences, and have demonstrated these concepts in the WebSifter prototype system [34].

Some research incorporates user domain knowledge for semantic search. For example, Aridor et al. [2] represent user domain knowledge as a small set of example web pages provided by users. Chakrabarti et al. adopted both a pre-defined (but modifiable) taxonomy and a set of example user-provided web pages as domain knowledge [6]. OntoBroker [8, 12, 13] uses an ontology in its search. The recent work on WebSifter [32-35], shows that the use of domain knowledge, agent-based services, and personalized ranking metrics can improve both precision and recall. Cercone et al discuss the use of machine translation, machine learning, and user interface design in intelligent search services [5].

2.2 Ontology Specification

An ontology is an explicit specification of a conceptualization. In an intelligent agent system, the ontology is a declarative formalism, the vocabulary for the representation of knowledge for a specific domain. Ontology definitions associate the names of entities in the universe of discourse (e.g., classes, relations, functions, or other objects) with human-readable text describing what the names mean, and formal axioms that constrain the interpretation and well-formed use of these terms. [16, 17]

The Knowledge Sifter approach posits a conceptual domain model, used in conjunction with a collection of light-weight and specialized ontologies that can be accessed by the user, or his agents, in formulating queries and more complex scenarios. Some ontologies are domain-independent, e.g., temporal/spatial concepts, while others are domain-dependent, e.g., an image metadata ontology such as the ISO 19115/19139 standard [26, 27].

We envision that the various scientific communities will continue to invest resources in creating such specialized ontologies using domain specific markup languages such as Microarray Markup Language (MAML) for gene expression data-bases, Protein Extensible Markup Language (PROXIML), Geography Markup Language (GML), and the Intelligence Community Markup Language [25].

Many of the new markup languages will incorporate type concepts such as RDF [9, 22, 36, 37] and XML Schema and there is growing acceptance Semantic Web [3, 19, 20] constructs such as DAML [1, 10, 21], OWL [11].

Organizational ontologies can be complemented with personal ontologies created by users over the course of their investigations. These reflect personal preferences regarding: 1) how concepts are related and organized, 2) preferred search engines, and 3) opinions regarding the authoritativeness of a source and the accuracy of its information. These preferences can be used to rank, sift and winnow the results returned from the heterogeneous data/knowledge sources.

Recently, the issue of creating an ontology for GRID environments has been proposed [51]. The authors point out that "GRID environments are service-oriented and emphasize operations that can be performed on data using associated metadata schemas, rather than focusing upon the content of metadata schemas and relationships between schema elements." In order for middleware services to be able to respond to service requests, the metadata (both schema and instance levels) must be available to that service. The metaphor for Knowledge Sifter is that each query has an associated instantiation which is exchanged by the agents and updated based on the services performed. This captures the pedigree and provenance of the entire collection of activities associated with the instance.

2.3 Semantic Web Services

Web services provide a means for computers and agents to discover, configure, invoke and use specialized programs that have been appropriately "wrapped" in the Web services protocols: Universal Description, Discovery and Integration (UDDI) [47], Simple Object Access Protocol (SOAP) [56], and Web Services Description Language (WSDL) [7].

Part of the DAML+OIL [14] effort is DAML-S, a trio of extensions to DAML designed to automate the specification and advertisement of semantic web services. DAML-S consists of a *Service Profile Ontology* for advertising the capabilities and requirements of a web service; a *Service Model Ontology* to describe how a service operates; and a set of *Service Groundings* which specify how an atomic web service is accessed. The emerging Semantic Web Services [40, 48] motivate the research for Knowledge Sifter Web services.

3 The Knowledge Sifter Agent Architecture

The rationale for using agents to implement intelligent search and retrieval systems is that agents can be viewed as autonomous and proactive. Each agent is endowed with certain responsibilities and communicates using an Agent Communication Language [15]. Recently, Huhns [24] has noted that agents can be thought of a Web services, and this is the approach we have taken to implement the agent community comprising Knowledge Sifter. The family of agents presented here is a subset of those incorpo

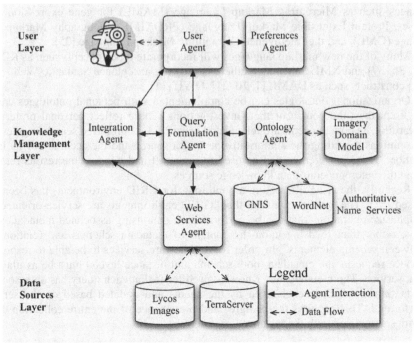

Fig. 1. The Knowledge Sifter Agent-Based Web Services Architecture

rated into the large vision for Knowledge Sifter. This work is motivated by earlier research into Knowledge Rovers [29, 30] performed at GMU. Note that the Knowledge Sifter architecture is quite general, as is its implementation to be discussed in section 5.

The Knowledge Sifter conceptual architecture is depicted in Figure 1. The architecture has three layers: User Layer, Knowledge Management Layer and Data Layer. Specialized agents reside at the various layers and perform well-defined functions. This collection of cooperating agents supports interactive query specification and refinement, query decomposition, query processing, integration, as well as result ranking and presentation. The Knowledge Sifter architecture is general and modular so that new ontologies and new information resources can be easily incorporated.

These services are described below.

3.1 User and Preferences Agents

The User Agent interacts with the user to elicit user preferences that are managed by the Preferences Agent. These preferences include the relative importance attributed to terms used to pose queries, the perceived authoritativeness of Web search engine results, and other preferences to be used by the Integration Agent. The Preferences Agent can also learn the user's preference based on experience and feedback related to previous queries.

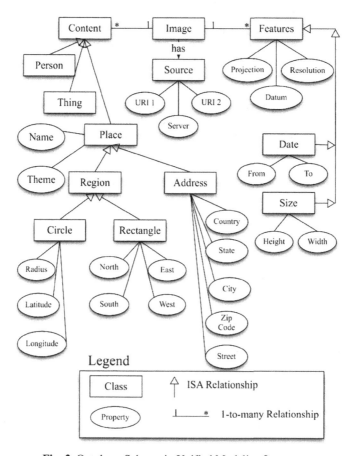

Fig. 2. Ontology Schema in Unified Modeling Language

3.2 Ontology Agent

The Ontology Agent accesses an imagery domain model which is specified in the
Web Ontology Language (OWL). In addition, there are two authoritative name services: Princeton University's WordNet and the US Geological Survey's GNIS. They
allow the Ontology Agent to use terms provided by the name services to suggest
query enhancements such as generalization or specialization. For example, WordNet
can provide a collection of synonyms for a term, while GNIS translates a physical
place in the US into latitude and longitude coordinates that are required by a data
source such as TerraServer. Other appropriate name and translation services can be
added in a modular fashion, and the domain model would be updated to accommodate
new concepts and relationships. We now discuss the various sources used by the Ontology Agent.

Imagery Domain Model Schema. The OWL schema for the imagery domain model, or ontology, is depicted as a UML diagram in Figure 2. The class Image is defined as having *source, content,* and file descriptive *features.* Subcategories of content are *person, thing,* and *place.* Since we are primarily interested in satellite and geographic images, the class *place* has two general attributes, *name* and *theme,* together with the subclasses *region* and *address.* The Region is meant to uniquely identify the portion of the Earth's surface where the place is located, either by a *rectangle* or a *circle.* In the case of a rectangle we need two latitude values (*north* and *south*) and two longitude values (*east* and *west*), while to specify a circle we need the *latitude* and *longtude* of its center point, and a *radius.* The *address* of our location is identified by *country, state, city, zip code* and *street.* Each image belongs to a specific online source, the *server,* and has *URI-1* as a unique identifier, together with a secondary *URI-2* for a thumbnail (if any). Some qualitative and quantitative attributes are also modeled as subclasses of the general class *features,* namely *resolution* (in square meters per pixel), *projection* and *datum* (for future GIS utilizations), a *date* range, and image *size* (with *height* and *width* expressed in pixels).

OWL Schema Specification. An OWL [55] specification of the imagery ontology utilizing RDF and XML was written to provide the conceptual schema of terms and relationships to assist users in instantiating queries. The instantiated schema was passed among the agents and was updated based on decisions and actions taken. To better illustrate how the taxonomy tree in Figure 1 can be converted into an OWL file, here follow some definitions extracted from of the RDF code. The first example shows how to specify that the class *Image* is participating in a relationship between the class *Content.* Such relationship is defined using the OWL nametag "ObjectProperty":

```
<owl:Class rdf:ID="Image">
    <owl:subClassOf rdf:resource="http://www.w3.org/2002/07/owl#Thing"/>
</owl:Class>
<owl:Class rdf:ID="Content">
    <owl:subClassOf rdf:resource="http://www.w3.org/2002/07/owl#Thing"/>
</owl:Class>
  <owl:ObjectProperty rdf:ID="HasContent">
      <owl:domain rdf:resource="#Image"/>
      <owl:range rdf:resource="#Content"/>
  </owl:ObjectProperty>
```

As a further example, it is shown how to define a subclass of an OWL class. In this case *Person* and *Thing* are set to be subclasses of the class *Content:*

```
<owl:Class rdf:ID="Person">
    <owl:subClassOf rdf:resource="#Content"/>
</owl:Class>
<owl:Class rdf:ID="Thing">
    <owl:subClassOf rdf:resource="#Content"/>
</owl:Class>
```

Each class or attribute can have a specific Datatype, which can be a simple XMLS type as in the following example, or a customized type created with the appropriate XMLS tags. The following specifies that the class *Person* has type "string":

```
<owl:DatatypeProperty rdf:ID="PersonName">
  <owl:domain rdf:resource="#Person"/>
  <owl:range rdf:resource="http://www.w3.org/2001/XMLSchema#string"/>
</owl:DatatypeProperty>
```

The full OWL schema specification may be accessed at:
http://www.scs.gmu.edu/~adamiano/csi710/ontology.txt

OWL schema extensions. The OWL schema depicted in Figure 1 captures the concepts that are needed to represent the data and metadata coming from our ontological sources (see section 3.4) and data sources (see section 3.6). However, it would be possible to manipulate and add other portions of ontologies coming from different sources and to integrate them with the existing OWL file. Using the power of RDF, it is reasonable to think of a "library" of ontologies, linked together by RDF relationships between the main upper-level classes. This library could be represented with a high-level RDF document in which the links between the ontologies were hard coded. On the other hand, that would require the Ontology Agent to support some intelligent search among different OWL files. This feature has not been included in the current Knowledge Sifter prototype, but is planned for future research.

Comments on Geospatial Standards and the Imagery Ontology. To enable the inter-operability and extensibility of our ontology and OWL specification, we evaluated the suitability of several existing and developmental metadata standards and image ontologies. Most were either too simplistic or far too detailed for our needs. However, two of the more detailed standards were examined in depth. The Content Standards for Digital Geospatial Metadata (CSDGM), FGDC, June 1994, and the International Standards Organization Technical Committee 211 Metadata Standards (ISO/TC 211). The ISO/TC 211 Metadata Standards were chosen despite being a work in progress. The documentation included a mapping from CSDGM to ISO. In fact, the ISO documentation included a recommendation to continue using the CSDGM until completion and approval. Direct and indirect participation and contributions are made to ISO/TC 211 by NGA, NIST, FGDC, INCITS, OGIS, and other academic, commercial, and governmental entities from several different countries. Furthermore, federal standards such as Spatial Data Transfer Standard (SDTS), FIPS 173, 1992, and many international standards such as The Digital Geographic Information Exchange Standard (DIGEST), January 1994, and International Hydrographic Organization Transfer Standard for Digital Hydrographic Data (IHO S-57), October 1995, were considered and used in the development.

The three documents of primary interest are currently still in development. ISO 19115 is the Geographic Information/Geomatics Metadata Standard. ISO 19139 is the XML Schema for the Dataset Metadata Implementation Standard for ISO 19115. ISO 19115 Part 2 is an Extension for inclusion of Imagery and Gridded Data. The purpose of these documents is to establish standards for geospatial information concerning "objects or phenomena that are directly or indirectly associated with a location relative to the Earth".

First, we developed a rudimentary ontology, identifying metadata requirements necessary to support access to our two sources. Our intent was to generate an OWL ontology by mapping our metadata requirements to specific elements in the ISO documents. For example, TerraServer has a metadata schema for its own database, and links to the data providers original metadata for data lineage.

For expediency, we implemented our proof-of-concept ontology knowing that we could convert the vocabulary and data types to be fully ISO compliant should those standards be supported by our sources in the future.

3.3 Authoritative Name Services

There are two authoritative name services used by the Ontology Agent: WordNet and GNIS.

Princeton University's WordNet. WordNet is a lexical database for the English language [44]. WordNet is already integrated in the existing version of Web Sifter. When the initial query instance, specifying whether a person, place, or thing, is sent to the Ontology Agent, it then consults WordNet to retrieve synonyms. The synonyms are provided to the Query Formulation Agent to request that the user select one or more synonyms. The decision is communicated to the Ontology Agent which updates the appropriate attribute in the instantiated version of the OWL schema. If the attribute value is the name of a class of type *place* then the Ontology Agent passes the instance to the USGS GNIS.

USGS Geographic Names Information System (GNIS). The USGS GNIS is a database of geographic names within the United States and its territories [54]. GNIS was developed by the USGS and the U.S. Board on Geographic Names to meet major national needs regarding geographic names and their standardization and dissemination. It is an integration of three separate databases, the National Geographic Names Data Base, the USGS Topographic Map Names Data Base, and the Reference Data Base. Records within the database contain feature name, state, county, geographic coordinates, USGS Geographic Map name, and others.

The user's search string is passed to the QueryGNIS web service. An optional *state* can be included to further localize the query. Then a query to the GNIS server is created by generating an appropriately formatted URL that contains the query data. The returned webpage is then parsed for results. There are four possible results pages, no result, a single result, multiple results, and too many results. Each page type is parsed differently. The GNIS limits the return values to less than 2000. When the number of results is greater than that threshold, the number of results is returned but no details are given. The web service user can obtain all these results. Results are then passed to the User Agent to select the preferred location.

For future development, the GNIS the database is available online and could be downloaded and implemented locally. In addition, other authoritative services should be included to yield a broader geographic coverage. For example, the GEOnet Names Server [46] covers much of the world.

3.4 Query Formulation Agent

The user indicates an initial query to the Query Formulation Agent. This agent, in turn, consults the Ontology Agent to refine or generalize the query based on the semantic mediation provided by the available ontology services. Once a query has been specified by means of interactions among the User Agent and the Ontology Agent, the Query Formulation Agent decomposes the query into subqueries targeted for the appropriate data sources. This involves semantic mediation of terminology used in the domain model ontology and name services with those used by the local sources. Also, query translation is needed to retrieve data from the intended heterogeneous sources.

For example, if the user specifies the domain of his search as *place*, Lycos and TerraServer will be chosen. In cases of *person* and *thing*, only Lycos will be chosen.
In the case of person and thing, the user is asked to choose a specific meaning from the list retrieved from WordNet, and then the synonym set and hypernym set regarding that particular meaning are retrieved. Synonyms can be chosen as alternate names. Hypernyms can be used to generalize the user's concept. The terms chosen by the user are used to query Lycos. For example, if the users specifies the concept 'Rushmore' the following synonym set is returned by WordNet:

```
Rushmore, Mount Rushmore, Mt. Rushmore - (a mountain
in the Black Hills of South Dakota; the likenesses of
Washington and Jefferson and Lincoln and Roosevelt
are carved on it)
```

In this case, the synonym set {Rushmore, Mount Rushmore, Mt. Rushmore} and the hypernym set {Mountain Peak} are retrieved from WordNet. If user chooses "Mount Rushmore" and "Mountain Peak", two different queries, "Mount AND Rushmore" and "Mountain AND Peak" are posed to Lycos, because the Lycos image search doesn't support the logical connector "OR" in search terms.

In the case of place, the user-selected synonym set and hypernym set are requested from GNIS server using a similar approach, that is, the queries ("Mount AND Rushmore" and "Mountain AND Peak") are posed to the GNIS server in order to collect a list of locations from which the user can choose. The user can specify a state to restrict the GNIS results. After the user chooses one specific location, the name of the location is also used to submit queries to the Lycos server. Concurrently, a query is sent to TerraServer Web service with the appropriate latitude and longitude for the selected place.

In our future research, we will endow the Query Formulation Agent with more rules and policies to help it to make more intelligent decisions about query specification and query optimization. For example, in the case of image databases, a strategy might be to query the image metadata, retrieve and view thumbnails, and then request the collection of selected images. In addition, Knowledge Sifter will have a repository of processed queries, instantiated and annotated according to the OWL schema. This information will be used by the Query Formulation Agent as a Case Base that can be searched and the results reused. For example, a user query might be specified in stages, and the Case Base could be used to retrieve a relevant query processing strategy, send a request to the Web Services Agent and the results returned for user consideration. If needed, the Ontology Agent could assist in query enhancement as described above.

3.5 Web Services Agent

The main role of the Web Services Agent is to accept a user query that has been refined by consulting the Ontology Agent, and decomposed by the Query Formulation Agent. The Web Service Agent is responsible for the choreography and dispatch of subqueries to appropriate data sources, taking into consideration such facets as: user preference of sites; site authoritativeness and reputation; service-level agreements; size estimates of subquery responses; and quality-of-service measures of network traffic and dynamic site workload.

The Web Services Agent transforms the subqueries to XML Protocol (SOAP) requests to the respective local databases and open Web sources (TerraServer or Lycos) that have Web Service published interfaces; this is the case for the TerraServer, while Lycos provides an HTTP interface.

3.6 Data Sources (Lycos and TerraServer)

Lycos. The Lycos server supports keyword-based image search via the web page http://multimedia.lycos.com. It makes use of both an image server and external data sources such as web pages for the image search. For a Lycos image search, no advanced search is supported and only conjunctions of terms are used. Therefore, the user cannot specify the image metadata such as *size* or *resolution*, so the results of search are limited. To address these problems the Query Formulation Agent generates a collection of conjunctive and disjunctive queries, while the evaluation and ranking process is left to the Integration Agent.

TerraServer. The TerraServer is a technology demonstration for Microsoft. There is a Web Service API for TerraServer. TerraServer is an online database of digital aerial photographs (DOQs – Digital Orthophoto Quadrangles) and topographic maps (DRGs – Digital Raster Graphics). Both data products are supplied by the U.S. Geological Survey (USGS). The images are supplied as small tiles and these can be made into a larger image by creating a mosaic of tiles. The demonstrator at terraserver-usa.com uses a mosaic of 2x3 tiles.

Our purpose is to take the ontology-enhanced query and generate specific subqueries for the TerraServer metadata. The resulting image identifiers and their metadata are wrapped into an instance of our image ontology. And an array of these is returned to the Web Service Agent to compile with other results.

Since our ontology currently specifies a single data point and a single resolution and the TerraServer only returns 200x200 pixel images, each query effectively returns at most one image (DOQ) and one map (DRG). We do want to give the user a bit more than that. So we can return image tiles surrounding our target and in adjacent resolutions.

In the future, there should be support for a range of values. Also, the service should consider generating mosaics of TerraServer image tiles, so the user can get bigger image results than just the 200x200 image. TerraServer is setup to allow this, but the assembly needs to occur on the application side.

3.7 Integration Agent

The Integration Agent is responsible for compiling the sub-query results from the various sources, ranking them according to user preferences, as supplied by the Preferences Agent, for such attributes as: 1) the authoritativeness of a source which is indicated by a weight – a number between 0 and 10 – assigned to that source, or 2) the weight associated with a term comprising a query. The following are the detail specification of similarity value assessment rules for each criterion.

Name:
If the name of the image exactly matches with user's term, then assign the value 10, a perfect match.

Else if the name of the image exactly matches one of synonym sets, then assign the value, 7.

Else if the name of the image includes the user's term, then give the value, 5.

Else if the name of image includes the one of synonym sets, then give the value, (10-5)/(# of Synonyms) for each synonym term.

Theme:
If the image theme (photo or map) matches the user's preference, then assign 10, else assign 0.

Location:

In case of a circle: Value $= \text{Max}(1 - \dfrac{\text{Distance}}{\text{Radius}}, 0)$

In case of rectangle: Value $= \text{Max}(1 - \dfrac{2 * \text{Distance}}{\text{Diagonal}}, 0)$

Date and Time:
If the time the image was taken is in period of user's preference, then assign 10,

Else assign a value between [0-9] according to the time difference between the user's preference and the date and time the image was taken.

Size:
Similarity Value $= 10 * (\text{width\_diff} * \text{height\_diff})$, where width_diff and height_diff are normalized value according to the size differences.

Resource:
If the source (Lycos or Terra) of image matches with user's preference, then give 10, else give 0.

Total Similarity:

$$\text{Value} = \sum_{c} \text{Sim}(c) * \text{Weight}(c)$$

where c denotes each criterion, and Sim(c) and Weight(c) denote similarity and user preference weight for each criterion, respectively.

The Integration Agent calculates each result's similarity by normalizing the total similarity value, ranks these results according to their similarity values, and returns the ranking information to the User Agent.

4 End-to-End Scenario

Consider the following scenario in which a user wishes to search for the term 'Rushmore'. This scenario is also used in the demonstration of the proof-of-concept prototype.

1. The user provides the User Agent with a query: 'Rushmore'.
2. The user identifies the term is being either a person, place or thing via radio buttons in the query form, see Figure 4. The user has chosen 'Place'.
3. The User Agent passes the query to Query Formulation Agent.
4. The Query Formulation Agent invokes the Ontology Agent to instantiate an OWL schema for the 'Place' with Name = 'Rushmore'.
5. The Ontology Agent chooses a service agent based on the initial query. In this case, it requests from WordNet a list of concepts for 'Rushmore'. WordNet then passes the results back to the Ontology Agent which then passes the results to the User Agent via the Query Formulation Agent for the user decision.
6. The user chooses the 'Mount Rushmore' concept, which has three synonyms ('Rushmore', 'Mt. Rushmore', and 'Mount Rushmore').
7. The Ontology Agent then submits the synonym set to the USGS Geographic Name Information Server and receives a list of candidate geographic coordinates.
8. The list of candidate coordinates is sent to the Query Formulation Agent and the user chooses the desired location.
9. The Ontology Agent then updates the OWL schema instance with the chosen latitude and longitude.
10. The Query Formulation Agent then passes the fully-specified query to the Web Service Agent.
11. The Web Services Agent forwards appropriate sub-queries to both Lycos and TerraServer. The TerraServer and Lycos data sources are queried, and the results are sent back to the Web Services Agent. The results are compiled into new OWL instances that describe image metadata.
12. All results are combined and sent to the Query Formulation Agent.
13. The Query Formulation Agent sends the result sets and the original query to the Integration Agent for ranking.
14. Within the Integration Agent the image metadata for each returned item is ranked using the weights and preferences provided by the Preferences Agent. The Preferences Agent maintains the user preferences.
15. The Integration Agent generates a score for each image result, and returns the scored list to the User Agent.
16. The User Agent then sorts the results by ranking and presents them to the user.
17. The user can then select an item from the list to download and view the image.

5 Knowledge Sifter Proof-of-Concept Implementation

The Knowledge Sifter proof-of-concept prototype has been implemented as an agent-based system, in which each agent is a Web service. Knowledge Sifter has been implemented as a web-application using the ASP and C# languages based on Microsoft .Net Framework. The W3C Document Object Model (DOM) utilized to deal with the

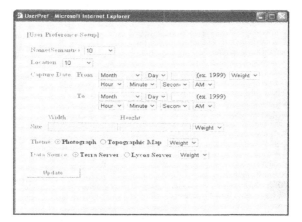

Fig. 3. User Preferences Pane

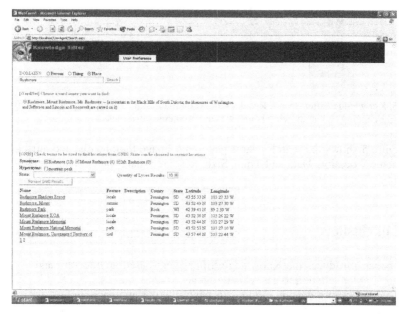

Fig. 4. Knowledge Sifter Query and Ontology Interface

XML representation of data by using MSXML technology. Each Agent implemented and deployed as a Web Service through the automation of Microsoft Visual Studio .Net and IIS server using a temporary UDDI. Furthermore, the automation provides the SOAP and WSDL specifications of each agent (Web Services).

Figure 3 shows the User Preferences pane in which users specify preferences and weights associated with semantic names, location, dates, image size, themes, and data sources.

Figure 4 shows the Web page for 1) query formulation, 2) consultation with WordNet and the selection of the synonyms for 'Rushmore" and 3) the results obtained from GNIS for those synonyms.

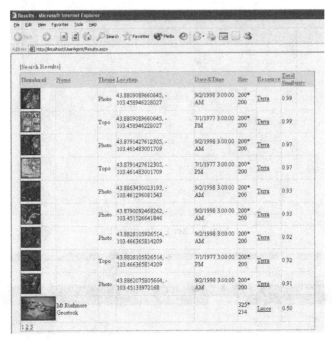

Fig. 5. Knowledge Sifter Search Results Page showing thumbnails of images ranked by similarity in descending order, showing sources, size and theme attributes

Figure 5 shows the search results page with image thumbnails, and attributes such as Theme, Location, Data and Time, Size, Resource (data source) and Total Similarity ranking.

6 Conclusions

This paper introduces the Knowledge Sifter agent-based architecture and a proof-of-concept implementation to access heterogeneous data sources.

The concept of a *domain ontology* is central to our approach, in fact, we envision a collection of cooperating ontological sources, accessed by the Ontology Agent that allow a user to pose queries to those data sources with needing to know the location of the supporting data, nor how the ontological concepts are materialized through an integration and ranking process.

The ontology is specified in the Web Ontology Language (OWL) and an XML-instance of the schema is passed among agents in Web services. This permits the agent to annotate the XML-instance so as to provide the *data/knowledge lineage* of a query, including the user preferences, the original query and its enhancements, decisions regarding query decomposition and the choreography of subqueries. This meta-data will be stored in a case repository for reuse. We term the concept having the history of an object traveling with it from agent-to-agent, its *digital-DNA*. We intend to expand this notion if future research. Basically, the idea is that a data-object will have its associated digital-DNA, so that it is equipped with knowledge regarding potential interactions with other objects, protocols for negotiation with agents, and rules that determine its behavior. The knowledge required for digital-DNA would be provided by the domain model schema and rules, as well as additional knowledge based on the type of object. This concept will become more important in the context of Grid databases.

Each agent is itself implemented as a Web service. As the Web evolves to the Semantic Web, we will see more ontologies developed in OWL, and we envision that mini-ontologies will be integrated into the existing ontology by means of a collection of RDF-relationships. The inclusion of a new data source will involve appropriate metadata mappings. Our current research includes the specification of a methodology using XTM Topic Maps [4, 50], to specify and merge multiple complementary ontologies in a "plug-and-play" fashion [45].

Future plans include enhancing the capabilities of the existing agents, as well as the investigation, specification, design, development and testing of new agents that will play the role of "staff" agents. These include a Web Services Choreography Agent, a Quality-of-Service Agent, and an Ontology Curation Agent, to deal with workflow management [39], system performance [41-43], and the evolution of the ontology via learning [38]. We are also investigating methods and tools for the dynamic configuration [23] of new sources into the Knowledge Sifter federation.

Finally, we plan to investigate Repository Services, based on XML-database technology, to store and manage the various artifacts that are produced within Knowledge Sifter, including queries, ontology schema instances, lineage, ranking, etc.

Acknowledgements. This work was sponsored by a NURI from the National Geospatial-Intelligence Agency (NGA). This work was also supported in part by the Advanced Research and Development Activity (ARDA). Any opinions, findings and conclusions or recommendations expressed in this material are those of the authors and do not necessarily reflect the views of the U. S. Government.

References

[1]   Ankolenkar, A., Hutch, F. and Sycara, K., Concurrent Semantics for the Web Services Specification Language DAML-S. in *Fifth International Conference on Coordination Models and Languages (Coordination 2002)*, (York, UK, 2002).

[2]   Aridor, Y., Carmel, D., Lempel, R., Soffer, A. and Maarek, Y.S., Knowledge Agent on the Web. in *Proceedings of the 4th International Workshop on Cooperative Information Agents IV*, (2000), 15-26.

[3]   Berners-Lee, T., Hendler, J. and Lassila, O. The Semantic Web: A new form of Web content that is meaningful to computers will unleash a revolution of new possibilities *Scientific American*, 2001, 34-43.

[4]   Biezunski, M. Introduction to the Topic Map Paradigm. in Park, J. and Hunting, S. eds. *XML Topic Maps: Creating and Using Topic Maps for the Web*, Addison Wesley, Boston, 2003.

[5]   Cercone, N., Hou, L., Keselj, V., An, A., Naruedomkul, K. and Hu, X. From Computational Intelligence to Web Intelligence *IEEE Computer*, 2002, 72-78.

[6]   Chakrabarti, S., Berg, M.v.d. and Dom, B., Focused Crawling: A New Approach to Topic-Specific Web Resource Discovery. in *Proceedings of the Eighth International WWW Conference*, (1999), Elsevier, 545-562.

[7]   Chinnici, R., Gudgin, M., Moreau, J.-J. and Weerawarana, S. Web Services Description Language (WSDL) Version 1.2 (http://www.w3.org/TR/wsdl12/), W3C, 2002.

[8]   Decker, S., Erdmann, M., Fensel, D. and Studer, R., ONTOBROKER: Ontology Based Access to Distributed and Semi-Structured Information. in *Database Semantics: Semantic Issues in Multimedia Systems (Proceedings of the 8th Working Conference on Database Semantics)*, (New Zealand, 1999).

[9]   Decker, S., Melnik, S., van Harmelen, F., Fensel, D., Klein, M., Broekstra, J., Erdmann, M. and Horrocks, I. The Semantic Web: the roles of XML and RDF. *IEEE Internet Computing, 4* (5). 63-73.

[10] Denker, G., Hobbs, J., Martin, D., Narayanan, S. and Waldinger, R., Accessing Information and Services on the DAML-Enabled Web. in *Second International Workshop on Semantic Web (SemWeb'2001)*, (Hong Kong, China, 2001).

[11] Fensel, D. Ontology-Based Knowledge Management *IEEE Computer*, 2002, 56-59.

[12] Fensel, D., Angele, J., Decker, S., Erdmann, M., Schnurr, H.-P., Staab, S., Studer, R. and Witt, A., On2broker: Semantic-Based Access to Information Sources at the WWW. in *Proceedings of the World Conference on the WWW and Internet (WebNet 99)*, (Honolulu, Hawaii, USA, 1999), 25-30.

[13] Fensel, D., Angele, J., Decker, S., Erdmann, M., Schnurr, H.-P., Studer, R. and Witt, A. On2broker: Lessons Learned from Applying AI to the Web, Institute AIFB, 1998.

[14] Fensel, D., van Harmelen, F., Horrocks, I., McGuinness, D.L. and Patel-Schneider, P.F. OIL: an ontology infrastructure for the Semantic Web *IEEE Intelligent Systems*, 2001, 38-45.

[15] Finin, T., Fritzson, R., McKay, D. and McEntire, R., KQML as an Agent Communication Language. in *International Conference on Information and Knowledge Management (CIKM-94)*, (1994), ACM Press.

[16] Gruber, T.R. Toward principles for the design of ontologies used for knowledge sharing. *International Journal of Human Computer Studies, 43* (5-6). 907-928.

[17] Gruber, T.R. A translation approach to portable ontologies. *Knowledge Acquisition, 5* (2). 199-220.

[18] Gu, J., Pedersen, T. and Shoshani, A., OLAP++: Powerful and Easy-to-Use Federations of OLAP and Object Databases. in *VLDB 2000, Proceedings of 26th International Conference on Very Large Data Bases*, (Cairo, Egypt, 2000), Morgan Kaufmann, 599-602.

[19] Heflin, J. and Hendler, J. A portrait of the Semantic Web in action *IEEE Intelligent Systems*, 2001, 54-59.

[20] Hendler, J. Agents and the Semantic Web. *IEEE Intelligent Systems, 16* (2). 30-37.

[21] Hendler, J. DAML: DARPA Agent Markup Language effort, (http://www.daml.org/), 2002.

[22] Hjelm, J. *Creating the semantic Web with RDF : professional developer's guide*. Wiley, New York, 2001.

[23] Howard, R. and Kerschberg, L., A Knowledge-based Framework for Dynamic Semantic Web Services Brokering and Management. in *International Workshop on Web Semantics - WebS 2004*, (Zaragoza, Spain, 2004), IEEE Computer Society.

[24] Huhns, M. Agents as Web Services *IEEE Internet Computing*, July/August 2002.

[25] ICMWG. Intelligence Community Metadata Working Group, 2003.

[26] ISO_TC_211_19115. Geographic Information - Metadata Part 2 - Metadata for imagery and gridded data, 2003.

[27] ISO_TC_211_19139. Geographic Information - Metadata - Implementation Specification, 2003.

[28] Kerschberg, L. Functional Approach to in Internet-Based Applications: Enabling the Semantic Web, E-Business, Web Services and Agent-Based Knowledge Management. in Gray, P.M.D., Kerschberg, L., King, P. and Poulovassilis, A. eds. *The Functional Approach to Data Management*, Springer, Heidelberg, 2003, 369-392.

[29] Kerschberg, L. (ed.), *Knowledge Management in Heterogeneous Data Warehouse Environments*. Springer, Munich, Germany, 2001.

[30] Kerschberg, L. The Role of Intelligent Agents in Advanced Information Systems. in Small, C., Douglas, P., Johnson, R., King, P. and Martin, N. eds. *Advanced in Databases*, Springer-Verlag, London, 1997, 1-22.

[31] Kerschberg, L., Gomaa, H., Menascé, D.A. and Yoon, J.P., Data and Information Architectures for Large-Scale Distributed Data Intensive Information Systems. in *Proc. of the Eighth IEEE International Conference on Scientific and Statistical Database Management*, (Stockholm, Sweden, 1996), IEEE Computer Society Press.

[32] Kerschberg, L., Kim, W. and Scime, A., Intelligent Web Search via Personalizable Meta-Search Agents. in *International Conference on Ontologies, Databases and Applications of Semantics (ODBASE 2002)*, (Irvine, CA, 2002).

[33] Kerschberg, L., Kim, W. and Scime, A. A Semantic Taxonomy-Based Personalizable Meta-Search Agent. in Truszkowski, W. ed. *Workshop on Radical Agent Concepts*, Springer-Verlag, Tysons Corner, 2002.

[34] Kim, W., Kerschberg, L. and Scime, A. Learning for Automatic Personalization in a Semantic Taxonomy-Based Meta-Search Agent. *Electronic Commerce Research and Applications (ECRA)*, *1* (2).

[35] Kim, W., Kerschberg, L. and Scime, A., Personalization in a Semantic Taxonomy-Based Meta-Search Agent. in *International Conference on Electronic Commerce 2001 (ICEC 2001)*, (Vienna, Austria, 2001), Elsevier Science.

[36] Klien, M. XML, RDF, and relatives *IEEE Intelligent Systems*, 2001, 26-28.

[37] Lassila, O. and Swick, R. Resource Description Framework (RDF) model and syntax specification (http://www.w3.org/RDF), World Wide Web Consortium, 1998.

[38] Maedche, A. and Staab, S. Ontology learning for the Semantic Web *IEEE Intelligent Systems*, 2001, 72-79.

[39] Marinescu, D.C. *Internet-based workflow management: toward a semantic web*. Wiley-Interscience, New York, 2002.

[40] McIlraith, S.A., Son, T.C. and Zeng, H. Semantic Web Services *IEEE Intelligent Systems*, 2001, 46-53.

[41] Menascé, D.A. QoS Issues in Web Services *IEEE Internet Computing*, 2002.

[42] Menascé, D.A., Almeida, V.A., Riedi, R., Ribeiro, F., Fonseca, R. and W. Meira Jr A Hierarchical and Multiscale Approach to Analyze E-Business Workloads. *Performace Evaluation*.

[43] Menascé, D.A., Dodge, R. and Barbará, D., Preserving QoS of E-commerce Sites Through Self-Tuning: A Performance Model Approach. in *ACM Conference on E-commerce*, (Tampa, FL, 2001).

[44] Miller, G.A. WordNet a Lexical Database for English. *Communications of the ACM*, *38* (11). 39-41.

[45] Morikawa, R. and Kerschberg, L., MAKO: Multi-Ontology Analytical Knowledge Organization based on Topic Maps. in *Fifth International Workshop on Theory and Applications of Knowledge Management*, (Zaragoza, Spain, 2004), IEEE Computer Society.

[46] NIMA. GEOnet Names Server (GNS), http://gnswww.nima.mil/geonames/GNS/index.jsp.

[47] OASIS. Universal Description, Discovery and Integration (http://www.uddi.org/specification.html), OASIS, 2002.

[48] Paolucci, M. and Sycara, K. Autonomous Semantic Web Services *IEEE Internet Computing*, Sept - Oct 2003, 34-41.

[49] Pedersen, T.B., Shoshani, A., Gu, J. and Jensen, C.S., Extending OLAP Querying to External Object Databases. in *CKIM 2000, Proceedings of the 2000 ACM CIKM International Conference on Information and Knowledge Management*, (McLean, VA, 2000), ACM, 405-413.

[50] Pepper, S. and Moore, G. XML Topic Maps (XTM) 1.0, http://www.topicmaps.org/xtm/1.0/, TopicMaps.org, 2001.

[51] Pouchard, L., Cinquini, L., Drach, B., Middleton, D., Bernholdt, D.E., Chanchio, K., Foster, I.T., Nefedova, V., Brown, D., Fox, P., Garcia, J., Strand, G., Williams, D., Chervanek, A.L., Kesselman, C., Shoshani, A. and Sim, A., An Ontology for Scientific Information in a Grid Environment: the Earth System Grid. in *CCGRID 2003*, (2003), 626-632.

[52] Seligman, L. and Kerschberg, L. Federated Knowledge and Database Systems: A New Architecture for Integrating of AI and Database Systems. in Delcambre, L. and Petry, F. eds. *Advances in Databases and Artificial Intelligence, Vol. 1: The Landscape of Intelligence in Database and Information Systems*, JAI Press, 1995.

[53] Sheth, A. and Larson, J. Federated Database Systems for Managing Distributed, Heterogeneous, and Autonomous Databases. *ACM Computing Surveys*, 22 (3). 183-236.

[54] USGS. USGS Geographic Names Information System (GNIS), http://geonames.usgs.gov/.

[55] W3C. OWL Web Ontology Language Overview, http://www.w3.org/TR/owl-features/. McGuinness, D.L. and van Harmelen, F. eds., W3C, 2003.

[56] W3C. XML Protocol Working Group (http://www.w3.org/2000/xp/Group/), World Wide Web Consortium, 2002.

Managing Grid Schemas Globally

Kimio Kuramitsu

CPDC, Kogakuin University
kuramitsu@cpd.kogakuin.ac.jp

Abstract. Sharing schemas is a shortcut to data interoperability, while in grid environments there are many difficulties such as schema disagreements and schema evolutions. We propose a new "mappings first, schemas later" schema model, named Grid Schema. The Grid Schema uses the idea of context-free mapping to modularize schemas and its translation rules. This is incorporated into its schema validation mechanism, which enables us to check the compatibility of different formed data. We show the flexibility of the Grid Schema in maintaining global schemas in a distributed, evolving, and multi-cultural environment.

1 Introduction

Data Grid has recently attracted an emerging attention to both scientific and business community. In their fields the amounts of data are increasing up to more than hundreds of terabytes [7]. It is too costly to maintain all the data in a single storage site. A sharing and delivery of the data in a Grid way could be a promising approach to the data explosion.

We consider *RFID Database* as a motivating example of Data Grid. RFID tag is an electronic tag, attached to the real-world object. Using RFIDs as an alternative to the barcodes, products can be uniquely identified. However, the length of the RFID identifier is at most 128 bits, so that it doesn't carry much information. Accordingly, RFID systems must work together with RDBMSs, or other database systems.

Manufacturers, intermediaries (brokers), resellers, or even customers would want to record several information associated with RFIDs. For simplicity, we assume these records are stored in relations, such as $R(\mathsf{rfid}, \mathsf{attr1}, \mathsf{attr2}, \mathsf{attr3}, \dots)$. A problem is that we are not going to agree on the schemas of these records (attributes). The schema varies from companies to companies or from products to products. It is impossible to assume a unified culture (or a language) in the schemas, because not a few products move across the national borders. Figure 1 shows an example of the movement of books that are stored in Data Grid. We need a transparent means of work together such distributed database in Data Grid, while Data Grid has traditionally focused on the effectiveness in data replica and data delivery.

We are developing the Grid Schema repository. The Grid Schema uses the idea of context-free mapping to modularize schemas and its translation rules. This is incorporated into its schema validation mechanism, which enables us

M. Bouzeghoub et al. (Eds.): ICSNW 2004, LNCS 3226, pp. 296–308, 2004.
© IFIP International Federation for Information Processing 2004

RFIDs Database

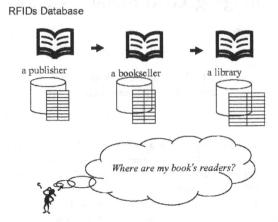

Fig. 1. Motivating Example of RFID Databases

to check the compatibility of different formed data. The management of different forms and representations help us evolve the schema repository as the grid environment changes.

The database community has long discussed schema mediation techniques [1,4,5,6,8,11,13,15]. That is, the schemas are allowed freely, and then maps are created to mediate between conflicted schemas. A rich history of this area has showed that creating maps is not easy, especially when the conflicts are *semantically* complicated. We consider that the mediation approach is unreasonably *inefficient* since data integration and translation are everywhere in Data Grid. That is why we have chosen a reverse approach, say, we first give vocabularies and their mappings to the users, and then the users create schemas over the vocabularies.

This paper models the Grid Schema and discusses the sharing of schemas in Data Grid. The rest of the paper proceeds as follows. In Section 2, we describe our basic ideas underlying Grid Schema. In Section 3, we formalize Grid Schema Model with a type-checking algorithm for schema resolution. In Section 4, we sketch the repository of Grid Schema, which is being implemented on top of RDBMS. In Section 5, we discuss the flexibility of Grid Schema in terms of the management of global schemas. In Section 6, we conclude the paper.

2   Context-Free Mapping

The idea underlying Grid Schema is "mappings first, schema later" – we share mappings before we create schemas. That is, the schemas are defined over *schema parts*, which are given with mappings to interoperate each other. A key is how to modularize the schema parts with keeping the reusability of its mappings. In this section, we informally introduce the idea of *context-free* mappings, which make the core of the Grid Schema model.

2.1 Modularization

The same information can be formed or represented in different ways – which causes the *schema conflict problem* [9, 12, 16, 17, 18]. We start by focusing on some conflicts between two simple data elements, say, labeled values. Here are two data elements, excerpted from different sources.

$$[\text{TEMPERATURE}, 40] [温度, 4]$$

Here we assume that these elements represent the same information, although they have different labels (we mean that the label "温度" represents temperature in Japanese) and different value representations (40F = 4C).

Schematic (or semantic) conflicts like the above very often occur between different databases. To reconcile the conflicts, we usually use the mapping to translate into a unified data representation. For example, we can specify a mapping rule between elements: the value X of TEMPERATURE $\longmapsto$ [温度, Y], where $Y = (X - 32) \times 5/9$.

The mapping rules are specified after the conflicts are identified. A problem with such rules is less reusability. Let suppose other similar elements, labeled as temperatur and temperatura instead of temperature. In each of different sources, we need to specify new rules, in spite of the fact that the rules might be the almost same. Note that the measurement of units would differ in each labeled element.

To improve the reusability, we focus first on the conversion between Fahrenheit and Celsius. This conversion is universal, or *context-free*, regardless of how the values are labeled. This means that the conversion of values *can be* independent of labels. Thus, we can compose the mapping rule between the elements by two discretely defined mappings:

- *Label mapping*: TEMPERATURE $\longmapsto$ 温度
- *Domain mapping*: $40 \longmapsto 4$ (by $Y = (X - 32) \times 5/9$)

We call the value conversion *domain mapping*, while we call the rest *label mapping*, known as the inter-schema correspondence. We assume that all parts in the Gird Schema are modularized in a way that they are mappable only by two types of context-free mappings.

It is important to note that labels are statically associated with *domains* in traditional data models; for example, in the relational model the domain of an attribute TEMPERATURE is determined by *dom*(TEMPERATURE). However, this is very problematic when we want to separate the specification of the label and domain mappings. Not all ones in the Grid use the same domain to represent values in TEMPERATURE. That is, we need a similar separation of domain semantics from the label on the data representation.

In the Grid Schema, we assume that the labels do not *a priori* involve any types of domains. Instead, domains should be given explicitly in an independent form, like [TEMPERATURE, *Fahrenheit*] or [TEMPERATURE, *Kelvin*].

Definition 1 (labels and domains). *We assume (in Grid Schema, defined later) that the structure of the data element is represented by two schema parts:*

- label *to identify the context of the element (what meaning the element carries), and*
- domain *to identify the domain of the element values (how to represent values).*

2.2 Limitations

The separation of the label and domain mappings is trivial when we look at the correspondence between only two data elements. But, when we have the broader scope for element sets, there are two types of schematic conflicts,[1] whose reconciles are not so simple. To keep the context-free modularity, we impose two limitations on the expressiveness of the Grid Schema.

Limitation 1. All labels have the first-class semantics.

Label mappings are not always context-free. This occurs when the meaning of a label depends on other elements. Let consider the following example.

phone-type: office   home-phone:

phone: 03-3812-2111 office-phone: 03-3812-2111

The meaning of phone depends on the value of phone-type, and then we cannot statically determine whether the phone should be mapped into office-phone/home-phone. Otherwise, we need a complex mapping rule, like phone $\longmapsto$ office-phone iff phone-type = office. Fortunately, we can carefully avoid such conflicts in modeling the data. To keep all label mappings context-free, we assume that all labels have the first-class semantics.

Limitation 2. Functional dependency has to be given within a source. Some label mappings need additional value (not domain) mappings. This mainly occurs when two or more elements are *isomorphic*. For example, consider the mapping from the departure element to nights. The scheme of domain mappings does not support the value mapping 2004-12-25 $\longmapsto$ 7.

arrival: 2004-12-19   check-in: 2004-12-19

departure: 2004-12-25   nights: 7

In the isomorphic conflict, it is not easy to avoid one of the occurrences because neither is definitive. We believe that label and domain mapping should be disparate in between different sources. To achieve our belief, let us suppose that the label check-out is defined in the right source. The label mapping departure $\longmapsto$ check-out is context-free, and then we can derive the value of nights from the functional dependency if it is formulated by nights = check-out − check-in. In this paper, we assume that we well formulate functional dependencies among labels within a source.

---

[1] We consider that one-to-many correspondence like name and (firstname, lastname) can be dealt with by extending domains to model multi values or a complex object.

3   Grid Schema Model

In representing data on the Data Gird, there are many formats available, ranging from relational data to XML. For simplicity, we assume that the all the data can be model by a flat relational structure including RFID, which would like $R(\mathsf{RFID}, attr1, attr2, ..)$. Here we highlight how to model a set of $attrs$ (without RFID) in each of the data structure.

3.1   Vocabulary

We start by defining the most fundamental schema part, a *vocabulary*. The vocabulary is the common structure to share the definition of both labels and data values (domains).

Definition 2. *A vocabulary is a finite set of terms, denoted $V = \{v_1, v_2, .., v_i, v_j, ..\}$, where there exists no two terms v_i, v_j that satisfy the mappings: $v_i \longmapsto v_j$ and $v_i \longmapsto v_j$. (That means the vocabulary has no inner-mappings.)*

Each vocabulary has a unique name, which we identify by the set name V. To distinguish the type of vocabularies, we also use S to denote a label vocabulary, and D for a domain vocabulary. In only domains, intensional set definitions and numerical terms are both allowed, like D_{name} or D_{USD}.

Example 1. The following D_1 is a vocabulary, while D_2 is not a vocabulary because we say fall $\longmapsto$ autumn (and autumn $\longmapsto$ fall).

$D_1 = \{\mathsf{spring, summer, fall, winter}\}$
$D_2 = \{\mathsf{spring, summer, fall, autumn, winter}\}$

The terms are *not simulatable*. That is, we are not certain which vocabulary a given term should belong to. For example, a term spring may belong to D_1, or other domains (as a mechanical part or a kind of water pool). We denote $D.v$ (or $S.l$) to explicitly represent the value v of D (or the label l of S).

A mapping is defined between two terms in different vocabularies. We write $D.v \longmapsto D'.v'$ for a rule that we can map $D.v$ into $D'.v'$. Similarly, we can map like $S.l \longmapsto S'.l'$. (We may map between labels and domain values, although it makes no sense.) If the mapping from D to D' is total, we simply write $D \longmapsto D'$.

All mappings are assumed to be *context-free*, as we described in Section 2. This is formalized below.

Definition 3 (context-free). *Suppose $[S.l, D.v]$.*

 – *If $S.l \longmapsto S'.l'$ is given, then we say $[S'.l', D.v]$ for arbitrary $D.v$.*
 – *If $D.v \longmapsto D'.v'$ is given, then we say $[S.l, D'.v']$ for arbitrary $S.l$.*

Note that we view the semantics of these mappings as a connection to *relative information capacity* [14]. Intuitively, the mapping $D.v \longmapsto D'.v'$ means $D.v$ is more informative than $D'.v'$. Also, we can rewrite $D'.v' \sqsubseteq D.v$ in terms of the capacity. We say the equivalence $D'.v' \equiv D.v$ if and only if $D'.v' \sqsubseteq D.v$ and $D.v \sqsubseteq D'.v'$. The equivalence is used to normalize mappings in a storage, which will be described in Section 4.

3.2 Data Representation

In the Grid Schema system, all data are represented over terms defined in vocabularies. We define the data object as follows.

Definition 4 (data). *The data (object) O is a finite set of data elements. Each data element is denoted as $[S.l, D.v]$, where the first term is a label in S and the last is a domain value in D. We presume that the order of the elements is meaningless.*

Example 2. The data can be represented over different label vocabularies or part of each vocabulary. Suppose two label vocabularies S_1 and S_2 are given:

$$S_1 = \{\text{title, author, isbn, publisher, year}\}$$
$$S_2 = \{\text{seller, listprice, salesprice, salesdate}\}$$
$$O_1 = \{\ [S_1.\text{title}, D_{EN}.\text{"Harry Potter and the Order of the Phoenix"}],$$
$$[S_1.\text{author}, D_{name}.\text{"J. K. Rowling"}],$$
$$[S_1.\text{isbn}, D_{isbn}.\text{043935806X}],$$
$$[S_2.\text{listprice}, D_{USD}.\text{30.00}],$$
$$[S_2.\text{salesprice}, D_{USD}.\text{12.00}]\ \}$$

We introduce the class C as a schema component. We use the class not only as a metadata to the underlying relational schema, but also as the view specification of a database application.

Definition 5 (class). *The class C is a finite set of attributes, each of which is a pair of label and domain name, denoted $(S.l, D)$.*

Example 3. The following C_1 is a class definition for the object O_1 above.
$$C_1 = \{\ (S_1.\text{title}, D_{EN}), (S_1.\text{author}, D_{name}), (S_1.\text{isbn}, D_{isbn}),$$
$$(S_2.\text{listprice}, D_{USD}), (S_2.\text{salesprice}, D_{USD})\}$$

We write $C.O$ if the data O is an instance of C, (that is, for each attribute $[S.l, D]$ in C the object O has the corresponding data element $[S.l, D.v]$.)

3.3 Type-Checking

Type-checking is of increasingly importance to data processing over the Data Grid. Specifically, a grid application needs to validate the structure of remote data (in distributed databases) before we process them. Here we should note that the remote data would differ from a schematic view that the application expects. The structural type-checking might reject most of the remote data.

The Grid Schema provides an advanced type-checking mechanism that is incorporated with mappings into the validation scheme. The underlying idea is the *compatibility*. Intuitively, we say that D_{USD} and D_{yen} are compatible because their values are mappable with each other. We apply this idea to check whether a given object is compatible to the Grid view C'.

Definition 6 (mapping-enhanced type-checking). *An data object C.O conforms to C' if and only if:*

- *C.O is an instance of C' ($C = C'$), or*
- *there exists a data instance $C'.O'$ that can be derived from $C.O \longmapsto C'.O'$.*

It is unrealistic of course that we specify mappings between all possible classes. The strength of Grid Schema is that we can check $C.O \longmapsto C'.O'$ from label mappings and domain mappings that are already defined. The algorithm is: $C.O) \longmapsto C'.O'$ is said if for each element $[S_i, l_i, D_j.v_j]$ in O there exists $[S_i'.l_i', D_j'.v_j']$ in O', such that $S_i.l_i \longmapsto S_i'.l_i'$ and $D_j.v_j \longmapsto D_j'.v_j'$.

Example 4. We suppose the following mappings are given, prior to the schema validation.

$$S_3.書名 \longmapsto S_1.\text{title}$$
$$S_3.著者 \longmapsto S_1.\text{author}$$
$$S_3.\text{ISBN} \longmapsto S_1.\text{isbn}$$
$$S_3.定価 \longmapsto S_2.\text{listprice}$$
$$S_3.定価 \longmapsto S_2.\text{salesprice}$$
$$D_{USD} \longmapsto D_{yen}$$

The following object O_2:

$O_2 = \{$ $[S_3.書名, D_{EN}.$"Harry Potter and the Order of the Phoenix"$]$,
$\quad [S_3.著者, D_{name}.$"J. K. Rowling"$]$,
$\quad [S_3.\text{ISBN}, D_{isbn}.043935806X]$,
$\quad [S_3.定価\ D_{yen}.2800]$,
$\quad [S_4.\text{TYPE}, D_{JISXB01}.\texttt{EnglishBook}]$ $\}$

is compatible to C_1, because we can translate it to $C_1.O_2'$:

$C_1.O_2' = \{$ $[S_1.\text{title}, D_{EN}.$"Harry Potter and the Order of the Phoenix"$]$,
$\quad [S_1.\text{author}, D_{name}.$"J. K. Rowling"$]$,
$\quad [S_1.\text{isbn}, D_{isbn}.043935806X]$,
$\quad [S_2.\text{listprice}, D_{USD}.\texttt{25.00}]$,
$\quad [S_2.\text{salesprice}, D_{USD}.\texttt{25.00}]$ $\}$

4   Grid Schema Repository

This section reviews implementation issues on the Grid Schema repository, and its inference engine.

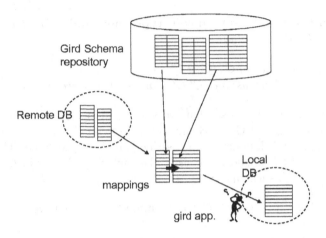

Fig. 2. An Architectural Overview of the Grid Schema repository

4.1 Overview

The Grid Schema repository delivers vocabularies and their mappings across the Grid. Figure 2 shows an architectural overview of the Grid Schema repository. For simplicity, we assume that the repository is centralized. (We do not consider the scalability and the locality issues in this paper.) The Grid Schema repository works together the OGSI-compliant services, such as GSI and MDS.

In designing grid databases, grid organizations first create the Grid Schema classes by choosing a collection of labels and domains from the repository. In cases of the lack of necessary vocabularies, they are allowed to add new vocabularies into the repository. In the end, all the classes are published as part of the Grid metadata in OGSI Monitoring and Discovery Services.

In accessing grid database, grid applications look for remote databases by using MDS. They check their class, compared to these database classes. If matched, remote data are moved and converted to the local database, or queries are translated into remote databases. Since the Grid Schema repository provides only mappings for the interoperability of grid databases, the efficiency of them in querying is beyond the scope of this paper.

4.2 Storing and Retrieval of Mappings

The Grid Schema repository must store huge volumes of terms and mappings. The advantage of the Grid Schema is that the model is so simple that we can easily maintain vocabularies on RDBMS. Intuitively, we can store all mappings in a relation; the mapping $D.v \longmapsto D'.v'$ can be rewritten by a relation $T(D, v, D', v')$.

More importantly, we can derive new mappings over existing T relations. The inference rules, supported in the Grid Schema, reflect the set and mapping theory (reflexivity and transitivity).

Definition 7 (inference rules). *We use* T *to denote the derived relations.*

I1. $T(D, v, D, v)$ *for all terms in the repository, and*

I2. $T(D_1, v_1, D_3, v_3)$ *if* $T(D_1, v_1, D_2, v_2)$ *and* $T(D_2, v_2, D_3, v_3)$

Although we represent mappings by T relations on RDBMSs, there would be many tips necessary to implement effective storage and mapping retrieval. Due to space constraint, we only describe the outline of our Grid Schema repository.

- *Normalization.* We classify all terms in the Grid Schema into normal vocabularies by equivalence class over $\equiv$. Normal domains are partially ordered over $\sqsubseteq$ in the whole Grid Schema (by Definition 2).
- *Partitioning.* We partition T relations by each of domain/range in mappings. The partitioned tables are called domain tables. (Partitioning table is a well-known technique to improve the selection operation.)
- *View Maintenance.* The inference rule **I2** is implemented with views that are equi-joined over domain tables.

5   Discussion

The Grid Schema works as a sort of *global schemas*. Building global schemas is one of the most straightforward means for data interoperability. In practice, however, it is awfully hard to maintain such schemas with keeping good interoperability over a distributing computing environment – where participants desire differently and schemas must update frequently.

Here we discuss the flexibility of the Grid Schema – how the Grid Schema helps us maintain global sharing, compared to existing schema sharing models, such as object-orientated (OO) models. It is important to note that the interoperability in global schemas depends not only on its schema model, but also on how to administrate schemas in a distributed manner. With an attention to the administration, we carefully set the following four situations (A1 $\sim$ A4).

- *A1. (Monolithic).* A central administrator is only allowed to design and modify global schemas. (e.g., EDIs).
- *A2. (Class-Subclass).* The schemas are developed in a hierarchal way. That is, local users are allowed to customize their own subclass schemas from super-class schemas that have been already published. (e.g., some practices under UML)
- **A3.** *(Object-Subclassing).* A significant variation of A2 is considerable in XML; the schema is virtually made by sub-classing on an instance of data. A typical example can be shown in XML namespaces where we combine an XML document with multiple XML schemas.
- **A4. (Grid Schema).** All users create their schemas, based on vocabularies in the Grid Schema. In addition, they are free to add new vocabularies to the repository if they specify mappings to existing related vocabularies.

Several difficulties in maintaining global schemas occur in cases of requirement mismatches and schema evolutions. Now we highlight three significant challenges (B1 ∼ B3), which very often appear in the administration of global schemas.

- **B1. (Evolving Element)**. Schemas must be evolved, when new requirements arise in the user side. For example, we imagine a brand-new travel frequency program, where some participants want to share the information, while others outside may not like to add modifications in the global schema.
- **B2. (Value Flexibility)**. It is important to allow representational variations on the Web environment, because all values can be not necessary standardized. For example, US people and European would not reach an agreement on how to write temperature in a unified way (i.e., Celsius vs. Fahrenheit). The value flexibility helps a rapid consensus building in the agreement.
- **B3. (renaming/localization/refactoring)**. A long-term use of global schemas requires the management of different naming schemes, ranging from a minor modification of errata naming to an extensive refactoring in the schema revision and merge. In addition, we have to make schemas internationalized, because labels in querying are a significant part of developing applications.

Table 5 summarizes our evaluation on the flexibility. The UPDATE column represents whether the schema update is centralized (C) or decartelized (D).

Table 1. Matrix of Agreement/Flexibility

	UPDATE	B1	B2	B3	safe
A1	C	o	x	x	o
A2	D	x	x	x	x
A3	D	o	x	x	x
A4	D	o	o	o	o

We begin with a general comment. In grid environments, the decentralized update is more desirable than the centralized one, since it doesn't limit chances in exploiting new data applications and services. In this light, the Grid Schema allow users to update their vocabularies, even though it runs on a central site.

Next, we take a look at each challenge. For convenience, we write $C \prec C'$ for the IS-A relationship in the OO model, that means C' is a (subclass of) C.

B1. (Evolving element). Suppose we want to add an element traveler-info to the existing schema. In the class-subclass style, the schema is created and updated in an incremental way (e.g., adding a new class C'' (that extends the traveler-info) between C and C', such that $C \prec C'' \prec C'$). Note that the modification of the class hierarchy may cause a name conflict between C'' and C'. In a case of A1, such a name conflict can be controlled by a single naming authority. In cases of A3 and A4, we can use namespaces to distinguish existing names from a new name.

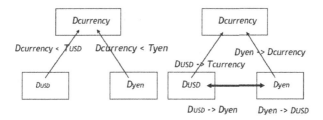

Fig. 3. Comparison of IS-A vs. Mapping

B2. (Value flexibility). Suppose we don't want to fix currency in price. In the class-subclass style, we usually define an abstract type $D_{currency}$, and then use its extended types, such as D_{usd} and D_{yen}. The variation is controlled by $D_{currency} \prec D_X$ – whether D_X is a subtype of $D_{currency}$. The problem is that the extended subtypes are not interoperable with each other. To sketch, suppose a grid application that only takes the values of D_{usd}. The application is not able to deal with values of D_{yen} even if values are validated by $D_{currency} \prec D_{yen}$. In contrast, the Grid Schema provides the mapping interoperability between D_{usd} and D_{yen}, and then allows the agent to understand D_{yen} by $D_{yen} \longmapsto D_{usd}$.

We consider that the semantics of mappings in the Grid Schema is more expressive than that of IS-A relation. The comparison is sketched in Figure 3.

B3. (renaming/localization/refactoring). Suppose some schemas of Japanese version need to run together with English schemas. It is very hard (or has largely been ignored) to deal with different naming schemes in the OO schema designs. The Grid Schema provides the mapping mechanism to the solution. That is, we can create Japanese vocabularies by just translating the English ones. More importantly, different versions are transparent to grid applications if they are compatible by the Grid Schema type-checking mechanism.

Finally, we would like to mention that the Grid Schema is *safe* in terms of the validation. That is, a grid application can safely use the validated data by the application class. On the other hand, the class-subclass extension is not safe in a sense that the extended types, although validated, are not always available in the application. The *polymorphism* may cause heterogeneous data at the representation level.

6   Conclusion

Sharing schemas is a shortcut to data interoperability, while in grid environments there are many difficulties such as schema disagreements and schema evolutions. We propose a new "mappings first, schemas later" schema model, named Grid Schema. The Grid Schema uses the idea of context-free mapping to modularize schemas and its translation rules. This is incorporated into its schema validation mechanism, which enables us to check the compatibility of different formed data. We showed the flexibility of the Grid Schema in maintaining global schemas in a distributed, evolving, and multi-cultural environment.

In this paper, we assume that all grid databases share global object identifiers (such as RFID). In the future, we will extend the sharing schema model to cover more generic data models for scientific databases and XML. In addition, our Grid Schema repository is developing for further experimental study. We would like to discuss the effectiveness, the scalability, and the extensibility of the repository through the development.

Acknowledgement. The author would like to thank all attendants in IC-SNW2004 for valuable comments.

References

1. S. Abiteboul, S. Cluet, and T. Milo. Correspondence and translation for heterogeneous data. In *Proceedings of 6th International Conference Database Theory - ICDT '97*, pages 351–363, 1997.
2. S. Abiteboul, R. Hull, and V. Vianu. *Foundations of Databases*. Addison-Wesley Publishing Company, 1995.
3. D. Carlson. *Modeling XML Applications with UML: Practical e-Business Applications*. Addison-Wesley, 2001.
4. T. Catarci and M. Lenzerini. Interschema knowledge in cooperative information systems. In *Proceedings of Conference on Cooperative Information Systems*, pages 55–62, 1993.
5. S. Cluet, C. Delobel, J. Siméon, and K. Smaga. Your mediators need data conversion! In *Proceedings of ACM SIGMOD International Conference on Management of Data - SIGMOD98*, pages 177–188, 1998.
6. S. B. Davidson and A. S. Kosky. Wol: A language for database transformations and constraints. In *Proceedings of the 13th International Conference of Data Engineering*, pages 55–65, 1997.
7. I. Foster, and C. Kesselman. *The Grid : Blueprint for a New Computing Infrastructure* . Morgan Kaufmann, 1998.
8. C. H. Goh, S. Bressan, S. Madnick, and M. Siegel. Context interchange: New features and formalisms for the intelligent integration of information. *ACM Transactions on Information Systems*, 17(3):270–293, 1999.
9. V. Kashyap and A. P. Sheth. Semantic and schematic similarities between database objects: A context-based approach. *VLDB Journal*, 5(4):276–304, 1996.
10. D. Lee and W. W. Chu. Comparative analysis of six xml schema languages. *Sigmod Record*, 29(3):76–87, 2000.
11. A. Y. Levy, A. Rajaraman, and J. J. Ordille. Querying heterogeneous information sources using source descriptions. In *Proceedings of the 22nd VLDB Conference*, pages 251–262, 1996.
12. W. Litwin, L. Mark, and N. Roussopoulos. Interoperability of multiple autonomous databases. *ACM Computing Surveys*, 22(3):267–293, 1990.
13. J. Madhavan, P. A. Bernstein, and E. Rahm. Generic schema matching with cupid. In *Proceedings of 27th International Conference on Very Large Data Bases – VLDB 2001*, pages 49–58, 2001.
14. Renée J. Miller, Yannis E. Ioannidis, and Raghu Ramakrishnan. The use of information capacity in schema integration and translation. In *Proceedings of 19th International Conference on Very Large Data Bases*, pages 120–133. Morgan Kaufmann, 1993.

15. T. Milo and Z. Zohar. Using schema matching to simplify heterogeneous data translation. In *Proceedings of 24th International Conference on Very Large Data Bases – VLDB 1998*, pages 122–133, 1998.
16. A. M. Ouksel and A. P. Sheth. Semantic interoperability in global information systems: A brief introduction to the research area and the special section. *SIGMOD Record*, 28(1):5–12, 1999.
17. E. Pitoura, O. Bukhres, and A. Elmagarmid. Object orientation in multidatabase systems. *ACM Computing Surveys*, 27(2):141–195, 1995.
18. A. P. Sheth and J. A. Larson. Federated database systems for managing distributed, heterogeneous, and autonomous databases. *ACM Computing Surveys*, 22(3):183–236, 1990.
19. V. Vianu. A web odyssey: from codd to xml. In *Proceedings of Symposium on Principles of Database Systems*, pages 1–15, 2001.

Relational Graphical Models of Computational Workflows for Data Mining

William H. Hsu

Department of Computing and Information Sciences, Kansas State University
Manhattan, KS 66506-2302
http://www.kddresearch.org, bhsu@cis.ksu.edu

Collaborative recommendation is the problem of analyzing the content of an information retrieval system and actions of its users, to predict additional topics or products a new user may find useful. Developing this capability poses several challenges to machine learning and reasoning under uncertainty. Recent systems such as *CiteSeer* [1] have succeeded in providing some specialized but comprehensive indices of full documents, but the kind of probabilistic models used in such indexing do not extend easily to information Grid databases and computational Grid workflows. The collection of user data from Grid portals [4] provides a test bed for the underlying IR technology, including learning and inference systems. To model workflows created using the *TAVERNA* editor [3] and *SCUFL* description language, the *DESCRIBER* system, shown in Figure 1, applies score-based structure learning algorithms, including Bayesian model selection and greedy search (cf. the K2 algorithm) adapted to relational graphical models. Figure 2 illustrates how the decision support front-end of *DESCRIBER* interacts with modules that learn and reason using probabilistic relational models,. The purpose is to discover interrelationships among, and thereby recommend, components used in workflows developed by other Grid users.

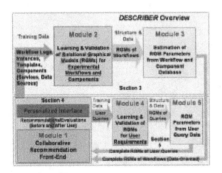

Fig. 1. *DESCRIBER* overview

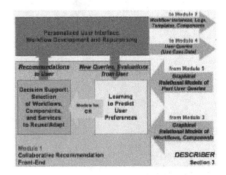

Fig. 2. Recommender component

In this work, we adapt score-based structure learning algorithms for discovering *relational graphical models* for domain-specific collaborative recommendation from scientific data and web service repositories, as well as use cases for software and data sets retrieved from them. Statistical evaluation is performed using validation user data over a larger set of *TAVERNA* workflows built using the same services. The object-relational representation of these transactional workflow models include probabilistic

M. Bouzeghoub et al. (Eds.): ICSNW 2004, LNCS 3226, pp. 309–310, 2004.
© IFIP International Federation for Information Processing 2004

graphical models, such as *Bayesian networks* and *decision networks*, that have recently been applied to a wide variety of problems in intelligent information retrieval, information extraction, and link analysis. [2] Our approach combines score-based algorithms for learning the structure of relational probabilistic models with existing techniques for constructing relational models of metadata about computational Grid services (including data sources, functions, and nested workflows).

As a motivating example of a computational genomics experiments, we use gene expression modeling from microarray data. DNA hybridization *microarrays*, also referred to as *gene chips*, are experimental tools in the life sciences that make it possible to model interrelationships among genes. A major challenge in bioinformatics is to discover gene/protein interactions and key features of a cellular system by analyzing microarray scans. Figure 3 depicts an example of a relational graphical model where each transactional workflow is mapped to one instance of an objectrelational schema as shown. Figure 4 shows another example, adapting the toy decision support network *DEC-Asia* to a relational extension of a decision network.

Our recent projects in computational genomics focus on the problem of automatically extracting gene regulatory dependencies from gene expression data sources such as cDNA microarrays. Most data resources we plan to use in developing *DESCRIBER* are in the public domain, while some are *TAVERNA* workflows [3] developed by $_{my}Grid$ project team [4].

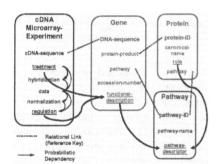

Fig. 3. Example relational model for bioinformatics domain

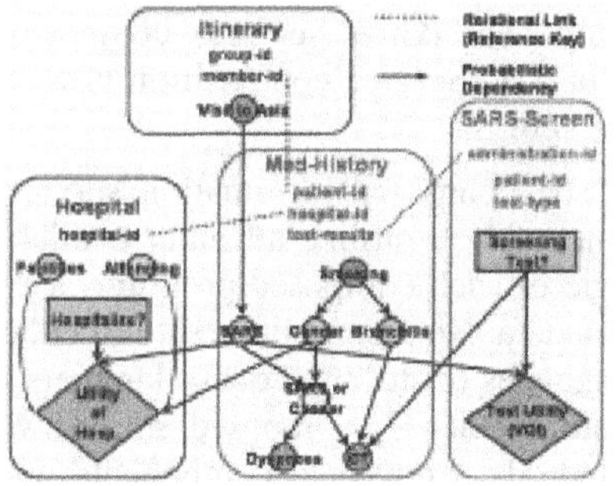

Fig. 4. Relational decision network for diagnostic utility (SARS-Screen)

References

1. Lawrence, S., Giles, C. L., & Bollacker, K. (1999). Digital libraries and autonomous citation indexing. *IEEE Computer, 32*(6):67-71.
2. Getoor, L., Friedman, N., Koller, D., & Taskar, B. (2002). Learning probabilistic models of link structure. *J. of Artificial Intelligence Research*, 3(12), 679-707.
3. Oinn, T., Marvin, D., & Rice, P. (2004). *TAVERNA* workflow editor for myGrid. Available from: http://taverna.sourceforge.net .
4. Stevens, R. D., Robinson, A. J., & Goble, C. A. (2003). myGrid: personalized bioinformatics on the information Grid (ISMB-2003). *Bioinformatics* 19:302-305.

InfoGrid: Information Resource Integration

Nikolaos Giannadakis, Mustafa Ghanem, and Y. Guo

Imperial College London
{ng300,mmg,yg}@doc.ic.ac.uk

Grid computing [3] constitutes the amalgamation of a drive towards the standardization of existing technologies that enable the collaboration of scientists overcoming restrictions of location, distance and compatibility. The aim is to exploit the full potential of resources, computational or informational. We aim to study how a network of distributed and heterogeneous grid resources could attain maximum adaptability to languages, models, scientific uses in a service composition based knowledge discovery environment. No language or data model assumptions are herein made. The presence of grid layers that can handle basic service registration, etc. tasks, service execution and data mobility is premised.

Accordingly, no assumption is made about the nature of the information that grid resources need to communicate. Emphasizing on the composing aspect, we move complexity from the query engine to the composition level by means of utilizing component (Grid Service) composition languages, composing service-based data resources. Service composition now becomes an information resource static integration tool.

The composed information services are essentially composed grid services and hence able to utilize all other available grid services. We assert that that execution logic of such composed programs should be enriched with logic for the provision of metadata. No assumptions should either be made for the type of metadata. Integration languages (distributed query languages) on top of the middleware can have their own requirements. A composed service will simply declare its supported languages or standards. Additional components will be created facilitating and being specialized for information resource composition.

Finally, a dynamic integration layer is proposed whereby an arbitrary integration language can declare its model and grid services which will transform a query expressed in it into a composite service that can be executed and return any results. Any such decomposing grid services will be mapping their operators to the corresponding grid services and ditto with any direct references to other resources.

From an information access point, our contribution is the proposed use of service composition and invocation layers as a means of integration with no language or model prerequisite. From a service composition view, we propose the introduction of dynamic metadata logic for services, built on top of existent composition capabilities. We aim to demonstrate that this approach can reproduce the integration capabilities of other approaches and, furthermore, that it is able to accommodate more complicated integration needs.

We are designing *InfoGrid* (the information integration effort of Imperial College's DiscoveryNet [4] project) which has the goal of addressing the needs of the scientific

M. Bouzeghoub et al. (Eds.): ICSNW 2004, LNCS 3226, pp. 311–312, 2004.
© IFIP International Federation for Information Processing 2004

community. In particular, bioinformatics and chemistry applications will constitute the application domains of our research.

Table 1. An overview of the resource characteristics for the basic information access approaches and that of InfoGrid.

Resources				
	JDBC resource	Discovery Link	OGSA-DAI	InfoGrid
Metadata language	Relational Db connection information	Special wrappers have to be available/ metadata is set statically during registration	Available through a Web Service interface	Any
Metadata model	A DatabaseMetaData Java object		XML Schema	Any
Invocation language	SQL	Handled internally by precompiled wrappers	SQL or XQuery	Any
Results model	A ResultSet object		Files (Tables or XML)	Any

Table 2. A summary of the integration approaches. We aim to prove that InfoGrid can reproduce all these.

Integration Approaches				
	JDBC	DiscoveryLink [1]	OGSA-DAI [2]	
Type	Bespoke	Federation	Query Based	Static & query based using the composition layer
Metadata	N/A (individual relational models)	Common Static Relational Model	Individual XML or relational models expressed in XML Schema	Metadata independent Using the
Language	SQL	SQL	OQL	For query based integration all languages that provide a decomposing service
Invocation	Orchestration	Abstracted	Decomposition into execution primitives with the aid of a service dictionary.	Grid execution layer

References

[1] Discovery link from IBM
[2] Open Grid Services Architecture Data Access and Integration (http://www.ogsadai.org.uk/)
[3] Global Grid Forum (http://www.gridforum.org/)
[4] DiscoveryNet project (http://ex.doc.ic.ac.uk/new/)

Semantic Annotation of Classification Data for KDD Support Services

Claudia Diamantini, Domenico Potena, and Maurizio Panti

Dipartimento di Ingegneria Informatica, Gestionale e dell'Automazione,
Università Politecnica delle Marche - via Brecce Bianche, 60131 Ancona, Italy
{diamanti,d.potena,panti}@diiga.univpm.it

Abstract. In order to guide the user in the correct and effective use of
tools, a KDD support system should posses a knowledge on the mapping
between certain characteristics of data (and the Data Mining task) and
the tools which could be profitably used. In this work, we want to dwell
upon this problem in the framework of the classification data mining
task, by showing an approach to extract some knowledge about the data
from the form of the decision border.

1 Introduction

In order to guide the user in the correct and effective use of Knowledge Discovery
in Databases (KDD) tools, a KDD support system should posses a knowledge
on the mapping between certain characteristics of data (and the Data Mining
task) and the tools which could be profitably used [4]. In this work, we want
to dwell upon this problem in the framework of the classification data mining
task, which reads: "find the (unknown) class an instance belongs to, out of
k predefined classes". In the literature, the problem is tackled from either a
knowledge representation [1] or knowledge induction [5] perspective. However,
these approaches do not exploit the information about the decision border, even
if it is known that the characteristics of the decision border define the type of
classification problem and a relationship exists between the characteristics of the
decision border and the performance of different classification architectures.

2 An Approach to Decision Boundary Characterization

We propose a method to derive an analytical description of (an approximation of)
the decision border. The method resorts to the nearest neighbor Vector Quantizer
Architecture with Euclidean distance (VQA), trained by the BVQ algorithm [3]
to induce a piecewise linear approximation of the true decision border. The
geometrical characteristics of the VQA allowed us to develop an algorithm to
extract the analytical Voronoi description in n-dimensional spaces, hence the
equations of hyperplanes and vertices of the decision regions.

Elaborating upon the analytical definition of decision borders, we are able to
extract any kind of geometrical characteristics of decision regions, for instance

M. Bouzeghoub et al. (Eds.): ICSNW 2004, LNCS 3226, pp. 313–315, 2004.
© IFIP International Federation for Information Processing 2004

describing both (1) topological and (2) geometrical properties. The former focuses on properties such as the Connected/Disconnected and the Open/Close properties of the regions. The latter refines the regions categorization describing features like: the surface area, volume, principal components ratio, convexity, volume/surface ratio, position in $\mathcal{R}^n$, and so on.

3 Applications

Geometrical characteristics of decision region can be associated to classification data as a sort of semantic annotation of the classification problem. This semantic description can be exploited to build intelligent services supporting the users in each step of the classification KDD process design, from the understanding and pre-processing of the input data, to the understanding of the discovered model.

In the framework of distributed KDD support systems [4], the semantic annotation of data can be exploited by linking it to information about the data mining techniques used to induce the model and their performances. To represent such information, suitable description languages and ontologies can be used, like the DAMON ontology [2]. Then, *Meta Learning Services* can be developed, to search, organize and elaborate such information, to find similarities between datasets on the basis of their decision borders, and correlations between groups of similar datasets and the performance of different data mining techniques. From the relationship between data characteristics and algorithms performances the Meta Learning Service can then extract meta-information about the learning process and exploit it to support the user, by suggesting the set of algorithms, or the typical parameter setting for a given algorithm, that have demonstrated the best performances on data similar in characteristics to a given dataset.

4 Conclusions

The paper presents a method to associate decision border information to classification data. This can be considered as a domain knowledge about the classification task, and we discuss how this information can be exploited in the framework of distributed KDD support systems. An important issue related with the method is the accuracy of border approximation needed for different applications. Qualitatively, it turns out for instance that an accurate model of the border is not needed to understand and to pre-process the data, while it is needed to build up a valid knowledge base registry. We are forming a set of experiments to test cost and quality of the method for the different applications.

References

1. Appice, A., Ceci, M. and Malerba, D. KDB2000: An Integrated Knowledge Discovery Tool. In *Data Mining III*, volume 6. WIT Press, 2002.
2. Cannataro, M. and Comito, C. A Data Mining Ontology for Grid Programming. In *Proc. 1st Work. on Semantics in Peer-to-Peer and Grid Computing*, 2003.

3. Diamantini, C. and Spalvieri, A. Quantizing for Minimum Average Misclassification Risk. *IEEE Trans. on Neural Networks*, 9(1):174–182, Jan. 1998.
4. Diamantini, C., Panti, M. and Potena, D. Services for knowledge discovery in databases. In *Int. Symp. of S.Caterina on Challanges in the Internet and Interdisciplinary Research*, volume 1, Jan. 29 - Feb. 1 2004.
5. Vilalta, R. and Drissi, Y. A perspective view and survey of meta-learning. *Artif. Intell. Rev.*, 18(2):77–95, 2002.

Role of the Ontologies in the Context of Grid Computing and Application for the Human Disease Studies*

Maja Hadzic and Elizabeth Chang

Curtin University of Technology, School of Information Systems,
GPO Box U1987 Perth,
Western Australia 6845, Australia
{hadzicm,change}@cbs.curtin.edu.au

1 Introduction

We describe the increasing impact of ontologies in the context of Grid computing for obtaining, comparing and analyzing distributed heterogeneous scientific data. The inherently autonomous and heterogeneous nature of the information resources forces applications to share data and services often without prior knowledge of their structure and functionality, respectively. Ontologies are needed to provide a way to capture and present in the computer, knowledge shared by all people in a certain community. Computer based ontologies may be seen as shared formal conceptualizations of domain knowledge and therefore constitute an essential resource for enabling interoperation in an open environment such as the Web on the Grid. We illustrate how ontologies can be developed for the knowledge domain of biomedical and bioengineering research. We chose the application domain of human disease research and control since it necessarily involves resources of phenotypic, genetic, environmental and treatment data.

2 Importance of Grid in the Biomedical Environment

Medical researchers consist of teams with heterogeneous members with different capabilities. There does not exist a unique organization that has all the required resources or skills and team members to be distributed around the globe. The Grid should enable resources sharing and usage co-ordination in dynamic, virtual, multi-institutional organizations [2]. Grid middleware provide the required distributed collaborative platform as well as easy access to resources. The source information covers different areas of interest with respect to human diseases in order to allow different user categories, each having specific intentions, to query the system. Another major advantage of using the Grid is that it respects complete autonomy of the existing ontology nodes. Each of the existing nodes can withdraw or join the Grid whenever it is

---

* This paper has been finalized during Maja's Hadzic research visit at the VUB STARLab in Brussels. The authors would like to thank Prof. Robert Meersman, Sven Van Acker, Andriy Lisovoy and other research team members of VUB STARLab for helpful discussions and useful suggestions.

M. Bouzeghoub et al. (Eds.): ICSNW 2004, LNCS 3226, pp. 316–318, 2004.
© IFIP International Federation for Information Processing 2004

necessary. This is very important when generating on request Specific Human Disease Ontologies.

3 Generic Versus Specific Human Disease Ontology, Using DOGMA Methodology

Our Generic Human Disease Ontology has four main branches: *(1) phenotype*, describing symptoms of a disease; *(2) treatment*, giving an overview of all treatments possible for that particular disease as well as treatment's efficiency; *(3) causes* responsible for that disorder, which can be environmental and/or genetical; *(4) types*, describing different types of a disorder

By combining grid services with a prototype of Generic Human Disease Ontology (GHDO), we extract and align the relevant information requested by an user from publication and medical databases, DNA and protein databases, research institutes, health departments, hospitals etc. This allows generating Specific Human Disease Ontologies (SHDO) for simple disorders such as SCA (sickle cell anemia) but, also for complex disorders such as MDD (manic-depressive disorder). The Generic Human Disease ontology stands here central as a link between multiple heterogeneous information resources on one side and the users on the other side. The specific information requested by user is accessed by using Grid services. Merging and aligning of this information to the Generic Human Disease Ontology results in Specific Human Disease Ontologies.

For the ontology design, we adopted the methodology of DOGMA [1]. In this approach database schema elements, as well as linguistical elements are represented as lexons combining the knowledge domain. Knowledge about their usage (such as constraints, rules, etc.) is kept rigorously separate and is specified as part of the formal commitment of an application to these lexons. This so-called double articulation [3] permits a high degree of scalability, an essential requirement for Grid-based computing. A second fundamental aspect of DOGMA is that it distinguishes data models (which are embedded in specific applications) from proper ontologies (this should be application-independent). The mapping of a data model to an ontology precisely constitutes its formal semantics, in fact reified as part of commitment.

4 Use Cases

We give some examples for the purpose of illustration of use and application of the Human Disease Ontologies. The Generic Human Disease Ontology with its four main branches (symptoms, treatments, causes and types) serves as a template. Grid services then "feed" applications committed to this ontology with relevant data required by a user which results in Specific Human Disease Ontologies. Researchers and physicians are strongly connected because they are working towards the same goal, but on different knowledge levels. The examples are intended to show typical, common problems researchers and physicians encounter.

5 Conclusion

We show how the combination of two different but complementary techniques, namely Grid computing and ontology, results in a dynamic and intelligent information system. The two approaches together, being complementary, enable the system as a whole.

References

1. Deray T., Verheyden P.: Towards a semantic integration of medical relational databases by using ontologies: a case study. In: Meersman R.: Semantic Ontology Tools in Information System Design. In: Ras Z., Zemankova M. (eds.): Proceedings of the ISMIS 99 Conference, Lecture Notes in Computer Science Vol. 1609, Springer-Verlag Heidelberg, (1999) 30-45.
2. Carole Goble: The Grid Needs you! Enlist Now. In: Robert Meersman, Zahir Tari, Douglas C. Schmidt (eds.): On the Move to Meaningful Internet Systems 2003, Confederated International Conferences DOA, CoopIS and ODBASE 2002 Irvine, California, USA, Proceedings. Lecture Notes in Computer Science, Springer-Verlag Heidelberg, ISBN 3-540-20498-9 (2003) 589-600.
3. Spyns P., Meersman R., Jarrar M.: Data modelling versus Ontology engineering. SIGMOD Record, Vol. 31, No. 4 (2002) 12-17.

Cluster Entries for Semantic Organization
of Peer-to-Peer Network*

Nicolas Lumineau[1], Anne Doucet[1], and Bruno Defude[2]

[1] LIP6 - 8, rue du Capitaine Scott 75 015 Paris, France.
{Nicolas.Lumineau,Anne.Doucet}@lip6.fr
[2] GET-INT - 9, rue Charles Fourier 91011 EVRY cedex, France
Bruno.Defude@int-evry.fr

1 Context

Techniques of pure flooding queries through a peer-to-peer network[1] reach their limits for data localization which are not replicated and stored through a high number of nodes. To improve implicitly the query routing towards relevant nodes in order to smartly recover all the relevant data, we propose to organize a peer-to-peer network in which the logical neighborhood of each node is built according to the semantic of its content. Indeed, the data we target, are semantically rich, easily classifiable with a field of interest, or a theme (e.g. "rock", "jazz", ... in music, or "hydrology", "ocean-ography",... in sciences of environment). The motivation of our approach is based on the fact users/providers query the network on the theme of the data they store. Thus, if a node contains many data about the theme "Hydrology", the query propagation is more efficient, if the neighbors of this node contain data about "Hydrology". In the prototype VENISE (serVicE for Node Insertion in Semantic clustErs), we propose a protocol of node insertion based on cluster entries to cluster a peer-to-peer network.

2 Semantic Representations

To build a network organized according to the semantic content of nodes, we define
– a set of *theme* statically established and used as common referential to semantically compare nodes.
– the semantic representation of each node, named *Thematic Vector*. The values of this vector contain the proportion of data stored on the node according to each theme.
– the semantic representation of each cluster, named *Aggregation Vector*. The values of this vector are learnt by a Machine Learning technique to take into account the aggregation of Thematic Vectors of nodes contained in the cluster and the semantic distance between clusters. Thus, a neural network is used as in the approach of self organizing maps[2] to classify nodes in cluster.

---

* This research is done in the context of the PADOUE project
(http://www-poleia.lip6.fr/padoue) financed by ACI GRID of French Research Minister
(htp://www-sop.inria.fr/aci/grid/public).

M. Bouzeghoub et al. (Eds.): ICSNW 2004, LNCS 3226, pp. 319–320, 2004.
© IFIP International Federation for Information Processing 2004

- An abstract entity to point on the node in charge of the physical insertion of a new node in the network, named *Cluster Entries*.

3 Protocol of Node Insertion

The process of node insertion is performed in three main steps:
- The relevant cluster entry selection: the thematic vector of the new node is compared (according to the least square method) with the aggregation vector of each cluster entry. This allows selecting the most relevant cluster entry.
- The physical node insertion: the node pointed by the selected cluster entry handle the physical insertion of the new node in the network (i.e. it is used as entry in the network).
- The cluster entries updating: the insertion of a new node in a cluster changes the content of a cluster. Thus, according to an algorithm of machine learning, the aggregation vectors of all cluster entries are updated.

The poster shows how machine learning technique can be used to organize a peer-to-peer network. Our main goal is to exploit the most relevant semantic in each level in a peer-to-peer network. To improve implicitly query propagation process, the semantic of node content is used to organize the network in order to reduce the number of hops necessary to resolve queries. In this way, to further improve the algorithm of query propagation we can use another semantic as experiences of user communities [3]. This allows to rout queries straightforwardly into relevant nodes with query solutions.

References

[1] Aberer, K., Hauswirth, M., Peer-to-Peer Information Systems: Concepts and Models, state-of-the-art, and Future Systems, Tutorial IEEE ICDE, 2002.
[2] Kohonen, T.,Exploration of very large databases by self-organizing maps. In Proceedings of ICNN'97, International Conference on Neural Networks, pages PL1-PL6. IEEE Service Center, Piscataway, NJ.
[3] Lumineau Nicolas, Doucet Anne, *Sharing Communities Experiences for Query Propagation in Peer-to-Peer Systems,* In 8th International Database Engineering and Applications Symposium (IDEAS'04), 7-9 Juillet 2004, Coimbra, Portugal.

A Peer-to-Peer Service Supporting Data Quality: Design and Implementation Issues

Diego Milano, Monica Scannapieco, and Tiziana Catarci

Dipartimento di Informatica e Sistemistica,
Universitá degli Studi di Roma "La Sapienza",
Via Salaria 113, Rome, Italy
{milano,monscan,catarci}@dis.uniroma1.it

Recent research has highlighted the importance of data quality issues in environments characterized by extensive data replication, such as Cooperative Information Systems (CISs). While high data quality is a strict requirement for CISs, the high degree of data replication that characterizes such systems can be exploited to improve the quality of data, as different copies of the same data may be compared in order to detect quality problems and possibly solve them.

The DaQuinCIS architecture [1] has been designed to manage data quality in cooperative contexts [2] and offers several quality-oriented services. Its core component, the *Data Quality Broker*, is in essence a data integration system that allows to access the best available quality data without having to know where such data are stored. It also allows diffusion of best quality data in the System, thus improving the overall quality of the CIS.

The Data Quality Broker is implemented as a peer-to-peer distributed service: each organization hosts a copy of the Data Quality Broker that interacts with other copies (see Figure 1, left side) playing both the roles of wrapper and mediator in the data integration architecture. Each copy of the Data Quality Broker is internally composed by four interacting modules (see Figure 1, right side).

The **Query Processor** performs query processing on the basis of a mapping specifically designed to exploit the presence of replicated data. To answer a query on the global schema, it submits appropriate data requests to multiple sources that provide overlapping sets of data. A record matching activity is performed on the global query result, and duplicated copies of the same data are compared in order to select or construct a best quality copy. Best quality copies are returned. Also, they are submitted to organizations having provided low quality copies of the same data.

The **Wrapper** translates the query from the language used by the broker to that of the specific data source. In this work the wrapper is a read-only module that accesses data and associated quality stored inside organizations without modifying them.

The **Transport Engine** is a communication facility that transfers queries and their results between the Query Processor module and data source wrappers. Another function it performs is the evaluation of the *availability* of data sources that are going to be queried for data. This feature is encapsulated into the

M. Bouzeghoub et al. (Eds.): ICSNW 2004, LNCS 3226, pp. 321–322, 2004.
© IFIP International Federation for Information Processing 2004

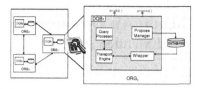

Fig. 1. The Data Quality Broker as a P2P system and its internal architecture

Transport Engine as it can be easily implemented exploiting Transport Engine's communication capabilities.

The **Propose Manager** receives feedbacks sent to organizations in order to improve their data.

The choice of a P2P architecture is motivated by the need of being as less invasive as possible in introducing quality controls in a cooperative system. The P2P paradigm is able to support the cooperation without necessarily involving consistent re-engineering actions.

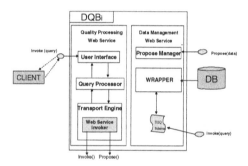

Fig. 2. The Data Quality Broker system architecture

The Data Quality Broker system architecture is based on web services technologies, supported by the the the J2EE 1.4 JAX-RPC API. Each copy of the Data Quality Broker is implemented by two web services, namely the Query Processing Web Service and the Data Manager Web Service as shown in Figure 2.

Some tests have been performed with two real data sets owned by Italian public administrations. The results we obtained show that the system is effective in improving the quality of data, with only a limited efficiency overhead.

References

1. The Data Quality in Cooperative Information Systems (DaQuinCIS) Project, http://www.dis.uniroma1.it/~dq/ .
2. M. Scannapieco, A. Virgillito, M. Marchetti, M. Mecella, and R. Baldoni, *The DaQuinCIS architecture: a Platform for Exchanging and Improving Data Quality in Cooperative Information Systems*, Information Systems **29** (2004), no. 7, 551–582.

Analysis Patterns for the Geographic Database Conceptual Schema: An Ontology Aided Approach
Extended Abstract

Guillermo Nudelman Hess, Cirano Iochpe, and José Palazzo Moreira de Oliveira

Universidade Federal do Rio Grande do Sul, Instituto de Informática
Porto Alegre, Brazil
{hess,ciochpe,palazzo}@inf.ufrgs.br

Conceptual modeling of Geographic Databases (GDB) has become a very important task due to both the increasing exchange and reuse of geographic information. Most of the GDB support a proprietary data model, specific for a particular system architecture. This design scenario leads to a non-reusable as well as implementation-dependent geographic database project. The reuse is especially interesting in GDB, since the precise modeling process can be of significant complexity. Furthermore, a wide set of real world entities must be represented in the database of most geographic applications. To support this kind of reuse, the analysis patterns methodology [2] is a very useful technique. Analysis patterns are the core of the conceptual modeling for the solution of a recurrent problem in a specific context. Having the patterns stored in a knowledge base that can be easily searched and updated, a designer is able to search, retrieve and reuse the most adequate concept representation that applies to a specific modeling process. To support this approach, a ontology can be used to play the role of the knowledge base mentioned above.

To support the recognition of analysis patterns automatically, the Knowledge Discovery in Databases (KDD) [1] is a candidate technology. This process can be briefly outlined as a sequence of steps or phases that can be revisited when necessary, an iterative process. In the preprocessing step, one of the main tasks is integration of all selected data. To reach a correct data preparation for mining, this schemata integration process must deal with syntactic and semantic heterogeneities. It must solve the unification problem of different representations used to describe the same real world phenomenon, and the relationships between them. The present work deals with this step. The architecture consists in a syntactic part, which intends to convert the different data models to the Geographic Markup Language (GML), which is used in our methodology as the canonical data model, since it is a standard for storing and exchanging geographical data.

To support the semantic phase of the pre-processing, we propose the use of an ontology to be used as the knowledge repository. In this sense, we developed semi-automate algorithm to search and update the ontology, illustrated in figure 1. In [3] there is a complete description of the algorithm.

To minimize the need of the expert intervention two parameters have to be set at the beginning of the algorithm execution: the minimum and the maximum accepted probabilities. Only the concepts having similarity probability higher than the minimum specified are shown to the expert. If one ore more of the ontology candidates have similarity probability higher than the maximum specified by the user,

M. Bouzeghoub et al. (Eds.): ICSNW 2004, LNCS 3226, pp. 323–324, 2004.
© IFIP International Federation for Information Processing 2004

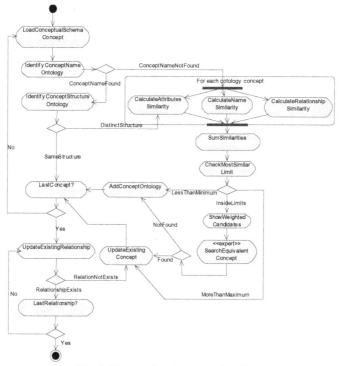

Fig. 1. The ontology's search algorithm

the one with the higher value is considered as equivalent (a synonym) of the input concept.

To perform the algorithm it is necessary to measure the similarity between two concepts, one from the input conceptual schema and the other from the ontology. Here we adopt a hybrid approach, combining syntactic matching between strings and semantic matching. In [3] the mathematical part of the similarity measurement is explained. It takes into account the name, attributes and relationships features of the concept

During this process, the original conceptual schema is kept unaltered and a new one is generated, in the canonical semantic format, and this is the one to be used later in the data mining. The ontology can also be dynamically updated depending on the concept's matches. Attributes and relationships can be added, and even new concepts may be inserted.

References

1. Fayyad, U.; Piatetsky-Shapiro, G.; Smyth, P. From Data Mining to Knowledge Discovery in Databases. In AI Magazine, v.17, n.3,p.37-54, 1996.
2. Fowler, M. Analysis patterns : reusable object models. Menlo Park: Addison-Wesley, 1997. 357 p. : il.
3. Hess, G.; Iochpe, C. Applying Ontologies in the KDD Pre-Processing Phase. In Proc. of 16th International Conference on Software Engineering and Knowledge Engineering (SEKE'04). Banff, Canada. June 2004 (to be published)

Author Index